THE BEST OF
FOOD&WINE
CHICKEN
COLLECTION

THE BEST OF
FOOD&WINE
CHICKEN
COLLECTION

American Express
Publishing Corporation
New York

Cover: Provençal Roast Chicken (page 64)

The Best of Food & Wine/CHICKEN COLLECTION
Designer: Loretta Sala
Assistant Editor: Martha Crow

American Express Publishing Corporation
Editor in Chief/Food & Wine: Mary Simons
Art Director/Food & Wine: Elizabeth Woodson
Managing Editor/Books: Kate Slate
Marketing Director: Elizabeth Petrecca
Production Manager: Joanne Maio Canizaro

Published by American Express Publishing Corporation
1120 Avenue of the Americas, New York, New York 10036

Manufactured in the United States of America

ISBN 0-916103-17-X

Table of Contents

The Incredibly Edible Chicken

When Herbert Hoover quoted Henry IV of France and told the American people that they would have "a chicken in every pot every Sunday," he was simply trying to reassure a mid-Depression populace that their lives would improve. At the time, chicken was almost as expensive as beef, and Sunday's chicken dinner was a treat. Little did President Hoover know of the Sanderses and Perdues who were to come or that some fifty years later the typical American would consume well over 50 pounds of chicken a year, and for a fraction of the cost of beef.

The reasons for chicken's popularity—then and now—are many:

★ Its tender, moist meat lends itself to all manner of cooking methods, from roasting and baking to poaching and braising.

★ Its flavor is just meaty enough to stand on its own but not so overwhelming that it doesn't go well with strong ethnic seasonings and all manner of sauces—from mild and creamy to assertive and spicy.

★ And last, but nowadays certainly not least, its light, white, lean meat appeals to those who are concerned about eating a healthier, lower-fat diet.

AT THE MARKET

Chicken is available commercially in a variety of ages, sizes and weights (see the chart at right for information on how best to use each of these types of chicken):

Poussins are baby chickens (*poussin* means chick in French) that weigh about 1 pound. In some areas of the country, they are sold as "squab chickens."

Broiler-fryers are about 1½ to 2 months old and may be male or female. The "fryer" refers to the chicken's age (as in small-fry), although many people mistakenly refer to this size chicken as a "frying" chicken. Broiler-fryers are the birds most commonly cut up and sold as individual parts, such as breasts and thighs, and account for about 90 percent of the chicken sold.

Roasters are larger than fryers and usually 3 to 5 months old. They are considered to be more flavorful (and fattier) and they have the highest ratio of meat to bone (chicken is about 41 percent edible).

Cornish game hens (also called **Rock Cornish hens**) are a special crossbreed that never get any bigger than about 1½ pounds. They are usually 4 to 6 weeks old.

Capons are the best of all roasting chickens (though they are not as easy to find in the market). Capons are castrated male chickens that are killed at between 4 and 8 months of age. They have a higher proportion of white breast meat, are plump in shape and have a thick layer of fat under the skin that melts during cooking to tenderize the bird as it cooks.

Stewing chickens or stewing hens are older, over one year, and hence tougher. Do not avoid stewing hens because of their age: They are highly flavorful and are

6

continued on page 8

TYPE	WEIGHT	SERVINGS	COST*	BEST USES
Broiler-Fryer (also called simply Broiler or Fryer)	2½-4 lbs.	2 to 4	3	Best for roasting, poaching, spit-roasting. Can be butterflied and broiled or grilled.
Cut-up (quartered or 8 pieces)	____	____	4	Best for sautéing, braising, frying. Also good for baking or broiling.
Whole Breasts, bone in	____	____	8	Same uses as cut up
Breast Halves, bone in	____	____	8	Same uses as cut up
Breast Halves, skinless, boneless	____	____	9-10	Best for poaching, sautéing and stir-frying. Can be broiled if basted.
Whole Legs (thigh and drumstick)	____	____	5	Same uses as cut up
Drumsticks	____	____	7	Same uses as cut up
Thighs	____	____	6	Same uses as cut up
Thighs, skinless, boneless	____	____	8-9	Best marinated and grilled
Wings	____	____	3	Best for frying or braising
Backs or Necks	____	____	1	Best for soups and stocks
Giblets (hearts and gizzards)	____	____	6	Best for soups and stocks
Livers	____	____	6	Best for sautéing. Also good for spreads or pâtés.
Young Roaster (also called Oven Roaster)	5-7 lbs.	4 to 6	5	Best for roasting
Poussin (baby chicken)	¾-1 lb.	1 to 2	9-10	Best for baking and spit-roasting. Also good butterflied and grilled or broiled.
Rock Cornish Game Hen	1-1½ lbs.	1 to 2	6	Same as poussins
Capon (castrated rooster)	4-8 lbs.	6 to 8	7	Best choice for roasting. Has extra meat on breast. Very tender and juicy.
Stewing Hen (also called Heavy Fowl)	3-8 lbs.	4 to 8	3	Best for soups and long-cooking stews

* *Because poultry prices vary widely with region of the country and point in history, the numbers listed above are merely to indicate relative costs, with 1 being the cheapest and 10 the most expensive.*

continued from page 6

good for slow-cooked dishes that use moist heat, such as stocks, soups, stews and braises. Also, chicken salad made from this tougher bird will be far better tasting that it would be if made from a younger broiler-fryer.

GRADING CHICKEN

The USDA inspects all chickens for wholesomeness; however, the grading of chickens raised and sold in-state is voluntary. All chickens transported across state lines must, by law, be graded. Grading is based on cosmetic factors, not on size, tenderness or age. Chickens that are whole, plump and pretty—with no rips or missing parts— will be graded A. Others will fall into the B or C categories—these are not generally available to the public.

BUYING CHICKEN

When buying chicken, remember that the color (yellow or white) has no bearing on the quality of the meat. Color varies with the diet and breed of the bird. Do look for a well-shaped, plump body; smooth, slightly moist, soft flesh; and a fresh smell. Fresh, dressed chicken stored at 35° is best. Frozen chicken is seldom as juicy, flavorful or tender as fresh chicken. If you have access to freshly slaughtered chickens, do not buy them (or at any rate, use them) until the next day. The flesh of freshly killed chickens does not relax until about 24 hours later; cooking a freshly killed chicken will produce a tough, stringy bird.

PREPARING CHICKEN FOR COOKING

Having purchased chicken at the market, remove the store packaging and rinse the chicken thoroughly. If the chicken will then be poached, there is no need to dry it. However, if the chicken is to be sautéed or roasted, it should be patted dry so it will brown properly.

If you do not intend to use the chicken right away,

rinse it, pat it dry, wrap it loosely in waxed paper and place it on a plate in the refrigerator. It is important to allow space for air to circulate around the meat. If there are giblets, wrap and store them separately. Or, for longer storage, rinse, pat dry and rewrap the chicken in freezer paper or waxed paper and then foil.

Most of the recipes in this book do not require much in the way of fancy techniques for preparing chicken for cooking. However, there are a couple of methods that it is helpful to know.

★ **Cutting up a chicken:** Buying a whole chicken, rather than pre-cut pieces, is by far the more economical. Cutting up a chicken into the 8 to 10 traditional serving pieces—2 breast halves (or 4 breast quarters), 2 drumsticks, 2 thighs, 2 wings—is easy; it also leaves you with the carcass, back and neck for making stock. For step-by-step photographs that lead you through the process, see page 19.

★ **Making chicken cutlets:** Pounding boneless chicken breasts into "cutlets" makes them cook faster and more evenly. To make cutlets, take a chicken breast half and fold out the strip of meat on the underside called the fillet. Place the chicken between two sheets of waxed paper and use a mallet, flat meat pounder or rolling pin to flatten the chicken to an even thickness of about ¼ inch.

★ **Trussing:** Although most people do not bother to truss a chicken, we recommend it. Trussing helps maintain the shape of the chicken, allows it to cook uniformly and, if the bird is stuffed, closes the cavity so that the stuffing is held inside.

★ **Boning legs:** Removing the bone from a whole leg (drumstick and thigh) provides a pocket in the dark meat that can be used for stuffing. When the French do this, they reform the stuffed leg into the shape of a small ham, thus the French name for this preparation, *jambonneau*, which means small ham. For step-by-step photographs, see page 18.

★ **Making "chicken lollipops":** In a technique borrowed from Chinese cooks, chicken lollipops are formed by scraping the meat on the third joint of the wing (the part closest to the chicken's body) toward one end of the bone to create what looks like a miniature drumstick. For step-by-step photographs, see page 20.

TESTS FOR DONENESS

Some controversy exists regarding the correct way to test for doneness. Some cooks use a meat thermometer and cook the bird to 165° (medium-well) to 180° (well-done). Others pinch or poke the thigh. Still others pierce the thickest part of the thigh all the way to the bone to see if the juices run clear. These methods are all viable. Wiggling the drumstick in the hip joint, on the other hand, is not a good test; by the time the leg moves in the socket, the bird is overcooked.

SALMONELLA

One of the commonest causes of food poisoning is infection by salmonella bacteria, which is present in about half of the raw poultry sold in this country. Proper storage, handling and cooking of poultry, however, eliminates the health hazard. Here are some simple guidelines for avoiding salmonella poisoning:

* Rinse chicken before cooking it. (See "Preparing Chicken for Cooking" at left.)

* After handling raw poultry, thoroughly wash your hands in hot soapy water before handling any other food. Also wash any utensils and scrub any cutting boards used in preparing the chicken. It's best to use a nonwooden cutting board if possible, as the cracks and crevices in wooden boards can harbor salmonella bacteria.

* Do not stuff poultry until just before roasting and remove the stuffing as soon as the bird is cooked (or cook the stuffing separately).

* If you use a pastry brush to baste raw poultry and intend to use any leftover basting mixture as a sauce to go with the chicken, be sure that you bring the sauce to a boil and simmer it for at least 3 minutes to kill any salmonella bacteria you may have introduced by dipping the pastry brush in it.

* Be sure that you do not undercook the chicken: It is the high heat of cooking that kills the salmonella bacteria; undercooked chicken, especially if it sits at room temperature, can still harbor salmonella.

MAKING CHICKEN STOCK

"Stock is everything in cooking, at least in French cooking," wrote Auguste Escoffier, the father of modern French haute cuisine. The legendary chef was hardly overstating the case: Well-prepared stocks are the foundation of numerous dishes, especially sauces. If a stock is weak and thin, no amount of added seasonings or thickening will cover up that fact.

Given its importance, the simplicity of making an excellent homemade stock is somewhat surprising. The basic principle of stockmaking is to simmer chicken bones and meat, seasoning vegetables and aromatics in water over low heat (French chefs speak of the stock "smiling" as the small bubbles lazily work their way to the surface). The flavors and the body-giving gelatin are extracted over a period of several hours, resulting in a rich, full-bodied broth.

Most butchers will part with chicken backs and necks quite cheaply. Even easier is to save and freeze the gizzards, hearts, carcasses, backs, necks and wing tips each time you prepare a whole chicken (livers, however, should be frozen separately for another use, as they darken and flavor stock unpleasantly). If you can get chicken feet, they provide a lot of natural gelatin. Live-poultry markets, sometimes still found in Chinese and Jewish neighborhoods, will often let you have them. (Before adding chicken feet to stock ingredients, blanch them in boiling water until the yellow skin peels off, 5 minutes or so; skin them and proceed.)

After preparing stock, cool it thoroughly, uncovered, before refrigerating it. Stocks keep well under refrigeration, provided they are re-boiled every three days or so to prevent spoilage. Or freeze stock in covered containers, and you can have it on hand for weeks. Always boil stock that has been frozen before using.

The following recipes for chicken stock represent several strengths of stock, ranging from simple Chicken Stock made only with "spare parts," to a Brown Chicken Stock in which the parts are browned first to add depth of flavor, to a Rich Chicken Stock in which whole chickens are used to make a really chickeny stock.

CANNED BROTH

There really is no substitute for a good homemade chicken stock. But with modern time pressures, having homemade chicken stock on hand may not be practical. One solution to this is to use canned chicken broth. Canned broths tend to be a great deal saltier than homemade broths. So, depending on how sensitive your palate is to sodium, you may want to use a low-sodium or reduced-sodium canned broth or dilute regular canned broth with water. Another trick for making canned broth more like homemade stock is to "freshen" the broth by simmering it with some cut-up vegetables and herbs (and perhaps even some chicken parts) before using it.

GLACE DE VOLAILLE

In addition to time constraints on most home cooks, there is also storage space to be considered when it comes to making homemade chicken stock. One solution to this—although it produces a more caramelized and slightly less delicate flavor in the long run—is to make what the French call *glace de volaille*, or poultry glaze. Poultry glaze is made by reducing chicken stock until it turns an amber color and is about the consistency of hot maple syrup. Pour the resulting glaze into an ice cube tray and freeze; then store the cubes in an airtight freezer container. To use the cubes, reconstitute them with water.

CHICKEN STOCK

The calf's foot called for here adds an incredible amount of gelatin—and thus body—to the stock.

Makes About 4 Quarts

5 pounds chicken necks, backs and bones
1 calf's foot, split (optional)
2 medium onions, quartered
2 carrots, coarsely chopped
2 celery ribs, coarsely chopped
3 garlic cloves, whole but bruised

3 leeks, green tops only, coarsely chopped
Bouquet garni: 10 parsley stems, ½ teaspoon thyme,
10 peppercorns and 1 bay leaf tied in cheesecloth

1. In a large stockpot, combine all of the ingredients. Add 4½ quarts of water. Bring to a boil over moderate heat, skimming off the foamy scum as it rises to the surface. Lower the heat to maintain a slow simmer. Cook, skimming occasionally, for 4 hours.

2. Strain the stock through a fine-mesh sieve lined with a double layer of dampened cheesecloth. Let cool to room temperature, then cover and refrigerate. Remove the congealed fat from the top before using.

—F&W

FREE-RANGE CHICKEN STOCK

Because free-range chickens are so full of flavor, they are excellent for making stock.

Makes About 2 Quarts

4 to 5 pounds free-range chicken backs,
wings and/or legs and thighs
1 onion, halved
1 carrot, quartered
1 imported bay leaf
½ teaspoon salt
¼ teaspoon thyme

1. In a large stockpot, place the chicken parts, onion, carrot, bay leaf, salt and thyme. Add 4 quarts of cold water and bring to a boil over high heat. Reduce the heat to moderately low and simmer, uncovered, for 4½ hours, skimming off the foam and fat occasionally.

2. Strain into a large saucepan and skim once more. Boil over high heat until the stock is reduced to 2 quarts. Let cool, cover and refrigerate for up to 3 days or freeze for up to 3 months.

—Molly O'Neill

RICH CHICKEN STOCK

Although this deliciously rich stock calls for two whole chickens in addition to chicken parts, the whole birds are removed as soon as they are cooked, so you can eat them as is or use the meat for other dishes, salads or sandwiches. Or substitute additional chicken parts for the whole chickens. Use this stock as a base for soups or sauces.

Makes About 3 Quarts

4 pounds chicken backs, necks
   and/or wings
2 whole chickens (about 3 pounds each),
   including necks and gizzards
3 large carrots, sliced
2 large onions, sliced
4 medium leeks—split lengthwise, rinsed and sliced
   crosswise (or substitute 1 extra onion)
2 celery ribs with leaves, sliced
Bouquet garni: 8 sprigs of parsley, 1 teaspoon thyme,
   1 bay leaf, ½ teaspoon peppercorns and 3 whole
   cloves tied in cheesecloth

1. Place the chicken parts in a large, heavy stockpot; place the whole chickens on top. Add 6 quarts of cold water and place over low heat. Heat to simmering, without stirring; for a clear stock, this should take about 1 hour. While the water is heating, skim off any scum that rises to the surface.

2. Add the carrots, onions, leeks, celery and bouquet garni. Simmer, partially covered, without stirring, for about 45 minutes. Remove both chickens. Continue simmering, without stirring, for about 4 hours, skimming occasionally. (Remove the meat from the chickens and return the bones to the pot.)

3. Ladle the stock carefully through a colander lined with several layers of dampened cheesecloth. Strain a second time, if desired, for an even clearer stock. If using the hot stock immediately, remove the fat by first skimming and then blotting the surface with paper towels, or use a degreasing utensil designed for that purpose.

Otherwise, let the stock cool to room temperature (be sure to let the stock cool uncovered); then cover and refrigerate. Remove the congealed fat from the top before using the stock. If it has been refrigerated for more than 3 days, bring it back to a boil and boil for 3 to 5 minutes before using it.

—F&W

BROWN CHICKEN STOCK

Use this rich, dark stock as the base for sauces to accompany poultry and game birds.

Makes About 1 Quart

3 to 4 pounds of chicken backs, wings
   and/or necks
1 medium onion, unpeeled and quartered
1 celery rib, coarsely sliced
1½ cups dry white wine
2 medium tomatoes, quartered
1 sprig of fresh thyme or ¼ teaspoon dried
½ bay leaf
½ teaspoon peppercorns

1. Preheat the oven to 500°. Place the chicken, onion and celery in a roasting pan and roast, turning the bones once or twice, until they are a dark, golden brown, about 30 minutes.

2. Transfer the chicken and vegetables to a stockpot. Deglaze the roasting pan with the wine and pour into the stockpot. Add the tomatoes, thyme, bay leaf, peppercorns, and enough water to cover by 1 inch. Bring to a boil over high heat, reduce the heat and simmer for 3 hours, skimming off the foam and fat occasionally as they rise to the top.

3. Strain the stock into a large saucepan; there should be about 2 quarts. Skim off any fat. Boil until reduced by half.

—F&W

Appetizers and First Courses

FRIED CHICKEN DRUMETTES WITH LEMON GRASS

If your market does not carry chicken wing sections labeled drumettes, buy 4 pounds of chicken wings. Cut off the meaty joints farthest from the tips; these are the drumettes. Reserve the remainder of the wings for stock.

4 to 6 Servings

2 pounds chicken drumettes
1 tablespoon dark soy sauce★
1½ teaspoons salt
*2 stalks of lemon grass★ (bottom third only),
  finely minced*
2 tablespoons dry sherry
1 tablespoon all-purpose flour
1 tablespoon cornstarch
2 teaspoons freshly ground black pepper
1 teaspoon crushed hot red pepper
¼ cup minced cilantro (fresh coriander)
2 cups peanut oil
Lemon Grass Dipping Sauce (recipe follows)
★Available at Asian markets

1. In a medium bowl, combine the chicken, soy sauce and salt. Toss to coat. Let marinate at room temperature, tossing occasionally, for 1 hour.

2. Put the lemon grass and sherry in a small heatproof bowl. Set in a steamer or on a rack in a saucepan over boiling water, cover and steam for 15 minutes.

3. Combine the flour, cornstarch, black pepper, hot pepper and cilantro. Toss to mix well. Add the seasoned flour and the lemon grass and sherry to the chicken. Toss well to coat evenly.

4. In a large skillet or wok, heat the oil to 375°. Add the chicken in batches without crowding and fry until golden brown, 5 to 7 minutes. Drain on paper towels and serve hot, with a bowl of Lemon Grass Dipping Sauce on the side.

———

—Bruce Cost

LEMON GRASS DIPPING SAUCE

Makes About ⅓ Cup

1 tablespoon peanut oil
*1 stalk of lemon grass★ (bottom third only),
  finely minced*
1½ teaspoons minced fresh ginger
2 tablespoons soy sauce
2 tablespoons rice vinegar
1 tablespoon Oriental sesame oil
1 teaspoon Chinese chile oil★
½ teaspoon sugar
★Available at Asian markets

In a small saucepan, heat the peanut oil over moderate heat. Add the lemon grass and ginger; sauté until fragrant, about 30 seconds. Remove from the heat and add the soy sauce, vinegar, sesame oil, chile oil and sugar. Stir to dissolve the sugar. Pour into a small bowl; let stand at room temperature for 1 hour before serving.

———

—Bruce Cost

BUFFALO CHICKEN WINGS WITH BLUE CHEESE SAUCE

4 to 6 Servings

2 tablespoons finely chopped onion
1 small garlic clove, minced
¼ cup minced parsley
1 cup mayonnaise
½ cup sour cream
¼ cup finely crumbled blue cheese
1 tablespoon fresh lemon juice
1 tablespoon white wine vinegar
¼ teaspoon salt

¼ teaspoon freshly ground black pepper

Pinch of cayenne pepper

1 stick (4 ounces) unsalted butter

¼ cup hot pepper sauce

24 chicken wings (about 4½ pounds)

About 1½ quarts vegetable oil or lard, for
deep-frying

Celery sticks, for garnish

1. In a medium bowl, combine the onion, garlic, parsley, mayonnaise, sour cream, blue cheese, lemon juice, vinegar, salt, black pepper and cayenne; whisk until blended. Cover and refrigerate the blue cheese sauce until 30 minutes before serving.

2. In a large skillet, melt the butter over moderately low heat and add the hot sauce; mix well and set aside. (This makes a medium-hot sauce. For a hotter or milder sauce, adjust the ingredients accordingly.)

3. Cut the wings into three pieces at the joints; discard the tips (or reserve for stock). Pat the chicken pieces dry.

4. In a deep-fryer or a heavy, deep skillet, heat the oil to 375°. Fry the chicken in batches for about 10 minutes, until browned and crisp. Drain on paper towels.

5. When all of the chicken has been fried, rewarm the hot sauce mixture in a large skillet. Add the chicken and toss to thoroughly coat each piece; turn off the heat, cover and let stand for 5 minutes.

6. Serve the chicken accompanied with the celery and the reserved blue cheese dressing for dipping.

———

—Janice Okun

CHICKEN WINGS WITH GARLIC SAUCE

This is a slightly more sophisticated version of *pollo al ajillo*, a dish that finds its way onto just about every restaurant menu in Spain. For easy serving, use chicken wings, although a whole chicken cut into bite-size portions can be used instead.

4 Servings

8 chicken wings (about 1½ pounds)

¼ cup olive oil

10 large garlic cloves

1 tablespoon brandy

½ teaspoon all-purpose flour

¼ cup dry white wine

¼ cup Chicken Stock (p. 10) or canned broth

Salt

1 tablespoon minced parsley

Pinch of saffron threads

3 peppercorns, coarsely cracked

1. Cut off the wing tips and reserve for stock. Divide the remaining wings at the joint into 2 pieces each.

2. In a large skillet, heat the oil until it begins to smoke. Add the chicken wings and whole garlic cloves and sauté over moderately high heat until the chicken and garlic are both golden, about 10 minutes. Remove the garlic as it colors and put it in a mortar or small bowl.

3. Add the brandy to the skillet and ignite with a match. As soon as the flames subside, sprinkle in the flour. Stir in the wine, stock and salt to taste. Cover and simmer for 10 minutes.

4. Meanwhile, mash the garlic. Add the parsley, saffron and peppercorns and mix to a paste. Scrape the mixture into the skillet, stir to combine and continue cooking, covered, for 10 minutes longer *(The dish can be made several hours ahead and reheated.)*

———

—Penelope Casas

VIETNAMESE STUFFED CHICKEN WINGS

It may be a surprise to you that the wings are put into room-temperature oil to fry, but they absorb a minimum of oil and will be very crisp.

Makes About 12

2 pounds chicken wings (about 12)
1 pound skinless, boneless chicken breast,
  thinly sliced crosswise
¼ teaspoon freshly ground white pepper
2 teaspoons cornstarch
½ teaspoon baking powder
¼ teaspoon sugar
1 tablespoon fish sauce (nuoc mam)*
1½ teaspoons vegetable oil, plus about 1 quart
  for deep-frying
1 large scallion, thinly sliced
¼ pound mushrooms, finely chopped
Nuoc Cham Dipping Sauce (recipe follows)
*Available at Asian markets

1. Cut apart the wings at the joint between the meaty "upper arm" and the double-boned "forearm;" reserve the meaty portion for another use. With a small sharp knife, scrape around the exposed joint of the chicken wings to loosen the meat. With your hand, work the meat down the double bone toward the wing tip, squeezing and pushing to separate the skin and meat from the bones. Snap the double bones off at the joint.

2. In a medium bowl, combine the chicken breast slices, white pepper, cornstarch, baking powder, sugar, fish sauce and 1½ teaspoons vegetable oil; mix to blend well. Cover and freeze until very firm, about 15 minutes.

3. In a food processor, puree the chicken breast mixture, scraping down the bowl once or twice, until very smooth and stiff, about 1 minute. Return the mixture to the bowl and stir in the scallion and mushrooms.

4. With oiled hands, hold a boned chicken wing in one hand and push the stuffing into the pocket, packing it in firmly and stuffing it gen-erously. Repeat, using all the filling and chicken wings. The wings should be slightly overstuffed.

5. Put 6 of the chicken wings into a large saucepan set over high heat. Add enough veg-etable oil to cover and cook, stirring occasion-ally, until the wings are golden brown and crisp, about 20 minutes. Remove the wings with tongs to drain on paper towels. Keep warm in a low oven while you fry the remaining wings.

6. Reduce the heat to moderate, add the re-maining stuffed chicken wings to the hot oil and cook until golden brown and crisp. about 15 minutes. Serve at once with Nuoc Cham Dipping Sauce on the side.

———————

—Marcia Kiesel

NUOC CHAM DIPPING SAUCE

This indispensable dipping sauce is served with every Vietnamese meal.

Makes About 2½ Cups

1 teaspoon crushed hot red pepper
1 tablespoon distilled white vinegar
½ cup fish sauce (nuoc mam)*
¼ cup fresh lime juice
1 small carrot—finely shredded, rinsed and
  squeezed dry
2 small garlic cloves, minced
½ cup sugar
*Available at Asian markets

1. In a small dish, soak the hot pepper in the vinegar for 2 minutes.

2. In a small bowl, combine the fish sauce, lime juice, carrot, garlic and sugar. Stir in 1½ cups warm water and the hot pepper-vinegar mixture. Stir until the sugar dissolves. Serve at room temperature. Store the sauce in a jar in the refrigerator for up to 3 days.

———————

—Marcia Kiesel

HOW TO MAKE CHICKEN LOLLIPOPS

1. Cut through the upper joint of each chicken wing to separate the large top section (the section closest to the body) from the lower portion and tip. Reserve this lower part for stock.

2. Cut through the tendons at the base of the narrower end of the wing section. Gently scrape the meat away from the bone toward the large end of the wing.

3. Bunch the meat up around the top of the bone to form a lollipop shape. For dishes that call for this technique, see Rosemary Chicken Lollipops with Spicy Tomato Dipping Sauce (photo below) or Oriental-Style Chicken Lollipops; both recipes are on page 21.

HOW TO MAKE JAMBONNEAUX

1. Cut through the meat down the inside of each thigh to expose the bone.

2. Starting at the top of the thigh and scraping against the bone, work the meat down to the leg joint.

3. Cut the tendons at the joint; do not cut through the skin.

4. Continue scraping down the leg bone, turning the meat inside out as you go.

5. At the lower part of the drumstick, use your fingers to pull the meat and skin down around the end of the bone.

6. Cut through the skin and remove the bones.

7. Remove the exposed tendons by grasping them with pliers or your fingers and pulling them out while scraping against them with a knife.

8. Turn the meat skin-side out and stuff the cavity.

9. Secure with a trussing needle and butcher's twine.

Sautéed Jambonneaux with Mushroom and Wild Rice Stuffing (p. 142).

1. Using a sharp boning knife, cut off the wing at the second joint, leaving the first joint attached to the body. Reserve the rest of the wing for making stock.

2. Pull the legs away from the body; cut through the inside at the top of the thigh bone. Pull the leg outward and cut to remove the whole leg from the body.

3. To separate the thigh from the drumstick, locate the thin line of fat that runs between the thigh and drumstick on the inside of the leg.

4. Angling the knife toward the drumstick, cut along the line of fat to find the joint. Cut through to separate the thigh and drumstick.

5. To help the dark meat cook in the same time as the light breast meat, slit the meat through to the bone along the bottom of the thighs and drumsticks.

6. Lay the chicken on its side with the front end toward you. Starting by the wing joint and slanting the knife down, make a cut the length of the chicken, from back to front.

7. Pull the breast meat (with wing joint attached) away from the body, scraping against the ribs to separate the meat from the bones.

8. With the chicken still on its side, use a knife to sever the back of the chicken from the remaining breast section (reserve the back for stock).

9. With a heavy knife, cut the remaining breast section crosswise into two even pieces.

ORIENTAL-STYLE CHICKEN LOLLIPOPS

For a step-by-step illustration of how to make chicken lollipops, see the photographs at left.

8 Servings

24 chicken wings (about 4 pounds)
1¼ cups soy sauce
½ cup honey
¼ cup vegetable oil
2 star anise pods, broken apart
2 tablespoons grated fresh ginger
3 medium garlic cloves, crushed through a press
20 peppercorns, coarsely cracked
½ teaspoon salt

1. Using a boning knife, cut through the upper joint of each wing, separating the large top section from the rest of the wing; reserve the lower section and the tips for making stock. Cut through the tendons at the base of the narrower end and, using the knife, gently scrape the meat from the bone, pushing it toward the large end. Pull the loosened meat around the top of the bone to form a ball or lollipop shape. Place the lollipops in a dish just large enough to hold them in a single layer.

2. In a medium bowl, combine the soy sauce, honey, oil, star anise, ginger, garlic, peppercorns and salt. Pour over the lollipops and marinate in the refrigerator, turning once or twice, for at least 4 hours or overnight.

3. Preheat the oven to 400°. Let the lollipops come to room temperature; then remove from the marinade and place them in a shallow roasting pan or baking dish. Pour ½ cup of the marinade over the lollipops and bake for 20 minutes, or until golden.

4. Meanwhile, place the remaining marinade in a small saucepan and bring to a boil over high heat. Boil for about 3 minutes, until slightly thickened. Let cool to room temperature and serve as a dipping sauce with the lollipops.

—John Robert Massie

ROSEMARY CHICKEN LOLLIPOPS WITH SPICY TOMATO DIPPING SAUCE

For a step-by-step illustration of how to make chicken lollipops, see the photographs at left.

8 Servings

24 chicken wings (about 4 pounds)
½ cup olive oil, preferably extra-virgin
1 tablespoon dried rosemary, crumbled
½ teaspoon salt
¼ teaspoon freshly ground pepper
Spicy Tomato Dipping Sauce (recipe follows)

1. Using a boning knife, cut through the upper joint of each wing, separating the large top section from the rest of the wing; reserve the lower section and the tips for making stock. Cut through the tendons at the base of the narrower end and, using the knife, gently scrape the meat from the bone, pushing it toward the large end. Pull the loosened meat around the top of the bone to form a ball or lollipop shape. Place the lollipops in a dish just large enough to hold them in a single layer.

2. Preheat the oven to 400°. In a medium bowl, combine the olive oil, rosemary, salt and pepper. Add the wings a few at a time and toss to coat.

3. Transfer the wings to a shallow roasting pan or large baking dish. Bake for 20 minutes, or until golden and lightly crisped. Serve with Spicy Tomato Dipping Sauce.

—John Robert Massie

SPICY TOMATO DIPPING SAUCE

Makes About 2½ Cups

1 can (28 ounces) Italian peeled tomatoes,
   seeded and drained
2 jalapeños, minced
2 large shallots, minced
1 small garlic clove, minced
1 teaspoon salt
¼ teaspoon freshly ground pepper
2 medium tomatoes—peeled, seeded and
   finely diced

In a blender or food processor, puree the canned tomatoes, jalapeños, shallots, garlic, salt and pepper. Puree until smooth, about 1 minute. Pour the puree into a bowl and stir in the diced tomatoes. Serve at room temperature.

—*John Robert Massie*

CHICKEN ROLLS WITH SPINACH AND FETA CHEESE STUFFING

The stuffed chicken rolls can be served either hot or cold. When cold, the rolls are easily sliced and make nice hors d'oeuvres.

8 Servings

3 tablespoons unsalted butter
1 garlic clove, minced
1 teaspoon rosemary, crumbled
1 cup chopped cooked spinach, squeezed dry
½ cup crumbled feta cheese
3 tablespoons fresh bread crumbs
1 egg yolk
½ teaspoon freshly ground pepper
8 skinless, boneless chicken breast halves

1. In a small skillet, melt the butter and add the garlic and rosemary; cook briefly over low heat. Do not allow the garlic to brown even slightly or it will impart a bitter taste.

2. In a medium bowl, combine the spinach and feta. Pour the butter mixture over the spinach; mix until thoroughly blended. Stir in the bread crumbs, egg yolk and pepper. Set the stuffing aside while you prepare the chicken breasts.

3. Using a meat pounder, mallet or rolling pin, pound or roll the 8 breast halves into 5- or 6-inch squares or ovals (the shape isn't important) about ¼ inch thick.

4. Using about ¼ cup for each breast half, divide the filling among the breasts, making a cylindrical shape down the center of each. Roll the chicken breast into a cylinder to enclose the filling and secure with a toothpick.

5. Add water to a steamer to 1 inch below the rack and bring it to a full, rolling boil. Place the chicken rolls on the rack, cover and steam for 15 minutes.

———

—*F&W*

CHICKEN MEDALLIONS WITH ROASTED RED PEPPER SAUCE

❦ Spanish red, such as Torres Coronas

12 to 18 Servings

12 skinless, boneless chicken breast halves
6 tablespoons unsalted butter
4 medium shallots, minced
2 large carrots, finely chopped
¾ pound mushrooms, stemmed and
   finely chopped
¾ teaspoon salt
¾ teaspoon freshly ground pepper
24 large spinach leaves
12 thin slices of prosciutto, cut crosswise in half
2 cups all-purpose flour
3 tablespoons olive oil
Roasted Red Pepper Sauce (recipe follows)

1. Pound each chicken breast between sheets of plastic wrap or two large heavy plastic bags until evenly ⅜ inch thick and rectangular in shape.

2. In a large skillet, melt the butter. Add the shallots and sauté over moderately high heat until translucent, about 1 minute. Add the carrots and mushrooms and sauté until most of the moisture from the mushrooms has evaporated, about 2 minutes. Season with ¼ teaspoon each of the salt and pepper.

3. Dip the spinach leaves in boiling water for about 10 seconds, until just limp but still bright green. Drain on paper towels and press out as much moisture as possible without tearing the leaves.

4. To assemble, place each chicken breast smooth-side down on the work surface. Cover with a piece of prosciutto and 1 or 2 spinach leaves. Spread about 2 tablespoons of the mushroom-carrot mixture on top in a thin even layer. Starting at one of the long sides, roll up. *(The recipe can be prepared ahead to this point. Wrap well and refrigerate. Remove from the refrigerator about 30 minutes before proceeding.)*

5. Season the flour with the remaining ½ teaspoon salt and ½ teaspoon pepper. Dredge the rolled chicken breasts in the seasoned flour and set on a rack for about 10 minutes to dry.

6. Preheat the oven to 375°. In a large heavy skillet, warm 1½ tablespoons of the oil over moderately high heat until shimmering. Add half the rolls seam-side down in a single layer and brown briefly on all sides; remove and set aside. Add the remaining 1½ tablespoons oil to the skillet and repeat with the remaining chicken.

7. Transfer the chicken to a baking sheet and roast for 8 to 10 minutes, until just cooked through. When cool enough to handle, slice crosswise into ¾-inch-thick medallions. Serve warm or at room temperature with Roasted Red Pepper Sauce as a condiment on the side.

—*Taste, San Francisco*

ROASTED RED PEPPER SAUCE

This sauce can be made a day or two ahead and refrigerated. Let return to room temperature before serving.

Makes About 2½ Cups

12 large red bell peppers
1 medium red onion, minced
2 garlic cloves, minced
Pinch of sugar
Pinch of salt
2 tablespoons vegetable oil

1. Preheat the oven to 500°. Place the peppers on a baking sheet and roast, turning frequently, until the skin is black and blistered all over, about 15 minutes. Seal the peppers in a plastic bag and let sit for at least 10 minutes.

2. Rub the skin off the peppers. Remove the stems, seeds and ribs. In a food processor, puree the peppers with the onion, garlic, sugar and salt.

3. In a large heavy skillet, heat the oil. Add the pepper puree and cook over moderate heat, stirring frequently, until slightly thicker than ketchup, about 15 minutes.

—*Taste, San Francisco*

CHICKEN-AND-SHRIMP WONTONS

Ideal for parties, wontons can be prepared ahead of time and fried just before serving.

Makes 48 Wontons

½ pound skinless, boneless chicken breast
¼ pound small shrimp, shelled and deveined
⅓ cup finely chopped onion
1 egg white
½ tablespoon soy sauce
1 teaspoon minced fresh ginger
½ tablespoon cornstarch
1 teaspoon sugar

½ cup water chestnuts, finely diced
1 egg yolk
48 wonton skins,★ thawed if frozen
Vegetable oil, for deep-frying
Duck sauce or sweet-and-sour sauce, for
  accompaniment
★Available at Asian markets

1. In a food processor, process the chicken, shrimp, onion, egg white, soy sauce, ginger, cornstarch and sugar until smooth, 30 seconds to 1 minute. Stir in the water chestnuts.

2. Shape the wontons: Place the egg yolk in a cup and stir in 1 tablespoon cold water. Center 2 teaspoons of the filling on one wonton skin. Moisten the edge of the skin all around with the egg-yolk mixture. Bring all four points upward to meet in the center. Pinch the seams together so that they protrude outward. Use the remaining filling to stuff the remaining wonton skins. Place them in a dish and cover tightly to prevent their drying out.

3. In a deep-fryer with a deep-frying basket inserted, heat about 3 inches of oil to 375°. Using a slotted spoon, place six or seven wontons into the basket in the oil and fry for about 2 minutes, or until golden brown and crisp and the chicken is cooked through. Remove with the basket and drain. Repeat with the remaining wontons. Serve hot with duck sauce or sweet-and-sour sauce.

———

—F&W

CURRIED SMOKED CHICKEN SALAD IN PHYLLO BASKETS

Smoked chicken, which is available at supermarket delis and specialty food shops, makes this a special salad. Be sure to use a good-quality curry powder.

❦ Spicy white, such as Alsace Gewürztraminer
  Makes 2½ Dozen

3 tablespoons unsalted butter, melted
5 sheets of phyllo dough
⅓ cup mayonnaise
2 tablespoons fresh lemon juice
1 tablespoon curry powder
1 cup finely diced cooked chicken breast,
  skinned and boned (about 5 ounces)
1 cup finely diced smoked chicken breast,
  skinned and boned (about 5 ounces)
1 carrot, shredded
1 celery rib, cut into ⅛-inch dice
1 tablespoon golden raisins, chopped
1 tablespoon diced roasted red pepper
1 scallion, thinly sliced

1. Preheat the oven to 350°. Lightly brush 2 miniature muffin tins, 1¾ inches in diameter, with 1 tablespoon of the melted butter.

2. Lightly brush 1 sheet of phyllo with some of the remaining melted butter. Lay another sheet of phyllo on top and brush lightly with butter; repeat with the remaining 3 phyllo sheets and melted butter. Using a 2½-inch round cutter, cut the stack of phyllo into 30 circles.

3. Place a phyllo circle in each prepared muffin cup and press the dough against the bottom and sides. Bake until the baskets are light brown, about 8 minutes. Remove from the oven and let cool in the pan on a rack before unmolding. *(The recipe can be prepared to this point up to 1 day ahead. Cover and store at room temperature.)*

4. In a medium bowl, combine the mayonnaise, lemon juice and curry powder. Add the cooked and smoked chicken, the carrot, celery, raisins, red pepper and scallion; toss to mix well. *(The recipe can be prepared to this point up to 6 hours ahead. Cover and refrigerate; let return to room temperature before proceeding.)*

5. Shortly before serving, fill each phyllo cup with 1 heaping tablespoon of the chicken salad. Serve slightly chilled or at room temperature.

—*Ridgewell's, Bethesda, Maryland*

MARINATED CHICKEN BREASTS ALEXANDRE

Here is a unique chicken-based first course, excellent for stimulating the appetite.

♆ Beaujolais Nouveau

4 to 6 Servings

2 pounds veal bones
3 cups canned chicken broth
4 skinless, boneless chicken breast halves
  (about 5 ounces each)
2 tablespoons sherry wine vinegar
2 tablespoons white wine vinegar
¼ cup olive oil
2 tablespoons corn or peanut oil
2 teaspoons Dijon-style mustard
1 tablespoon fresh lemon juice
1 teaspoon Cognac or other brandy
2 whole cloves
1 medium shallot, finely minced
2 tablespoons minced fresh chives
2 tablespoons minced fresh tarragon or 2
  teaspoons dried
Salt and freshly ground pepper
1 cup green beans, cut into 2-inch lengths,
  for garnish
1 large tomato, quartered and seeded,
  for garnish
12 very thin slices black truffle (optional)

1. In a large saucepan, simmer the veal bones, 1 cup of the chicken broth and water to cover for 1 hour, skimming the foam from the top occasionally. Strain and skim off the fat. Measure out 1 cup of the veal broth to use in the marinade in Step 3; reserve the remainder for another use.

2. In a large deep skillet or heatproof casserole, arrange the chicken breasts in a single layer. Add the remaining 2 cups chicken broth and enough water, if necessary, just to cover. Heat to a bare simmer, cover and poach gently until the breasts are barely pink in the center, 8 to 10 minutes. Remove, drain and pat dry.

3. Meanwhile, make the marinade: In a small bowl, whisk the reserved 1 cup of veal broth, the sherry wine vinegar, white wine vinegar, olive oil, corn oil, mustard, lemon juice and Cognac until blended. Stir in the cloves, shallot, chives and tarragon. Season with salt and pepper to taste.

4. With a very sharp knife, cut each chicken breast *horizontally* into 3 thin slices. Arrange the slices in a single layer in a large nonreactive pan or baking dish. Pour the marinade over the chicken; turn to coat both sides. Marinate, turning the slices every 30 minutes, for at least 1 and up to 3 hours.

5. Serve the chicken at room temperature, sauced with a little of the marinade. Garnish each plate with some green beans and a tomato quarter, dressed with the marinade. Decorate each piece of chicken with a slice of black truffle, if desired.

—*Georges Blanc, La Mère Blanc, Vonnas, France*

PALMIERS OF CHICKEN WITH ORANGES AND LEEKS

Inspired by the classic *palmiers*, which are small Parisian cookies made with puff pastry, our version uses chicken breasts and orange segments. It makes an elegant first course.

6 Servings

5 tablespoons olive oil, or 2 tablespoons olive
   oil and 3 tablespoons walnut oil
1½ cups chopped leeks (white portions only)
2½ tablespoons Chinese salted black beans,★
   rinsed and coarsely chopped
6 small skinless, boneless chicken breast halves
   (about 4 ounces each)
2 navel oranges, peeled and segmented
Orange segments, watercress leaves and
   chutney, for garnish
★Available at Asian markets

1. In a skillet, heat 3 tablespoons of the olive oil (or 2 tablespoons olive oil and 1 tablespoon walnut oil). Add the leeks and sauté for 1 minute over moderate heat. Add the beans and sauté until the leeks are soft, 2 to 3 minutes.

2. Between sheets of waxed paper, pound the chicken breasts until they are about ¼ inch thick (or slightly less) and oval-shaped; carefully peel off the waxed paper. Brush one side of each cutlet with some of the remaining oil and then spread it with about ¼ cup of the leek mixture, leaving a ¼-inch border all around. Place an orange segment near each end of each chicken oval and turn the ends of the chicken over the oranges to meet in the center. Then fold the chicken in half to enclose the oranges. Tie the roll closed at each end with string and place in a steamer. Cover and steam for 10 minutes.

3. Cool the *palmiers* to room temperature, cover and then chill. Just before serving, remove the string and cut them crosswise into ½-inch-thick slices. Serve cold or at room temperature garnished with the orange segments, watercress leaves and chutney.

———

—F&W

CHICKEN WITH GARLIC CREAM IN PHYLLO TULIP CUPS

This savory filling with its mild garlic flavor and creamy sauce is for prebaked phyllo shapes. Sandwiched between phyllo sheets, cut into decorative rounds it makes a delightful luncheon dish.

6 Servings

8 garlic cloves, finely chopped
3 shallots, finely chopped
¾ cup dry white wine
10 black peppercorns
1½ cups heavy cream
1 tablespoon vegetable oil
6 skinless, boneless chicken breast halves, cut
   into 1-inch cubes and patted dry
⅜ teaspoon salt
3 tablespoons unsalted butter
3 tablespoons finely chopped parsley
Pinch of freshly ground white pepper
4 sheets of phyllo dough
4 tablespoons clarified butter

1. In a medium saucepan, combine the garlic, shallots, wine and peppercorns. Bring to a boil and cook over moderately high heat until the liquid is reduced to about 1 tablespoon. Add the cream and boil until reduced by about half. Strain through a fine sieve, pressing down on the solids to extract all the liquid. *(The sauce can be prepared to this point several hours ahead.)*

2. In a large skillet, heat the oil over high heat until it starts to smoke. Add the chicken and toss in the oil to coat. Reduce the heat to moder-

ately high and sauté, tossing occasionally, until lightly browned outside, 3 to 4 minutes. Remove to a plate and season lightly with ⅛ teaspoon of the salt. Cover loosely and set aside in a warm place.

3. Reheat the cream sauce to a simmer. Remove from the heat and whisk in the butter 1 tablespoon at a time. Add the parsley, white pepper, remaining ¼ teaspoon salt and any juices from the chicken.

4. Preheat the oven to 375°. Working with 1 sheet of phyllo at a time (keep the remainder covered with plastic wrap and a damp towel), lightly brush with clarified butter. Cover with a second sheet of dough and another coating of butter. Repeat until all 4 of the sheets of phyllo have been brushed with butter (not all of the butter will be used).

5. Cut the stack of buttered phyllo into 12 squares. Brush the insides of muffin cups with some of the remaining clarified butter. Press each phyllo square into a muffin cup, pressing the bottom flat and folding excess dough to create a petal effect on the sides. Bake in the bottom third of the oven for about 12 minutes, until light golden brown.

6. Fill the tulip cups with the chicken cubes and coat with the sauce.

—F&W

CORN CREPE CAKE WITH CHICKEN CHILE FILLING
4 Servings

2 eggs
½ cup milk
½ cup corn kernels, fresh or frozen
½ cup all-purpose flour
¼ cup yellow cornmeal
2 tablespoons corn oil, plus oil for cooking
  the crêpes
½ teaspoon salt
⅛ teaspoon freshly ground pepper
2 teaspoons sugar
1 teaspoon cumin
2 tablespoons olive oil
½ medium onion, chopped
1 garlic clove, minced
2 plum tomatoes—peeled, seeded and chopped
2 tablespoons chopped cilantro (fresh coriander)
1½ cups finely diced cooked chicken
3 scallions, thinly sliced
1 jalapeño (fresh or pickled)—seeded, ribbed
  and cut into slivers
¼ cup freshly grated aged Monterey Jack or
  Parmesan cheese
½ cup shredded Monterey Jack cheese
2 tablespoons sour cream, plus additional sour
  cream for serving

1. In a blender or food processor, combine the eggs, milk, corn and ½ cup of water. Puree until smooth. Add the flour, cornmeal, 2 tablespoons corn oil, the salt, pepper, sugar and cumin. Mix until blended. Refrigerate, covered, for about 1 hour before using.

2. Heat a 6- to 7-inch crêpe pan over moderate heat. Brush with a little corn oil. Pour about 3 tablespoons of corn crêpe batter into the center of the pan and swirl to cover the bottom evenly. Cook for about 1 minute, until the bottom of the crêpe is lightly browned. Turn and cook for about 10 seconds, until dry and spotted brown

on the other side. Repeat until the batter is used up, stacking the finished crêpes between sheets of paper towels.

3. Preheat the oven to 400°. In a medium skillet, heat the olive oil. Add the onion and garlic and sauté over moderate heat until the onion is translucent, about 3 minutes.

4. Add the tomatoes and cilantro and cook, stirring occasionally, until the sauce thickens, about 10 minutes. Remove from the heat and stir in the chicken, scallions and jalapeño.

5. To assemble, use 6 crêpes. (Freeze any extras for another use.) Mix together the grated and shredded cheeses. Place one crêpe on a lightly oiled baking sheet. Spread about one-fifth of the chicken mixture evenly over the crêpe. Sprinkle with 2 tablespoons of the cheese. Place another crêpe on top and lightly press to flatten. Repeat with remaining filling, cheese and crêpes. Spread 2 tablespoons of sour cream on top and sprinkle on the remaining cheese.

6. Bake for 10 to 15 minutes, until the cheese melts and the crêpes and filling are heated through. Let rest for 5 minutes. Use a large spatula to transfer the "cake" to a serving platter. Cut into wedges and pass a bowl of sour cream on the side.

—*Jeanette Ferrary & Louise Fiszer*

JAPANESE STEAMED CUSTARD WITH CHICKEN

Here's a fresh, protein-rich custard of Japanese extraction, a dish popular enough in Japan to warrant special, lidded custard cups. If you cannot find these at Oriental import shops, you can improvise by using sturdy, heatproof, 8-ounce coffee mugs (such as those made of stoneware, earthenware, or porcelain) and aluminum foil as a cover. When you remove the cups from the steamer, don't be alarmed if the custard is not as firmly set as you are accustomed to; these custards are extremely light and soft.

8 Servings

3 eggs
2¼ cups Chicken Stock (p. 10) or
  canned broth
¾ cup bottled clam juice
1½ tablespoons plus 2 teaspoons dark shoyu
  (Japanese soy sauce)★
2 tablespoons mirin (sweet rice wine),★ dry
  sherry or sake
4 ounces skinless, boneless chicken breast, cut
  into 8 equal pieces, each measuring ½ by ½
  by 2 inches
4 medium shrimp—shelled, halved lengthwise
  and deveined
32 nameko or enoki mushrooms★
16 small sprigs of watercress
8 canned ginkgo nuts,★ peeled
  and rinsed
★ Available at Asian markets

1. In a medium bowl, beat the eggs; beat in the chicken stock and clam juice and stir until the mixture is well blended. Stir in 1½ tablespoons of the soy sauce and the mirin; set the mixture aside.

2. Set eight 8-ounce custard cups out on a work surface. Place the remaining 2 teaspoons soy sauce in a small cup. Dip the chicken pieces and shrimp halves into the soy sauce and divide them among the 8 cups. Place 4 *nameko* mush-

rooms, 2 sprigs watercress and 1 ginkgo nut in each cup.

·3. Pour ½ cup of the egg mixture into each custard cup and cover. Fill the bottom of a steamer (large enough to accommodate all 8 cups) with hot water; it should come no farther than 1 inch below the steamer rack. Bring the water to a full, rolling boil. Carefully set the custard cups on the steamer rack, cover and steam at a full boil for 5 minutes. Lower the heat to moderate and steam for an additional 6 minutes. Cool for 5 minutes and serve.

———

—F&W

CHICKEN AND BROCCOLI TARTS

It is important that the glaze used to finish the tarts be freshly made and still hot. To ensure this, it is best to assemble all the tarts completely and then to glaze them all at once. If you do not want to make all four tarts, simply halve the ingredients and freeze the extra pastry dough.

To cut the tarts at serving time, use a long, heavy, sharp knife and apply pressure to it along the back of the blade (rather than using a sawing motion) so as not to disturb the design.

Makes Four 5-by-10-Inch Tarts

4 Butter Pastry Tart Shells (recipe follows)
1 cup mayonnaise
1 teaspoon basil
1 teaspoon oregano
2 tablespoons finely minced parsley
12 cooked broccoli florets, each about
  2 inches long
4 skinless, boneless chicken breast halves,
  cooked and chilled
40 carrot rounds, cooked
32 strips (¼ by 2¼ inches) green bell
  pepper, cooked
1 large roasted red pepper, cut into 36 small
  diamond shapes
2 level teaspoons cornstarch

¾ cup Chicken Stock (p. 10) or canned broth,
  degreased and at room temperature

1. Bake the tart shells and set aside.

2. Meanwhile, in a medium bowl, blend the mayonnaise, basil, oregano and parsley.

3. Using a small spoon, gently spread each tart shell with one-fourth of the herb mayonnaise, bringing it just to the rim.

4. Slice the broccoli florets lengthwise, including the stems, to create 12 tree-shaped cross-sections. Cut each chicken breast half lengthwise into 4 slices. Then cut each of these in half crosswise and trim one end of each into a neat U-shape. Finally, cut half of the U-shaped pieces of chicken in half again.

5. With a short side of a tart shell toward you, make two horizontal rows of carrot rounds to divide the tart into thirds. Make a border for each carrot row, top and bottom, with bell pepper strips.

6. In each third of the tart, place two broccoli slices, stem-end toward you, so they look like trees side by side. Between the two "trees," place a U-shaped piece of chicken. Fill in the space on the other sides of the broccoli trees with the half-U chicken shapes. Place a red pepper diamond in the middle of each piece of chicken.

7. Make the glaze: In a small saucepan, combine the cornstarch and stock. Cook over moderate heat, stirring constantly, until the mixture comes to a full boil. Remove from the heat and carefully spoon some of the glaze over each tart. Cool the tarts to room temperature and then chill them, uncovered, for at least an hour; if necessary to hold longer, cover them loosely with plastic wrap or aluminum foil.

———

—Jim Fobel

BUTTER PASTRY TART SHELLS

Makes Four 5-by-10-Inch Shells

3 cups all-purpose flour
½ teaspoon salt
2 sticks (8 ounces) unsalted butter,
  well chilled
⅓ cup vegetable shortening
½ cup plus 1 tablespoon ice water
1 egg yolk, for glazing

1. Place the flour and salt in a large mixing bowl. Cut the butter into very thin slices and submerge them in the flour. Using a pastry blender or two knives, rapidly blend the flour and butter together until the mixture resembles coarse meal. Using the same procedure, blend in the shortening. Do not allow the mixture to get warm, or it will not make a flaky pastry. Refrigerate it if necessary.

2. Toss some ice cubes with the ice water before measuring it to make sure that it is as cold as possible. Sprinkle half the ice water over the flour mixture and stir rapidly with a fork. Sprinkle the remaining water over the pastry and continue mixing rapidly with the fork only until blended; do not overwork the dough.

3. Divide the dough in half. Flatten each half onto a separate sheet of waxed paper; wrap each tightly and refrigerate for at least 2 hours to firm the dough.

4. Make the tart shells: Preheat the oven to 400°. Out of paper, cut a 5-by-10-inch rectangle for a pattern.

5. Working on a lightly floured surface, roll out half the chilled pastry into a 12-inch square. It should be about ⅛ inch thick or slightly more. Work quickly so that the dough does not soften.

6. Using a paring knife to cut around the pattern, cut out two rectangles of dough. Also cut out eight ¼-inch-wide strips, four that are 9½ inches long and four that are 5 inches. (Refrigerate the pastry scraps for another use.) Using a lightly floured spatula, transfer the two pastry rectangles to an ungreased baking sheet.

7. Beat the egg yolk with 1 teaspoon water in a cup to make a glaze. Using a small brush or your fingertip, moisten the top of the outer edge of one pastry rectangle. Then edge the rectangle with four corresponding strips of pastry, laying the strips flat so that a ⅛-inch-deep rim is formed around the rectangle. Brush the top of the rim with more glaze. Repeat the procedure to make a second tart shell.

8. Repeat Steps 5 through 7 with the remaining pastry to make two more tart shells.

9. Prick the bottoms of the tart shells all over with a fork and bake them for 12 to 15 minutes, or until they are golden brown and crisp. Remove the baking sheets from the oven and allow the shells to cool for about 5 minutes. Then, using a spatula, carefully transfer them to a wire rack and allow them to thoroughly cool. The tarts may be left at room temperature for one day, loosely covered with aluminum foil.

———————

—*Jim Fobel*

CHICKEN PANCAKES WITH PEAR SALSA

It's best not to make these too large. They cook quickly, so it's not a chore.

8 Servings

6 medium chicken thighs (1¾ pounds total)
1¼ teaspoons salt
¾ teaspoon freshly ground pepper
1 medium Idaho potato
1 small onion, coarsely grated
2 tablespoons all-purpose flour
2 dashes of hot pepper sauce
3 eggs, lightly beaten

2 tablespoons unsalted butter
2 tablespoons safflower oil
Pear Salsa (recipe follows)

1. Preheat the oven to 375°. Season the chicken with ½ teaspoon each salt and pepper. Put the thighs snugly, skin-side up with the skin stretched out, in a baking dish. Bake for 35 minutes, or until the juices run clear when pricked with a knife. Turn off the heat and leave the chicken in the oven for another 45 minutes without opening the door.

2. When the chicken is cool enough to handle. remove the skin and bones and discard. Chop the chicken coarsely. *(The recipe can be prepared to this point up to 1 day ahead. Cover and refrigerate.)*

3. Peel the potato, grate it and squeeze out as much liquid as possible. In a medium bowl, combine the potato, onion, flour, hot sauce, remaining ¾ teaspoon salt and ¼ teaspoon pepper. Mix to blend well. Add the chicken and eggs and mix.

4. In a large nonstick skillet, melt the butter in the oil over moderate heat until hot but not smoking. Drop rounded tablespoons of the batter into the skillet, allowing room for them to spread. Cook over moderately high heat, until golden on the bottom and set, about 4 minutes. Turn over, flatten slightly with a spatula and cook until golden on the bottom, about 2 minutes longer. Serve the pancakes on a warmed platter with the Pear Salsa on the side.

———————

—*Lee Bailey*

PEAR SALSA

I have made this same recipe with peaches, and it is equally good. However, I'd save that for summer when peaches are at their best. If you prefer your salsa very zesty, add more scallions and jalapeño pepper.

Makes About 3 Cups

2 plum tomatoes
2 firm pears, preferably Bosc—peeled, cored
  and cut into ¼-inch dice
1 tablespoon fresh lemon juice
6 large scallions, chopped
1 tablespoon minced, seeded jalapeño
¼ cup plus 2 tablespoons extra-virgin
  olive oil
2 tablespoons sherry wine vinegar
1 teaspoon honey

1. Blanch the tomatoes in a medium saucepan of boiling water for 1 minute. Rinse under cold running water to cool. Slip the skins off, cut the tomatoes in half and scoop out the seeds. Slice the tomatoes into ¼-inch julienne strips.

2. In a medium bowl, toss the pears with the lemon juice. Add the tomatoes, scallions and jalapeño; toss to mix well.

3. In another medium bowl, whisk together the oil, vinegar and honey. Drizzle over the pears and toss to coat. *(The recipe can be prepared ahead to this point. If you are having it within 3 hours, set aside at room temperature; up to 1 day ahead, cover and refrigerate.)* Serve with a slotted spoon, allowing most of the juice to drain off.

———————

—*Lee Bailey*

CHICKEN AND SPINACH CAKES WITH SHIITAKE MUSHROOM SAUCE

If the fresh shiitakes called for here are not available, any other wild mushrooms could be used in their place.

❦ The earthy, savory richness of the sauce is best paired with a flavorful but not overbearing red, such as a Charles Shaw Harvest Wine or Parducci Pinot Noir.

8 Servings

¼ cup plus 2 tablespoons olive oil
¾ pound shallots, thinly sliced
¼ pound bacon, coarsely chopped
1½ pounds skinless, boneless chicken breast,
    cut into ½-inch cubes
1 package (10 ounces) frozen chopped spinach,
    thawed and squeezed dry
¾ cup heavy cream
1½ cups fresh bread crumbs
1½ teaspoons freshly ground black pepper
¼ teaspoon salt
¼ teaspoon cayenne pepper
1 tablespoon unsalted butter
2 pounds fresh shiitake mushrooms, stemmed
    and thinly sliced
½ teaspoon thyme
1 can (10½ ounces) low-sodium chicken broth

1. In a large saucepan, heat 2 tablespoons of the olive oil. Add the shallots and cook over moderate heat, stirring occasionally, until lightly golden, 8 to 10 minutes. Set aside.

2. Place the bacon in a food processor and pulse until finely chopped. Transfer the bacon to a large bowl. Add half of the chicken to the processor and pulse until minced. Add the minced chicken to the bacon in the bowl. Repeat with the remaining chicken cubes.

3. To the bowl, add the spinach, 6 tablespoons of the heavy cream, ⅓ cup of the bread crumbs, ½ cup of the cooked shallots, 1 teaspoon of the black pepper and the salt and cayenne. Mix well to thoroughly blend the ingredients. Form the mixture into 16 little round cakes.

4. Preheat the oven to 400°. In a shallow bowl, mix the remaining bread crumbs with the remaining ½ teaspoon black pepper. Coat the cakes with the seasoned bread crumbs.

5. In a large skillet, heat 2 tablespoons of the olive oil over moderately high heat. Add 8 of the cakes and fry, turning once, until browned, about 3 minutes per side. Transfer to a baking sheet. Repeat with 1 more tablespoon of the olive oil and the remaining 8 chicken cakes. Bake the cakes for 10 to 12 minutes, until firm.

6. Meanwhile, reheat the shallots over high heat. Stir in the butter, mushrooms, thyme and the remaining 1 tablespoon olive oil. Cover and cook, stirring frequently, until the mushrooms soften and begin to brown, 4 to 5 minutes.

7. Stir in the chicken broth and the remaining 6 tablespoons heavy cream and bring to a boil; cook until the sauce reduces and lightly coats the back of a spoon, 8 to 10 minutes. Season the sauce with salt and pepper to taste.

8. To serve, place 2 chicken cakes on each of 8 warmed plates and spoon a generous amount of mushrooms and sauce on top.

———————————

—*Bob Chambers*

CHICKEN QUENELLES
WITH MUSHROOM
DUXELLES

🍷 Vouvray Sec or California Dry Chenin Blanc

8 Servings

4 tablespoons unsalted butter
¼ cup minced shallots
2 cups (6 ounces) finely chopped mushrooms
¼ cup all-purpose flour
½ cup Chicken Stock (p. 10) or
*   canned broth*
1 pound skinless, boneless chicken breast, cut
*   into 1-inch pieces and chilled*
¾ teaspoon salt
Pinch of freshly ground white pepper
Pinch of cayenne pepper
5 egg whites, chilled
1 cup heavy cream, chilled
Beurre Blanc (recipe follows)

1. In a medium skillet, melt 2 tablespoons of the butter over moderate heat. Add the shallots and mushrooms and sauté, stirring, until the mushrooms have given up their juice and are reduced in volume by half, about 5 minutes. Set aside the mushroom duxelles.

2. In a medium saucepan, melt the remaining 2 tablespoons butter over moderately low heat. Add the flour and cook, stirring, for 5 minutes without browning to make a roux. Whisk in the stock, bring to a boil and cook, stirring, until thickened and smooth, about 1 minute. Remove the thickened flour base from the heat and let cool to room temperature.

3. In a food processor, grind the chicken to a smooth paste, 3 to 4 minutes. Scrape down the sides of the bowl and add the salt, white pepper and cayenne. Mix to blend well, about 30 seconds. Add the cooled flour base and mix until well blended, about 30 seconds.

4. Scrape the mixture into a large bowl set over ice. With a wooden spoon, beat in the egg whites, one at a time. Gradually beat in the heavy cream, about 1 tablespoon at a time. Continue to beat over ice for 1 to 2 minutes to lighten the mixture. Cover and refrigerate for at least 15 minutes to chill well. *(The recipe can be prepared ahead to this point and refrigerated overnight.)*

5. Spread 4 sheets of parchment paper (12 by 9 inches) on a flat surface. Spoon one-quarter of the chicken mixture (about 1 cup) in a 6-by-2-inch strip down the middle of one sheet of parchment. Make a deep groove down the center of the chicken and neatly fill with one-quarter (about ¼ cup) of the duxelles. With a rubber spatula, gently lift the long edges of the chicken mixture up and over the filling to completely enclose it and form a filled roll. Wrap the roll in the parchment paper by folding over the two long sides and pinching and tying the two short ends with string to form a sausage shape. Do not wrap too tightly; allow some room for expansion as the mixture cooks. Repeat to form 3 more rolls with the remaining ingredients.

6. Fill a large deep skillet with 3 inches of water; bring to a simmer. Gently lower the rolls into the simmering water and poach, turning after 10 minutes, for about 20 minutes, or until firm.

7. Remove the rolls, unwrap and drain on paper towels. Slice each roll crosswise on the diagonal into 10 slices. Arrange 5 overlapping slices on each plate and coat lightly with Beurre Blanc.

—F&W

BEURRE BLANC

If not served immediately, this sauce can be kept warm in a pan of hot—not simmering—water for up to 30 minutes.

Makes About 1½ Cups

2 tablespoons minced shallots
¼ cup dry white wine
¼ cup white wine vinegar
3 sticks (12 ounces) cold unsalted butter, cut into tablespoons
½ teaspoon salt
⅛ teaspoon freshly ground white pepper

1. In a heavy nonreactive saucepan, combine the shallots, wine and vinegar. Bring to a boil over high heat and boil until the liquid is reduced to 1 tablespoon, 4 to 5 minutes.

2. Remove from the heat and whisk in 4 tablespoons of the butter, 2 tablespoons at a time, until incorporated. Return the pan to very low heat and gradually whisk in the remaining butter, 2 tablespoons at a time. Season with the salt and pepper.

—F&W

CHICKEN-HAZELNUT QUENELLES

6 to 8 Servings

QUENELLE MIXTURE:
1 pound skinless, boneless chicken breast
⅓ cup hazelnuts
1½ teaspoons salt
¾ teaspoon white pepper
1½ teaspoons sage leaves, crumbled
2 egg whites
2¼ cups heavy cream

SAUCE:
3 cups Chicken Stock (p. 10) or canned broth
1 cup dry white wine
½ cup coarsely chopped onion
½ cup coarsely chopped carrot
Bouquet garni: 8 white peppercorns, 3 sprigs of parsley, 1 bay leaf and ½ teaspoon sage leaves tied in cheesecloth
1½ cups heavy cream
¼ cup tomato paste
Salt and freshly ground white pepper

1. Prepare the quenelle mixture: Cut the chicken breasts into ½-inch pieces. In a food processor, finely grind the hazelnuts using an on-and-off motion. Remove the nuts and set them aside. Refrigerate the chicken and the container and blade of the processor for about 10 minutes.

2. Place the chicken, salt, pepper and sage in the chilled container fitted with the steel blade and process for about 1 minute. Add the egg whites and hazelnuts and process 30 seconds longer. With the machine still running, add the cream in a slow, steady stream and process until it is incorporated, about 1 minute. Transfer the mixture to a glass or stainless-steel bowl and chill until ready to cook.

3. Prepare the sauce: In a medium saucepan, place the stock, wine, onion, carrot and bouquet garni. Bring the mixture to a boil, reduce the heat slightly and simmer for 30 minutes. Remove the bouquet garni. Put the mixture through a food mill or push it through a sieve with a wooden spoon; place the sauce in a saucepan.

4. In a small bowl, slowly add the cream to the tomato paste, whisking constantly. When the mixture is smooth, add it to the sauce. Bring the sauce to a boil over moderate heat and cook until it is reduced to about 1½ cups. Remove the pan from the heat, stir in salt and pepper to taste and keep the sauce warm.

5. Poach the quenelles: Bring 2 inches of salted water to a simmer in a shallow pan. Working in batches, use two soup spoons dipped in hot water to form oval shapes of the quenelle mixture. Gently slide the ovals off the spoon into the simmering water; simmer for 3 to 4 minutes on each side. Lift the quenelles out with a slotted spoon, drain on paper towels and keep warm on a heated platter until all have been cooked. Divide the sauce among the individual plates, top with the quenelles and serve.

—F&W

TOMATO RAVIOLI WITH FENNEL SAUSAGE AND CHICKEN FILLING

These ravioli can be sauced with either of the two sauces—Béchamel Sauce with Parmesan or Creamy Tomato Sauce—that follow.

12 Servings

FILLING:
2 tablespoons olive oil
2 skinless, boneless chicken breast halves (about 5 ounces each)
1¼ pounds sweet Italian sausage, casings removed
2 garlic cloves, crushed through a press
¼ cup heavy cream
Salt and freshly ground pepper

TOMATO PASTA:
About 2½ cups all-purpose or bread flour
5 tablespoons tomato paste
2 whole eggs
1 egg yolk
2 teaspoons olive oil
Pinch of salt

1. Make the filling: In a medium skillet, heat the oil. Add the chicken breast and sauté over moderate heat, turning once, until lightly browned and resistant to the touch, about 10 minutes. Remove from the skillet and let cool.

2. Add the sausage to the skillet and sauté over moderate heat, stirring to break up the meat, for 4 minutes. Add the garlic and cook until the meat begins to brown and there is no trace of pink, about 2 to 3 minutes longer. With a slotted spoon, remove the sausage from the skillet. Let cool to room temperature.

3. Cut the chicken into pieces; place in a food processor. Add the sausage, garlic and cream and process for about 1 minute, until well blended. Season with salt and pepper to taste.

4. Make the pasta: Place 2½ cups of flour in a medium bowl. Make a well in the center and add the tomato paste, whole eggs, egg yolk, oil and salt. Using your fingers or a fork, mix together the ingredients in the well.

5. Gradually work in the flour until the mixture is blended and the dough begins to mass and pull away from the side of the bowl. It should be soft, pliable and slightly sticky. If the dough is too dry and stiff or will not absorb all the flour, add up to 2 tablespoons water, 1 teaspoon at a time. If it is too wet and sticky, add additional flour, 1 tablespoon at a time.

6. Turn the dough out onto a lightly floured surface and knead for 8 to 10 minutes, until smooth and elastic.

7. Divide the dough into sixths. Working with one piece at a time, pat the dough into a rectangle roughly 6 by 4 inches. Knead the dough by passing it through a pasta machine at the widest setting 2 or 3 times, until it is silky smooth and no longer sticky.

8. Continue to pass the dough through the pasta machine, reducing the space between the rollers by one number each time, until the pasta has passed through the thinnest setting.

9. Cut the band of dough crosswise into two even lengths. Place one strip of dough on a flat work surface. Spoon or pipe mounds (about 1½ teaspoons) of filling onto the strip of dough, about ½ inch in from the edges and spaced about ½ inch apart.

10. Paint the exposed areas of dough lightly with water. Drape the second sheet of dough on top and shape the ravioli with your fingers, pressing out the air and sealing the edges. Cut the ravioli apart with a sharp knife, a jagged pastry wheel or a ravioli stamp. Repeat with the remaining dough and filling.

11. Cook the ravioli, 12 at a time, in a large pot of boiling salted water until the pasta is al dente, 6 to 7 minutes; the filling will be hot and cooked. Do not overcrowd or the ravioli may stick.

—*John Robert Massie*

CREAMY TOMATO SAUCE
Makes About 1½ Cups

1 can (35 ounces) Italian peeled tomatoes,
  drained
Bouquet garni: 5 sprigs of parsley, ½ teaspoon
  thyme and 5 peppercorns tied in cheesecloth
¾ cup heavy cream
½ teaspoon salt
Freshly ground pepper

1. Place the tomatoes in a blender or food processor and puree until smooth. Strain through a coarse-mesh sieve to remove the seeds.

2. In a large skillet, bring the tomato puree with the bouquet garni to a boil over moderate heat. Boil, uncovered, for 5 minutes to reduce slightly. Stir in the cream and add the salt. Discard the bouquet garni. Season with additional salt and pepper to taste.

—*John Robert Massie*

BECHAMEL SAUCE WITH PARMESAN
Makes About 1½ Cups

2 cups milk
Bouquet garni: 5 sprigs of parsley,
  ¼ teaspoon thyme and ½ bay leaf tied
  in cheesecloth
2 tablespoons unsalted butter
3 tablespoons all-purpose flour
½ teaspoon salt
Pinch of freshly ground white pepper
Pinch of freshly grated nutmeg
½ cup freshly grated Parmesan cheese

1. In a medium saucepan, bring the milk with the bouquet garni to a boil.

2. Meanwhile, in another heavy, medium saucepan, melt the butter over moderate heat. Add the flour and cook, stirring, for 1 to 2 minutes without browning to make a roux.

3. Whisking constantly, strain the boiling milk into the roux. Return to the boil and cook, whisking, until the sauce is thickened and smooth, 3 to 4 minutes. Season with the salt, pepper and nutmeg and stir in the cheese.

—*John Robert Massie*

A Good Roast Chicken (p. 60).

Double Chicken Soup (p. 42).

Sesame Oat Chicken (p. 146).

Crispy Balsamic Chicken Wings (p. 246).

Soups
and
Stews

BURMESE LEMON CHICKEN SOUP

This is a typical Burmese soup, consumed almost like a beverage throughout the meal.

4 Servings

4 cups Chicken Stock (p. 10) or 2 cups
  canned broth diluted with 2 cups water
2 tablespoons finely diced red bell pepper
1 tablespoon finely diced medium-hot
  green chile
½ inch of fresh ginger, peeled and minced
1 garlic clove, minced
2 teaspoons fish sauce (nuoc mam)★
1 scallion, thinly sliced
1 tablespoon chopped cilantro (fresh coriander)
1 tablespoon fresh lemon juice
★Available at Asian markets

In a medium saucepan, combine the chicken stock, bell pepper, chile, ginger, garlic and fish sauce. Bring to a boil, reduce the heat to low and simmer, uncovered, for 10 minutes. Stir in the scallion, cilantro and lemon juice and serve hot or warm.

—*Copeland Marks*

DOUBLE CHICKEN SOUP

Finally, a chicken soup that tastes the way chicken soup used to taste—like chicken. This version is so rich, you won't be able to put down your spoon.

4 Servings

One 4½-pound chicken, preferably free-range
5 carrots, quartered lengthwise
4 leeks (white and tender green), quartered
  lengthwise
4 celery ribs, cut into 2-inch pieces
3 parsnips, quartered lengthwise
2 imported bay leaves, crumbled
1 teaspoon salt
½ teaspoon whole peppercorns

Free-Range Chicken Stock, chilled (p. 10)
Freshly ground black pepper

1. In a large heavy saucepan or stockpot, place the chicken, carrots, leeks, celery, parsnips, bay leaves, salt and peppercorns. Add the chicken stock and 4 cups of water. Bring slowly to a boil over moderately low heat. Reduce the heat to a simmer and cook, uncovered, skimming off the foam and fat occasionally, until the chicken is tender, about 1 hour.

2. Strain the soup and transfer the chicken and vegetables to a warm platter. Cover loosely with foil.

3. Return the broth to the pan and bring to a boil over high heat. Boil until reduced to 6 cups, 30 to 40 minutes. Season with additional salt and freshly ground pepper to taste.

4. To serve, carve the chicken. In 4 warmed soup bowls, place slices of white and dark meat, carrots, leeks, celery and parsnips. Ladle on the broth and serve hot.

—*Molly O'Neill*

GRANDPA'S HEARTY CHICKEN SOUP

The secret to this traditional chicken soup, adapted from my father-in-law's recipe, is long, slow simmering. A pullet (young hen) is used instead of a fowl or stewing chicken because its meat is moist and tender. Chicken backs and wings are added for additional flavor. The pullet and stock are made the first day, and the soup is finished the next day. The stock can be used as a base for countless combinations of ingredients. Kreplach (meat or cheese-filled noodle dumplings) or matzo balls (traditional for Passover but good anytime) would be right at home in this soup.

8 to 10 Servings

One 3½- to 4-pound pullet or chicken
1 pound chicken backs or wings
2 large onions, halved

5 large carrots, halved crosswise

4 large celery ribs with leaves, halved crosswise,
  plus additional leaves from the bunch

3 small rutabagas or 3 medium turnips (about
  1½ pounds), peeled and halved

1 cup (packed) fresh dill with stems

2 cups fine egg noodles (3 ounces)

¼ cup finely chopped parsley

Salt and freshly ground pepper

1. In a large heavy stockpot, combine the pullet, chicken backs, onions, carrots, celery and its leaves, rutabagas and dill. Add about 3½ quarts of cold water to just cover the chicken and vegetables. Bring to a boil over high heat. Immediately reduce the heat to low so that the liquid barely simmers. Simmer, partially covered, skimming as necessary, until the pullet is cooked through, about 1 hour.

2. Transfer the pullet to a plate; let cool slightly. Test the carrots, celery and rutabagas for doneness with a fork; the rutabagas may need about 10 minutes more but the carrots and celery will probably be done. When the vegetables are just tender, transfer 4 carrot halves, 4 celery halves and 2 rutabaga halves to a plate to cool. Let the rest of the vegetables continue to simmer, partially covered, in the stock.

3. Pull most of the meat from the pullet and cut it into strips about 1 inch long. Cut the cooled carrots and celery into ½-inch chunks and the rutabagas into ½-inch dice. Cover the chicken and vegetables and refrigerate overnight.

4. Return the chicken bones and skin to the stockpot and continue simmering, partially covered, for at least 3 more hours. For a very full-bodied soup, simmer the stock for a total of 6 hours. Strain the stock through a fine strainer into a large saucepan; discard the solids. Let the stock cool completely, then cover and refrigerate overnight.

5. The next day, in a medium saucepan of boiling salted water, cook the noodles until al dente, about 6 minutes. Drain, rinse under cold running water and set aside.

6. Skim the fat from the surface of the stock and discard. Reheat the stock over moderately high heat until it is liquefied. Add the noodles and the reserved chicken and vegetables. Cook until heated through, about 15 minutes. Stir in the parsley and season with salt and pepper to taste. Serve hot in large soup bowls. *(The soup can be made up to 3 days ahead. Let cool, cover and refrigerate. Reheat slowly before serving.)*

—*Susan Shapiro Jaslove*

CHICKEN, CHARD, LETTUCE AND TWO-POTATO SOUP

The Swiss chard in this hearty Sunday-night soup has a potent enough flavor to remain distinctive even after simmering with the other vegetables.

  6 Servings

One 4½- to 5-pound chicken

7 large celery ribs with leaves, chopped

1½ pounds Swiss chard

4 tablespoons unsalted butter

¾ cup coarsely chopped scallions

2 large baking potatoes (about 1 pound),
  peeled and cut into ½-inch dice

1 small head of Boston lettuce

1 large sweet potato (about 12 ounces), peeled
  and cut into ½-inch dice

1 tablespoon salt

¾ teaspoon ground coriander

½ teaspoon freshly ground black pepper

⅛ teaspoon cayenne pepper

1. Stuff the chicken with 3 cups of the celery and place in a stockpot or large flameproof casserole. Add 10½ cups water, or enough to cover, and the remaining celery. Bring to a boil over high heat, reduce the heat to moderately low

and simmer, partially covered, until the bird is fork tender, 1 to 1½ hours. Remove from the heat and let the chicken cool in the liquid.

2. When the chicken is cool enough to handle, remove the meat in large pieces, coarsely chop and set aside. Discard the skin and return the bones and celery from inside the bird to the liquid in the pot. Bring to a simmer and cook, uncovered, for 1 hour, or until reduced to 8 cups. Strain the stock into a large bowl. Skim off the fat, let cool and refrigerate until ready to use. *(The recipe can be made to this point up to 1 day ahead. Refrigerate the stock and chicken separately. Skim any congealed fat from the liquid before proceeding.)*

3. Strip the leaves from the chard and set aside; chop the stems into ½-inch pieces. In a stockpot or large flameproof casserole, melt the butter. Add the scallions and cook over low heat, uncovered, until softened but not browned, about 5 minutes. Add about ¾ cup of the stock along with the baking potatoes and chard stems. Cover and cook over low heat until the potatoes and chard are almost tender, about 8 minutes.

4. Tear the chard leaves and lettuce into bite-size pieces. Add the chard leaves, lettuce, sweet potato, salt, coriander, black pepper and cayenne to the potatoes and chard stems. Cover and cook over low heat, stirring once, until the sweet potato is almost tender, about 8 minutes.

5. Add the remaining 7¼ cups stock and the chicken to the vegetables. Simmer until the vegetables are tender and the chicken is heated through, about 5 minutes. Season with additional salt and cayenne pepper to taste. Let stand for about 15 minutes before serving.

—Lee Bailey

FENNEL-SCENTED CHICKEN SOUP WITH SPINACH

6 to 8 Servings

1 tablespoon olive oil
6½ cups chopped fennel (with tops, 2 to 3 medium bulbs)
1 medium leek (white and tender green), coarsely chopped
3 garlic cloves, unpeeled
1 sprig of fresh thyme or ¼ teaspoon dried
1½ imported bay leaves
5 peppercorns
3 cups Chicken Stock (p. 10) or canned broth
1⅔ cups diced red potato
1¼ pounds skinless, boneless chicken breast, cut into ½-inch dice
½ cup coarsely chopped scallions (white and tender green)
4 cups (firmly packed) shredded fresh spinach
Salt

1. In a large nonreactive saucepan, heat the oil. Add 6 cups of the fennel, the leek, garlic, thyme, bay leaves and peppercorns. Stir to coat with the oil. Cover and cook the vegetables over low heat, stirring occasionally, until softened but not browned, about 10 minutes.

2. Add the chicken stock and 3 cups of water. Simmer, partially covered, for 45 minutes.

3. Strain the broth through a sieve lined with several layers of dampened cheesecloth, pressing down on the solids to extract as much liquid as possible.

4. Return the broth to the saucepan and bring to a boil. Add the potato and cook until the potato is just tender, about 10 minutes.

5. Add the chicken, scallions and remaining ½ cup fennel and cook until the chicken is cooked through, about 5 minutes.

6. Bring the soup back to a boil, stir in the spinach and cook until just wilted and heated through, about 1 minute. Adjust the seasoning with salt to taste.

———

—F&W

MUSHROOM-CHICKEN SOUP WITH BACON AND LEEKS

We recommend using slightly old mushrooms with opened caps and exposed dark gills for this recipe. They will contribute a fuller mushroom flavor to the soup. Avoid packaged mushrooms with chemical preservatives.

6 to 8 Servings

1½ teaspoons unsalted butter
3 onions (about ¾ pound), unpeeled
  and chopped
2 garlic cloves, unpeeled and chopped
½ pound plum tomatoes, quartered, plus 1
  cup diced plum tomatoes
1¼ pounds mushrooms, finely chopped
3 cups Chicken Stock (p. 10) or canned broth
5 peppercorns
1½ imported bay leaves
6 slices bacon
1 pound skinless, boneless chicken breast, cut
  into ½-inch dice
3 cups sliced leeks (white and tender green)
1 cup diced celery
1½ cups cooked rice

1. In a large saucepan, melt the butter over moderate heat. Add the onions and cook, covered, until translucent, about 5 minutes.

2. Add the garlic, quartered tomatoes, mushrooms, stock, peppercorns, bay leaves and 3 cups of water. Bring to a boil, reduce the heat to low and simmer, partially covered, for 45 minutes, skimming occasionally.

3. Meanwhile, in a large skillet, cook the bacon over moderately high heat until crisp, about

10 minutes. Drain on paper towels; crumble and set aside.

4. Strain the broth through a sieve lined with several layers of dampened cheesecloth, pressing down on the solids to extract as much liquid as possible.

5. Return the broth to the saucepan and bring to a boil. Add the chicken, leeks and celery and bring back to a boil. Reduce the heat to moderately low and simmer until the chicken is cooked through, about 5 minutes.

6. Stir in the rice and cook until heated through, about 1 minute. Add the diced tomatoes and cook for another minute. Just before serving, stir in the crumbled bacon.

———

—F&W

SMOKY ONION-CHICKEN SOUP WITH PINTO BEANS

6 to 8 Servings

2 tablespoons unsalted butter
2 large Spanish onions (2 pounds),
  coarsely chopped
3 garlic cloves, unpeeled
5 peppercorns
1½ imported bay leaves
3 cups Chicken Stock (p. 10) or
  canned broth
1 smoked ham hock (about ½ pound)
1 cup dry white wine
2½ cups julienned carrots
2 cups finely shredded green cabbage
1¼ pounds skinless, boneless chicken breast,
  cut into ½-inch dice
½ cup julienned scallions
1⅔ cups cooked pinto beans
Salt

1. In a large nonreactive saucepan, melt the butter over moderate heat and add the onions, garlic, peppercorns and bay leaves. Cook, un-

covered, until the onions are golden, 10 to 15 minutes.

2. Add the chicken broth, 2 cups of water and the ham hock. Bring to a boil, reduce the heat and simmer, partially covered, for 45 minutes to extract the flavors.

3. Add the wine to the saucepan. Bring to a boil again, then reduce the heat to low and simmer, uncovered, for 3 minutes. Strain the broth through a sieve lined with several layers of dampened cheesecloth, pressing down on the solids to extract as much liquid as possible.

4. Return the broth to the saucepan and bring to a boil. Add the carrots and cabbage and cook until the carrots are cooked through, about 10 minutes.

5. Add the chicken and scallions and cook until the chicken is cooked through, about 5 minutes.

6. Add the beans and cook until heated through, about 1 minute. Adjust the seasoning with salt to taste.

———————

—F&W

CHICKEN SOUP WITH SAUSAGE, RICE AND YELLOW SQUASH

6 to 8 Servings

1 tablespoon olive oil
5 cups coarsely chopped celery plus 1 cup sliced celery
2 medium leeks, finely chopped (about 2½ cups), plus ½ cup julienned leek (white and tender green)
2 garlic cloves, unpeeled and lightly bruised
4 cups Chicken Stock (p. 10) or canned broth
1 imported bay leaf
½ teaspoon thyme
6 peppercorns

¼ pound fully cooked garlic sausage, such as kielbasa, diced
1 pound skinless, boneless chicken breast, cut into ½-inch dice
3½ cups diced yellow squash
1⅔ cups cooked basmati or other aromatic rice

1. In a large saucepan, heat the oil. Add the chopped celery and chopped leeks, cover and cook over moderate heat until the vegetables are softened and translucent, about 5 minutes. Add the garlic, stock, bay leaf, thyme, peppercorns and 2 cups of water.

2. Bring to a boil, then reduce the heat to low and simmer, partially covered, for 45 minutes, skimming occasionally.

3. Strain the broth through a sieve lined with several layers of dampened cheesecloth, pressing down on the solids to extract as much liquid as possible.

4. Return the broth to the saucepan and bring to a boil. Add the sausage and cook for 2 minutes.

5. Add the chicken, the 1 cup sliced celery and ½ cup julienned leek. Cook until the chicken is cooked through, about 5 minutes.

6. Add the squash and rice and cook until heated through, about 1 minute.

———————

—F&W

KENTUCKY CHICKEN, MUSHROOM AND RICE CHOWDER

♟ Look for an off-dry white, such as Chenin Blanc, to act as a simple foil for the medley of hearty flavors in this soup. From California, Hacienda or Villa Mt. Eden would work well.

6 Servings

One 2½- to 3-pound chicken
1 unpeeled onion, halved
1 large carrot, thickly sliced
1 large celery rib, coarsely chopped
1 parsnip, thickly sliced

4 sprigs of parsley plus chopped parsley,
  for garnish
8 whole peppercorns
6 cups Chicken Stock (p. 10) or canned broth
6 ounces mushrooms, sliced (2½ cups)
1 tablespoon plus 1 teaspoon fresh lemon juice
2 tablespoons unsalted butter plus
  1 teaspoon, softened
3 medium leeks (white and tender green),
  thinly sliced
1 garlic clove, minced
¼ cup chopped red bell pepper
½ cup rice
1 teaspoon all-purpose flour
1 cup heavy cream, at room temperature
Pinch of freshly grated nutmeg
Salt and freshly ground black pepper

1. Place the chicken in a saucepan just large enough to hold it. Add the onion, carrot, celery, parsnip, parsley sprigs, peppercorns, chicken stock and 2 cups of water. Bring to a boil over high heat. Reduce the heat to moderate, cover and simmer until the chicken is tender, about 50 minutes.

2. Transfer the chicken to a plate and let cool slightly. Remove the meat from the bones and set aside.

3. Return the skin and bones to the saucepan and cook over moderate heat until the stock has reduced to 6 cups, about 15 minutes. Strain the stock and discard the solids. Shred enough of the chicken to yield 1 cup; reserve the remaining chicken for another use.

4. Meanwhile, toss the mushrooms with 1 tablespoon of the lemon juice and set aside for 10 minutes.

5. In a large saucepan, melt 2 tablespoons of the butter over moderately high heat. Add the mushrooms and cook, stirring frequently, until the mushrooms release their liquid and are lightly browned, about 5 minutes. Reduce the heat to moderately low and stir in the leeks, garlic and red bell pepper. Cook, stirring occasionally, until the vegetables are slightly softened, about 5 minutes. Stir in the reserved chicken stock and the rice and bring to a boil. Reduce the heat to low, cover and cook until the rice is tender, about 20 minutes.

6. In a small bowl, mix the flour with the 1 teaspoon softened butter until blended; set aside.

7. Scoop ½ cup of the chowder into a blender. Add the cream and blend until smooth. Return the puree to the chowder and whisk in the flour mixture. Bring to a boil over moderate heat. Reduce the heat to low and simmer gently for 10 minutes. Stir in the shredded chicken, nutmeg and the remaining 1 teaspoon lemon juice. Season with salt and black pepper to taste and simmer for 3 minutes longer. Ladle the chowder into bowls and sprinkle with the chopped parsley.

—*Phillip Stephen Schulz*

ANA'S CIORBA

This recipe for *ciorba*, a cross between a soup and a stew, is from Ana Cotaescu, a wonderful Rumanian cook of our acquaintance.

8 Servings

One 3½- to 4-pound chicken, cut into 8
  pieces
2 medium carrots, coarsely grated
1 green bell pepper, cut into thin strips 1½
  inches long
1 red bell pepper, cut into ¼-inch squares
8 scallions, chopped
2 medium tomatoes, chopped
¼ pound green beans, as thin as possible, cut
  into 2-inch lengths
1 cup small cauliflower florets (about 4 ounces)
2 cups Chicken Stock (p. 10) or low-sodium
  canned broth
1 teaspoon salt
½ teaspoon freshly ground white pepper
½ cup chopped fresh dill
½ cup chopped parsley

4 ounces dry egg vermicelli
2 egg yolks
⅔ cup sour cream
¼ cup fresh lemon juice

1. In a large nonreactive saucepan, combine the chicken, carrots, green and red bell peppers, scallions, tomatoes, green beans and cauliflower. Add the stock, salt, white pepper and 3 cups of water. Bring to a boil over moderate heat. Reduce the heat to low and simmer, partially covered, skimming occasionally, until the chicken is tender, about 1 hour.

2. Add the dill, parsley and vermicelli. Cook until the noodles are tender, about 5 minutes. Remove from the heat and set aside for 5 minutes. Skim off any fat that rises to the surface.

3. In a small bowl, beat the egg yolks and sour cream until blended. Gradually whisk in ¼ cup of the hot cooking liquid. Stir the mixture back into the hot *ciorba*. Stir in the lemon juice and season with additional salt and white pepper to taste and serve hot. *(The recipe can be made 1 day ahead. Let cool completely, then cover and refrigerate. Reheat gently before serving. Do not boil.)*

———

—F&W

CHICKEN BOUILLABAISSE

Originally, bouillabaisse (*fish* bouillabaisse, that is) was a very humble dish, made by fishermen on the rocks or on the beach, from whatever fish they thought difficult to sell. Sometimes the fishing was so bad that they did not bring back much for the family meal. Housewives then coped, substituting a chicken from the backyard. I find it important to choose a good wine in order to give this dish a distinctive flavor. I prefer Domaines Ott, Blanc de Blancs, from Provence.

4 Servings

One 5-pound roasting chicken, cut into 8
  serving pieces

1 bottle (750 ml) dry white Provençal wine
2 cups Chicken Stock (p. 10) or
  canned broth
1 cup Madeira wine
1 garlic clove, peeled but whole
3 sprigs of parsley
2 bay leaves
6 small white onions, peeled and halved
½ teaspoon saffron threads, ¼ teaspoon
  powdered saffron or ½ teaspoon turmeric
12 green olives, pitted
6 large tomatoes, peeled and quartered
12 slices of French bread

1. In a large saucepan, bring about 2 quarts of water to a boil. Add the chicken parts. When the water begins to boil again, lower the heat and cook the chicken for 10 minutes (the idea is that you should get rid of excess fat). Drain. Let the chicken cool, then remove and discard the skin. Reserve the chicken.

2. In a Dutch oven or a large saucepan, heat the wine over moderately high heat for a moment or two, just until near simmering (don't let it boil). Add the chicken broth, Madeira, garlic, parsley, bay leaves, onions and saffron. Let simmer for 15 minutes.

3. Add the chicken and simmer 45 minutes, then add the olives and tomatoes.

4. While the chicken is cooking, trim the crusts from the bread and dry the slices well in a 350° oven.

5. When the chicken is tender, choose a large earthenware or thick china dish large enough to hold the bread slices in one layer. Spread the bread in the dish, then pour the chicken bouillabaisse over the slices and serve, piping hot, with the same white wine (chilled) that you used for cooking.

———————

—Monique Guillaume

"NOUVELLE"
BRUNSWICK STEW

Three southern states with Brunswick counties—Virginia, Georgia and North Carolina—lay claim to originating Brunswick stew. Though the territorial dispute has yet to be settled, it is certain that the first renderings of the dish contained a mixed bag of game plentiful in the Old South: squirrel, rabbit, venison and wild turkey. Today beef, pork or chicken often are substituted for the game. Here is a "nouvelle" version that separates the stew into its elements.

▼ California Petite Sirah, such as Fetzer Mendocino Special Reserve

6 Servings

12 chicken drumsticks
¼ pound smoked ham, cut into ¼-inch dice
1 can (35 ounces) Italian peeled tomatoes, with their juice
1 teaspoon salt
1½ teaspoons freshly ground black pepper
¼ teaspoon cayenne pepper
1 large onion, coarsely chopped
3 large all-purpose potatoes, cut into ½-inch dice
4 or 5 ears yellow sweet corn, cut into thirds
3 tablespoons unsalted butter
10 ounces fresh okra, cut into ¼-inch slices
1 package (10 ounces) frozen baby lima beans
1 to 3 teaspoons Worcestershire sauce, to taste
1 tablespoon minced parsley

1. Put the chicken, ham, tomatoes and their juice, ½ teaspoon of the salt, 1 teaspoon of the black pepper, the cayenne pepper and onion into a large, nonreactive, flameproof casserole and bring to a simmer. Cook, covered, over low heat for 30 minutes.

2. Add the potatoes and cook for 30 to 45 minutes longer, until the potatoes begin to fall apart and thicken the sauce.

3. About 10 minutes before the stew is finished, cook the corn in a large pot of boiling salted water until tender, 8 to 10 minutes. Drain and loosely cover with foil to keep warm.

4. Meanwhile, melt the butter in a large skillet over moderate heat. Add the okra and sauté for 3 minutes. Add the lima beans, reduce the heat to low and cook until the vegetables are tender, about 3 minutes longer. Season with the remaining ½ teaspoon salt and pepper. Keep warm over very low heat.

5. Season the stew with 1 teaspoon Worcestershire sauce. Taste and add more as desired. Heap the stew in the center of a deep heated platter. Surround with alternating bunches of corn and green vegetables. Garnish with the parsley.

———

—Judith Olney

CHICKEN AND SAUSAGE
STEW WITH PARSLEY
AND LEMON

This is a crowd-pleasing stew, full of hearty flavors and textures. It can be prepared completely in advance and will probably be the better for it. It is generously liquid by intent. Serve with lots of crusty semolina bread for mopping up the sauce.

▼ Simi Rosé of Cabernet Sauvignon

6 Servings

8 tablespoons olive oil
1 pound sweet Italian sausages, pricked all over
One 2½- to 3-pound chicken, cut into 8 serving pieces, giblets reserved
1 teaspoon salt
½ teaspoon freshly ground pepper
2 medium onions, finely chopped
3 celery ribs with leafy tops, cut on the diagonal into 1-inch pieces
4 large garlic cloves, minced
1½ teaspoons oregano
1 teaspoon thyme
1 bay leaf
3 tablespoons all-purpose flour
1 cup dry white wine

2 cups Chicken Stock (p. 10) or canned broth
1 can (28 ounces) Italian peeled tomatoes,
* with their juice*
1 pound medium mushrooms, stemmed
1 cup Calamata olives
½ cup chopped flat-leaf parsley
1 tablespoon finely julienned lemon zest

1. In a large, nonreactive, deep skillet or flame-proof casserole, warm 2 tablespoons of the oil over moderate heat. Add the sausages and the chicken giblets and cook, turning occasionally, until well browned, about 10 minutes. Transfer the sausages to a bowl; leave the giblets in the skillet.

2. Add the chicken pieces, skin-side down, and season with ½ teaspoon of the salt and ¼ teaspoon of the pepper. Cook until golden brown, about 5 minutes. Turn, season with the remaining ½ teaspoon salt and ¼ teaspoon pepper and brown on the other side, about 5 minutes longer. Transfer to the bowl with the sausages. Discard the giblets and pour off any oil from the pan.

3. Return the pan to moderate heat. Add 3 tablespoons of the oil, the onions, celery, garlic, oregano, thyme and bay leaf. Reduce the heat to moderately low, cover and cook, stirring occasionally, until the onions are soft and golden, 15 minutes. Uncover, sprinkle the vegetables with the flour and cook over very low heat, stirring, for 5 minutes without allowing the flour to color to make a roux.

4. Gradually whisk in the wine. Add the stock and the tomatoes (crushing them with your fingers) and their juice. Bring to a boil over moderately high heat, stirring; reduce the heat to a simmer, partially cover and cook until the liquid is slightly thickened, about 30 minutes.

5. Cut the reserved sausages on the diagonal into 1-inch pieces. Add the sausages and chicken to the pan. Simmer uncovered until the chicken is very tender, about 30 minutes.

6. Meanwhile, in a large skillet, heat the remaining 3 tablespoons oil. Add the mushrooms and sauté over moderately high heat, until the mushrooms begin to yield their juice, about 5 minutes. Season with salt and pepper to taste and remove from the heat.

7. When the chicken is tender, transfer it with a slotted spoon to a serving bowl; cover to keep warm. Add the mushrooms, their juices and the olives to the sauce. Simmer for 5 minutes. *(The stew may be prepared to this point 1 day ahead. Pour the sauce over the chicken, let cool to room temperature, then cover and refrigerate. Reheat the stew gently, stirring, until hot.)*

8. Skim off any fat. Stir the parsley into the sauce and pour it over the chicken. Sprinkle the lemon zest on top.

———————————

—Michael McLaughlin

CHICKEN FRICASSEE
WITH ARTICHOKES AND
PEARL ONIONS
🍷 Chianti, such as Badia a Coltibuono
4 to 6 Servings

1 lemon plus ¼ cup fresh lemon juice
6 medium artichokes
One 3½- to 4-pound chicken, cut into 8
* serving pieces*
½ teaspoon salt
¼ teaspoon freshly ground pepper
2 tablespoons unsalted butter
2 tablespoons vegetable oil
¾ pound pearl onions, blanched and peeled
¾ pound small mushrooms or quartered large
* mushrooms*
½ cup dry white wine
½ cup Chicken Stock (p. 10) or low-sodium
* canned broth*
1 cup heavy cream
1 bay leaf
2 tablespoons chopped parsley

1. In a large nonreactive saucepan, squeeze the lemon into 2 quarts of water. Add the lemon

halves to the water. Trim the artichokes by first snapping off the tough outer leaves. Then, using a stainless steel knife, cut off the stems; cut the crown to within about 1½ inches of the base. Drop the trimmed artichokes into the saucepan.

2. Bring to a boil over moderately high heat and cook the artichokes until just tender when pierced with a knife, about 25 minutes. Remove from the heat and let them cool in the cooking liquid. When cool enough to handle, scoop out the hairy chokes with a spoon. Cut the hearts into quarters and set aside. *(The hearts can be prepared up to 1 day ahead. Return the artichoke hearts to their cooking liquid, cover with plastic wrap and refrigerate overnight.)*

3. Season the chicken pieces with the salt and pepper. In a large nonreactive skillet or flame-proof casserole, melt the butter in the oil over moderately high heat. Add the chicken and cook, turning, until browned on all sides, about 10 minutes. Remove from the skillet and set aside.

4. Add the pearl onions to the skillet and cook, tossing frequently, until evenly browned, about 10 minutes. Using a slotted spoon, remove from the skillet and set aside.

5. Add the mushrooms to the skillet and cook, tossing frequently, until lightly browned, about 8 minutes. Using a slotted spoon, remove from the skillet and set aside.

6. Drain any fat from the skillet. Pour in the white wine and bring to a boil, scraping up any browned bits from the bottom of the pan. Add the chicken stock and cook until the liquid is reduced to 3 tablespoons, about 5 minutes.

7. Pour in the cream and add the artichoke hearts, chicken, onions, mushrooms and bay leaf. Reduce the heat to moderately low and simmer for 35 minutes. Stir in the ¼ cup lemon juice and season with salt and pepper to taste. Sprinkle with the parsley just before serving.

—*John Robert Massie*

CHICKEN FRICASSEE WITH CHERRIES AND SHERRY VINEGAR

8 Servings

6 medium carrots, cut into 1½-inch lengths

5 small white turnips, peeled and quartered lengthwise

Salt

½ pound green beans, halved crosswise if long

8 chicken breast halves or 8 chicken legs with thighs, or a mixture of both (about 8 ounces each)

¼ cup plus 1½ tablespoons all-purpose flour

¼ cup olive oil

Freshly ground pepper

3 tablespoons unsalted butter

1 shallot, minced

¾ cup sherry vinegar

¾ cup Brown Chicken Stock (p. 11)

1 jar (5 ounces) cherries preserved in sherry vinegar★ (see Note), drained

1 teaspoon tarragon

★Available at specialty food stores

1. With a small paring knife or vegetable peeler, carve the carrots and turnips into ovals about 1½ inches long and 1 inch in diameter. Put the two vegetables into separate small saucepans, add water to cover and ½ teaspoon salt to each and bring to a boil over moderate heat. Reduce the heat and simmer until just tender, allowing 5 to 10 minutes of cooking time for each. Drain the vegetables thoroughly.

2. Cook the beans in a small saucepan of boiling water with ½ teaspoon salt until tender but still slightly crunchy, 4 to 6 minutes. Rinse under cold running water and drain thoroughly; set aside.

3. Preheat the oven to 450°. If using chicken legs, separate the thighs and drumsticks. Dredge the chicken pieces in ¼ cup of the flour. Heat the oil in a large, nonreactive, ovenproof skillet. Add enough of the chicken to fit in a single layer,

sprinkle with salt and pepper and sauté over high heat, turning often, until browned all over, about 5 minutes. Drain on paper towels. Repeat with the remaining chicken. When all the pieces are browned, return them to the skillet and place it in the oven. Bake, turning once or twice, for 20 to 25 minutes, or until the juices run clear when pierced with a fork. Transfer the chicken to a platter and cover with aluminum foil to keep warm.

4. Reheat the vegetables in a steamer or in the oven while you finish the sauce.

5. Blend 1 tablespoon of the butter with the remaining 1½ tablespoons flour to make a beurre manié. Discard the fat from the skillet. Add the shallot and vinegar and bring to a boil over moderately high heat. Pour in the stock and whisk in enough of the beurre manié, 1 or 2 teaspoons at a time, to thicken the sauce so it coats a spoon lightly.

6. Lower the heat, add the cherries and tarragon and simmer for 2 to 3 minutes. Season with salt and pepper to taste. Remove from the heat and stir in the remaining 2 tablespoons butter, in small pieces.

7. To serve, arrange some carrot and turnip ovals and a small serving of beans on each plate with the chicken. Spoon the sauce and cherries over the chicken.

NOTE: If cherries preserved in sherry vinegar are not available, marinate 1 can (17 ounces) dark, sweet, pitted cherries in sherry vinegar to cover (about ¾ cup) for 12 to 24 hours. Drain before using.

—*Anne Willan*

GIBELOTTE OF CHICKEN WITH LARDONS AND YELLOW TURNIPS

Gibelotte comes from the Old French word *gibecier*, which meant hunting and has lent its name to the *gibecière*, the bag held on the hunter's back to carry game. The word *gibelotte* is used synonymously with *fricassée*, but it most commonly refers to game and rabbit rather than chicken. This recipe is inspired by memory as well as by an old recipe from Marin, a famous 18th-century French cook.

🍷 Red Rhône, such as St-Joseph

6 to 8 Servings

2 chickens (3 to 3½ pounds each), quartered
1 medium onion, grated
1 tablespoon all-purpose flour
1 cup dry white wine
1 teaspoon salt
½ teaspoon fresh thyme or ¼ teaspoon dried
½ teaspoon freshly ground pepper
½ pound lean salt pork, in 1 piece
2 large yellow turnips or rutabagas (about 3½ pounds)
¼ cup rinsed and drained capers
1 tablespoon fresh lemon juice
3 or 4 anchovy fillets, mashed to a paste
2 tablespoons chopped fresh chervil or parsley

1. Heat 2 large skillets over moderately high heat. Add the chicken, skin-side down, in a single layer and cook until the skin is nicely browned and most of the fat has been rendered, about 15 minutes. Turn the pieces over and brown on the other side, 3 to 5 minutes longer. Transfer the chicken pieces to a platter. Drain the rendered fat into a bowl and reserve.

2. In a large flameproof casserole, heat 1 tablespoon of the chicken fat. Add the grated onion and sauté over moderate heat until golden brown, about 3 minutes. Add the flour and cook, stirring for 1 minute. Whisk in the wine, salt, thyme,

pepper and 1 cup of water. Bring to a boil, whisking until smooth. Reduce the heat and simmer for 3 minutes.

3. Add the browned chicken to the sauce. Return to a boil, reduce the heat to a simmer, cover and cook for 20 minutes.

4. Transfer the chicken to a platter; reserve the sauce. When the chicken is cool enough to handle, remove the bones from the breast. (The leg, thigh and wing bones stay in.) Return the chicken to the sauce. *(The recipe can be made to this point up to 1 day ahead. Refrigerate, covered.)*

5. Meanwhile, cut the salt pork into 1-by-¼-inch strips, or lardons. Put the lardons in a medium saucepan, cover with water and bring to a boil. Drain and rinse under running water; drain well.

6. In a small skillet, heat 1 tablespoon of the reserved chicken fat. Add the lardons and cook over moderate heat, partially covered to prevent splattering, until well browned, 6 to 8 minutes. Remove the lardons with a slotted spoon and drain on paper towels.

7. Peel the turnips and cut into 1½-inch cubes. Round the edges of each piece with a knife. Put the turnip pieces in a large saucepan and add cold water to cover. Bring to a boil and cook for 5 minutes; drain.

8. In a large skillet, heat 3 tablespoons of the reserved chicken fat. Add the turnips and cook over moderate heat, tossing occasionally, until nicely browned, 8 to 10 minutes. Remove the turnips from the heat and set aside with the lardons until serving time. *(The lardons and turnips can be prepared to this point up to 4 hours ahead. Set them aside at room temperature.)*

9. To finish the dish, add the turnips and lardons to the chicken in its sauce. Bring to a boil, reduce the heat to a simmer, cover and cook for 10 minutes to reheat and blend the flavors. Add the capers, lemon juice and anchovies. Bring to a boil. Arrange the chicken and vegetables on a platter and garnish with the chopped chervil.

———

—*Jacques Pépin*

RAGOUT OF CHICKEN WITH BLACK OLIVES AND ONION JAM

Braised on the bone with browned onions and olives, free-range chicken stays moist and picks up a heady aroma. Serve this dish with buttered egg noodles.

♟ Light California red, such as Sinskey or Mark West Pinot Noir

8 Servings

2 chickens (4½ to 5½ pounds each),
  preferably free-range
2 cups all-purpose flour
1 teaspoon salt
½ teaspoon freshly ground pepper
6 tablespoons unsalted butter
4 pounds large white onions, thickly sliced
2 cups (about 1 pound) oil-cured black olives,
  pitted (see Note)
4 cups Free-Range Chicken Stock (p. 10)
½ cup dry sherry
2 tablespoons grated lemon zest
2 teaspoons thyme

1. Cut off the wing tips from the chickens. Cut each chicken into 8 pieces: Cut off the legs and separate the drumsticks and thighs. Cut out the backbone and separate the two breasts on the bone with the wings attached. Using a heavy sharp knife, cut crosswise through the bone of each breast to cut into 2 pieces.

2. Preheat the oven to 325°. In a medium bowl, combine the flour, salt and pepper. Dredge the chicken pieces in the seasoned flour. In a large flameproof casserole, melt 4 tablespoons of the butter over moderately high heat. Add the coated chicken in 3 batches and cook, turning, until browned, about 4 minutes on each side. As the chicken is cooked, transfer it to a bowl. Wipe out the casserole with paper towels.

3. In the casserole, melt the remaining 2 tablespoons butter over moderate heat. Add the onions, cover and cook until softened, about 15

minutes. Uncover and cook, stirring occasionally, until caramelized to a golden brown, about 25 minutes.

4. Add the olives, chicken stock, sherry, lemon zest and thyme and bring to a boil. Add the chicken pieces. Cover and bake, stirring occasionally, until the chicken is tender, about 1 hour and 15 minutes.

5. Remove the chicken and boil the liquid until the sauce thickens slightly, 5 to 10 minutes. Season with additional salt and pepper to taste. Return the chicken to the casserole.

NOTE: Oil-cured olives can be very salty and may need to be blanched: Place the olives in a medium saucepan, cover with cold water and bring to a boil over high heat. Drain and rinse under cold water. If still too salty, repeat.

—*Molly O'Neill*

CHICKEN DRUMSTICK RAGOUT WITH BELL PEPPERS AND ARTICHOKES

The skillet supper below, particularly the use of chicken legs, stirs a fond memory of growing up. In a house with three hungry boys, there could never be enough drumsticks on a normal chicken to satisfy us all. If you can find red, green and yellow peppers, they make this creamy fricassee a gorgeous presentation. (If not, use whatever you have on hand; the flavor will be fine.) Serve with white rice and hot garlic bread.

🍷 A crisp Italian white, such as Pinot Grigio

4 to 6 Servings

16 chicken drumsticks (about 4 pounds)
1 cup all-purpose flour
1 stick (4 ounces) unsalted butter
1 teaspoon salt
½ teaspoon freshly ground black pepper
2 medium onions, chopped
4 garlic cloves, minced
1 teaspoon thyme
1 teaspoon basil
1 imported bay leaf
2 cups Chicken Stock (p. 10) or canned broth
1 cup dry white wine
1 large red bell pepper, quartered
1 large green bell pepper, quartered
1 large yellow bell pepper, quartered
1 package frozen artichoke hearts, thawed
  and drained
1 cup heavy cream

1. Dredge the chicken in the flour; shake off any excess. In a large skillet or flameproof casserole, melt 4 tablespoons of the butter over moderate heat. Working in batches, add the legs, season with the salt and black pepper and cook, turning, until lightly browned, about 10 minutes for each batch. As they brown, transfer the legs to a dish and set aside.

2. Add 2 tablespoons of butter to the pan. Stir in the onions, garlic, thyme, basil and bay leaf. Reduce the heat to moderately low, cover and cook, stirring occasionally, until the onions are tender, 10 to 15 minutes.

3. Return the chicken to the skillet. Add the stock and wine and bring to a boil. Reduce the heat to moderately low, cover, and simmer, turning the legs occasionally, until very tender, about 40 minutes. Remove to a bowl.

4. Meanwhile, in a medium skillet, melt the remaining 2 tablespoons butter over moderately high heat. Add the bell peppers, season with a pinch of salt and pepper and cook, tossing frequently, until lightly browned, about 5 minutes. Add the artichoke hearts and cook for 2 minutes. Transfer the chicken, peppers and artichokes to a bowl.

5. Strain the cooking liquid and return it to the skillet. Place over high heat, stir in the cream and bring to a boil. Boil until the liquid is reduced by one-third, about 15 minutes. Season with salt and pepper to taste. Return the chicken, peppers and artichokes to the skillet. Simmer gently until heated through, about 5 minutes.

—*Michael McLaughlin*

YELLOW CHICKEN CURRY

Chicken curries are traditionally prepared in Thailand with the chicken either cut into parts or hacked through the bone, Chinese style, into bite-size pieces. If the chicken is to serve a large number of people, then the latter style is preferable. You will need a heavy cleaver to penetrate the bones, or ask the butcher to do it for you.

♟ Alsace Gewürztraminer

8 Servings

3 pounds chicken parts, skinned and cut through the bone into large bite-size pieces
3 cups Thin Coconut Milk (p. 56)
2 tablespoons fish sauce (nam pla, nuoc mam or patis)★
½ cup Yellow Curry Paste (recipe follows)
4 thin slices (quarter-size) peeled fresh ginger
4 dried hot red chiles (optional)
2 cups Thick Coconut Milk (p. 56)
2 tablespoons chopped cilantro (fresh coriander)
★Available at Southeast Asian and some Chinese markets

1. In a wok set over moderately high heat, combine the chicken pieces, Thin Coconut Milk and fish sauce. Bring the mixture to a gentle boil. Reduce the heat to low and simmer uncovered, stirring occasionally, until the chicken is no longer pink but still juicy, about 20 minutes.

2. Using a slotted spoon, remove the chicken pieces from the wok and set aside covered loosely with foil to keep warm. Blend the Yellow Curry Paste into the liquid. Add the ginger and chiles. Increase the heat to moderate and boil the sauce, stirring occasionally, until it is reduced by one-third, about 10 minutes.

3. Return the chicken to the wok and simmer for 5 minutes longer. Add the Thick Coconut Milk, increase the heat to moderately high and cook, stirring, for 3 minutes. Pour into a serving bowl and sprinkle with the cilantro.

—*Jennifer Brennan*

YELLOW CURRY PASTE

This paste, which is mostly used for chicken curries in Thailand, gets its yellow tinge from turmeric. The use of this spice indicates that the curry has been influenced by the Indian traders who have come to Thailand during the last two centuries.

Makes About ½ Cup

8 dried hot red chiles, seeded and broken into pieces, or 2 teaspoons cayenne pepper
1 tablespoon coriander seeds or 1 tablespoon ground coriander
2 teaspoons cumin seed or 2 teaspoons ground cumin
1 teaspoon whole black peppercorns or 1 teaspoon freshly ground black pepper
6 garlic cloves, minced (about 2 tablespoons)
4 shallots, minced (about ¼ cup)
1 stalk of fresh lemon grass,★ minced, or grated zest of 1 lemon (about 2 teaspoons)
1 tablespoon minced cilantro (fresh coriander) stems and roots (do not use leaves)
1½ teaspoons turmeric
1 teaspoon ground galingale (laos root, ka)★ or ½ teaspoon ground ginger
1 teaspoon salt

2 teaspoons shrimp paste (kapi trassi)* or
Chinese shrimp sauce, or 2 teaspoons
anchovy paste
2 tablespoons vegetable oil
*Available at Southeast Asian and some
Chinese markets

1. In a spice mill or mortar, grind the chiles, coriander, cumin seed and black peppercorns to a powder. (Omit this step if using ground spices.)

2. Transfer the ground spices to a food processor (or continue with the mortar and pestle). Add the garlic, shallots, lemon grass, cilantro, turmeric, galingale, salt, shrimp paste and oil. Process to as fine a paste as possible.

3. Transfer the paste to a jar and cap tightly. Store in the refirgerator for up to 3 months.

—*Jennifer Brennan*

COCONUT MILK

Coconut milk is made by pressing a mixture of shredded coconut and hot water through a strainer. The first pressing yields Thick Coconut Milk. A second pressing will yield Thin Coconut Milk. Combining the liquid from both pressings is similar to mixing cream and skim milk to yield whole milk.

Makes About 3 Cups

1 coconut
4 cups hot water (see Note)

1. Preheat the oven to 350°. Place the coconut in a small baking dish and cook until the outer shell cracks in several places, about 30 minutes.

2. Wrap the hot coconut in 3 layers of kitchen towels. Using a small hammer, pound the wrapped coconut until it breaks open.

3. Unwrap the coconut and discard the liquid inside. Using a strong dull knife, pry the hard, outer shell away from the coconut meat. Using a vegetable peeler, remove the thin brown skin from the coconut.

4. Cut the white coconut meat into 1-inch pieces. Place in a food processor and process until shredded (there will be about 3 cups).

5. Make the Thick Coconut Milk: Pour 2 cups of the hot water over the coconut and process for 1 minute. Transfer to a fine strainer set over a large bowl and press with a rubber spatula or wooden spoon. This should yield about 1½ cups.

6. Make the Thin Coconut Milk: Return the reserved shredded coconut to the food processor. Add 2 cups of hot water and process for 1 minute. Transfer the coconut to a fine strainer set over a large bowl and press the mixture through. Yields about 1½ cups.

NOTE: For an even richer coconut milk, use milk instead of water.

—*Marcia Kiesel*

CHICKEN CURRY CALCUTTA STYLE

This curried chicken dish can easily be made ahead and reheated.

🍷 Chilled lager beer

4 Servings

1 tablespoon corn or peanut oil
½ medium onion, coarsely chopped
2 medium garlic cloves, minced
1 teaspoon minced fresh ginger
2 teaspoons curry powder
½ teaspoon crushed hot red pepper
One 3½-pound chicken, cut into 8 or 10
  serving pieces
½ cup coarsely chopped tomato, fresh or
  canned
1 tablespoon cider vinegar
2 teaspoons dark brown sugar

½ teaspoon salt

1 medium red potato, peeled and cut into ½-
   inch cubes

1. In a large deep skillet or flameproof casserole, heat the oil. Add the onion, garlic and ginger and fry over moderate heat, stirring, until the onion is softened and translucent, about 2 minutes.

2. Add the curry powder and hot pepper and stir over the heat for a few seconds.

3. Add the chicken pieces and fry, turning once, until golden, about 2 minutes on each side.

4. Add ¾ cup of water, the tomato, vinegar, brown sugar, salt and potato. Simmer, uncovered, turning the chicken occasionally, until the meat is tender, 30 to 35 minutes.

———————————

—*Copeland Marks*

SWEET-AND-SOUR CHICKEN WITH CARROTS

This unusual "dry curry," which is moist but has very little sauce, originated in the Jewish community of Calcutta. It is traditional to remove the skin from the chicken, which produces an almost fat-free dish. If you prefer to leave the skin on, degrease the sauce just before serving.

8 to 10 Servings

3 tablespoons corn or peanut oil

4 medium carrots, finely shredded

2 medium onions, thinly sliced

3 garlic cloves, minced

1½ tablespoons minced fresh ginger

¾ teaspoon turmeric

1½ teaspoons salt

2 chickens (3 pounds each), skinned and cut
   into 8 serving pieces each, giblets reserved

3 imported bay leaves

6 cardamom pods, lightly cracked

⅓ cup fresh lemon juice

2 tablespoons light brown sugar

1. In a large skillet, heat 1½ tablespoons of the oil over moderately low heat. Add the carrots and sauté until wilted, about 3 minutes. Set aside.

2. In a large flameproof casserole, heat the remaining 1½ tablespoons oil. Add the onions, garlic, ginger, turmeric and salt and cook until the onions are soft and translucent, 2 to 3 minutes. Add the chicken and cook, turning, until white all over, 8 to 10 minutes.

3. Add 1½ cups of water, the bay leaves and cardamom. Cover and cook, turning the chicken occasionally, for 15 minutes. Add the sautéed carrots and continue to cook for 10 minutes. Add the lemon juice and sugar; stir well and cook, partially covered, over moderately low heat, until the chicken is so tender it is almost falling off the bone, about 10 minutes.

4. Uncover and boil over moderately high heat until the liquid is almost evaporated, 5 to 10 minutes. Season with additional lemon juice and sugar to taste if desired.

———————————

—*Copeland Marks*

CHICKEN AND SAUSAGE GUMBO

The Patout family has also been known to make this gumbo with turkey instead of chicken to take full advantage of Thanksgiving leftovers.

♀ With this down-home dish, serve a fine American beer, such as Anchor Steam.

6 Servings

One 3-pound chicken

1 teaspoon unsalted butter

1 onion, unpeeled and quartered, plus 1 large
   onion, peeled and finely chopped

1 carrot, quartered

2 celery ribs—1 quartered, 1 finely chopped

1 sprig of parsley

1 cup all-purpose flour

½ teaspoon salt
¼ teaspoon cayenne pepper
¼ teaspoon freshly ground black pepper
⅛ teaspoon freshly ground white pepper
½ cup corn oil
1 green bell pepper, finely chopped
1 pound smoked pork sausage, sliced
Louisiana hot sauce
Chopped scallion greens and chopped parsley,
 for garnish

1. Cut the chicken into 8 pieces; reserve the backbone, wing tips, neck and gizzards. In a large heavy saucepan, melt the butter over moderately high heat. Add the reserved giblets and trimmings and the quartered onion, carrot and quartered celery. Cook, stirring, until browned, about 5 minutes. Add the parsley sprig and 6 cups of water. Bring to a boil, reduce the heat to moderate and simmer for 1 hour; strain the broth and discard the solids.

2. In a large plastic bag, combine ½ cup of the flour with the salt, cayenne and black and white pepper. Add the chicken pieces, a few at a time, and shake until well coated. Remove the chicken and reserve any remaining seasoned flour.

3. In a large heavy skillet, heat 2 tablespoons of the oil. Add the chicken pieces and cook over high heat, turning once, until browned, 4 to 5 minutes per side. Remove the chicken and set aside.

4. Add the remaining 6 tablespoons oil to the skillet and whisk to scrape up any browned bits from the bottom of the pan. When the oil begins to smoke, gradually whisk in the remaining ½ cup flour plus the reserved seasoned flour. Reduce the heat to moderate and whisk until the roux becomes a dark red-brown, 3 to 4 minutes. Remove the skillet from the heat and stir in half of the chopped onion, celery and green pepper; stir until the roux stops browning and cools slightly, 3 to 5 minutes.

5. In a large casserole, combine the reserved broth and enough water to equal 8 cups. Add the remaining chopped onion, celery and green pepper and bring to a boil over high heat. Stir in the roux, 1 spoonful at a time. Reduce the heat to moderate and simmer for 45 minutes.

6. Add the chicken and the sliced sausage and cook until the chicken is very tender, about 45 minutes longer. (If the gumbo thickens too much, add a little water.) Remove from the heat; let stand for 20 minutes.

7. Skim off all of the fat that rises to the surface and season the gumbo with salt, pepper and hot sauce to taste. Sprinkle the scallion greens and chopped parsley over the gumbo. Serve with rice.

—Alex Patout, Patout's, New Iberia, Louisiana

Roast Chicken

A GOOD ROAST CHICKEN

This recipe is deceptively simple. The roast chicken, perfumed with rosemary and basted with sweet butter, can be the mainstay of a superb family dinner or can serve as the centerpiece of the most elegant dinner party. If you want crisp skin, turn the oven up to 375° for the last 10 minutes of roasting.

℗ Choose a light red that will not overwhelm the mildness of the chicken, such as Caymus Special Selection or Carneros Creek Pinot Noir.

4 Servings

One 4½- to 5½-pound chicken, preferably
  free-range
3 sprigs of fresh rosemary or 1½ teaspoons
  dried
4 tablespoons unsalted butter, cut into 4
  pieces, at room temperature
2 teaspoons coarse (kosher) salt
1 teaspoon coarsely ground pepper

1. Preheat the oven to 325°. Loosen the breast skin from the meat. Place 1 sprig of the rosemary (or ¼ teaspoon dried) and 1 tablespoon of butter under the skin on each side of the breast. Place the remaining sprig of rosemary (or 1 teaspoon dried) in the cavity. Truss the bird. Rub the remaining 2 tablespoons butter over the chicken and sprinkle all over with the salt and pepper.

2. Place the chicken, breast-side up, in a roasting pan. Roast for 45 minutes. Baste and continue roasting, basting every 15 minutes, until the bird is golden brown, the juices run clear and the internal temperature of the thigh reaches 170°, about 1 hour longer.

3. Transfer the chicken to a warm platter, cover loosely with foil and let rest for about 15 minutes before carving.

—*Molly O'Neill*

CARAWAY CHICKENS WITH LIGHT GRAVY

Savory and succulent, these buttery roast chickens taste of the caraway seeds that are tucked under their skins before roasting. The seeds enhance the light, flavorful gravy, too. Make the caraway butter several hours or even a day ahead of time so it can chill before you prepare the chickens.

12 Servings

1 tablespoon plus 2 teaspoons caraway seeds
1 stick (4 ounces) unsalted butter, at room
  temperature
2 large roasting chickens (about 6 pounds each)
About 1 cup Chicken Stock (p. 10), canned
  broth or water
3 tablespoons all-purpose flour
¼ cup dry white wine
Salt and freshly ground pepper

1. Place 1 tablespoon of the caraway seeds in a mortar, spice grinder or blender and pulverize. In a small bowl, beat the butter until fluffy. Stir the caraway powder into the butter to blend. On a square of aluminum foil, form the caraway butter into a log about the size of a stick of butter. Wrap tightly, twisting the ends of the foil, and refrigerate until solid, at least 1 hour.

2. Preheat the oven to 350°. Place the chickens, breast-side up, on a work surface. Beginning near the main cavity, carefully slip your fingers between the skin and breast meat and gently work apart to separate almost to the neck area of each bird; be careful not to tear the skin. Cut three-quarters of the chilled caraway butter into thin slices and, dividing equally, slide it under the skin of each breast half. Toss 1 teaspoon of the remaining 2 teaspoons whole caraway seeds into the cavity of each chicken. Truss the chickens with string and place them breast-side up on a rack in a large shallow roasting pan.

3. Melt the remaining caraway butter in a small saucepan over low heat. Brush the chickens with half of the melted caraway butter.

4. Roast the chickens in the center of the oven for 30 minutes. Brush with the remaining caraway butter and continue to roast, basting with the pan drippings every 20 minutes, for about 1½ hours longer, or until the internal temperature reaches 165° to 170°. Transfer to a large platter to rest for 10 minutes while the juices settle.

5. Meanwhile, pour the drippings from the roasting pan into a heatproof bowl or large measuring cup. Carefully pour the juices from the cavities of the birds and any that have accumulated on the platter into the bowl. Spoon 3 tablespoons of fat from the surface of the drippings into a medium, nonreactive skillet and set aside. Skim off and discard any remaining fat from the cooking juices. There will be about 1 cup of juice remaining. Add enough stock or water to make a total of 2 cups; reserve.

6. Add the flour to the chicken fat in the skillet and stir over moderate heat until bubbling; cook for 2 minutes without coloring to make a roux. Pour in the reserved chicken juices and the wine. Whisk constantly over moderate heat until the gravy boils and thickens slightly. Simmer, stirring constantly, for 3 minutes; remove from the heat. Season with salt and pepper to taste.

7. To serve, carve the chickens; arrange on a platter and accompany with the hot gravy.

—*Jim Fobel*

ROASTED CHICKEN WITH ACHIOTE AND GARLIC SAUCE

Robert Del Grande, chef and co-owner at Cafe Annie in Houston, likes to serve this dish with a watercress salad dressed in walnut oil.

❡ Although roasted chicken is normally amenable to just about any wine match, the garlic sauce here tunes the dish toward an herbaceous, crisp Sauvignon Blanc, such as Iron Horse or Silverado, to match the pungency.

4 Servings

4 cups Chicken Stock (p. 10) or canned broth
¾ cup orange juice
½ cup achiote seeds (annatto seed)★
One 3½-pound chicken
5 garlic cloves, peeled, plus 2 heads
  of garlic, unpeeled
1 tablespoon paprika
1¼ teaspoons salt
2 medium onions, sliced
2 large sweet potatoes (about 1 pound each),
  peeled and quartered
2 tablespoons unsalted butter, melted
1 tablespoon fresh lime juice
1 teaspoon coarsely cracked pepper
★Available at Latin American markets

1. In a medium saucepan, combine 1 cup of the chicken stock, the orange juice, achiote seeds and 1 cup of water. Bring to a boil over moderate heat. Cook until the achiote seeds are soft and the liquid is almost entirely evaporated, about 25 minutes.

2. Meanwhile, using a sharp heavy knife, cut the chicken along both sides of the backbone; remove and discard. Pushing down with both hands, press the chicken flat. Remove and discard any excess fat and large protruding bones.

Turn the chicken over. Make a small incision through the skin between the leg and the lower end of the breast on each side. Slide the ends of the drumsticks through the holes to secure the legs in place.

3. Transfer the achiote mixture to a blender and add the 5 peeled garlic cloves, the paprika, ¼ teaspoon of the salt and 1 more cup of the chicken stock. Puree the achiote marinade until smooth, about 1 minute.

4. Preheat the oven to 350°. Separate the heads of garlic into cloves. Butter the bottom of a large roasting pan. Cover the bottom of the pan with the onion slices and the unpeeled garlic cloves. Place the chicken, skin-side up, on top of the onion and garlic.

5. Brush the chicken liberally with the achiote marinade. Arrange the sweet potatoes around the chicken. Roast, basting with the melted butter and pan juices every 15 minutes, until the chicken is browned outside and the juices run clear when the thickest part of the thigh is pricked, about 1 hour and 15 minutes.

6. Transfer the chicken and sweet potatoes to a carving board and cover with foil to keep warm.

7. Squeeze the roasted garlic cloves into a blender, discarding the skins. Add the roasted onions, any juices from the roasting pan, the remaining 2 cups chicken stock and the lime juice. Puree until smooth. (Add a little water to thin if desired.)

8. Transfer the sauce to a medium saucepan and stir in the remaining 1 teaspoon salt and the cracked pepper. Rewarm the sauce over low heat, stirring, until heated through.

9. Quarter the chicken and divide among 4 warm dinner plates. Serve with the sweet potatoes and garlic sauce.

—*Robert Del Grande, Cafe Annie, Houston*

SIMPLE ROAST CHICKEN WITH PARSLEY AND LEMON

♆ Beaujolais-Villages or a light California Zinfandel, such as Simi

4 Servings

1 lemon
One 3½-pound chicken
½ teaspoon salt
½ teaspoon freshly ground pepper
10 sprigs of parsley with stems
5 tablespoons unsalted butter, melted

1. Preheat the oven to 400°.

2. Squeeze the juice of the lemon into the cavity of the chicken; reserve the lemon rinds. Turn the bird to moisten all over inside with the juice.

3. Season the inside of the chicken with ¼ teaspoon each of the salt and pepper. Stuff the squeezed lemon rinds and the parsley into the cavity. Truss the chicken.

4. Baste well with one-third of the melted butter. Sprinkle with the remaining ¼ teaspoon each salt and pepper.

5. Put the bird on its side on a rack and roast for 25 minutes, basting with one-third of the remaining butter halfway through. Turn the bird over and roast on the other side for 25 minutes longer, basting again halfway through. Turn the bird breast-side up, baste one last time and roast for 15 minutes, until the juices of the thigh run clear when pierced. Remove from the oven and let rest for 10 minutes before carving.

—*John Robert Massie*

ROAST CHICKEN WITH GOAT CHEESE, HONEY AND THYME

4 Servings

One 3-pound chicken
1 teaspoon coarse (kosher) salt
½ teaspoon coarsely cracked black pepper
12 large sprigs of fresh thyme or
 2 teaspoons dried
1 head of garlic, cloves separated but unpeeled
1 tart green apple, such as Granny Smith,
 peeled and quartered
1 onion, quartered
4 whole shallots, unpeeled
4 tablespoons unsalted butter
¼ cup honey
¼ cup cider vinegar
1 cup dry white wine
2 ounces mild goat cheese, such as Montrachet
¼ cup heavy cream

1. Preheat the oven to 450°. Sprinkle the cavity of the chicken with ¼ teaspoon each of the salt and pepper. Place half the thyme and half the garlic cloves in the cavity. Truss the chicken. Rub the skin with the remaining ¾ teaspoon salt and ¼ teaspoon pepper.

2. Place the chicken in a roasting pan. Surround with the apple, onion, shallots and remaining garlic cloves. Roast for 30 minutes.

3. Meanwhile, in a small heavy saucepan, combine the butter, honey and vinegar. Cook over moderate heat, stirring frequently, until the butter is melted, to make a basting sauce.

4. Baste the chicken every 5 to 10 minutes as it roasts for about 30 minutes longer, or until the juices run clear when the thigh is pricked to the bone. Turn the vegetables occasionally to coat with drippings so that they will be evenly caramelized.

5. Turn off the oven. Remove the chicken, shallots and garlic cloves to a heatproof platter, cover loosely with foil and return to the oven to keep warm.

6. Place the roasting pan on top of the stove. Add the wine and bring to a boil, scraping up any browned bits from the bottom and sides of the pan and mashing the apples and onion into the sauce.

7. Strain the sauce into a medium saucepan and return to a boil. Strip the leaves from the remaining thyme and mince. Stir the thyme, goat cheese and cream into the sauce. Boil until slightly thickened, about 5 minutes.

8. To serve, remove the thyme and garlic from inside the chicken and discard. Carve the chicken into serving pieces and arrange on a platter. Surround with the caramelized garlic and shallots. Pass the sauce separately.

—*Robert Del Grande, Cafe Annie, Houston*

THYME-ROASTED CHICKEN WITH ONIONS AND POTATOES

℣ California Chardonnay, such as Simi, or Beaujolais Nouveau

4 to 6 Servings

1 stick (4 ounces) unsalted butter, softened
1 large onion, coarsely chopped
½ teaspoon salt
½ teaspoon freshly ground pepper
1 tablespoon fresh thyme leaves or
 1 teaspoon dried
One 3-pound chicken
6 medium all-purpose potatoes, quartered

1. In a large ovenproof skillet, preferably cast iron, melt 1 tablespoon of the butter over moderately high heat. Add the onion, ¼ teaspoon of the salt and a pinch each of the pepper and thyme.

Cook, tossing frequently, until the onion is lightly browned, about 10 minutes. Remove from the skillet and let cool to room temperature.

2. In a small bowl, combine the remaining 7 tablespoons butter, ¼ teaspoon of the salt, a pinch of pepper and the remaining thyme; blend well.

3. Preheat the oven to 400°. Using your fingers, gently loosen the breast, thigh and leg skin of the chicken. Rub 4 tablespoons of the thyme butter under the skin.

4. Stuff the cavity with the browned onion and truss the chicken. Rub the skin with 1 tablespoon of the thyme butter. Place the chicken in the skillet.

5. Toss the potatoes with the remaining thyme butter and arrange around the chicken. Set the skillet, uncovered, in the oven and bake for 1 hour and 15 minutes, or until the juices run clear when the thigh of the chicken is pierced.

—*John Robert Massie*

PROVENCAL ROAST CHICKEN

Whether or not this chicken is authentically Provençal, it evokes hill towns and hearty suppers. If the recipe were written in French, it would call for *un beau poulet*. I start with the *beau*-est chicken I can find—plump and fresh— flavor it with oranges and basil, give it a massage with melted butter and fragrant olive oil, and fit it into a dutch oven. When cooked through, the chicken is moist and aromatic, with juices that can be served au naturel or used as the base for a gravy. If any chicken remains, serve it the following day cold, doused with pureed anchovies, garlic and olive oil.

4 Servings

1 tablespoon unsalted butter
1 tablespoon olive oil
1½ teaspoons salt
¾ teaspoon freshly ground pepper
6 juice oranges
One 3½-pound chicken
1 large onion, thinly sliced
6 sprigs of basil, or substitute fresh rosemary
 or thyme
2 garlic cloves, unpeeled and smashed
1 tablespoon Cognac or other brandy
Orange slices and basil leaves, for garnish

1. Preheat the oven to 375°. In a small saucepan, melt the butter in the olive oil over moderate heat. Add ½ teaspoon of the salt and ¼ teaspoon of the pepper and set aside.

2. Squeeze the juice from 4 of the oranges and reserve; this should yield about 1 cup. Save the shell from 1 of the juiced oranges. Thinly slice the 2 remaining whole oranges crosswise.

3. Work your fingers between the skin and flesh of the chicken breasts and thighs to separate without tearing the skin. Slip 1 of the orange slices under the skin of each thigh and 2 under each breast. Season the cavity with ½ teaspoon of the salt and ¼ teaspoon of the pepper. Fill the cavity with the reserved orange shell, 4 slices of the onion and 1 sprig of the basil. Truss the bird with string and rub all over with the seasoned melted butter and olive oil.

4. In a lightly buttered ovenproof casserole or dutch oven, combine the remaining orange slices, onion slices, basil sprigs and the garlic cloves. Season with the remaining ½ teaspoon salt and ¼ teaspoon pepper. Toss to mix well.

5. Place the chicken in the pan and pour in ¼ cup of the reserved orange juice. Cover and roast for 15 minutes. Baste with ¼ cup more orange juice. Re-cover and cook, basting with the accumulated pan juices every 15 minutes, for 1 hour longer.

6. Remove the pan from the oven and increase the oven temperature to 425°. Strain the pan juices into a nonreactive saucepan and set aside. Return the chicken to the oven and roast uncovered, basting once or twice, until nicely browned, about 20 minutes.

7. Meanwhile, add the remaining ½ cup orange juice to the reserved pan juices and boil over moderately high heat until reduced by half, about 7 minutes. Add the Cognac and boil for 1 minute longer. Carve or quarter the chicken and moisten with a little of the sauce. Garnish with orange slices and basil leaves. Pass the remaining sauce separately.

———————————

—Dorie Greenspan

CLAY POT CHICKEN WITH GARLIC AND HERBS

This is a family favorite because all my children love garlic and chicken. They learned from their mother, who likes chicken so much and makes it so often that when they were little, they even thought pork and veal were chicken.

❦ California Chardonnay, such as Vichon or Kendall-Jackson Vintner's Reserve

   4 Servings

   One 4½- to 6-pound roasting chicken
   Salt and freshly ground pepper
   6 sprigs of fresh thyme or ½ teaspoon dried
   6 sprigs of parsley
   2 imported bay leaves
   1 tablespoon unsalted butter, at room
     temperature
   1 medium onion, sliced
   1 medium carrot, sliced
   1 celery rib, sliced
   40 unpeeled garlic cloves (about 2 heads)
   4 fresh or dried whole sage leaves
   1 sprig of fresh tarragon or ¼ teaspoon dried
   Toasted country bread, for serving

1. Cover a 2- to 3-quart clay pot with cold water and let soak for 15 minutes.

2. Meanwhile, sprinkle the inside of the chicken lightly with salt and pepper. Place 2 thyme sprigs (or a pinch of dried), 2 parsley sprigs and 1 bay leaf into the cavity and truss the bird. Rub the butter all over the chicken and sprinkle lightly with salt and pepper.

3. Drain the clay pot and add the onion, carrot and celery. Set the chicken on top of the vegetables and scatter the garlic cloves around the bird. Scatter around the sage leaves, tarragon sprig and the remaining 4 sprigs of thyme (or dried thyme), 4 sprigs of parsley and 1 bay leaf.

4. Cover the clay pot and place it in a cold oven. Turn the oven temperature to 475° and cook the chicken for about 1 hour and 20 minutes or until the juices run clear when a thigh is pierced. Uncover and cook for about 10 minutes longer to brown the breast. Transfer the bird and the garlic cloves to a warmed platter, cover loosely with foil and let them rest for about 15 minutes.

5. Strain the cooking juices into a sauceboat and keep warm. Carve the chicken and serve with the garlic cloves on the side. Let each person squeeze the garlic from its skin onto the toasted bread.

———————————

—Patrick Clark

CANTONESE ROAST CHICKEN

This chicken was designed to be used for Cantonese Chicken Salad (p. 253), but it is delicious on its own, straight out of the oven, served with your favorite chicken side dishes.

   4 Servings

   1½ tablespoons distilled white vinegar
   3 tablespoons dry white wine
   1 tablespoon Oriental sesame oil
   1 teaspoon salt
   ¼ teaspoon freshly ground pepper
   One 3½-pound chicken
   4 large garlic cloves, sliced ¼ inch thick

1. Preheat the oven to 375°. In a bowl, combine the vinegar, wine, sesame oil, salt and pepper. Rub this mixture all over the chicken in-

side and out. Place half of the garlic in the cavity of the chicken. Set the bird on a rack in a roasting pan, breast-side up. Add the remaining garlic and ¾ cup of cold water to the pan.

2. Roast the chicken for 30 minutes. Lower the heat to 350° and roast for 15 minutes longer. Turn the chicken over and roast for 30 minutes longer. If the pan looks dry, add boiling water, ¼ cup at a time. Turn the chicken breast-side up and roast for another 30 minutes or until the juices run clear when a thigh is pierced. Set aside to cool slightly before serving.

—*Eileen Yin-Fei Lo*

ROAST CHICKEN WITH FIG-GIBLET SAUCE

♟ A big and rich Pinot Noir is the right match for this richly sauced chicken. Full-flavored bottlings, such as Chalone or Edna Valley from California or Elk Cove "Wind Hill" from Oregon would do beautifully.

4 Servings

One 5-pound roasting chicken
½ lemon, cut in half
2 tablespoons unsalted butter, softened
Salt and freshly ground pepper
½ cup dry red wine, preferably Pinot Noir
8 large garlic cloves, unpeeled
2 large or 3 small dried figs, preferably
  Calimyrna
1 teaspoon chopped fresh tarragon
2 teaspoons chopped fresh chives

1. Preheat the oven to 400°. Place the chicken in a roasting pan just large enough to accommodate it. Place the lemon quarters in the cavity of the bird. Rub 1 tablespoon of the butter all over the chicken and sprinkle lightly with salt and pepper. Pour the wine into the roasting pan and add ½ cup of water. Scatter the garlic cloves and figs around the chicken and roast in the middle of the oven for 30 minutes to brown the bird.

2. In a small bowl, combine the remaining 1 tablespoon butter with the tarragon and chives. Season with a pinch of salt and pepper. Cover and refrigerate.

3. After 30 minutes, reduce the oven temperature to 350° and baste the chicken. Roast for 10 minutes longer and then add ½ cup of water to the pan. Continue to roast, basting occasionally and turning the figs to keep them moist, until a thermometer inserted in the inner thigh registers 160°, about 50 minutes longer.

4. Pour the juices from inside the chicken into the roasting pan and transfer the chicken to a warm platter. Remove the figs and garlic and set aside on a plate. Pour all of the pan juices into a measuring cup and with a small ladle, skim the fat from the surface.

5. Set a small, coarse strainer over a small nonreactive saucepan. Put the garlic cloves in the strainer and pour over the degreased pan juices. With a rubber spatula, push the cooked garlic through the strainer into the juices, scraping the garlic from the underside of the strainer into the juice. Discard the garlic skins.

6. To carve the chicken, cut off the legs and cut the drumsticks from the thighs at the joint using a sharp knife. Cut off the wings. Slice the breast meat off the bone. Pour any accumulated juices into the sauce. Arrange the chicken on a warmed platter and cover loosely with foil.

7. Cut the figs into ¼-inch dice and add them to the sauce. Heat the sauce over moderate heat until hot. Remove from the heat and whisk in the chilled herb butter, bit by bit, until the sauce is smooth and thickened slightly. Season with salt and pepper to taste and serve separately in a sauceboat.

—*Marcia Kiesel*

AROMATIC ROAST CHICKEN

The stuffing for this roast chicken has been placed under the skin rather than in the cavity, which makes for more succulent breast meat and shortens the cooking time.

☙ Red Rioja

6 to 8 Servings

One 5-pound chicken
2 teaspoons salt
¾ teaspoon freshly ground pepper
1 cup dry bread crumbs
½ teaspoon grated lemon zest
2 tablespoons minced parsley
1 large garlic clove, minced
2 tablespoons olive oil
1 lemon, cut in half
3½ tablespoons unsalted butter, melted

1. Preheat the oven to 450°.

2. Place the chicken, breast-side up, on a work surface. Using your fingers and working from the cavity toward the neck, carefully loosen the skin covering the breast to make a pocket. Rub the interior and exterior of the chicken with 1½ teaspoons of the salt and ½ teaspoon of the pepper.

3. In a small bowl, combine the bread crumbs with the lemon zest, parsley, garlic and remaining ½ teaspoon salt and ¼ teaspoon pepper. Stir in the olive oil. Using your fingers, insert this stuffing under the skin of the entire breast. Place the lemon halves in the cavity of the chicken and truss the bird.

4. Place the chicken, breast-side up, on a rack in a shallow roasting pan and brush it with 1 tablespoon of the melted butter. Roast for 10 minutes. Reduce the temperature to 375° and turn the chicken on its side. Baste with ½ tablespoon more of the butter, roast for another 20 minutes, turn it on its other side and baste with another ½ tablespoon butter. Cook another 20 minutes, turn the chicken breast-side down, baste with another ½ tablespoon butter and cook another 20 minutes. Turn the chicken breast-side up, baste with the remaining 1 tablespoon butter and cook a final 30 minutes, or until the juices run clear when the thigh is pierced with a fork or a meat thermometer inserted into the thickest part of a thigh registers 165°.

5. Reserving the pan juices, transfer the chicken to a serving platter and allow it to rest for 10 to 15 minutes. In the meantime, pour the pan juices into a small bowl and allow the fat to rise to the top. Skim or pour off most of the fat. Carve the bird and serve with the degreased pan juices.

———

—F&W

APRICOT- AND SHIITAKE-STUFFED CHICKEN WITH TURNIPS

This dish can also be made with two large chicken breasts instead of a whole chicken. Preheat the oven to 375° and cook the chicken and vegetables together for 50 minutes.

☙ Alsace Riesling, such as Trimbach

4 Servings

4 tablespoons unsalted butter
1 small onion, minced, plus 2 medium
  onions, quartered
¼ pound prosciutto, coarsely chopped
½ cup dried apricots
¼ pound fresh shiitake mushrooms (or 1 ounce
  dried, reconstituted), stemmed and minced
⅔ cup fresh bread crumbs
¼ teaspoon salt
One 3- to 3½-pound chicken
1 tablespoon vegetable oil
½ teaspoon freshly ground pepper

1¾ pounds white turnips, peeled and
   cut into 1-inch cubes
4 small carrots, halved on the diagonal

1. In a small skillet, melt the butter over moderately low heat. Add the minced onion and cook until softened, 3 to 4 minutes.

2. Preheat the oven to 425°. In a food processor, combine the prosciutto and apricots. Process until finely chopped; scrape into a bowl. Add the mushrooms, the cooked onion, the bread crumbs and salt and toss to combine.

3. With your fingers, loosen the chicken breast skin and lightly pack the stuffing under the skin in an even layer. Place the chicken in a large oval gratin dish or roasting pan. Brush with the oil. Sprinkle the pepper over the chicken and bake for 20 minutes.

4. Remove the roasting pan from the oven and reduce the temperature to 375°. Place the turnips, quartered onions and carrots around the chicken and toss the vegetables with the fat in the pan. Return to the oven and bake until the vegetables are tender, about 50 minutes.

———————

—Mary Lynn Mondich

ROAST CHICKEN STUFFED WITH SAUSAGE AND ARMAGNAC PRUNES

The Armagnac-soaked prunes in this chicken recipe from Brittany, France, impart a subtle perfume to the filling.

   4 Servings

1 cup pitted prunes (about 6 ounces),
   cut in half
½ cup Armagnac or other brandy
4 tablespoons unsalted butter
2 medium onions, finely chopped
3 celery ribs, finely chopped
8 garlic cloves, minced
2 tablespoons olive oil

8 ounces lean ground pork
2 teaspoons chopped fresh thyme or ½
   teaspoon dried
1 teaspoon freshly grated nutmeg
Salt and freshly ground pepper
One 4-pound chicken

1. In a small bowl, combine the prunes and Armagnac; set aside, covered, for 1 hour or overnight to plump.

2. Preheat the oven to 475°. In a large saucepan, melt 2 tablespoons of the butter over moderate heat. Add the onions and cook, stirring occasionally, until softened but not browned, about 5 minutes.

3. Add the celery and garlic and cook for 5 minutes more. Transfer the vegetables to a medium bowl.

4. Wipe out the saucepan and pour in the olive oil. Add the ground pork and cook, stirring, over high heat until the pork has lost its redness and is cooked through, 3 to 5 minutes.

5. Add the pork to the cooked vegetables. Stir in the thyme, nutmeg, prunes and Armagnac. Season with salt and pepper to taste. Let cool before proceeding.

6. Season the cavity of the chicken with ¼ teaspoon each salt and pepper. Fill the cavity with the pork stuffing. Close the cavity and secure with string, wrapping it tightly around the legs.

7. Rub the chicken with the remaining 2 tablespoons butter and place it, breast-side up, in a roasting pan. Roast for 10 minutes, reduce the heat to 400° and cook for 1¼ hours, or until golden brown and the juices run clear when the thigh is pierced with a knife. Cover loosely with foil and let rest before carving.

———————

—Joyce Goldstein

ROAST CAPON WITH PLUM AND PEAR STUFFING

8 Servings

½ pound mild pork sausage
½ cup chopped celery
4 or 5 medium red or purple plums, coarsely chopped (2 cups)
2 large pears, peeled and chopped (2 cups)
¼ cup minced parsley
1 cup sliced scallions (white and some of the green)
¾ cup chopped walnuts
¾ cup dry bread crumbs
3 egg yolks
1 teaspoon tarragon
1 teaspoon salt
¼ teaspoon freshly ground pepper
One 8-pound capon or roasting chicken
Melted butter

1. Preheat the oven to 400°.

2. Crumble the sausage into a large, heavy skillet; add the celery and sauté about 5 minutes, or until the celery softens.

3. Remove from the heat and stir in the plums, pears, parsley, scallions, walnuts, bread crumbs, egg yolks, tarragon, salt and pepper. Mix the stuffing with your hands or a large spoon until the egg yolks are blended in.

4. Season the body and neck cavities of the capon with a little salt and pepper. Loosely pack both cavities with the stuffing. Secure the neck skin with a skewer; tie the legs together with kitchen string. Brush the outside of the capon with a little melted butter; sprinkle lightly with salt.

5. Place the capon on a rack in a roasting pan. Roast for 30 minutes. Reduce the oven temperature to 350° and roast an additional 1½ to 2 hours. If the bird begins to brown too quickly, cover it with a tent of aluminum foil. Occasionally baste the bird with the pan drippings. The capon is done when a meat thermometer inserted in the thickest part of the thigh, without touching the bone, reaches 180°.

———

—F&W

ROASTED CAPON WITH SHIITAKE MUSHROOM AND CHICKEN LIVER STUFFING

It's best to start preparing this dish two days in advance. First make the stuffing and let it marinate overnight in the refrigerator. The next day cook the stuffing. Then, all you'll have to do is stuff and roast the birds and make the sauce.

8 Servings

1 pound fresh shiitake mushrooms, stemmed and minced
½ pound chicken livers, trimmed and finely chopped
5 to 6 large shallots, minced (¾ cup)
½ cup minced parsley
2 tablespoons minced garlic
2 tablespoons minced chives
1 tablespoon fresh thyme or 1½ teaspoons dried
1½ teaspoons coarse (kosher) salt
¾ teaspoon freshly ground pepper
1 stick (4 ounces) unsalted butter, at room temperature
2 tablespoons olive oil
1 cup freshly grated Gruyère cheese (about 3 ounces)
One 9- to 10-pound capon (reserve wing tips and neck trimmings for the Enriched Stock)
Enriched Stock (recipe follows)

1. In a medium bowl, combine the mushrooms, chicken livers, shallots, parsley, garlic and chives. Add 1 teaspoon of the fresh thyme (or ½ teaspoon dried) and the salt and pepper; mix well. Cover and refrigerate for 6 hours or overnight to blend the flavors.

2. In a large skillet, melt 2 tablespoons of the

butter in the oil over moderately high heat. Add the stuffing mixture and reduce the heat to low. Cover tightly and cook, stirring occasionally, until the mushrooms release their liquid and the liver is cooked through, about 10 minutes.

3. Remove from the heat and let cool to room temperature. Stir in the Gruyère cheese and season with salt and pepper to taste. Cover and refrigerate until cold.

4. Meanwhile, in a small bowl, blend 4 tablespoons of the butter with the remaining 2 teaspoons fresh thyme (or 1 teaspoon dried).

5. Preheat the oven to 425°. Loosen the breast and thigh skin of the bird with your hands and place the stuffing under the skin; press gently to evenly distribute it. Set the capon in a roasting pan, without trussing, and spread the thyme butter over the breast and thighs.

6. Roast the capon for 15 minutes, then reduce the temperature to 400° and roast, basting occasionally, for about 1¼ hours, or until an instant-read thermometer inserted in a thigh registers 170°.

7. Remove the capon from the oven and carve off the leg-thigh pieces. Transfer them to a smaller pan and roast for 30 minutes longer, basting occasionally. Set the breast on a large platter and cover loosely with foil while you prepare the sauce. Carve the legs and thighs and slice the breast carefully so that each slice has some stuffing.

8. Pour all the juices from the roasting pan into a small saucepan, scraping in all the browned bits from the bottom of the pan. Skim the fat from the surface. Stir in the Enriched Stock and bring to a boil over high heat. Boil, skimming as necessary, until reduced to 1 cup, about 3 minutes. Remove from the heat and whisk in the remaining 2 tablespoons butter. Season with salt and pepper to taste and strain into a sauceboat. Place capon slices on each of 8 heated dinner plates and pass the sauce separately.

—*Lydie Marshall*

ENRICHED STOCK
Makes 1 Cup

2 tablespoons unsalted butter
*Reserved wing tips and neck trimmings from
  the capon (see above)*
2 shallots, coarsely chopped
1 carrot, coarsely chopped
¼ pound mushrooms, coarsely chopped
6 sprigs of parsley
2 cups low-sodium canned broth

1. In a large skillet, melt the butter over high heat. Add the reserved wing tips and necks and cook, stirring occasionally, until well browned all over, about 10 minutes. Add the shallots, carrot, mushrooms and parsley and cook for 5 minutes longer, stirring occasionally.

2. Add 1 cup of the broth to the skillet and bring to a boil. Reduce the heat to moderate and boil until reduced by half, about 5 minutes.

3. Add the remaining 1 cup of stock and boil until 1 cup of liquid remains, about 5 minutes longer. Strain and let cool, then refrigerate. Skim off all the fat that congeals on the surface. *(The stock can be made 1 day ahead.)*

—*Lydie Marshall*

ROASTED CHICKEN BREASTS WITH PROSCIUTTO AND LEMON

Serve this flavorful dish with simple buttered mashed potatoes or rice and buttered green beans tossed with pistachios. If you have any chicken left over, thinly slice it and serve cold.

❦ A lively, fruity California Chenin Blanc, such as Folie à Deux or Pine Ridge, makes a nice contrast to the prosciutto and lemon flavors of this dish.

8 Servings

1½ sticks (6 ounces) unsalted butter,
  at room temperature

4 ounces thinly sliced prosciutto, finely chopped

1 tablespoon grated lemon zest

½ teaspoon salt

½ teaspoon freshly ground black pepper

¼ cup finely chopped parsley

4 large whole chicken breasts, bone in (1 to
 1¼ pounds each)

2 tablespoons olive oil

2 large shallots, minced

2 garlic cloves, crushed

2 medium carrots, minced

1 small green bell pepper, minced

6 cups Chicken Stock (p. 10) or low-sodium
 canned broth

Juice of 1 lemon

½ cup crème fraîche

1½ teaspoons arrowroot dissolved in 1
 tablespoon of water

1. Preheat the oven to 450°. In a small bowl, combine the butter with the prosciutto, lemon zest, salt, black pepper and the parsley. Divide the seasoned butter into 8 equal portions.

2. Using your fingers, carefully loosen the skin from the chicken breasts without tearing. Pat one portion of the seasoned butter under the skin of each breast half, spreading it evenly.

3. Place the chicken breasts on a rack set over a baking sheet. Roast in the middle of the oven for about 30 minutes, basting frequently with the drippings, until golden brown and firm to the touch but still juicy. Cover with foil and keep warm.

4. Meanwhile, in a large nonreactive skillet, heat the olive oil. Add the shallots and cook over moderate heat until translucent, about 3 minutes. Add the garlic and cook for 1 minute more. Stir in the carrots and green pepper and cook until slightly softened, about 2 minutes.

5. Add the chicken stock, lemon juice and crème fraîche to the pan and bring to a boil over high heat; boil until the sauce reduces to 2 cups, 15 to 20 minutes.

6. Gradually add the arrowroot mixture and simmer, stirring constantly, until the sauce thickens, about 1 minute. Season with salt and pepper to taste.

7. To serve, cut the stuffed chicken breasts off the bones in one piece with a long, thin, sharp knife, using the breastbones as a guide. Place 1 breast half on each of eight warmed plates and spoon the sauce on top.

———————————

—Bob Chambers

CORNISH HENS WITH FRESH APRICOT AND WATER CHESTNUT STUFFING

♥ California Cabernet Sauvignon, such as Fetzer
 4 Servings

5 tablespoons unsalted butter

½ cup brown rice

1¾ cups Chicken Stock (p. 10) or
 canned broth

2½ teaspoons salt

1 large onion, chopped

1 teaspoon sugar

2 teaspoons minced garlic

¾ cup diced fresh apricots (about 3 medium)

½ cup chopped parsley

½ cup diced water chestnuts

½ teaspoon curry powder

½ plus ⅛ teaspoon freshly ground pepper

4 Cornish game hens (1 to 1¼ pounds each)

1 tablespoon olive oil

1. In a medium saucepan, melt 2 tablespoons of the butter over moderately low heat. Add the rice and cook, stirring once or twice, for 5 minutes. Add the chicken stock and ½ teaspoon of the salt. Bring to a boil, cover and simmer over moderately low heat until the rice has absorbed the stock, about 30 minutes. Transfer to a bowl.

2. Meanwhile, melt the remaining 3 tablespoons butter in a medium skillet over moderately low heat. Add the onion and sugar and cook, stirring occasionally, until the onion is golden, about 10 minutes. Add the garlic and cook for 1 minute longer. Add to the bowl of rice.

3. Add the apricots, parsley, water chestnuts, curry powder and ⅛ teaspoon of the pepper and mix thoroughly.

4. Preheat the oven to 450°. Rub the hens inside and out with the olive oil; season with the remaining 2 teaspoons salt and ½ teaspoon pepper. Loosely fill the cavities of the hens with the stuffing; sew or skewer closed. Place the stuffed hens, breast-side up, on a rack in a roasting pan and roast for 20 minutes. Reduce the heat to 350° and cook for another 30 to 40 minutes, or until the juices run clear when the thigh joint is pierced with a fork. Remove the hens from the roasting pan and let rest 10 minutes before serving.

———————

—F&W

CORNISH GAME HENS WITH DILL STUFFING
6 Servings

6 Cornish game hens (1 to 1¼ pounds each),
  livers reserved
1 tablespoon olive oil
Salt and freshly ground pepper
1 stick (4 ounces) plus 3 tablespoons
  unsalted butter
¼ cup dry white wine
½ cup minced scallions (4 to 6)
1½ cups dry bread crumbs
1 egg, beaten
½ cup minced fresh dill or 2 tablespoons dried
  dillweed

1. Preheat the oven to 450°.

2. Remove the livers and reserve. Rub the skins all over with the olive oil and season the hens inside and out with salt and pepper.

3. In a small skillet, heat 1 tablespoon of the butter until sizzling. Add the livers and sauté over high heat, turning, until browned on all sides, about 2 minutes. Remove the livers from the skillet, cut them into small pieces and set them aside.

4. Pour the wine into the skillet used to cook the livers and heat, scraping loose the browned bits in the bottom of the skillet. Remove from the heat.

5. In a large bowl, place the scallions, bread crumbs, beaten egg, dill, 1 teaspoon salt, ¼ teaspoon pepper and 1 stick of the butter. Pour the wine from the skillet over the ingredients in the bowl and stir them with a fork. Lightly mix in the chopped livers.

6. Loosely stuff each hen with about ½ cup of the stuffing.

7. Place the stuffed hens in a roasting pan and roast for 20 minutes. Reduce the heat to 350° and cook for another 30 to 40 minutes, or until the juices run clear. Remove the hens from the roasting pan, reserving the drippings and arrange the hens on a platter.

8. Pour all the drippings from the roasting pan into a measuring cup and degrease. Transfer the cooking juices to a small saucepan; add ½ cup water and the remaining 2 tablespoons butter. Simmer the sauce only until the butter is melted. Add salt and pepper to taste. Serve hot along with the stuffed Cornish hens.

———————

—F&W

Stir-Fry of Chicken,
Red Peppers, Arugula
and Prosciutto (p. 158).

Chicken Stir-Fry with Summer Squashes (p. 157) and Clay Pot Chicken with Olives (p. 119).

Broiled Chicken and Caraway (p. 84).

CORNISH GAME HENS WITH ORANGE STUFFING

6 Servings

6 Cornish game hens (1 to 1¼ pounds each)
1½ tablespoons vegetable oil
1½ teaspoons salt
½ teaspoon freshly ground pepper
1 stick (4 ounces) unsalted butter
1 cup chopped onion
2 sweet Italian sausages, cooked and
  finely chopped
1½ cups dry bread crumbs
1 tablespoon grated orange zest
1¼ cups orange juice
½ cup minced parsley
1 egg, lightly beaten

1. Preheat the oven to 450°. Rub the hens with the oil and sprinkle them with 1 teaspoon of the salt and ¼ teaspoon of the pepper.

2. In a large skillet, melt the butter over moderate heat. Add the onion and sauté until translucent, about 10 minutes. Remove the skillet from the heat and stir in the sausage, bread crumbs, orange zest, ½ cup of the orange juice, ½ teaspoon of the salt, the remaining ¼ teaspoon pepper and the parsley; then stir in the egg.

3. Using about ½ cup of stuffing for each hen, loosely stuff the cavities. Secure the legs by tying them together with kitchen string and place the hens in a flameproof roasting pan just large enough to hold them. Roast for 30 minutes, reduce the oven temperature to 350° and continue roasting for an additional 20 to 30 minutes, or until the juices run clear when the thigh is pierced with a fork. Remove the hens from the roasting pan, reserving the drippings and arrange them on a platter.

4. Pour off and discard the fat from the roasting pan, leaving the juices and browned bits behind in the pan. Place the pan over low heat and deglaze it with the remaining ¾ cup orange juice. Stirring constantly, bring the mixture to a boil. Remove the pan from the heat and stir a pinch of pepper. Pour into a sauceboat and serve hot, along with the stuffed hens.

————

—F&W

CITRUS CORNISH HENS

These succulent little birds are glamorized by the addition of sweet-tart grapefruit. For best success, choose juicy grapefruits that feel heavy for their size. I like to serve the hens with a simple rice pilaf or wild rice and a buttered green vegetable, such as broccoli or peas.

♟ Alsace Riesling, such as Trimbach or Zind-Humbrecht

4 Servings

4 large pink grapefruits
4 tablespoons unsalted butter, at room
  temperature
4 Cornish game hens (1 to 1¼ pounds each)
1 cup Madeira
Salt and freshly ground pepper
½ cup chopped pistachio nuts
  (about 2½ ounces)

1. Preheat the oven to 375°.

2. Grate the yellow zest from 2 of the grapefruits, leaving the bitter white pith. In a small heatproof bowl, pour boiling water over the grated zest and let stand for 1 minute. Drain well.

3. In a small bowl, combine the grapefruit zest with the butter. Blend well. Spread 1 tablespoon of grapefruit butter under the breast skin of each hen.

4. Using a sharp knife, peel and section all 4 grapefruits, cutting in between the membranes. Squeeze the membranes over a bowl and set aside ¼ cup of the grapefruit juice.

5. Stuff the cavities of the hens with half of the grapefruit sections. Reserve the remaining sections for garnish.

6. Truss the hens and place in a medium roasting pan. Baste the birds with the reserved grapefruit juice and bake for 1 hour, basting every 15 minutes. The hens are done when the juices run clear when a thigh is pricked. Transfer the birds to a warmed platter and cover loosely with aluminum foil.

7. Using a bulb baster, remove any fat from the juices in the roasting pan. Set the pan over moderate heat, add the Madeira and bring to a boil. Reduce to a simmer and cook, stirring, until the sauce is thickened, 3 to 4 minutes. Strain the sauce and season with salt and pepper to taste.

8. Remove the trussing strings from the hens. Halve each bird lengthwise and discard the grapefruit sections. Arrange the hens on a serving platter or on individual plates. Garnish with the reserved fresh grapefruit sections and sprinkle the pistachio nuts on top. Pass the sauce separately.

—*W. Peter Prestcott*

HERBED CORNISH GAME HENS

Stuffing fresh herbs and butter under the breast skin provides wonderful flavor and bastes the white meat during roasting. Without the sauce, this dish can also be served at room temperature or cold.

🍷 Crisp white, such as Iron Horse Fumé Blanc

6 Servings

1 stick (4 ounces) unsalted butter
¼ cup plus 1 tablespoon minced basil
¼ cup plus 1 tablespoon minced parsley
2 tablespoons minced fresh mint
½ teaspoon salt
½ teaspoon freshly ground black pepper
⅛ teaspoon cayenne pepper
3 tablespoons Dijon-style mustard
3 Cornish game hens (1 to 1¼ pounds each)
1½ cups dry red wine
3 tablespoons minced shallots

1. In a small bowl, beat 3 tablespoons of the butter until softened. Add ¼ cup each of the basil and parsley, 1 tablespoon of the mint and the salt, black pepper and cayenne. Beat until well blended; then beat in 2 tablespoons of the mustard. Set the herb butter aside.

2. Rinse the hens inside and out; pat dry. Loosen the breast skin of each bird from the meat, without tearing the skin. Spread one-third of the herb butter under the breast skin of each bird. Truss the hens.

3. In a small bowl, blend 1 tablespoon of the butter with the remaining 1 tablespoon mustard. Rub 2 teaspoons of this mixture over each hen and sprinkle lightly with salt and pepper. *(The Cornish game hens can be prepared to this point up to 1 day ahead. Cover tightly with plastic wrap and refrigerate. Let return to room temperature before roasting.)*

4. Preheat the oven to 400°. Melt 2 tablespoons of the butter. Place the hens on their sides in a roasting pan and roast for 25 minutes, basting twice with the melted butter. Turn the birds to their other side and roast for 25 minutes longer, basting twice with the melted butter. Increase the oven temperature to 450°, turn the hens breast-side up and roast for 5 minutes. Transfer to a platter and remove the strings.

5. Pour the pan drippings and the juices from the cavities into a small bowl. Skim the fat off the top.

6. Add the wine to the roasting pan and bring to a boil over high heat, stirring to scrape up any browned bits from the bottom of the pan. Cook for 1 minute. Strain the sauce into a small saucepan.

7. Add the shallots to the saucepan and cook over moderately high heat until the liquid is reduced by half. Stir in the degreased juices and

remove from the heat. Swirl in the remaining 2 tablespoons butter and the remaining 1 tablespoon basil, parsley and mint. Season with salt, pepper and cayenne to taste.

8. Cut each bird in half lengthwise and serve with a small spoonful of sauce.

—*Mary Marshall Hynson*

ROAST CORNISH HENS WITH GARLIC CREAM
8 Servings

7 tablespoons unsalted butter
1 tablespoon all-purpose flour
1½ teaspoons Dijon-style mustard
1 teaspoon thyme
1 teaspoon marjoram
1 teaspoon imported sweet paprika
4 Cornish game hens (1 to 1¼ pounds each),
* patted dry*
Coarse (kosher) salt and freshly ground pepper
1 tablespoon peanut oil
2 small onions, halved
1¼ cups Chicken Stock (p. 10) or
* canned broth*
8 large garlic cloves
1½ cups heavy cream
Watercress, for garnish

1. Preheat the oven to 450°. In a small bowl, blend 1 tablespoon of the butter into the flour to make a beurre manié.

2. In another bowl, combine the mustard, thyme, marjoram and paprika. Truss the hens and rub them all over with the mustard–herb mixture. Season lightly with salt and pepper.

3. Spread 2 tablespoons of the butter and the oil in a small roasting pan. Set the hens in the pan on their sides. Arrange the onions around the hens and pour in ¼ cup of the stock. Roast the hens in the middle of the oven for 30 to 40 minutes, turning once and basting every 10 minutes with the pan juices and an additional 2 tablespoons of the chicken stock. The hens are done when the thighs are pierced and the juices run clear. Transfer the hens to a cutting board with tongs, cover loosely with foil and let stand for about 15 minutes before serving.

4. Meanwhile, in a small saucepan of boiling water, blanch the garlic cloves for 1 minute; drain. Add fresh water to the saucepan, bring to a boil and add the blanched garlic cloves. Cook until tender, about 10 minutes; drain well.

5. In a food processor, puree the garlic cloves. Add the cream and process until thick, about 1 minute. Set aside.

6. Discard the onions in the roasting pan and pour the juices into a bowl. Skim off as much fat as possible. Return the juices to a saucepan and add the remaining chicken stock. Boil over moderately high heat until the liquid reduces to ¾ cup, about 7 minutes.

7. Whisk in the garlic cream and boil to reduce slightly, about 5 minutes. Gradually whisk in the beurre manié, bit by bit, then remove the pan from the heat and gradually whisk in the remaining 4 tablespoons butter. Season the sauce with salt and pepper to taste.

8. Remove the strings from the hens, cut them in half and place on individual plates. Spoon some of the sauce around the hens and garnish with the watercress. Pass the remaining sauce separately.

—*Perla Meyers*

SKILLET-ROASTED CORNISH GAME HENS ON A BED OF POLENTA

Cornish game hens are stuffed with sprigs of fresh sage and served over polenta.

4 Servings

2 Cornish game hens (1 to 1¼ pounds each)
Salt and freshly ground pepper
4 sprigs of fresh sage or 6 dried leaves
2½ tablespoons unsalted butter
1½ tablespoons olive oil
3 cups Chicken Stock (p. 10) or 1½ cups
  canned broth diluted with 1½ cups water
1 cup instant polenta
¼ cup boiling water

1. Preheat the oven to 350°. Season the game hens inside and out with a pinch of salt and pepper. Stuff 1 sprig of sage (or 3 dried leaves) into each bird and truss with kitchen string.

2. In a large ovenproof skillet, melt 1½ tablespoons of the butter in the oil over high heat. Cook the birds, turning, until browned evenly all over, 8 to 10 minutes.

3. Turn the birds breast-side up, cover the skillet and place it in the oven. Cook until the birds are tender and the thigh juices run clear when pierced with a fork, 20 to 25 minutes. Transfer to a warm plate and cover loosely with foil.

4. In a medium saucepan, bring the stock to a boil over high heat. Add the remaining 1 tablespoon butter. Gradually stir in the polenta. Cook, stirring constantly, for 5 minutes. Add the boiling water and cook for 5 minutes longer.

5. Cut the game hens in half and reserve any cooking juices that escape. Stir the juices into the polenta. Spoon the polenta onto a large platter and arrange the hens on top. If you are using fresh sage, garnish the platter with the remaining sprigs.

—*John Robert Massie*

SMALL CHICKENS MARINATED IN TEQUILA AND LIME

This unusual marinade moves the margarita from the bar to the kitchen and results in moist and savory chickens every time. The birds can be cooked entirely in the oven, or they can be removed about 10 minutes early and finished on a grill over savory wood. They're good hot or at room temperature.

▼ The tartness of the marinade and chiles in the accompanying salad calls for cold pitchers of a refreshing beer, such as Carta Blanca.

4 Servings

4 poussins (baby chickens) or
  Cornish game hens (about 1¼ pounds each),
  backbones removed
½ cup fresh lime juice
⅓ cup golden tequila
¼ cup olive oil
2 tablespoons Cointreau
2 garlic cloves, minced
¼ teaspoon salt
⅛ teaspoon freshly ground pepper

1. Flatten the chickens with the palm of your hand. In a large bowl, combine the lime juice, tequila, olive oil, Cointreau and garlic. Add the chickens and turn to coat with the marinade. Cover and marinate, turning once or twice, for up to 2 hours at room temperature or overnight in the refrigerator. Let return to room temperature before cooking.

2. Preheat the oven to 400°. Remove the chickens from the marinade and arrange them skin-side up in a shallow baking dish. Season with the salt and pepper. Bake on the upper rack of the oven, basting occasionally with the marinade, until the skin is golden and the juices from the thighs, pricked at their thickest, run pinkish-yellow, 25 to 30 minutes.

—*Michael McLaughlin*

POUSSINS WITH WILD RICE

This recipe is representative of the Midwest harvest. Because poussins are not always available, Cornish game hens can be used as a somewhat larger substitute. When properly cooked, the wild rice in this dish is still somewhat chewy.

❦ The moist birds and nutty rice would be complemented by a full-bodied, round California Chardonnay, such as McDowell.

4 Servings

1½ *cups wild rice*
4 *cups Chicken Stock (p. 10), canned low-*
 sodium broth or water
Salt
1 *tablespoon goose fat or butter*
1 *large shallot, minced*
10 *ounces mushrooms, finely chopped*
 (about 2 cups)
1 *teaspoon finely grated lemon zest*
½ *teaspoon coriander seeds, crushed*
2 *tablespoons plus 1 teaspoon fresh lemon juice*
Freshly ground pepper
½ *cup hazelnuts (3 ounces)*
4 *poussins (about 1 pound each) or Cornish*
 game hens (about 1¼ pounds each)
1 *tablespoon extra-virgin olive oil*
2 *tablespoons minced flat-leaf parsley*

1. In a large saucepan, combine the wild rice and stock and bring to a boil over high heat. Reduce the heat to moderately low and cook, covered, until most of the water is absorbed and about two-thirds of the rice kernels have burst and are somewhat chewy but not hard, 35 to 50 minutes (the cooking time varies dramatically, depending on the age and quality of the rice). Check the rice occasionally as it cooks and add more water if necessary. If you prefer more tender rice, cook for 5 to 10 minutes longer, but do not overcook the rice or it will become mushy. Season to taste with salt.

2. While the rice is cooking, melt the goose fat in a large skillet over moderate heat. Add the shallot and cook, stirring constantly, until translucent, about 2 minutes. Add the mushrooms and cook, stirring occasionally, until they have released all their liquid and it has evaporated, about 6 minutes. Add the lemon zest, coriander seeds and 1 tablespoon of the lemon juice.

3. Stir in the cooked rice and season to taste with salt and pepper. Partially cover and keep warm. *(The rice can be made up to 1 day ahead; cover and refrigerate. Reheat in a 325° oven.)*

4. Preheat the oven to 450°. On a baking sheet, toast the hazelnuts for about 5 minutes, until golden. Let cool, then rub them together in a kitchen towel to remove the skins. Coarsely chop the nuts; set aside. Leave the oven on.

5. Season the cavities of the birds with salt and pepper and 1 tablespoon of the lemon juice. Truss the birds, then rub them all over with the olive oil.

6. Place the birds breast-side up in a roasting pan with space between them. Roast in the upper part of the oven, basting every 10 to 15 minutes, for about 30 minutes. Reduce the heat to 350° and continue roasting until the skin is golden, the thigh juices run clear when pierced with a sharp knife and an instant-reading thermometer inserted into the thickest part of a thigh reads 160°, about 15 minutes longer for smaller birds and 20 minutes for larger birds. Transfer the birds to a platter and set aside. Cover with foil to keep warm.

7. Place the roasting pan with the pan juices over two burners and heat over moderately high heat until beginning to smoke, about 30 seconds. Pour in ½ cup of water and scrape the bottom of the pan with a wooden spoon to loosen the browned bits. Add the remaining 1 teaspoon lemon juice and boil until brown and syrupy, about 2 minutes. Season to taste with salt and pepper and transfer to a gravy boat.

8. Just before serving, stir the reserved hazelnuts into the wild rice. Spoon the rice onto 4 warmed dinner plates and sprinkle the parsley on top. Place the birds on top of the rice. Pass the pan juices separately and serve at once.

———————————

—Susan Herrmann Loomis

ROASTED POUSSINS WITH CARROTS AND PARSNIPS

If you have a hard time finding poussins (baby chickens), use Cornish game hens instead.

❦ With this roasted chicken dish, serve a light Pinot Noir, such as Domaine Dujac Morey St-Denis from Burgundy, Saintsbury Garnet from California or Bethel Heights from Oregon.

8 Servings

3 pounds small carrots, trimmed,
*   or large carrots, cut into 5-by-1-inch*
*   sticks*
3 pounds small parsnips, trimmed,
*   or large parsnips, cut into 5-by-1-inch*
*   sticks*
¼ cup olive oil
Salt and freshly ground pepper
8 poussins (about 1 pound each)
2 lemons, quartered
8 sage leaves
16 garlic cloves, crushed and peeled

1. Preheat the oven to 450°. Toss the carrots and parsnips with 2 tablespoons of the oil and place in a single layer in a large shallow roasting pan or 2 smaller ones that will fit on one oven shelf. Season with salt and pepper. Roast for 15 minutes, shaking the pan every 5 minutes.

2. Meanwhile, loosen the breast skins of the poussins with your fingers. Cut 1 thin slice from each lemon quarter, top with 1 sage leaf and place under the breast skin of each bird. Season the cavities with salt and pepper and place 2 garlic cloves and 1 lemon quarter in each. Using kitchen string, tie the legs of each poussin together to give the birds a nice shape. Brush them with the remaining 2 tablespoons olive oil.

3. Set the poussins on top of the vegetables and roast for 20 minutes. Reduce the temperature to 350° and continue roasting, basting the birds and vegetables with the pan juices every 10 minutes, for about 25 minutes longer. The poussins are done when the skin is golden and the juices run clear when the thighs are pierced. Transfer the birds and vegetables to plates or a large platter and remove the trussing strings. Degrease the pan juices and spoon them on top.

———————————

—Elizabeth Woodson

Broils,
Grills
and
Barbecues

THYME-BROILED BUTTERFLIED CHICKEN

4 Servings

One 3½-pound chicken
1 tablespoon olive oil
1 teaspoon cayenne pepper
1 teaspoon thyme

1. Preheat the broiler.

2. Using poultry shears or a sharp cleaver, split the chicken down the center of the back from neck to tail; spread the chicken open butterfly-fashion and cut off the wing tips.

3. Rub the skin with the olive oil. Place the chicken, skin-side down, on a broiler pan and broil 4 inches from the heat for 15 minutes.

4. Turn the chicken over and sprinkle it with the cayenne and thyme. Broil for an additional 5 minutes, or until the skin is crisp and the juices run clear when the thigh is pierced with a fork.

———

—F&W

BROILED CHICKEN AND CARAWAY

This savory chicken makes a beautiful presentation served with apple and red onion slices that have been sautéed in butter, painted with a little of the glaze and sprinkled with caraway seeds. Plums, peaches or any other firm fruit can also be used.
❧ Cabernet Sauvignon, such as Beringer State Lane

2 to 4 Servings

2 tablespoons unsalted butter
3 tablespoons minced onion
1 teaspoon caraway seeds
½ teaspoon salt
¼ teaspoon freshly ground pepper
One 3½-pound chicken
2 teaspoons corn oil
1 can (6 ounces) frozen apple juice
  concentrate, thawed

1. In a small skillet, melt the butter. Add the onion, caraway seeds, ¼ teaspoon of the salt and the pepper. Cook over low heat until the onions are just softened, 2 to 3 minutes. Set aside to cool.

2. Using a pair of poultry shears, cut out the backbone of the chicken to butterfly the bird. Gently loosen the breast, thigh and leg skin by working your fingers carefully underneath. Using a sharp knife, score the thickest part of the meat along the back center of the thigh and leg down to the bone (this allows the legs to cook roughly as fast as the breast).

3. Preheat the broiler and broiler pan. Stuff the onion mixture under the chicken skin, spreading as evenly as possible. Sprinkle the skin with the remaining ¼ teaspoon salt.

4. Brush the hot broiler pan with the oil and place the chicken on it skin-side up. Broil about 5 inches from the heat until well browned, about 10 minutes.

5. Meanwhile, in a small saucepan, boil the apple juice concentrate until reduced by about one-fourth to a syrupy glaze, about 5 minutes.

6. Reduce the oven temperature to 375°, transfer the chicken to the middle of the oven and roast for 10 minutes. Brush the bird with the apple glaze. Roast for 10 minutes longer, basting twice. Serve hot or at room temperature.

———

—Anne Disrude

GRILLED CHILE CHICKEN

The fiery chile peppers inserted under the skin of the chicken to heighten the effect of the sauce are removed before serving.

6 Servings

4 ancho chiles, seeded
4 red bell peppers
2 tablespoons olive oil
1 small onion, chopped
6 garlic cloves—2 minced, 4 cut in half
2 tablespoons curry powder
1 teaspoon fennel seeds, crushed
1 teaspoon cumin
2 teaspoons sweet paprika
⅓ cup strongly brewed coffee
1½ cups Chicken Stock (p. 10) or
   canned broth
1 stick (4 ounces) unsalted butter,
   cut into pieces
½ cup fresh orange juice
¼ cup fresh lime juice
3 broiling chickens (2½ pounds each),
   backbones removed
18 small dried red chile peppers, split and
   seeded
6 sprigs of cilantro (fresh coriander)
3 small unpeeled oranges, halved and
   thinly sliced

1. Place the ancho chiles in a small bowl and add enough boiling water to barely cover them. Let stand for 30 minutes. Drain and when cool enough to handle, remove the skins.

2. Roast the bell peppers directly over a gas flame or as close to the heat of a broiler as possible, turning frequently, until the skin is charred all over. Enclose the peppers in a paper bag and let stand for 10 minutes. Remove the stems, seeds and skins, wiping away any blackened particles with a damp cloth.

3. In a medium nonreactive saucepan, heat the olive oil. Add the onion and minced garlic and cook over low heat, stirring frequently, until softened but not browned. 3 to 5 minutes.

4. Add the curry powder, fennel seeds, cumin and paprika. Cook, stirring frequently, for 3 minutes.

5. Add the brewed coffee and the chicken stock. Bring to a boil. Add the peeled ancho chiles and the roasted bell peppers and simmer, stirring occasionally, for 30 minutes.

6. Pour the mixture into a blender or food processor. Add the butter and puree until smooth. Return to the saucepan. Blend in the orange juice, lime juice and additional stock to thin the sauce if necessary. Set the sauce aside, covered, to keep warm.

7. Preheat the broiler. Rub the chickens with the halved garlic cloves and stuff the small, split dried chiles under the skin. Place the chickens, skin-side up, on a baking sheet and broil about 5 inches from the heat for 15 minutes, turning them with tongs every 3 to 4 minutes. Move the chickens to a lower rack about 7 inches from the heat and cook for 10 to 12 minutes, turning twice, until the skin is browned and the juices run clear.

8. To serve, split the chickens in half and remove the chiles from under the skin. Ladle the sauce over the chicken. Garnish the plates with a sprig of cilantro and thin slices of orange.

—Barbara Figueroa, Sorrento Hotel, Seattle

GRILLED MARINATED CHICKEN BREASTS

Although there is some marinating time (about 3 hours) required, this grilled chicken dish is nearly effortless.

6 Servings

¾ cup fresh lemon juice
¾ cup vegetable oil
¼ cup minced onion
1½ teaspoons salt
¼ teaspoon thyme
2 tablespoons green peppercorn mustard
12 skinless, boneless chicken breast halves
  (4 to 5 ounces each)

1. In a medium bowl, combine the lemon juice, oil, onion, salt, thyme and mustard.

2. With a sharp knife, score both sides of each breast in a cross-hatch pattern about ⅛ inch deep. Pour one-third of the marinade into a shallow glass bowl. Add half the chicken in a single layer and cover with another third of the marinade. Put the remaining breasts in a layer on top and pour on the remaining marinade. Cover with plastic wrap and refrigerate for 2 hours, turning occasionally. Remove from the refrigerator for 1 hour before cooking to bring to room temperature.

3. Meanwhile, preheat the broiler. Arrange the chicken on a broiler pan and grill about 4 inches from the heat for 3 minutes. Turn and grill for another 3 minutes, or until the juices run clear when pierced with a sharp knife. Make sure not to overcook. Transfer to a warmed platter and cover loosely with foil until ready to serve.

—*Lee Bailey*

CHICKEN BREASTS WITH TOASTED MUSTARD SEED SAUCE

To match the delicacy of the chicken, try a dry Chenin Blanc with its faint peachy flavor. Look for Chappellet or Villa Mt. Eden.

6 Servings

2 cups heavy cream
3 tablespoons Dijon-style mustard
¾ teaspoon salt
1 teaspoon freshly ground pepper
1½ tablespoons yellow mustard seeds
6 boneless chicken breast halves, with the skin
  on (about 6 ounces each)
2 teaspoons fresh lemon juice
3 large scallions, thinly sliced

1. In a heavy medium saucepan, bring the cream to a boil over high heat. Reduce the heat to low and cook, stirring occasionally until the cream is slightly thickened and reduced to 1¼ cups, about 10 minutes.

2. Remove the cream from the heat and whisk in the mustard, ¼ teaspoon of the salt and ½ teaspoon of the pepper. *(The sauce can be made ahead to this point up to 4 hours in advance. Whisk it occasionally to keep a skin from forming.)*

3. Meanwhile, in a small skillet, toast the mustard seeds over moderately high heat, shaking the pan until they are lightly browned and begin to pop. Immediately transfer the seeds to a plate to cool.

4. Preheat the oven to 500°. Place the chicken breasts on a broiler pan, skin-side up, and season with the remaining ½ teaspoon salt and ½ teaspoon pepper. Bake on the top rack of the oven until the chicken has only a trace of pink in the center, about 12 minutes.

5. Turn the broiler on and broil the chicken until the skin is browned and crisp, about 1

minute. Let the chicken stand for 2 to 3 minutes while you reheat the sauce over low heat. Stir the lemon juice, scallions and mustard seeds into the sauce.

6. To serve, arrange a chicken breast on each of 6 dinner plates. Spoon the sauce on top.

———————

—*Marcia Kiesel*

CHICKEN BREASTS WITH GINGER AND LEMON

The chicken for this elegant ginger dish needs to marinate overnight, so plan accordingly.

♟ Alsace Riesling, such as Hugel or Faller Frères, or Ockfener Bockstein

4 Servings

1¾ cups diagonally sliced scallions
⅓ cup chopped unpeeled fresh ginger, or ½
*   cup fresh ginger peelings, plus 1½ teaspoons*
*   grated, peeled fresh ginger*
2 garlic cloves, chopped
Zest of 1 lemon, removed with a vegetable
*   peeler in 1-inch-wide strips*
½ teaspoon salt
½ teaspoon freshly ground pepper
4 skinless, boneless chicken breast halves
*   (about 5 ounces each)*
1 cup Chicken Stock (p. 10) or canned broth
½ cup dry white wine
¼ cup Stone's Original Ginger-Flavored
*   Currant Wine★ or sweet white wine*
1 stick (4 ounces) cold unsalted butter, cut into
*   12 pieces, plus 1 tablespoon butter, melted*
2 tablespoons fresh lemon juice
★Available at most liquor stores

1. In a shallow baking pan, toss together 1 cup of the scallions, the chopped unpeeled ginger, the garlic, lemon zest, salt and pepper.

2. Add the chicken to the scallion mixture, turning to season both sides. Cover tightly with plastic wrap and refrigerate overnight.

3. Pick out the lemon zest and blanch it in 1 cup of boiling water for 3 minutes. Drain and rinse under cold, running water. Cut the zest into long, thin strips.

4. Scrape the seasonings from the chicken and the baking pan into a small nonreactive saucepan. Place the chicken back in the baking pan, cover and set aside.

5. Add the chicken stock, dry white wine and ginger-currant wine to the saucepan. Bring to a boil over high heat, reduce the heat to low, cover and simmer for 20 minutes. Pour through a strainer into a small bowl, pressing on the solids. Pour the liquid into a clean small saucepan; there will be about 1¼ cups. Bring to a boil and continue to cook over high heat until the liquid is reduced to ¼ cup, about 10 minutes.

6. Remove from the heat and whisk in the cold butter, 1 piece at a time, adding each piece just as the previous one is almost incorporated. (If necessary, return to low heat briefly, whisking to produce a creamy emulsion.)

7. Stir the remaining ¾ cup scallions, the lemon zest, lemon juice and grated peeled ginger into the sauce. Season with additional salt and pepper to taste.

8. Lightly brush the chicken breasts on both sides with the melted butter. Transfer to a broiler pan lined with foil and broil about 6 inches from the heat, for 4 to 5 minutes per side, or until just cooked through, moist with no trace of pink. Transfer to serving plates or a platter.

9. Gently reheat the sauce, if necessary, and spoon over the chicken.

———————

—*Jane Helsel Joseph*

DEVILED CHICKEN PAILLARDE WITH ZUCCHINI

🍷 Rosé, such as Château de Selle

2 Servings

*2 large skinless, boneless chicken breast halves
  (about 7 ounces each)*
2 tablespoons olive oil
½ teaspoon thyme
½ teaspoon coarsely cracked pepper
1 medium zucchini, cut into 24 thin slices
*2 large tomatoes, halved lengthwise and cut
  into 24 thin half-moon slices*
*1 medium onion, halved lengthwise and cut
  into 24 thin half-moon slices*
½ teaspoon ground coriander
½ teaspoon salt
2 tablespoons plus ½ teaspoon dry white wine
¼ teaspoon dry mustard
1 teaspoon Dijon-style mustard
2 tablespoons coarse white bread crumbs

1. Preheat the oven to 375°. Between two layers of plastic wrap, pound each chicken breast to a ¼ inch thickness. In a small bowl, combine 1 tablespoon of the olive oil, the thyme and ¼ teaspoon of the pepper. Paint both sides of each breast with the seasoned oil and set aside.

2. On a baking sheet with sides, arrange overlapping slices of the zucchini, tomato and onion in 4 rows, alternating the vegetables so that each row contains 6 slices each of zucchini, tomato and onion. Sprinkle with the remaining ¼ teaspoon pepper, the coriander and ¼ teaspoon of the salt. Paint with the remaining 1 tablespoon oil. Sprinkle with 2 tablespoons of the wine.

3. Bake for 15 minutes, basting twice with the pan juices, until the onion is softened. Remove from the oven and cover with aluminum foil to keep warm.

4. Preheat the broiler and set the broiler pan about 4 inches from the heat. In a bowl, combine the dry mustard with the remaining ½ tea-spoon wine; stir until smooth. Blend in the Dijon-style mustard.

5. Oil the hot broiler pan. Lay the chicken breasts on it and broil, turning once, for 1 minute on each side. Remove the chicken from the broiler; leave the heat on. Brush the mustard sauce on both sides of the breasts. Return the chicken to the pan and sprinkle one side with the remaining ¼ teaspoon salt and the bread crumbs. Return the chicken to the broiler and cook until the bread crumbs are browned, 1 to 2 minutes.

6. To serve, place each chicken breast in the center of a warmed plate. Lay a row of the baked vegetables on either side of the breast.

———————

—Alain Sailhac

SESAME CHICKEN

The marinade here has the same flavor as the traditional sauce for cold spicy noodles with sesame sauce. Running the chicken breasts under the broiler gives them an almost black, crusty exterior and a wonderful flavor. The chicken needs marinating for about 24 hours, so plan accordingly.

6 Servings

¾ cup Oriental sesame paste★
⅓ cup brewed Chinese black tea
¼ cup dark soy sauce★
1½ tablespoons Chinese chile oil★
3 medium garlic cloves, crushed through a press
2 tablespoons Oriental sesame oil
2 tablespoons sugar
2 tablespoons red wine vinegar
½ cup thinly sliced scallions
2 pounds skinless, boneless chicken breast
1 bunch of watercress, for garnish
★Available at Asian markets

1. In a small bowl, combine the sesame paste, tea, soy sauce, chile oil, garlic, sesame oil, sugar and vinegar. Whisk until well blended. Stir in the scallions.

2. Place the chicken in a large glass baking dish. Pour the marinade over the chicken. Turn to coat well. Cover and refrigerate for 24 hours. Let the chicken return to room temperature before proceeding.

3. Preheat the broiler. Place the chicken on a broiler pan. Broil the chicken about 3 inches from the heat, turning carefully so as not to break the crust, for about 5 minutes on each side, until the outside is slightly charred and the chicken is still juicy but no longer pink.

4. Let rest for 10 minutes. Cut into 1-inch cubes. Serve warm or at room temperature, garnished with the sprigs of watercress.

—*Karen Lee & Alaxandra Branyon*

GOLDEN BROILED CHICKEN

This chicken dish makes ideal picnic fare. Not only does it taste wonderful at room temperature, but this cornmeal crisped fowl holds up well when made the day before, sparing the cook a last-minute scramble in the kitchen.

🍷 Crisp, light white, such as Hacienda Dry Chenin Blanc or Hogue Cellars Chenin Blanc

8 Servings

2 garlic cloves, bruised
½ teaspoon salt
½ teaspoon freshly ground black pepper
½ teaspoon cayenne pepper
1 teaspoon fresh rosemary, minced, or ½ teaspoon dried, crumbled
3 tablespoons fresh lemon juice
2 tablespoons yellow cornmeal
½ cup vegetable oil
2 chickens (about 3½ pounds each), cut into 8 serving pieces each

1. In a small bowl, mash the garlic and salt to a paste. Add the black pepper, cayenne, rosemary, lemon juice and cornmeal and mash until fairly smooth. Stir in the oil until blended.

2. Place the chicken in a large shallow dish and spoon the seasoned cornmeal over the pieces, spreading to coat evenly. Let stand uncovered at room temperature for 1 hour.

3. Preheat the broiler. Place the chicken, skin-side up, on a broiler pan and broil, about 5 inches from the heat, until the juices run clear when pricked with a fork, about 20 minutes per side.

—*Phillip Stephen Schulz*

CHICKEN TERIYAKI

Accompany this broiled chicken dish with steamed rice and a salad.

4 Servings

½ cup mirin (sweet rice wine)★
¾ cup sake
½ cup dark shoyu (Japanese soy sauce)★
2 tablespoons shredded fresh ginger
1 medium garlic clove, minced
1 teaspoon sugar
12 chicken thighs (3 pounds), skinned and boned to yield 1½ pounds
½ cup peanut oil
¼ cup plus 2 teaspoons cornstarch
¼ cup all-purpose flour
★Available at Asian markets

1. In a blender or food processor, combine the mirin, sake, soy sauce, ginger, garlic and sugar and blend until the ginger and garlic are pulverized, about 1 minute. Strain the marinade into a bowl, pushing on the solids with a wooden spoon to extract as much liquid as possible.

2. Cut the chicken meat into pieces about ¾ by ¾ by 1 inch and soak them in the marinade for 10 minutes.

3. Preheat the broiler. In a large heavy skillet, warm the peanut oil over moderately high heat until almost smoking.

4. Meanwhile, combine ¼ cup of the cornstarch and the flour in a paper bag. Drain the chicken in a strainer or colander set over a bowl;

reserve 1 cup of the marinade. Place the chicken pieces in the bag and shake to coat them. Place about half the pieces in the hot oil and fry them for 1 to 1½ minutes, or until crisp and golden on one side. Quickly turn them over with tongs and fry for 30 seconds more. Transfer the pieces to paper towels to drain and fry the remaining chicken in the same manner.

5. Place the reserved marinade in a small saucepan. Whisk in the remaining 2 teaspoons cornstarch, stirring until dissolved. Place the pan over moderate heat and cook, stirring constantly, until the sauce is smooth and thickened.

6. Place the chicken pieces on a broiling pan. Drizzle the top of the chicken with about ⅓ cup of the teriyaki sauce. Broil 4 to 5 inches from the heat for 1 to 2 minutes, or until the sauce is bubbling. Serve with the remaining sauce.

———

—F&W

SPICY GRILLED CITRUS CHICKEN

In a sense, the zesty marinade used to flavor the chicken breasts is related to Mexican *sangrita* because the same ingredients—tomato, orange and lime—are combined to make a luscious barbecue sauce with a kick of hot pepper and a lick of honey. The chicken must marinate for about 12 hours, so plan accordingly.

6 Servings

1 can (6 ounces) frozen orange juice
  concentrate, thawed
½ cup canned tomato puree
¼ cup honey
1 teaspoon minced orange zest
1 teaspoon minced lemon zest
1 teaspoon minced lime zest
3 tablespoons fresh lemon juice
3 tablespoons fresh lime juice
4 garlic cloves, crushed through a press
1 teaspoon thyme leaves
¾ teaspoon cayenne pepper
¾ teaspoon freshly ground black pepper
1 teaspoon salt
6 chicken breast halves, bone in (about 8
  ounces each)

1. In a large bowl, combine the orange juice concentrate, tomato puree, honey, orange zest, lemon zest, lime zest, lemon juice, lime juice, garlic, thyme, cayenne, black pepper and salt. Mix to blend well.

2. Add the chicken and turn to coat. Cover and refrigerate for 12 hours, or overnight.

3. Light a charcoal fire. When the coals are glowing, place a lightly oiled grill about 5 inches above the fire and heat for 5 minutes. Remove the chicken from the marinade; reserve the marinade. Place the chicken, bone-side down, on the grill. Cook for 5 minutes.

4. Meanwhile, pour the marinade into a small nonreactive saucepan and bring to a boil over moderate heat. Boil for 1 minute. After the chicken has cooked for 5 minutes, spoon some of the marinade over each piece and turn. Grill, basting with the marinade and turning every 5 minutes, for 20 to 30 minutes, until the chicken is white throughout but still juicy.

———

—Jim Fobel

GRILLED TANDOORI-STYLE CHICKEN

The first time I made tandoori chicken for James Beard, he took one bite and said casually, "This has two marinades, how interesting." With his sharp palate, he knew immediately. A properly made tandoori chicken does, indeed, have two marinades—one of just salt and lime juice, and another containing yogurt, onion, garlic, ginger, green chiles and garam masala (see Note).

4 to 6 Servings

2½ pounds chicken drumsticks and thighs
2 teaspoons coarse (kosher) salt
1½ juicy lemons, cut into quarters

¾ cup plain yogurt
½ medium onion, peeled and
  quartered
5 garlic cloves
¾-inch cube fresh ginger, peeled
  and quartered
½ fresh hot green chile, roughly sliced
2 teaspoons garam masala (see Note)
2 sticks (8 ounces) unsalted butter, melted
Lemon wedges, for accompaniment

1. On the morning or evening before you plan to serve this dish, make two diagonal incisions, about 1 inch long, on each side of the chicken pieces. The slits should be deep enough to reach the bone.

2. Spread the chicken pieces on one or two platters. Sprinkle with 1 teaspoon of the salt, then squeeze the juice from three lemon quarters over them. Lightly rub the salt and lemon juice into the slits. Turn the chicken pieces over and do the same with the remaining salt and lemon juice. Set aside for 20 minutes.

3. In a food processor or blender, blend the yogurt, onion, garlic, ginger, green chile and garam masala. You should have a smooth paste. Empty the paste into a large bowl.

4. Coat the chicken well with the marinade, making sure it penetrates the slits. Cover and refrigerate from 5 to 24 hours.

5. When ready to serve, heat a charcoal grill until the coals become grayish on top and very hot. Arrange the chicken pieces 5 inches from the heat and grill about 15 to 20 minutes a side, or until the chicken is just cooked through. Baste very frequently with the melted butter.

6. Serve hot with lemon wedges.

NOTE: Garam masala is a ground spice mixture available in Indian and other specialty food stores, as well as from many mail-order houses across the country. However, it tastes best when made at home. To make it, finely grind 1 tablespoon cardamom seeds, a 1-inch piece of cinnamon stick, one-third of a whole nutmeg and 1 teaspoon each whole cloves, peppercorns and black cumin seeds. Store in a tightly lidded jar at room temperature.

—*Madhur Jaffrey*

CHICKEN MAKHANI

In India, tandoori chicken is either served whole, to be torn up and eaten with a tandoori bread called *naan*, or cut into serving pieces and doused with a quickly made sauce containing butter, tomatoes, cream, ginger and toasted cumin. This is what is known as chicken makhani.

The sauce for this dish can be made while the tandoori chicken is grilling.

4 to 6 Servings

1 teaspoon cumin seeds
1 cup canned tomato sauce
1-inch cube of fresh ginger, peeled
  and grated to a fine pulp
1 cup heavy cream
1 teaspoon garam masala (see Note above)
¼ teaspoon salt
1 fresh hot green chile, sliced into very
  fine rounds
¼ teaspoon cayenne pepper
1 tablespoon minced cilantro
  (fresh coriander)
1 tablespoon fresh lemon juice
1 stick (4 ounces) unsalted butter
Grilled Tandoori-Style Chicken (at left)
Sprigs of cilantro, for garnish

1. In a small, ungreased skillet, dry-roast the cumin seeds over medium heat, stirring until they turn a shade darker. Use a mortar and pestle, or a spice mill, to grind the seeds finely.

2. In a bowl, combine the tomato sauce, ginger, heavy cream, garam masala, salt, green chile, cayenne, cilantro, lemon juice and roasted cumin seeds.

3. In a large skillet, melt the butter. Add the ingredients from the mixing bowl to the hot butter,

bring to a simmer and cook over medium heat for 1 minute.

4. Add the Grilled Tandoori-Style Chicken pieces, stirring once to coat and briefly rewarm them.

5. Transfer the coated chicken to a warm serving platter and spoon additional sauce evenly over the top. Garnish with cilantro sprigs and serve immediately.

—*Madhur Jaffrey*

TERIYAKI CORNISH HENS

These little birds offer big taste, especially after they are marinated in the refrigerator for a day. Don't be alarmed by the large quantity of ginger. It contributes great flavor.

4 Servings

4 large Cornish game hens (about 1½
  pounds each)
¾ cup chopped fresh ginger
  (about 4 ounces)
2 tablespoons minced garlic
½ cup sugar
1 cup sake
½ cup soy sauce

1. The day before you want to grill the game hens, cut along each side of the spine to free the backbones and discard. Flatten the birds slightly with a mallet or side of a cleaver or with the bottom of a cast-iron skillet.

2. In a blender or food processor, combine the ginger, garlic, sugar, sake and soy sauce. Puree until smooth. Pour the marinade into a large nonreactive baking dish. Add the hens and turn. Marinate in the refrigerator for at least 24 hours, turning occasionally.

3. Light a charcoal fire. When the coals are glowing but covered in gray ash, drain the hens and put them bone-side down on the grill, about 5 inches from the heat. Grill, turning every 5

minutes or so, until the skin is well browned and the thigh juices run clear when the meat is pricked, 18 to 25 minutes.

—*Jim Fobel*

JAPANESE CHICKEN YAKITORI

🍷 Kirin or Sapporo beer
  6 Servings

¾ cup soy sauce
¾ cup sake
1 tablespoon sugar
1 tablespoon crushed, peeled ginger, passed
  through a garlic press
1¾ pounds skinless, boneless chicken breast,
  cut into 1-inch squares
12 chicken livers (about 12 ounces), trimmed
  and halved
12 scallions (white and light green),
  each cut into 2 pieces

1. Light the charcoal or preheat the broiler. In a medium bowl, stir the soy sauce, sake, sugar and ginger until the sugar dissolves. Add the chicken, chicken livers and scallions and toss to coat. Let marinate at room temperature for 15 minutes, turning once or twice.

2. Thread the chicken cubes, scallions and chicken livers onto 6 long, metal skewers, alternating the ingredients and dividing evenly. Reserve the marinade.

3. Grill 4 to 6 inches over hot coals, basting several times with the marinade and turning once, until the chicken is slightly crisp on the outside, but the livers are still tender and moist inside, 8 to 10 minutes.

—*F&W*

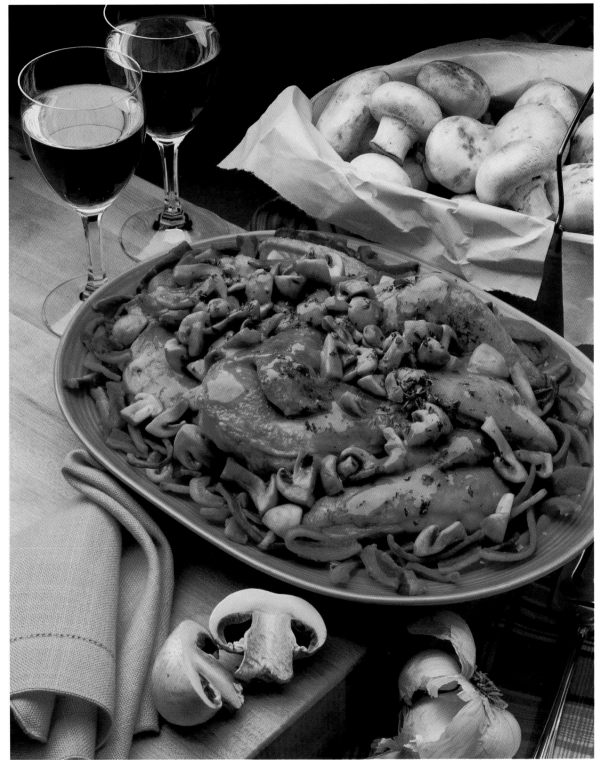

Coq au Riesling (p. 168).

Peanut-Fried Drumsticks with Curried Cucumbers (p. 149).

SLOW-FIRE SMOKED CHICKEN

If you won't be eating the chicken immediately, let it cool, then set it on a plate and cover loosely with waxed paper to allow it to breathe. For best flavor and texture, use a free-range or kosher chicken.

♟ To harmonize with but not overwhelm the mild chicken, try a fragrant, light Pinot Noir, such as Clos du Bois from Sonoma.

2 to 3 Servings

One 3½- to 4-pound chicken
1 lemon, halved
1 teaspoon salt
2 teaspoons freshly ground Szechuan peppercorns★ or 1 teaspoon freshly ground black pepper
1 garlic clove, crushed
2 tablespoons unsalted butter
2 shallots
3 sprigs of fresh rosemary or ½ teaspoon dried
1 tablespoon extra-virgin olive oil
★Available at Asian markets

1. Start the fire in a grill with a cover.
2. Remove the fat from the tail end of the chicken. Squeeze half of the lemon into the cavity and sprinkle in ½ teaspoon of the salt and 1 teaspoon of the Szechuan pepper (or ½ teaspoon of the black pepper). Then place the 2 lemon halves, garlic, butter, shallots and rosemary in the cavity. Rub the chicken with the olive oil and the remaining ½ teaspoon salt and 1 teaspoon Szechuan pepper (or ½ teaspoon black pepper). Skewer the chicken closed at both ends.

3. Brush the grill rack with oil. Place the chicken, breast-side up, in the center of the grill and cover, leaving all the vents wide open. Cook the chicken for 1¼ to 1½ hours, turning it with a wide spatula every 15 to 20 minutes. The chicken is done when it is evenly browned and the juices run clear when a thigh is pierced. If the chicken seems to be cooking too fast and getting too dark too soon, move it to the side of the grill where the heat is less intense.

4. Transfer the chicken to a platter and let rest for 15 minutes before carving. If you'll be serving the chicken the next day, let it cool completely, cover and refrigerate.

———————————

—*Karen Lee & Alaxandra Branyon*

CALIFORNIA-STYLE BARBECUED CHICKEN

Serve the chicken with a salsa made with chopped fresh pineapple, minced fresh or pickled jalapeño, lemon juice and chopped cilantro.

4 Servings

¾ cup pineapple juice or apricot nectar
½ cup (packed) light brown sugar
½ cup ketchup
½ cup cider vinegar
1 tablespoons cornstarch
2½ pounds chicken parts

1. Light a charcoal fire.
2. In a medium nonreactive saucepan, combine ½ cup of the pineapple juice, the brown sugar, ketchup and vinegar. Bring to a boil over moderate heat, stirring occasionally.

3. In a small bowl, dissolve the cornstarch in the remaining ¼ cup juice. Whisk into the hot sauce, and simmer, stirring constantly, until the sauce is thickened and slightly translucent, about 3 minutes.

4. When the coals are ready (glowing but covered with ash), grill the chicken pieces 4 inches from the heat, turning once, for 6 minutes. Baste with the barbecue sauce and continue grilling—basting liberally and turning every 5 minutes—until the chicken is cooked through, 20 to 30 minutes longer.

—F&W

EGYPTIAN GRILLED STUFFED GAME HENS

In Egypt, this traditional recipe is made with squab or poussins (baby chickens), but this recipe calls for the more readily available game hens. The birds may also be cooked in a 375° oven, turning and basting as described above, for 1 hour to 1 hour 15 minutes.

4 Servings

2 medium onions, grated, plus 1 small onion,
  finely chopped
½ cup fresh lemon juice
2 teaspoons salt
4 Cornish game hens (1 to 1¼ pounds each),
  livers reserved
4 tablespoons unsalted butter
½ cup finely chopped walnuts
2 cups fireek (Egyptian cracked wheat) or
  bulgur wheat★
2 tablespoons dried mint
Freshly ground pepper
1½ cups Chicken Stock (p. 10) or
  canned broth
2 tablespoons olive oil
★Available at Middle Eastern markets and
  health food stores

1. In a large bowl, combine the grated onions, lemon juice and salt. Place the hens in the onion marinade and turn to coat well all over. Cover and let marinate at room temperature, turning the hens every 20 minutes, for 2 hours (or up to 4 hours in the refrigerator; let return to room temperature before grilling).

2. Finely chop the reserved livers. In a medium skillet, melt the butter over moderate heat. Add the chopped onion, livers and walnuts and cook, stirring frequently, until the onion is lightly browned, 5 to 7 minutes.

3. Add the bulgur, mint and salt and pepper to taste; cook, stirring, for 3 minutes. Add the stock, bring to a boil, reduce the heat and simmer, stirring often, for 5 minutes. Remove from the heat and let cool for 5 minutes.

4. Remove the hens from the marinade, scraping any excess marinade back into the bowl; reserve the marinade. Loosely fill the hens with stuffing. (Reserve extra stuffing to reheat and serve as a side dish.) Truss the hens, closing the body cavity securely.

5. Light the charcoal. Rub the hens all over with the oil. Place them breast-side up on the grill 4 to 6 inches above hot coals and cook for 5 minutes. Turn onto one side and grill for 5 minutes; turn onto the other side and grill for another 5 minutes. Turn the hens breast-side down and grill for 5 minutes longer. Baste with the reserved marinade. Repeat the entire procedure, basting with the marinade each time you turn the birds, about 3 more times, until they are cooked through and the thigh juices run clear, a total of 1 to 1½ hours, depending on whether you are using an open or covered-kettle grill.

—Citadel Grill, Ramses Hilton, Cairo, Egypt

ALL–AMERICAN BARBECUED CHICKEN

If you have time, marinate the chicken in the cooled barbecue sauce for up to 6 hours before grilling.

4 Servings

1 can (6 ounces) tomato paste
1 cup dry vermouth
⅓ cup fresh lemon juice
⅓ cup tarragon vinegar
⅓ cup honey
¼ cup Worcestershire sauce
3 tablespoons Dijon-style mustard
2 tablespoons soy sauce
1 tablespoon hot pepper sauce
1 teaspoon ground cumin
2 tablespoons unsalted butter
1½ tablespoons olive oil
1 medium onion, minced
4 garlic cloves, minced
1 bay leaf
2½ pounds chicken parts

1. In a medium bowl, mix the tomato paste, vermouth, lemon juice, vinegar, honey, Worcestershire sauce, mustard, soy sauce, hot sauce and cumin until blended.

2. In a medium nonreactive saucepan, warm the butter and oil over moderate heat. Add the onion and garlic and sauté, stirring, until softened and translucent, about 4 minutes.

3. Add the sauce mixture and the bay leaf and simmer, uncovered, over moderately low heat, stirring occasionally until thickened, about 20 minutes.

4. Light a charcoal fire. When the coals are ready (glowing but covered with ash), grill the chicken pieces 4 inches from the heat, turning once, for 6 minutes. Baste with the barbecue sauce and continue grilling—basting liberally and turning every 5 minutes—until the chicken is cooked through, 20 to 30 minutes longer.

———

—F&W

MIDDLE EASTERN DEVILED CHICKEN

Serve the chicken with tabbouleh salad and toasted pita bread.

4 Servings

1 tablespoon olive oil
½ small onion, chopped
4 large garlic cloves, chopped
1 teaspoon crushed hot red pepper
1 cup beef broth
1 can (6 ounces) tomato paste
½ cup plus 2 tablespoons honey
1½ teaspoons thyme
1½ teaspoons oregano
1 large bay leaf, crumbled
1 teaspoon salt
½ teaspoon freshly ground black pepper
2½ pounds chicken parts

1. In a medium saucepan, heat the oil over moderate heat. Add the onion, garlic and hot pepper and sauté, stirring occasionally, until the onion begins to turn golden, about 3 minutes.

2. Add the broth, tomato paste, honey, thyme, oregano, bay leaf, salt and black pepper and bring to a boil. Reduce the heat to low and simmer, stirring occasionally, 12 to 15 minutes. Strain into a bowl.

3. Light a charcoal fire. When the coals are ready (glowing but covered with ash), grill the chicken pieces 4 inches from the heat, turning

once, for 6 minutes. Baste with the barbecue sauce and continue grilling—basting liberally and turning every 5 minutes—until the chicken is cooked through, 20 to 30 minutes longer.

———————

—F&W

SHERRIED CHICKEN WITH STICKY-LICK-IT BARBECUE SAUCE

The sherry marinade brings depth of flavor to the chicken and is then used to make a sticky barbecue sauce. The chicken must marinate for about 6 hours, so plan accordingly.

❦ Chilled rosé, such as McDowell Zinfandel Blanc or Simi Rosé of Cabernet Sauvignon

4 Servings

2 cups dry sherry
¼ cup fresh lemon juice
2 bay leaves
2 large garlic cloves, crushed through a press
1 small onion, finely chopped
One 4-pound chicken, cut into 8
  serving pieces
1 can (15 ounces) tomato puree
¼ cup honey
3 tablespoons light molasses
1 teaspoon salt
½ teaspoon cayenne pepper
½ teaspoon thyme
¼ teaspoon freshly ground black pepper
2 tablespoons white wine vinegar

1. In a large bowl, combine the sherry, lemon juice, bay leaves, garlic and onion. Add the chicken and toss well. Cover and marinate in the refrigerator for 6 hours, or overnight.

2. Drain the chicken, reserving the marinade. In a heavy, medium nonreactive saucepan, combine the reserved marinade with the tomato puree, honey, molasses, salt, cayenne, thyme and black pepper. Bring to a boil over moderate heat. Reduce the heat to moderately low and cook, stirring occasionally, until the sauce is thick and rich and reduced to 2 cups, 35 to 45 minutes. Remove from the heat and stir in the vinegar. Remove the bay leaves.

3. Light a charcoal fire. Grill the chicken over glowing hot coals for 10 minutes, turning 2 or 3 times. Spoon some of the sauce over the pieces and continue grilling, basting liberally with sauce and turning every 5 minutes, until cooked through, 20 to 30 minutes longer.

———————

—Jim Fobel

Baked Chicken Dishes

SPICED HONEY WINGS WITH POPPY AND SESAME SEEDS

This dish is made with just the meatiest portion of the wing, which is sometimes called the drumette. Save the rest of the wings in the freezer for making stock.

8 Servings

24 chicken wings
1 tablespoon dry mustard
1 teaspoon ground ginger
¼ teaspoon allspice
1 teaspoon salt
1 teaspoon freshly ground pepper
⅓ cup poppy seeds
⅓ cup sesame seeds
⅓ cup honey

1. Preheat the oven to 400°. Line a baking sheet with foil and set a rack on top. Remove the tip and mid-section from the wings and reserve for stock. Pat the remaining wing sections (the drumettes) dry with paper towels.

2. In a large bowl, combine the mustard, ginger, allspice, salt, pepper, poppy seeds, sesame seeds and honey; stir well. Toss the drumettes in the honey mixture until thoroughly coated. Transfer them to the rack in the baking pan and bake for 20 minutes.

3. Turn the drumettes and bake for 20 minutes longer. Remove from the oven.

4. Preheat the broiler. Broil the drumettes 4 to 5 inches from the heat, watching them carefully and turning once, for 1 to 2 minutes per side, or until nicely browned. Serve hot.

—*Bob Chambers*

BAKED CHICKEN WINGS AND DRUMSTICKS WITH SEASONED SALT

6 Servings

2 teaspoons Szechuan peppercorns
1 teaspoon whole black peppercorns
1½ teaspoons salt
¼ teaspoon freshly grated nutmeg
¼ teaspoon ground cloves
¼ teaspoon cinnamon
4 pounds chicken wings and drumsticks
2 tablespoons peanut oil

1. Preheat the oven to 400°.

2. In a small skillet, heat the Szechuan and black peppercorns until fragrant, 1 or 2 minutes. Crush the peppercorns in a mortar or blender and place in a small bowl.

3. Stir in the salt, nutmeg, cloves and cinnamon.

4. Rub the chicken wings and drumsticks with the oil and place them in a single layer in a shallow roasting pan. Sprinkle the seasoned salt evenly over the top of the chicken pieces and bake for 45 minutes, or until the chicken is crisp and golden.

5. Transfer to a serving dish and serve.

—*F&W*

COLD-HOT CHICKEN LEGS

 Firestone Rosé of Cabernet Sauvignon

6 Servings

1 stick (4 ounces) unsalted butter
2 tablespoons olive oil
12 chicken drumsticks
6 tablespoons hot Dijon-style mustard
3 pickled jalapeños, about 2 inches long
3 tablespoons fresh lime juice
2 teaspoons cumin
4 cups fresh bread crumbs
Yogurt Sauce (recipe follows)

1. In a large skillet, melt 4 tablespoons of the butter in the oil over moderately high heat. Add the drumsticks and sauté, turning, until browned on all sides, about 5 minutes. Remove from the pan; reserve the fat.

2. In a blender or food processor, combine the mustard, jalapeños, lime juice and cumin. Mix until smooth. With the machine on, slowly drizzle in enough of the reserved fat until the mixture is the consistency of mayonnaise.

3. Paint the drumsticks with the mustard mixture and let stand at room temperature for at least 2 hours.

4. Preheat the oven to 350°. Roll the drumsticks in the bread crumbs to coat all over. Place on a rack in a baking pan. Bake for 15 minutes.

5. Meanwhile, melt the remaining 4 tablespoons butter. Drizzle over the drumsticks. Bake for another 15 minutes. Remove from the oven and let cool. Serve at room temperature or refrigerate and serve cold. Serve with the Yogurt Sauce.

—*W. Peter Prestcott*

YOGURT SAUCE
Makes About 2½ Cups

1 cup plain yogurt
1 cup sour cream
2 tablespoons fresh lime juice
3 tablespoons finely minced scallions (white and tender green)
¼ teaspoon freshly ground white pepper
1 teaspoon coarse (kosher) salt

Combine all the ingredients in a bowl and refrigerate, covered, for several hours or overnight.

—*W. Peter Prestcott*

DRUMSTICKS ALONG THE MOHAWK

These drumsticks can be baked several hours ahead and reheated under the broiler just before serving. They are also good at room temperature, but the skin won't be as crisp. The chicken must be marinated for a minimum of 2 hours, but it can also marinate for up to 2 days.

❦ Spicy white, such as Mirassou Gewürztraminer
4 Servings

⅓ cup Dijon-style mustard
2 garlic cloves, crushed through a press
1 tablespoon Worcestershire sauce
1 tablespoon vegetable oil
1½ teaspoons hot pepper sauce
1 teaspoon paprika
8 chicken drumsticks, skin slashed at ½-inch intervals

1. In a small bowl, combine the mustard, garlic, Worcestershire sauce, oil, hot sauce and paprika; mix well.

2. Dip each drumstick in the sauce and arrange in a shallow glass dish. Pour any extra sauce over the chicken. Cover with plastic wrap and marinate in the refrigerator for at least 2 or up to 48 hours. Let the chicken return to room temperature before cooking.

3. Preheat the oven to 375°. Bake the chicken for about 35 minutes, or until the outside is browned and the juices run clear when the thickest part is pricked to the bone.

4. Preheat the broiler. Broil the drumsticks 4 inches from the heat for about 2 minutes on each side to crisp the skin. Serve warm.

—*F&W*

BAKED JAMBONNEAUX WITH ITALIAN-STYLE STUFFING

For step-by-step photographs that show how to make *jambonneaux*, see page 18.

🍷 Italian Chardonnay, such as Santa Margherita

6 Servings

3 tablespoons olive oil, preferably extra-virgin
1 large garlic clove, minced
⅔ cup dry bread crumbs, preferably from
  Italian bread
⅓ cup minced prosciutto or good-quality cured
  ham (about 1½ ounces)
½ cup freshly grated Parmesan cheese
1½ tablespoons chopped fresh basil or 2½
  teaspoons dried
1 tablespoon chopped parsley
⅛ teaspoon freshly ground pepper
1 egg, lightly beaten
6 large chicken legs with thighs attached, at
  least 10 ounces each

1. In a small skillet, heat 1 tablespoon of the olive oil. Add the garlic and cook over low heat until the garlic is fragrant but not browned, about 1 minute.

2. Remove from the heat and add the bread crumbs. Scrape the mixture into a medium bowl and stir in the prosciutto, Parmesan, basil, parsley and pepper. Add the egg and mix lightly to combine.

3. Using a boning knife, cut through the meat down the inside of each thigh to expose the bone. Starting at the top and scraping against the bone, gently work the thigh meat down to expose the leg joint. Carefully cut the tendons at the joint, taking care not to pierce the skin. Continue to scrape the meat off the leg bone, turning it inside out as you go. As you reach the lower part of the drumstick where the meat is thin, use your fingers to pull the meat downward around the bone. Cut through the skin and remove the bones, reserving them for stock. Remove the white ten-dons by pulling them out with small pliers or your fingers while scraping against the tendon with a knife.

4. Preheat the oven to 375°. Divide the stuffing into 6 equal portions. Turn the legs skin-side out. Spoon the stuffing into the cavity of each chicken leg. Fold down the top flap of the thigh, wrapping the meat around the stuffing so that each leg resembles a small ham, and tuck the thigh flap into the skin of the leg. With a trussing needle and butcher's twine, sew the skin together to seal or fasten securely with a rounded toothpick. Rub the skin with the remaining 2 tablespoons olive oil and place the *jambonneaux*, seam-side down without crowding, in a shallow baking pan lined with foil.

5. Bake for 25 to 30 minutes, until light golden. Drain on paper towels. Remove the strings or toothpicks before serving. Serve whole or halved lengthwise.

—*John Robert Massie*

BAKED CHICKEN WITH CELERY SAUCE

This chicken is unusual in that it bakes actively for only 30 minutes. However, it sits in the still-hot oven and finishes cooking there. The result is tender and moist pieces of chicken that are warm and flavorful.

6 Servings

3 cups coarsely chopped celery
Salt
10 medium chicken thighs (about 2 pounds)
2 whole small chicken breasts, cut in half
  (about 1½ pounds)
14 sprigs of fresh chervil (optional) plus 1
  teaspoon chopped fresh chervil or
  ½ teaspoon dried
Freshly ground pepper
About ¼ cup crème fraîche

1. Preheat the oven to 375°. Cover the bottom

of a lasagna dish with the celery. Salt the chicken thighs and breasts very generously (including the areas under the skin where possible); if fresh chervil is available, tuck a sprig under the skin of each piece. Pack the chicken parts tightly together, skin-side up, in a single layer that completely covers the celery. Arrange any loose skin so that it completely covers the meat. Sprinkle generously with pepper.

2. Bake the chicken, uncovered, for 30 minutes. Turn off the oven (do not open the door) and let the chicken sit in the warm oven for 1½ hours.

3. Just before serving, transfer the celery pieces to a food processor; keep the chicken and juices warm in the oven. Add the chopped chervil to the celery and puree. If the puree is very liquid, drain briefly in a sieve. Otherwise, transfer to a small heavy saucepan, add ¼ cup crème fraîche and correct the seasoning if necessary. Cook over moderate heat until warmed through; if the sauce seems too thick, add more crème fraîche and thin with some of the chicken juices from the baking dish. Serve a generous spoonful of the sauce with each piece of chicken.

———————————

—Lee Bailey

CHICKEN THIGHS STUFFED WITH RICE, SAUSAGE AND PECANS

One of the best things about this dish, aside from its flavor, is that it rests in the oven for so long that when it is served, it seems effortless.

🍷 Dry, spicy California Gewürztraminer, such as Gundlach-Bundschu

6 to 8 Servings

1¼ cups rice
¼ pound andouille or hot Italian sausage
2 tablespoons unsalted butter
1 small onion, coarsely chopped
¼ cup coarsely chopped green bell pepper
1¼ cups toasted pecans, coarsely chopped

¼ cup minced scallion (white part with 1 inch of green)
2 tablespoons minced parsley
¼ teaspoon thyme
¾ teaspoon salt
½ teaspoon freshly ground black pepper
1 egg, lightly beaten
16 chicken thighs, boned, with the skin on
½ teaspoon paprika

1. Preheat the oven to 375°. In a small saucepan, cook the rice in 3 cups of water over moderate heat until tender, about 20 minutes. Rinse under cold water; drain.

2. In a small saucepan of water, simmer the sausage over moderate heat for 10 minutes. Drain and coarsely chop.

3. In a large skillet, melt the butter over moderate heat. Add the onion and green pepper and cook until softened but not browned, about 5 minutes. Remove from the heat and stir in the pecans, scallion, parsley and the cooked rice and sausage. Season with the thyme, ½ teaspoon of the salt and ¼ teaspoon of the black pepper. Mix in the egg.

4. Season the chicken thighs on both sides with the remaining ¼ teaspoon each salt and black pepper and the paprika. Place a rounded tablespoon of the stuffing in the center of each thigh and fold the meat and skin over to enclose the stuffing. Place the thighs, seam-side down, in a large buttered baking dish in 2 long rows, leaving an open space down the center of the dish. Pack the leftover stuffing into the center space between the rows. Cover the stuffing with a narrow strip of foil.

5. Bake the chicken thighs for 35 minutes. Turn the oven off, but leave the chicken inside without opening the door for 1 hour. Remove the thighs and stuffing to a warm platter, skim the fat off the pan juices and pour over the chicken.

———————————

—Lee Bailey

PEACH-GLAZED CHICKEN THIGHS

For a wonderful summer supper, serve this slightly sweet chicken with rice or pasta and a garden vegetable salad.

❦ Choose a fragrant, off-dry Chenin Blanc, with its slightly peachy flavor, to perfectly complement this mild tart-sweet chicken dish. A Robert Mondavi Chenin Blanc or even an NV Wildman sparkling Vouvray (made from Chenin Blanc) has enough fruitiness.

2 to 3 Servings

2 large peaches
6 chicken thighs
½ teaspoon salt
¼ teaspoon freshly ground pepper
2 teaspoons olive oil
2 teaspoons honey
1 tablespoon red wine vinegar
2 tablespoons sliced scallion greens

1. Peel and chop 1 peach and place in a medium bowl. Mash the peach with a fork. Place the chicken thighs in the bowl and toss to coat well. Cover and let stand at room temperature for 2 hours or refrigerate for up to 6 hours; let return to room temperature before proceeding.

2. Preheat the oven to 350°. Remove the chicken from the marinade and pat dry with paper towels. Season the chicken with the salt and pepper.

3. In a large ovenproof skillet, heat the olive oil over high heat. Add the chicken, skin-side down, and cook until the skin is deep brown and crisp, about 5 minutes. Turn the thighs and place the skillet in the oven. Bake until tender, about 15 minutes.

4. Peel and slice the remaining peach. Remove the chicken thighs from the skillet. Pour off any fat from the pan and return the chicken to the skillet. Place over high heat until the chicken begins to sizzle. Add the honey; toss to coat the thighs. Cook, stirring, until the honey begins to brown and stick to the bottom of the pan, about 1 minute. Add the vinegar and peach slices. Stir to loosen the browned bits from the bottom of the pan and turn to glaze the chicken, about 1½ minutes. Remove the thighs to a platter, place the peach slices in the middle and garnish with the scallion.

—*Marcia Kiesel*

CHICKEN WITH GARLIC, CAPERS AND PARMESAN CHEESE

❦ A light red, such as Valpolicella

3 to 4 Servings

¼ cup olive oil
6 large garlic cloves, sliced
6 chicken thighs
2 teaspoons thyme
2 teaspoons coarsely cracked pepper
½ teaspoon salt
1 tablespoon capers, chopped
¼ cup freshly grated Parmesan cheese

1. Preheat the oven to 350°. In a large heavy skillet, warm the oil over moderate heat until shimmering. Add the garlic and sauté, stirring, until golden, about 3 minutes. Remove from the oil with a slotted spoon and finely chop.

2. Season the chicken thighs on both sides with the thyme and pepper. Reheat the oil in the skillet over moderate heat until rippling. Add the chicken and sauté until golden, about 10 minutes on each side. Remove from the heat and drain briefly on paper towels. Season with the salt.

3. Combine the capers and chopped garlic and spread on top of the chicken thighs. Sprinkle with the cheese and arrange on a baking sheet. Bake until the cheese melts and the chicken is cooked through, about 15 minutes.

—*Anne Disrude*

FARM-STAND DINNER IN A PACKET
4 Servings

6 small links of spicy, dried sausage such as
  chorizo, cut into ¼-inch slices
4 small zucchini, stem ends trimmed
4 small ears of sweet corn, shucked
4 small tomatoes
4 skinless, boneless chicken breast halves
  (about 6 ounces each), lightly pounded
½ cup dry white wine
4 tablespoons unsalted butter, cut into small
  pieces
1 tablespoon coarse (kosher) salt
2 teaspoons freshly ground pepper
4 sprigs of fresh rosemary

1. Preheat the oven to 450°. Cut out 4 pieces of aluminum foil, 14 by 20 inches each. Lay slices of 1 sausage in the center of each piece of foil. Arrange the zucchini, corn and tomato on top of the sausage. Place the chicken breast over the vegetables. Dividing evenly, top with the remaining sausage. Sprinkle the meat and vegetables with the wine, dot with the butter and season with the salt and pepper. Top each with a sprig of rosemary.

2. Fold up to seal each pouch tightly, but allow room for steam to form as it cooks. Bake in the preheated oven for 25 minutes. Serve at once.

————————

—*Molly O'Neill*

PAPILLOTE OF CHICKEN WITH KALE AND PROSCIUTTO
🍷 Dry Chenin Blanc, such as Chappellet
2 Servings

3 tablespoons extra-virgin olive oil
2 cups chopped kale, turnip greens or mustard
  greens
Salt and freshly ground pepper
2 skinless, boneless chicken breast halves
  (about 5 ounces each)
1 thin slice of prosciutto, cut in half

1. Preheat the oven to 400°. Fold two 15-by-20-inch sheets of butcher's paper, parchment or aluminum foil in half crosswise to make 15-by-10-inch rectangles. Using scissors, cut each rectangle into a heart shape with the fold running vertically down the center. Open up the hearts and brush each with ½ tablespoon of the oil.

2. Toss the kale with 1 tablespoon of the olive oil. Season lightly with salt and pepper. Dividing evenly, place in the middle of one side of each heart.

3. Fold out the small fillet from each breast to even the thickness of the chicken. With a sharp knife, make 4 deep, evenly spaced cuts crosswise on the diagonal.

4. Roll up each piece of prosciutto and cut each into 4 pieces. Tuck 1 spiraled piece of prosciutto into each cut in the chicken. Place on top of the greens. Season the chicken lightly with salt and pepper. Drizzle the remaining 1 tablespoon oil on top.

5. Fold the paper over the chicken and beginning at the top of each heart, make a series of tight overlapping folds to seal the papillotes.

6. Place the papillotes on a cookie sheet and bake for 10 minutes (if the breast is larger than 5 ounces increase the time to 12 minutes). Serve hot.

———————

—*Anne Disrude*

GINGERED CHICKEN BREASTS

Boneless chicken breasts lend themselves to being cut into medallions for easy and attractive serving when entertaining a crowd. Chutneys are a wonderful accompaniment.

15 to 20 Servings

16 skinless, boneless chicken breast halves
   (about 6½ pounds)
½ cup soy sauce
5 scallions, chopped
¼ cup vegetable oil
3 tablespoons sherry vinegar
3 tablespoons chopped parsley
2 tablespoons ground ginger
1 tablespoon Oriental sesame oil
Assorted chutneys, for accompaniment

1. Place the chicken breasts in a single layer in nonreactive baking pans or large shallow baking dishes.

2. In a small bowl, mix the soy sauce, scallions, vegetable oil, vinegar, parsley, ginger and sesame oil. Pour the mixture over the chicken, turning the breasts to coat evenly. Set aside to marinate for at least 1 hour at room temperature or overnight, covered, in the refrigerator.

3. Preheat the oven to 350°. Bring the chicken to room temperature if refrigerated. Bake, with the marinade, for about 25 minutes, until the chicken is firm with a light spring to the touch. Halfway through cooking, check to make sure the chicken is not dry. If necessary, add a small amount of water to the baking pans or baking dishes. *(The recipe can be prepared to this point up to 1 day ahead. Cover and refrigerate.)*

4. Leave the chicken breasts whole or slice them on the diagonal into medallions. Serve warm or at room temperature. Serve the chutneys alongside.

———————

—*Paul Grimes*

CHICKEN BREASTS STUFFED WITH MORELS

Boned chicken breasts stuffed with morels are a classic combination. In the following recipe, imported dried black morels have been used for the stuffing. The soaking liquid from the morels is used in the sauce.

♀ California Cabernet Sauvignon, such as Clos du Val

4 Servings

½ ounce imported dried black morels
4 skinless, boneless chicken breast halves
½ teaspoon salt
¼ teaspoon freshly ground pepper
11 tablespoons unsalted butter
4 medium shallots, minced
½ cup crème fraîche or heavy cream
½ pound fresh black morels, or
   reconstituted dried
1 teaspoon fresh lemon juice
1½ tablespoons all-purpose flour
1 cup Chicken Stock (p. 10) or canned broth
4 sprigs of fresh tarragon or
   ¼ teaspoon dried

1. In a medium bowl, soak the dried morels in 1 cup of warm water for 30 minutes, until the mushrooms are softened.

2. Meanwhile, remove the small fillets from each breast half; reserve. Using a sharp knife, cut a pocket in the thickest part of each breast half. Sprinkle with ¼ teaspoon of the salt and ⅛ teaspoon of the pepper and set aside.

3. Preheat the oven to 400°. Using a slotted spoon, lift the morels from the soaking liquid;

reserve the soaking liquid. Rinse the morels carefully under running water to remove any sand and grit. Dry and chop them.

4. In a heavy medium skillet, melt 2 tablespoons of the butter over moderate heat. Add the shallots and sauté until softened and translucent, 2 to 3 minutes. Add the chopped morels, a pinch of salt and pepper and ¼ cup of the crème fraîche and simmer, covered, for 10 minutes, or until tender. Set aside to cool.

5. Strain the reserved soaking liquid through a paper coffee filter or double thickness of dampened cheesecloth and set aside.

6. Stuff the shallot-morel mixture into the pockets of the 4 pieces of chicken. Stuff the reserved fillets into the opening of each pocket to close them.

7. Trim the stems from the fresh morels. Rinse them quickly in water and drain. Split or quarter them depending on their size. In a medium skillet, melt 3 tablespoons of the butter over moderate heat. Add 1 tablespoon of the morel soaking liquid, a pinch of salt and pepper and the fresh morels. Cover and braise for 15 minutes, stirring occasionally, until tender.

8. Meanwhile, melt 4 tablespoons of the butter and pour it into a medium baking dish. Arrange the stuffed chicken breasts in the dish in a single layer. Sprinkle with the lemon juice and 2 tablespoons of the morel soaking liquid. Cover with foil and bake for 10 minutes.

9. Meanwhile, prepare the sauce. In a small saucepan, melt the remaining 2 tablespoons butter over moderate heat. Add the flour and cook, stirring, for 2 minutes without coloring to make a roux. Whisk in the stock, the remaining morel liquid, the remaining ¼ cup crème fraîche and the tarragon. Bring to a boil, whisking constantly. Reduce the heat to moderately low and simmer for 15 minutes. Remove the tarragon sprigs. Season the sauce with the remaining ¼ teaspoon salt and ⅛ teaspoon pepper. Add the braised morels to the sauce and heat through.

10. Remove the chicken from the oven.

Arrange the chicken on a platter and strain the cooking juices from the dish into the sauce. Pour the sauce over the chicken.

————————

—*Lydie Marshall*

CHICKEN BREASTS STUFFED WITH SAUSAGE AND LEMON ZEST

These aromatic chicken breasts would be delicious with buttered green beans and a rice pilaf for a spring supper.

♇ Fruity white, such as Gaston Huet Vouvray, or Robert Mondavi Chenin Blanc

6 Servings

3 tablespoons olive oil
1 medium onion, finely chopped
1 garlic clove, minced
¼ pound hot Italian sausage
¼ pound sweet Italian sausage
2 teaspoons tarragon
2 tablespoons tomato paste
½ cup brandy
1 cup fresh bread crumbs
2 tablespoons minced parsley
1 tablespoon grated lemon zest
Pinch of salt
4 whole boneless chicken breasts, with the skin on, pounded lightly to flatten
3 tablespoons unsalted butter
½ cup dry white wine

1. Preheat the oven to 450°. In a large skillet, heat the oil over high heat. Add the onion and garlic, reduce the heat to low, cover and cook until the onion is very soft but not browned, about 20 minutes.

2. Meanwhile, put the hot and sweet sausages in a medium saucepan with water to cover. Bring to a boil, reduce the heat to moderate and simmer until the sausages are cooked through, about 15 minutes. Drain well and coarsely chop.

3. Add the sausages, tarragon, tomato paste

and brandy to the skillet and cook, stirring occasionally, until most of the brandy has evaporated, about 5 minutes. Scrape the sausage mixture into a large bowl and stir in the bread crumbs, 1 tablespoon of the parsley, 2 teaspoons of the lemon zest and the salt.

4. Spoon one-fourth of the stuffing onto each chicken breast. Gather the sides around the stuffing to form a ball shape, and secure with wooden skewers.

5. In a large ovenproof skillet, melt 2 tablespoons of the butter over high heat. When the foam subsides, add the chicken breasts, rounded-side down, and cook until well browned, about 5 minutes; turn the breasts over and put the skillet in the oven. Bake for 25 minutes, or until the chicken breasts are white throughout but still juicy.

6. Transfer the chicken breasts to a large platter. Pour off the fat from the skillet and set it over high heat. Add the white wine and bring to a boil, scraping up any browned bits from the bottom of the pan. Boil until reduced to 3 tablespoons, about 3 minutes. Remove from the heat and stir in the remaining 1 tablespoon parsley and 1 teaspoon lemon zest.

7. Remove the skewers from the chicken and cut into slices about ⅜ inch thick. Pour any accumulated juices into the skillet and stir in the remaining 1 tablespoon butter. Drizzle the sauce over the chicken.

—*W. Peter Prestcott*

CHICKEN BREASTS DOMINICANA

8 Servings

3 large yams
1 stick (4 ounces) unsalted butter, cut into
  small pieces, at room temperature
¾ cup finely chopped cilantro (fresh coriander),
  no stems
2 to 3 teaspoons cumin
2 tablespoons fresh lemon juice
Salt and freshly ground pepper
6 whole skinless, boneless chicken breasts
Vegetable oil and butter, for frying
1 cup all-purpose flour
2 lemons, cut into wedges

1. Preheat the oven to 400°. Bake the yams in their jackets for about 1 hour, until quite tender. When cool enough to handle, split the yams, scoop out the pulp and puree it in a food processor until smooth. You should have a generous 2 cups of pulp.

2. Add the butter, cilantro, cumin, lemon juice and salt and pepper to taste. Chill the yam filling until the butter has set.

3. Remove the fillet from the underside of each chicken breast and set aside. On a slightly wet cutting surface (or between two sheets of waxed paper), use a mallet or cleaver to pound the breasts lightly to about a ⅜-inch thickness. Also pound the fillets. If the breasts are halved, overlap the edges by about 1 inch. Place about ⅓ cup of the yam filling in the center of each breast, then top with a flattened fillet. Fold the sides of the breast neatly over the filling, pressing together to form an evenly rounded package. Place on a baking sheet, cover with plastic wrap and chill for an hour or so.

4. Preheat the oven to 450°. In a large ovenproof skillet, heat a ⅛-inch layer of oil and butter (1 part oil to 2 parts butter) until the bubbling subsides.

5. On a plate, combine the flour with 1½ tea-

spoons salt and ½ teaspoon pepper. Dredge the breasts in the flour mixture, shaking off the excess, then place them, seam-side up, in the pan. Cook over medium heat for about 3 minutes, then carefully turn the breasts seam-side down and continue to cook another 2 minutes. Place the pan in the oven and cook the breasts 10 minutes, or until they are firm and slightly puffy. Serve hot, with the lemon wedges.

—Alan Lieb

SPICY STUFFED CHICKEN BREASTS

Tomatoes are naturally high in sodium. Drying them concentrates their flavor and intensifies the impact of their acidic sweetness. Some brands of dry, unmarinated sun-dried tomatoes contain small amounts of residual salt from the drying process. Blanching and rinsing the tomatoes well removes most of the added salt.

❦ The sun-dried tomatoes and the other piquant accents here point to a Pinot Noir, such as Clos du Val or Louis M. Martini.

4 Servings

1 ounce (about 12) dry, unmarinated sun-
  dried tomato halves
1 tablespoon cumin seeds
3 garlic cloves, minced
1 jalapeño pepper, seeded and minced
2 teaspoons finely grated lemon zest
1 teaspoon freshly ground black pepper
¼ cup plus 1 tablespoon sour cream
¼ cup chopped cilantro (fresh coriander)
8 large boneless chicken breast halves, with the
  skin on (about 8 ounces each)
½ teaspoon pure chile powder
1 tablespoon olive oil

1. In a small saucepan, add enough water to just cover the sun-dried tomatoes and bring to a boil over moderately high heat. Reduce the heat to low and simmer until the tomatoes are tender but still slightly chewy, about 3 minutes. Drain the tomatoes, rinse well under cold running water and drain again thoroughly. Cut into ¼-inch dice and set aside.

2. In a small skillet, toast the cumin seeds over moderately high heat, shaking the pan occasionally, until the seeds darken slightly and become very aromatic, about 1 minute. Set aside ½ teaspoon of the seeds. On a work surface or in a mortar with a pestle, finely chop or pound the remaining 2½ teaspoons cumin seeds. If using a mortar, blend in the garlic, jalapeño, lemon zest and black pepper to form a paste. Blend in the sour cream, cilantro and sun-dried tomatoes. Alternatively, combine the chopped seeds with the above ingredients in a bowl. Divide the stuffing into 4 equal portions.

3. Carefully run your fingers under the breast skin to loosen the flesh. Put one-fourth of the stuffing under the skin of each breast and press gently to distribute the filling evenly. Season the chicken breasts on both sides with the reserved ½ teaspoon cumin and the chile powder. *(The chicken breasts can be stuffed 1 day ahead. Store, covered, in the refrigerator.)*

4. Allow the chicken breasts to come to room temperature if refrigerated. Preheat the oven to 450°. In a large ovenproof skillet, heat the olive oil over high heat. When the oil begins to smoke, add the chicken breasts, skin-side down, and cook until the skin is browned and crisp, about 5 minutes. Turn the chicken over and place the skillet in the oven. Bake until the chicken feels firm to the touch but still juicy, about 8 minutes. Remove the chicken to a warm plate and let rest for 5 minutes before slicing. Cut the breasts on a diagonal into ¼-inch slices or serve whole if desired.

—Marcia Kiesel

DILLED DIJON CHICKEN

To develop a fuller herbal flavor, marinate the dill-coated chicken in the refrigerator for 2 to 3 hours before proceeding to Step 2.

🍷 Sauvignon Blanc, such as Dry Creek

4 Servings

3 pounds chicken parts
3 tablespoons chopped fresh dill or 1 tablespoon dried dillweed
4 tablespoons unsalted butter
¼ cup Dijon-style mustard
Freshly ground pepper

1. Preheat the oven to 350°. With your fingers, rub the chicken pieces all over with the dill.

2. In a small saucepan, melt the butter over low heat. Remove from the heat and stir in the mustard until smooth.

3. Sprinkle the chicken with pepper on all sides. Turn the pieces skin-side down and spread with half of the mustard-butter mixture. Arrange skin-side down in a single layer in 1 or 2 baking dishes.

4. Bake the chicken for 25 minutes. Remove from the oven, turn the pieces over and quickly spread the skin side with the remaining mustard-butter mixture. Return to the oven and bake until golden, 25 to 30 minutes. Serve hot or cold.

—*F&W*

PROVENCAL CHICKEN WITH 40 CLOVES OF GARLIC

The garlic in this dish cooks so long that it mellows and is luscious spread on grilled or toasted French bread rounds.

🍷 Alsace Pinot Blanc, such as Hugel

6 to 8 Servings

2 chickens (3 pounds each), cut into 8 pieces each
½ teaspoon salt
1 teaspoon freshly ground pepper
¾ cup extra-virgin olive oil
2½ teaspoons herbes de Provence (½ teaspoon each dried marjoram, oregano and summer savory and 1 teaspoon dried thyme), or use all thyme
40 whole garlic cloves, unpeeled
1 loaf of French or Italian bread, sliced and toasted

1. Preheat the oven to 375°. Season the chicken pieces with the salt and ½ teaspoon of the pepper. In a large flameproof casserole, heat 2 tablespoons of the olive oil over moderately high heat. Add the chicken in batches and brown evenly, about 3 minutes on each side.

2. Remove the casserole from the heat. Return all of the chicken to the casserole and add the herbes de Provence, garlic, remaining ½ cup plus 2 tablespoons olive oil and ½ teaspoon pepper. Toss to coat well. Place aluminum foil over the casserole and cover with the lid. Bake, without removing the lid, for 1 hour and 10 minutes.

3. Serve the chicken with the garlic cloves, to be spread onto the toasted French or Italian bread.

—*Peter Kump*

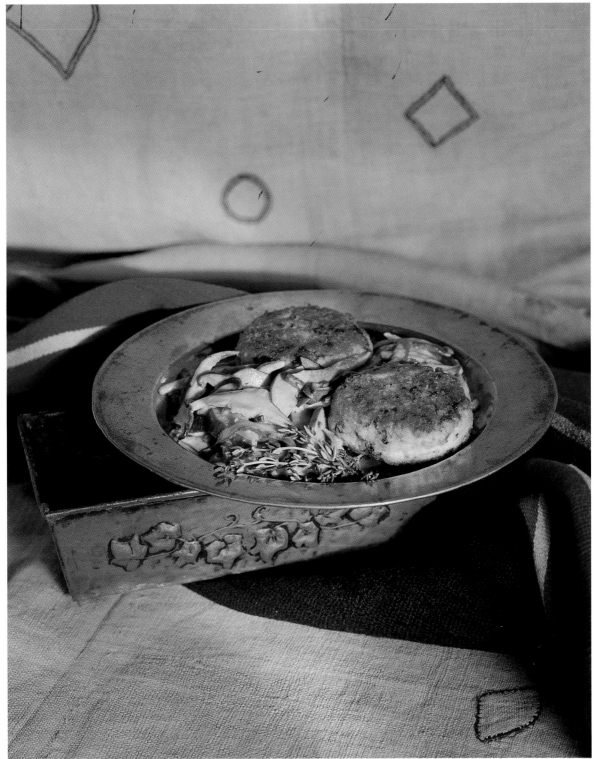

Chicken and Spinach Cakes with Shiitake Mushroom Sauce (p. 32).

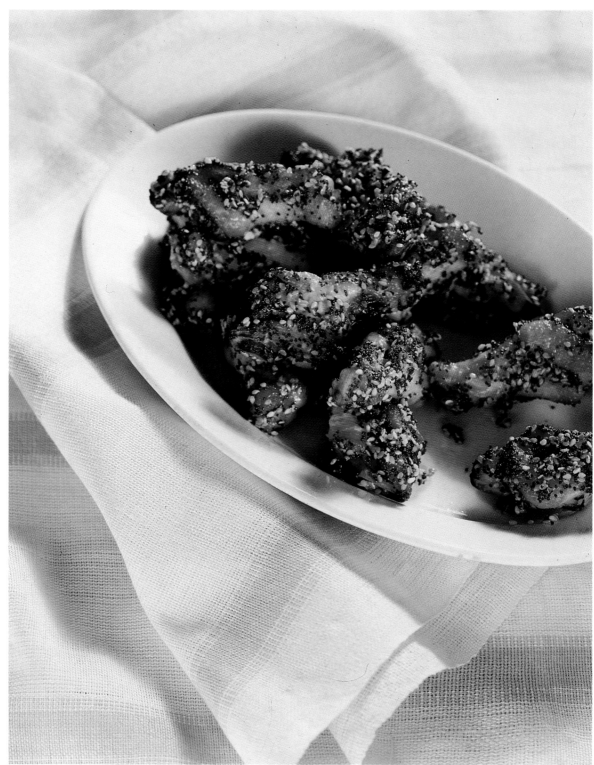

Spiced Honey Wings with Poppy and Sesame Seeds (p. 102).

MUSTARD CHICKEN

Although this chicken dish is delicious served hot, it is even better at room temperature and can be eaten cold. If it is made the day before, the flavors will develop and the chicken can be reheated.

♟ Pouilly-Fumé, such as Ladoucette, or California Fumé Blanc, such as Chateau St. Jean

4 Servings

One 3-pound chicken, cut into 8 serving pieces
½ cup Dijon-style mustard
2 eggs, lightly beaten
2½ cups fresh bread crumbs
1 tablespoon paprika
1 teaspoon tarragon
1 teaspoon freshly ground pepper
3 tablespoons unsalted butter
3 tablespoons olive oil
⅓ cup fresh lemon juice

1. Make a slit at the main joint of each wing and remove the skin from the larger portion of the wing. Remove and discard the skin from the remaining chicken pieces. In a large bowl, toss the chicken with the mustard to coat. Cover and marinate at room temperature, tossing occasionally, for 30 minutes.

2. Preheat the oven to 375°. Place the eggs in a shallow bowl. In a pie pan or shallow dish, combine the bread crumbs with the paprika, tarragon and pepper.

3. One at a time, dip the mustard-coated chicken pieces into the egg and then roll in the crumb mixture to coat evenly; place in a shallow baking dish large enough to hold the chicken in a single layer.

4. In a small saucepan, melt the butter in the olive oil over low heat. Remove from the heat and stir in the lemon juice. Spoon half of the lemon butter over the chicken pieces. Bake for 30 minutes. Spoon the remaining lemon butter over the chicken and bake for about 30 minutes longer, until the chicken is cooked through and the juices run clear when the thickest part of a thigh is pierced with a fork. Let rest for at least 15 minutes before serving.

———

—Jim Fobel

BAKED CHICKEN AND POTATOES WITH ROSEMARY AND LEMON

4 Servings

3 tablespoons olive oil
2½- to 3-pound chicken, cut into 8 serving pieces
3 medium baking potatoes, scrubbed and cut into 1½-inch chunks
1 garlic clove, minced
2 teaspoons rosemary, crumbled
6 tablespoons fresh lemon juice
½ teaspoon salt
¼ teaspoon freshly ground pepper

1. Preheat the oven to 400°. Grease a large ovenproof skillet or baking pan with 1 tablespoon of the oil. Toss the chicken and potatoes with the remaining 2 tablespoons oil and arrange in the skillet in an even layer.

2. Sprinkle with the garlic, rosemary and 4 tablespoons of the lemon juice. Cover the skillet loosely with aluminum foil.

3. Bake for 30 minutes. Uncover and bake for 15 minutes longer, turning the chicken pieces occasionally to brown evenly.

4. To serve, divide the chicken among 4 plates and sprinkle with the remaining 2 tablespoons lemon juice; season with the salt and pepper. Spoon some of the pan juices over each plate.

———

—James W. Brown

SPICY BAKED SPINACH CHICKEN

Although free-range chickens have more flavor and leaner meat, this dish can certainly be made with a regular, supermarket-variety chicken. Just be sure to remove and discard any excess fat from the chicken before baking.

4 to 6 Servings

5 tablespoons unsalted butter, at room temperature
¼ cup crumbled feta cheese
1 package (10 ounces) frozen chopped spinach, thawed and squeezed dry
½ teaspoon minced fresh jalapeño
One 4½- to 5½-pound chicken, preferably free-range—thighs and legs separated, breast quartered
¼ cup Dijon-style mustard
1 cup fresh bread crumbs
½ teaspoon salt
¼ teaspoon freshly ground pepper

1. In a food processor, combine 3 tablespoons of the butter, the feta cheese, spinach and jalapeño pepper. Puree until smooth. Transfer to a small bowl and refrigerate until firm, about 10 minutes.

2. Wipe the chicken pieces. Carefully separate the skin from the meat and stuff 1 tablespoon of the spinach mixture under the skin of each piece of chicken. Pat the skin in place. Slather the chicken with mustard and place skin-side up on a baking sheet. Refrigerate for 30 minutes. Meanwhile, preheat the oven to 350°.

3. Season the bread crumbs with the salt and pepper. Place in a shallow bowl and roll each piece of mustard chicken in the crumbs. Return the chicken to the baking sheet. Dab each piece with the remaining 2 tablespoons butter. Bake in the preheated oven for 1½ hours, or until the skin is golden and crisp and the meat is falling from the bones.

—*Molly O'Neill*

BAKED CHICKEN SMOTHERED WITH GARLIC AND HERBS

In this simple but spectacular dish, the chicken is cooked unsupervised with its "aromatics," all sealed together in a pot. The sealed pot is opened to reveal a perfectly cooked bird, fragrant with garlic and green herbs. The chicken is served with some of the cooked garlic cloves, whose sweet, succulent puree can be eaten on bread, or directly on the meat.

4 Servings

One 3-pound chicken
Salt and freshly ground pepper
40 cloves of garlic (about 4 heads)
1 teaspoon rosemary, crumbled
2 bay leaves, crumbled
1 teaspoon marjoram
1½ teaspoons thyme (wild thyme, if possible)
1 cup olive oil
3⅓ cups all-purpose flour

1. Sprinkle the chicken lightly, inside and out, with salt and pepper. Truss the chicken with kitchen string. Place the chicken in a flameproof casserole that will hold it comfortably.

2. Preheat the oven to 350°. Pull off the outer skin of the garlic cloves, leaving in place the last, thin layer of peel. Scatter the cloves of garlic over and around the chicken, then sprinkle everything with the rosemary, crumbled bay leaves, marjoram and thyme. Drizzle the olive oil over and around the chicken and seasonings, then give everything a quick toss with your hands so that the herbs and oil are distributed evenly. Place the cover on the casserole.

3. Prepare the flour paste: Place the flour in a bowl and gradually stir in enough water (about 2 cups) to make a smooth, pliable paste. Form a long rope of the paste about 2 inches thick. Press the rope firmly over the opening between casserole and lid, making a close seal. (This paste is for sealing purposes only and is not eaten.)

4. Bring the contents of the covered casserole to a lively simmer over moderate heat on top of the stove—you will hear the oil begin to sizzle after a couple of minutes. Place the casserole in the oven and bake for 1½ hours.

5. At serving time, take the sealed casserole to the table. Break the seal with a knife and open the pot. Lift the chicken onto a platter, remove the trussing strings and carve it, accompanying each portion with a share of the garlic cloves and a spoonful of the fragrant oil.

———————

—*Michèle Chassagne*

CLAY POT CHICKEN WITH OLIVES

Parslied egg noodles and a green vegetable or two are a good accompaniment for this savory chicken.

❦ Zinfandel, such as Sutter Home

4 to 6 Servings

20 tiny white boiling onions, peeled
1 tablespoon olive oil
One 3½-pound chicken
2 imported bay leaves
Zest of 1 navel orange
6 whole garlic cloves, bruised and peeled
2 sprigs of fresh rosemary or ½
* teaspoon dried*
20 Calamata olives, halved and pitted
20 green olives, halved and pitted
¼ teaspoon coarsely ground pepper
¾ cup Chicken Stock (p. 10) or canned broth
¼ cup dry vermouth
2 teaspoons arrowroot

1. Soak the clay pot top and bottom in cold water for 15 minutes.

2. Cook the onions in a large pot of salted boiling water until almost tender, about 5 minutes. Drain well. Heat 1 teaspoon of the oil in a small skillet. Add the onions and sauté over high heat, shaking the pan, until browned all over.

3. Stuff the chicken with 1 bay leaf, half of the orange zest, 2 garlic cloves and 1 sprig of rosemary. Truss the chicken. Rub the chicken with the remaining 2 teaspoons olive oil and place inside the pot. (If the bottom surface is not glazed, fold a piece of parchment or waxed paper to fit the bottom so the chicken doesn't stick.)

4. Distribute the onions, olives, remaining orange zest, bay leaf, rosemary and 4 garlic cloves around the chicken. Sprinkle with the pepper and pour on the broth and vermouth.

5. Cover and place the clay pot in the middle of a cold oven. Turn the oven on to 450° and bake the chicken for 1 hour. Remove the lid and bake uncovered for 15 minutes longer to brown the skin.

6. To serve, transfer the chicken to a carving board and cut into pieces. Arrange on a platter. Remove the onions and olives with a slotted spoon and scatter over the chicken. Skim the fat off the top of the cooking juices and pour into a small saucepan. Dissolve the arrowroot in 2 tablespoons of cold water and stir into the juices. Reheat, stirring until slightly thickened. Serve this light gravy with the chicken.

———————

—*Anne Disrude*

HAKKA "SALT-BAKED" CHICKEN WITH GINGER SAUCE

This is the most famous dish in the Hakka cuisine of Fukien province—a whole chicken that is "baked" in a cocoon of hot salt and emerges exceedingly juicy and not at all salty. It is the southern cousin of the well-known northern Chinese dish "Beggar's Chicken," which is baked in clay.

3 to 4 Servings

One 3½- to 4-pound chicken
5 slices (quarter-size) fresh ginger
2 medium scallions, cut into 1½-inch lengths
1½ tablespoons Chinese rice wine
* or dry sherry*

*5 sprigs of cilantro (fresh coriander) plus
  additional sprigs for garnish*
5 points of a star anise pod
*1 tablespoon Rose Dew Liqueur or
  Wu Chia Pi Chiew (see Note) or extra dry
  vermouth or vodka*
4½ pounds coarse (kosher) salt
Hakka Ginger Sauce (recipe follows)

1. Clean the chicken thoroughly. Rinse well with cold water and pat dry inside and out.

2. Smash the ginger and scallions with the broad side of a knife blade. Rub the cavity of the chicken with the rice wine and stuff with the ginger, scallions, cilantro and star anise. Truss the cavity and neck shut to retain the juices during baking.

3. Brush the liqueur evenly over the skin. Place the chicken, breast-side up, on a rack in a cool, airy place for about 2 hours, until the skin is dry to the touch.

4. Truss the chicken with string, bringing the legs and wings close to the body to make a compact shape. Wrap in a single layer of loose-weave cheesecloth and bring two sides up to overlap ½ inch on top. Bring up the loose ends and tie them tightly together with string. The chicken should be tightly wrapped in a neat ball.

5. Place the salt in a large heavy stockpot or spun-steel wok that will hold the chicken snugly. Heat over moderately high heat, stirring frequently, until the salt is very hot to the touch, 5 to 10 minutes. Scoop out and reserve all but 1 inch of salt (about 6 cups). Place the chicken in the pot, breast-side up, and cover completely with the reserved hot salt.

6. Cover the pot, reduce the heat to moderate and "bake" the chicken on top of the stove undisturbed for 1½ to 2 hours, or until the juices run clear. (Check the doneness by brushing off the salt from the thigh and piercing with a sharp knife. If the juices run pink, re-cover with salt and continue to bake 15 to 30 minutes longer.)

7. Push the salt aside and gently pull out the chicken, holding the knotted cheesecloth on top. Try not to tip the chicken, to reserve the juices. Carefully transfer the chicken to a platter and remove the cheesecloth. Remove the trussing strings and use chopsticks or tongs to extract and discard the seasonings from the inside of the chicken.

8. Serve the chicken hot, tepid or at room temperature. Chop Chinese-style into bite-size pieces or carve Western-style. Garnish, if desired, with fresh sprigs of cilantro and serve with the Hakka Ginger Sauce.

NOTE: Rose Dew Liqueur (Mei Kuei Lu Chiew) and the untranslatable Wu Chia Pi Chiew are available in Chinese liquor stores. Bottled in squat brown crocks, they have an inimitable taste, the former heady with the aroma of roses. Both are a walloping 99 proof.

—*Barbara Tropp*

HAKKA GINGER SAUCE

This is the traditional accompaniment to Salt-Baked Chicken, often made with a gingery powder that has a distinctly medicinal taste. This variation uses fresh ginger in its place.

Makes About ¼ Cup

1 packed tablespoon finely minced fresh ginger
2 tablespoons corn or peanut oil
¼ teaspoon coarse (kosher) salt

Put the ginger in a small heavy saucer. Heat the oil over moderate heat until it sends up a wisp of smoke, then scrape it evenly over the ginger. Stir to combine, sprinkle with the salt, then stir to blend. Serve warm or at room temperature.

—*Barbara Tropp*

Sautés

CHICKEN CUTLETS WITH PINE NUTS AND LIME

Thin slices of turkey breast may be substituted for the chicken in this recipe.

4 Servings

*4 skinless, boneless chicken breast halves
  (about 5 ounces each)*
2 tablespoons minced parsley
1 tablespoon minced pine nuts
1½ teaspoons grated lime zest
½ teaspoon minced garlic
¼ cup all-purpose flour
1 teaspoon tarragon
Salt and freshly ground white pepper, to taste
3 tablespoons unsalted butter
1½ tablespoons olive oil
¾ cup dry white wine
1 tablespoon fresh lime juice
1 lime, thinly sliced

1. Place a chicken breast half, smooth-side down, on a sheet of waxed paper. Fold out the small fillet to the side of the larger portion of the breast, slitting along the attachment if necessary so that it lies flat. Remove the tendon and trim off any fat or connective tissue. Place a second sheet of waxed paper on top and pound with a meat pounder or heavy rolling pin until the chicken flattens out to a thin, even cutlet, about ⅛ inch thick.

2. In a small bowl combine the parsley, pine nuts, ½ teaspoon of the lime zest and the minced garlic.

3. On a sheet of waxed paper, mix the flour with the remaining 1 teaspoon lime zest, the tarragon, salt and pepper. Dust the chicken in the seasoned flour; shake off the excess and place the cutlets on a clean sheet of waxed paper.

4. In a large skillet, heat the butter and oil over moderately high heat until the butter melts and sizzles. When the butter stops sizzling, reduce the heat to moderate and add 2 of the cutlets to the skillet. Sauté the chicken for about 45 seconds on each side, or until lightly browned. Transfer the cutlets to a heatproof dish as they are finished and keep warm in a 200° oven. Sauté the remaining cutlets in the same manner.

5. Pour the wine into the skillet. Cook, scraping up any browned bits clinging to the bottom of the pan, until the wine is reduced to ½ cup, about 2 minutes. Stir in the lime juice and the pine nut mixture.

6. Remove the chicken from the oven and with tongs, dip each cutlet in the sauce in the skillet. Arrange the cutlets on dinner plates or a platter. Spoon the remaining sauce in the skillet over the chicken and garnish with the lime slices.

———

—*F&W*

SAUTEED CHICKEN WITH LEMON SAUCE

4 Servings

4 tablespoons unsalted butter
1 tablespoon vegetable oil
*4 skinless, boneless chicken breast halves
  (about 5 ounces each), pounded ¼ inch thick*
2 teaspoons all-purpose flour
½ cup dry white wine
3 tablespoons fresh lemon juice
Salt and freshly ground pepper
2 tablespoons finely chopped parsley

1. In a large skillet, melt the butter in the oil over moderate heat until foamy. Working in batches, as necessary, sauté the chicken cutlets for 1 minute on each side. Remove the chicken to a plate and cover loosely to keep warm.

2. Off the heat, sprinkle the flour over the drippings in the skillet. Stir well to incorporate the flour. The mixture should be smooth, without

lumps. Place the skillet over moderate heat and cook, stirring constantly, for 2 minutes to make a roux. Whisk in the wine and lemon juice. Bring to a boil, reduce the heat and cook, stirring, for 2 minutes, until the sauce is thickened and smooth. Season with salt and pepper to taste.

3. Return the four chicken cutlets to the skillet and turn to coat with the sauce. Reduce the heat to low and simmer gently for 2 to 3 minutes, or until just cooked through. Transfer the chicken and sauce to a warm serving platter; sprinkle with the parsley.

—W. Peter Prestcott

SAUTEED CHICKEN
WITH MADEIRA SAUCE
4 Servings

4 tablespoons unsalted butter
1 tablespoon vegetable oil
4 skinless, boneless chicken breast halves
  (about 5 ounces each), pounded ¼ inch thick
¼ cup minced onion
1 small garlic clove, minced
½ cup Madeira
2 tablespoons fresh lemon juice
Salt and freshly ground pepper

1. In a large skillet, melt the butter in the oil over moderate heat until foamy. Working in batches, as necessary, sauté the chicken cutlets for 1 minute on each side. Remove the chicken to a plate and cover loosely to keep warm.

2. Add the onion and garlic to the skillet and sauté over moderate heat until the onion is soft and translucent, about 2 minutes.

3. Pour in the Madeira and cook, stirring, for 2 minutes; add the lemon juice and cook for 1 minute longer to blend the flavors. Season with salt and pepper to taste.

4. Return the four chicken cutlets to the skillet and turn to coat with the sauce. Reduce the heat to a bare simmer and cook gently for 2 to 3 minutes, or until the chicken is just cooked through. Serve with the sauce spooned over the top.

—W. Peter Prestcott

SAUTEED CHICKEN
WITH ARTICHOKE AND
BLACK OLIVE SAUCE
4 Servings

1 package (8 ounces) frozen artichoke hearts
4 tablespoons unsalted butter
1 tablespoon vegetable oil
4 skinless, boneless chicken breast halves
  (about 5 ounces each), pounded ¼ inch thick
½ cup finely chopped onion
3 tablespoons all-purpose flour
1 to 1⅓ cups Chicken Stock (p. 10) or
  canned broth
¾ cup dry white wine
2 teaspoons white wine vinegar
12 large, pitted black olives, coarsely chopped
  (about ¾ cup)
1 teaspoon rosemary, crumbled
Salt and freshly ground pepper
2 tablespoons chopped parsley

1. Place the artichoke hearts in boiling water to cover and cook for 5 to 8 minutes, or until just tender. Drain, chop coarsely and set aside.

2. In a large skillet, melt the butter in the oil over moderate heat until foamy. Working in batches, as necessary, sauté the chicken cutlets for 1 minute on each side. Remove the chicken to a plate and cover loosely to keep warm.

3. Add the onion to the skillet and sauté over moderate heat until soft and translucent, about 2 minutes. Remove the skillet from the heat and sprinkle the flour over the onion. Mix well to coat. Return to moderate heat and cook, stir-

ring, for 2 minutes. Gradually stir in 1 cup of the broth; then add the wine. Bring to a boil, reduce the heat and cook, stirring, for 2 to 3 minutes, until the sauce thickens.

4. Add the vinegar, olives, rosemary and reserved artichoke hearts; cook until heated through, about 2 minutes. Season with salt and pepper to taste. If the sauce is too thick, stir in ¼ to ⅓ cup more broth.

5. Return the four chicken cutlets to the skillet and turn to coat with the sauce. Reduce the heat to a bare simmer and cook gently for 2 to 3 minutes. Serve with the sauce spooned over and around the chicken and sprinkle with the parsley.

—*W. Peter Prestcott*

SAUTEED CHICKEN WITH CHERRY SAUCE
6 Servings

1 can (8 ounces) Bing cherries, drained, with
  ½ cup of the juice reserved
1 tablespoon plus 1 teaspoon cornstarch
6 tablespoons unsalted butter
1½ tablespoons vegetable oil
6 skinless, boneless chicken
  breast halves (about 5 ounces each),
  pounded ¼ inch thick
¾ cup thinly sliced scallions (white part and
  about 2 inches of the green)
½ cup coarsely chopped walnuts
1 cup Chicken Stock (p. 10) or canned broth
½ cup dry red wine
1 tablespoon fresh lemon juice
Salt and freshly ground pepper

1. In a small bowl, stir the cherry juice with the cornstarch until the mixture is smooth; set aside.

2. In a large skillet, melt the butter in the oil over moderate heat until foamy. Working in batches, as necessary, sauté the chicken cutlets for 1 minute on each side. Remove the chicken to a plate and cover loosely to keep warm.

3. Add the scallions to the skillet and sauté over moderate heat, stirring, until softened, about 3 minutes. Add the walnuts and cook, stirring, for 3 minutes. Pour in the stock and wine and cook for 4 minutes longer.

4. Give the cornstarch mixture a stir and slowly whisk it into the sauce. Cook, stirring, until the sauce thickens. Add the cherries and cook until just heated through, about 2 minutes. Add the lemon juice and season with salt and pepper to taste.

5. Return the chicken cutlets to the skillet and turn to coat with the sauce. Reduce the heat to low and simmer for 2 to 3 minutes, or until the chicken is just cooked through. Serve surrounded by the sauce and the cherries.

—*W. Peter Prestcott*

CHICKEN CUTLETS WITH CURRIED CREAM SAUCE
Here is a simply sauced chicken sauté that is easily made within 30 minutes.
2 Servings

2 skinless, boneless chicken breast halves,
  pounded ¼ inch thick
½ teaspoon salt
3 tablespoons unsalted butter
¼ pound mushrooms, quartered
⅓ cup half-and-half or light cream
¼ teaspoon curry powder
⅛ teaspoon paprika
⅛ teaspoon freshly ground pepper
1 tablespoon chopped parsley, for garnish
Lemon wedges, for accompaniment

1. Season the chicken breast halves on both sides with the salt.

2. In a medium heavy skillet, warm 2 tablespoons of the butter over moderately high heat until sizzling. Add the chicken breasts and sauté, turning once, until lightly colored, about 1 minute

per side (the chicken will finish cooking later). Transfer to a warm platter and cover with foil.

3. Add the remaining 1 tablespoon butter and heat until sizzling. Add the mushrooms and sauté, stirring, until softened, 1 to 2 minutes. Increase the heat to high and add the half-and-half, curry powder, paprika and pepper. Boil, uncovered, until reduced to about ¼ cup, 3 to 5 minutes.

4. Reduce the heat to low and return the chicken breasts to the skillet, along with any meat juices from the platter. Simmer until the chicken is hot and cooked through, about 2 minutes. Transfer to the platter and pour the sauce with the mushrooms on top. Sprinkle the chopped parsley on top and serve with lemon wedges.

———

—F&W

MIXED SKILLET GRILL
This grill can be served on a platter, but it's more appealing (and convenient) to serve it from the skillet.

♟ Rioja, such as C.U.N.E.

2 Servings

3 tablespoons olive oil
1 tablespoon Dijon-style mustard
¼ teaspoon thyme
2 large skinless, boneless chicken breast, pounded ¼ inch thick
2 baby eggplants, halved lengthwise, or 1 small eggplant, quartered lengthwise
Salt
4 sticks of mozzarella cheese (1½ by ½ inch)
4 large radicchio leaves
2 basil leaves, minced, or ¼ teaspoon dried oregano
Freshly ground pepper
2 small zucchini, halved lengthwise
1 large plum tomato, halved crosswise

1. In a small bowl, combine 2 teaspoons of the olive oil with the mustard and thyme; blend well. Brush the chicken breast halves on both sides with the mustard mixture. Cover and refrigerate for 1 to 4 hours.

2. With a sharp knife, score the eggplant halves in a diamond pattern and sprinkle with a little salt. Set aside cut-side down.

3. Place a piece of mozzarella on each radicchio leaf. Top each piece of cheese with one-fourth of the minced basil and a sprinkle of salt and pepper. Roll the cheese up in the radicchio and set aside.

4. Remove the chicken from the refrigerator. Heat a 12-inch cast-iron skillet over high heat for 5 minutes.

5. Pat the eggplant dry and paint the cut sides with 1 tablespoon of the olive oil. Place them in the skillet and cook over high heat, turning, until they are softened and well browned all over, about 10 minutes. Remove the eggplant to a platter.

6. Brush the cut sides of the zucchini with 1 teaspoon of the olive oil. Place in the skillet and cook, turning, until browned on both sides, 3 to 4 minutes. Season with salt and pepper to taste and set aside on the platter.

7. Brush the cut sides of the tomato halves with 1 teaspoon of the olive oil, place in the skillet and cook until browned on the bottom, about 1 minute. Set aside on the platter.

8. Add the chicken to the skillet and cook for 2 minutes on the first side; turn and cook 1 minute on the second side, or until browned and cooked through. Season with salt and pepper to taste. Add to the platter.

9. Brush the radicchio rolls with the remaining 2 teaspoons olive oil and place seam-side down in the skillet. Cook for 30 seconds on the first side; turn the rolls over and remove from the heat.

10. Arrange the chicken and vegetables in the skillet to keep them warm. Serve directly from the skillet.

———

—Anne Disrude

CHICKEN CUTLETS IN TARRAGON CRUMBS WITH LIME JUICE

6 Servings

*6 skinless, boneless chicken breast halves
(about 5 ounces each)*
2 eggs
1½ cups dry bread crumbs
1 tablespoon tarragon
1 teaspoon salt
½ teaspoon freshly ground pepper
4 tablespoons olive oil
4 tablespoons unsalted butter
2 limes, cut into wedges

1. Pound the chicken breast halves between sheets of waxed paper to a thin cutlet about 6 by 8 inches. Carefully peel off the waxed paper.

2. In a shallow bowl, beat the eggs. In another shallow bowl, combine the bread crumbs, tarragon, salt and pepper.

3. Dip each cutlet first in egg and then in the crumbs, Pressing the crumbs lightly so that they adhere. Place the cutlets on a wire rack and refrigerate, uncovered, for 1 hour.

4. In a large heavy skillet, warm the oil over moderate heat; stir in the butter until melted. Increase the heat to moderately high. When the fat is almost smoking, add 2 or 3 of the cutlets, depending on the size of the skillet, and sauté them for about 1 minute on each side, or until they are crisp and golden brown. Do not overcook. Drain on paper towels, and sauté the remaining cutlets in the same manner. Serve hot with the wedges of lime, to be squeezed over the cutlets.

—*F&W*

CHICKEN CUTLETS PARMESAN

These chicken cutlets are delicious served hot or cold, sprinkled with plenty of fresh lemon juice. They also make a tasty sandwich, served at room temperature on a crusty roll with slices of ripe tomato, mayonnaise and ground pepper.

4 Servings

*4 skinless, boneless chicken breast halves
(about 5 ounces each)*
¼ cup all-purpose flour
2 eggs
3 tablespoons milk
*1½ cups fresh bread crumbs (made from 4
slices firm-textured white bread),
dried in the oven*
*1 cup freshly grated Parmesan cheese
(4 ounces)*
⅓ cup fruity olive oil
2 lemons, quartered

1. Place a chicken cutlet, smooth-side down, on a sheet of waxed paper. Fold out the small fillet to the side of the larger portion of the breast, slitting along the attachment if necessary so that it lies flat. Remove the tendon and trim off any fat or connective. tissue. Place a second sheet of waxed paper on top and pound with a meat pounder or heavy rolling pin until the chicken flattens out to a thin, even cutlet, about ⅛ inch thick.

2. Dust the chicken cutlets in the flour on a sheet of waxed paper; shake off any excess. Set aside on a clean sheet of waxed paper.

3. Lightly beat the eggs and milk with a fork in a shallow dish. Mix the bread crumbs and cheese and place on a large plate.

4. One by one, dip the chicken cutlets into the egg mixture, then coat both sides with the bread crumb mixture, pressing the crumbs firmly with your hands to make sure they adhere. Place the cutlets on a small tray or between sheets of waxed paper and refrigerate 45 minutes to 1 hour.

5. Remove the chilled cutlets and, in order to minimize sticking when they are fried, make shallow crosshatching marks through the coating on both sides with a sharp knife. Refrigerate for at least another 30 minutes.

6. About 15 minutes before you plan to cook the cutlets, remove them from the refrigerator to allow them to come to room temperature. Heat ¼ cup of the oil in a heavy, medium skillet, preferably nonstick, over moderate heat until the oil is almost smoking. Sauté the cutlets one at a time, without crowding, for about 45 seconds on each side, or until golden brown. If a cutlet sticks at all when you start to turn it, don't force it; simply wait a few seconds and try again. When the crust is properly browned, it turns easily. Add more oil as needed for final cutlets.

7. Drain the cooked cutlets on paper towels. (They can be kept in a very low oven for up to 30 minutes.) Arrange them on dinner plates or a platter and garnish with lemon wedges.

———

—F&W

SAUTEED CHICKEN BREASTS WITH COGNAC AND CREAM SAUCE

This sauce, which begins with a deglazing of the pan used to sauté the chicken breasts, can take a number of different turns. For a mustard sauce, add 1 to 2 tablespoons of Dijon mustard along with the crème fraîche. For a green peppercorn sauce, add 1½ tablespoons of drained green peppercorns. For a tarragon sauce, add 1½ tablespoons minced fresh tarragon or 2 teaspoons dried.

4 Servings

4 skinless, boneless chicken breast halves
  (about 5 ounces each)

Salt and freshly ground pepper
2 tablespoons unsalted butter
1 tablespoon oil
2 tablespoons chopped shallots or scallions
¼ cup Cognac or other brandy, Bourbon
  or whiskey
1 cup Chicken Stock (p. 10) or canned broth
1 cup crème fraîche or heavy cream

1. Dry the chicken breasts thoroughly and sprinkle them lightly with salt and pepper.

2. In a large skillet, heat the butter in the oil until quite hot. Add the chicken breasts, being careful not to crowd them.

3. Immediately lower the heat and sauté slowly until just tender, turning every 5 minutes or so; this should take 12 to 16 minutes. Remove the chicken to a plate and cover loosely to keep warm.

4. Pour off the excess fat from the skillet. Add the shallots and sauté until softened, about 1 minute.

5. Add the Cognac and carefully light it at arm's length with a match. Allow the Cognac to flame, scraping up the browned bits from the pan until the flames die down. Add the chicken stock and boil, uncovered, over high heat until the stock has reduced to a thick, syrupy glaze.

6. Add the crème fraîche or heavy cream and boil over moderately high heat until reduced to a thick golden cream (as it begins to thicken, you may wish to lower the heat slightly to avoid scorching). The sauce is done when it is thick enough to cling to food without running.

———

—F&W

CHICKEN BREASTS WITH LIME BUTTER

2 Servings

2 large skinless, boneless chicken breast halves
  (about 6 ounces each)
Salt and freshly ground white pepper
2 tablespoons vegetable oil
Juice of 1 lime, or more if needed
6 tablespoons unsalted butter, cut into
  small pieces
6 chives, minced
1 teaspoon minced fresh dill (no stems)

1. Sprinkle each breast half lightly with salt and white pepper on both sides. In a small skillet, heat the oil until it is very hot but not smoking. Place the chicken into the hot oil, skinned-side down and sauté over moderately high heat until lightly browned, about 2 minutes. Carefully flip the breasts over, cover the skillet and lower the heat to very low. Cook for 5 to 6 minutes, or until the breasts have just cooked through; they should be slightly springy to the touch.

2. When the chicken has just cooked through, remove it to a warm plate. Pour off all the oil from the skillet. Use a paper towel to blot the excess oil, but leave any browned bits in the bottom of the pan.

3. Add the lime juice to the pan over moderately low heat, scraping up the browned bits with a wooden spoon. When the lime juice just begins to bubble, add the pieces of butter, swirling the pan over low heat until the butter becomes opaque and forms a thickish sauce. Add the chives and dill to the sauce and a few more drops of lime juice to taste, if you like.

4. To serve, cut each half chicken breast crosswise on the bias to form three small "scallops." Spoon a small puddle of sauce in the center of the plate and place the chicken on top. Serve hot.

—Jean-Jacques Jouteux

CHICKEN BREASTS WITH CREME FRAICHE AND LIME

❦ Chilled Provençal rosé, such as Domaines Ott

4 Servings

4 large skinless, boneless chicken breast halves
  (about 6 ounces each)
¼ cup clarified butter
2 shallots, minced
¾ cup Chicken Stock (p. 10) or canned broth
⅔ cup crème fraîche
3 tablespoons fresh lime juice
Salt and freshly ground pepper
4 tablespoons cold unsalted butter
2 limes, thinly sliced, for garnish

1. Trim off all excess fat and remove the tendons from each chicken breast.

2. In a large nonreactive skillet, heat the clarified butter. Add the chicken breasts and sauté over moderate heat, turning once, until cooked through, firm and springy to the touch and light golden in color, 8 to 10 minutes. Transfer the chicken to a warm plate and cover to keep warm.

3. Add the shallots to the skillet. Cook over moderately low heat until softened but not browned, about 1 minute. Add the chicken stock, increase the heat to high and boil until reduced to ¼ cup.

4. Add the crème fraîche and continue to boil gently until reduced by half, about 5 minutes. Add the lime juice. Season with salt and pepper to taste. Remove from the heat and whisk in the cold butter, 1 tablespoon at a time.

5. Cut each chicken breast crosswise on the diagonal into 5 or 6 slices. Arrange the chicken slices on 4 warm plates, coat lightly with the sauce and garnish each plate with several slices of lime.

—Amandier de Mougins, Mougins, France

LEMON CHICKEN WITH CAPERS AND PINE NUTS

Serve this with steamed broccoli and drizzle it with some of the sauce from the pan.

❦ A tart, zesty dish like this is nicely contrasted by a rich, round Chardonnay with its own lemony overtones, such as Girard or De Loach.

4 Servings

¼ *cup pine nuts*
4 *boneless chicken breast halves, with the skin on (about 6 ounces each)*
½ *teaspoon salt*
½ *teaspoon freshly ground pepper*
1 *tablespoon extra-virgin olive oil*
½ *cup dry white wine*
1½ *tablespoons fresh lemon juice*
1 *tablespoon capers*
3 *tablespoons unsalted butter*

1. Preheat the oven to 400°. Spread the pine nuts on a baking sheet and toast in the oven until golden brown, about 4 minutes. Set aside to cool.

2. Gently pound each boneless chicken breast half between 2 sheets of waxed paper until flattened to an even ¼ inch. Season with the salt and pepper.

3. In a large nonreactive skillet, heat the olive oil over moderately high heat until almost smoking. Add the chicken breasts, skin-side down, and cook until golden brown, about 5 minutes. Turn the breasts over and cook until white throughout but still moist, about 3 minutes. Arrange the chicken on a large warmed platter. Cover loosely with foil to keep warm. Pour off the fat from the skillet.

4. Add the wine to the skillet and bring to a boil, scraping up any browned bits from the bottom of the pan. Cook over high heat until reduced by half, about 3 minutes.

5. Add the lemon juice and capers. Remove from the heat and whisk in the butter, 1 tablespoon at a time. Pour any accumulated juices from the chicken platter into the sauce. Pour the sauce over the meat and sprinkle with the pine nuts.

———————

—*Nora Carey*

SAUTE OF CHICKEN BREASTS WITH GORGONZOLA AND FRESH HERBS

❦ Dry Chenin Blanc, such as Chappellet

4 Servings

6 *skinless, boneless chicken breast halves (about 5 ounces each)*
Salt and freshly ground white pepper
Flour, for dredging
2 *tablespoons unsalted butter*
2 *teaspoons peanut oil*
⅓ *cup plus 3 tablespoons Chicken Stock (p. 10) or canned broth*
3 *ounces Gorgonzola cheese*
1 *cup heavy cream*
Beurre manié (optional): 1 tablespoon softened unsalted butter blended to a paste with 1 tablespoon flour
2 *tablespoons minced fresh tarragon*
2 *tablespoons minced fresh chives*

1. Season the chicken breasts lightly with salt and white pepper. Dredge lightly in flour; shake off the excess.

2. In a large heavy skillet, melt the butter in the oil over high heat. Add the chicken breasts and sauté, turning once, until browned on the outside (they will still be quite pink inside), 2 to 3 minutes per side.

3. Reduce the heat to moderately low. Add 3 tablespoons of the chicken stock, cover and cook for 5 minutes. With a slotted spoon, transfer the chicken to a plate.

4. Meanwhile, in a food processor, puree the Gorgonzola with ¼ cup of the cream.

5. Add the remaining ⅓ cup stock to the skillet. Cook over high heat, scraping the bottom of the pan, until the sauce reduces to a glaze, about 2 minutes. Add the remaining ¾ cup cream and cook, stirring, until reduced to ½ cup, about 5 minutes.

6. Whisk in the Gorgonzola cream. If the sauce seems thin, bring to a boil and whisk in bits of the beurre manié until the sauce lightly coats a spoon. Add the tarragon and season with salt and pepper to taste. *(The recipe can be prepared to this point up to 2 hours ahead.)*

7. Add the chicken breasts to the sauce, cover and cook over low heat until just heated through, about 2 minutes. Transfer to a serving platter and spoon the sauce over the chicken. Sprinkle with the chives.

—*Perla Meyers*

PEPPERED CHICKEN BREASTS WITH ROSEMARY AND GARLIC

❦ Barbaresco, such Gaja, or California Sauvignon Blanc, such as Groth

4 Servings

2 tablespoons fresh lemon juice
2 tablespoons olive oil
½ teaspoon rosemary, crumbled
⅛ to ¼ teaspoon crushed hot red pepper,
  to taste
½ to 1 teaspoon coarsely cracked black pepper,
  to taste
4 garlic cloves, crushed
4 skinless, boneless chicken breast halves
  (about 5 ounces each)
1 teaspoon unsalted butter
1 teaspoon vegetable oil
¼ teaspoon salt

1. In a glass dish just large enough to hold the chicken breasts, combine the lemon juice, olive oil, rosemary, hot pepper, black pepper and garlic. Add the chicken breasts and let marinate at room temperature, turning once or twice, for 1 hour.

2. Remove the chicken from the marinade and pat dry. In a large skillet, melt the butter in the oil. Add the chicken, smooth-side down, and sauté over moderate heat, turning once, for 4 to 5 minutes on each side, until lightly browned and cooked through. Season with the salt. Serve hot or warm.

—*Anne Disrude*

CHICKEN BREASTS WITH ANAHEIM CHILE BUTTER, CORN AND PEPPERS

All-American ingredients add freshness to this flavorful chicken.

❦ The piquancy of the chile butter on the chicken suggests a fruity, dry but simple white for contrast, such as Chappellet Dry Chenin Blanc.

8 Servings

¼ cup vegetable oil
2 large Anaheim chiles
½ jalapeño or 1 serrano pepper
1 small garlic clove
2 tablespoons fresh lemon juice
1¾ teaspoons salt
6 tablespoons unsalted butter
1 medium red bell pepper, cut into ¼-inch dice
1 medium green bell pepper, cut into
  ¼-inch dice
4 cups corn kernels, preferably fresh
3 sage leaves, preferably fresh, finely chopped
8 boneless chicken breast halves, with
  the skin on
Sprigs of cilantro (fresh coriander), for garnish

1. In a medium skillet, heat the vegetable oil

until very hot. Using long tongs, add the Anaheim chiles to the pan, being careful to avoid any splattering oil. Cook the chiles, turning, until the skins turn white, about 1 minute. Transfer the chiles to a plate lined with paper towels; reserve the oil.

2. When the chiles are cool enough to handle, remove and discard the skins, seeds and ribs. Place the chiles in a blender. Add the jalapeño pepper, garlic, lemon juice and ¼ teaspoon of the salt. Puree until smooth. With the machine on, add 4 tablespoons of the butter, 1 tablespoon at a time, and blend until smooth. Transfer the butter to a sheet of plastic wrap and roll into a 4-inch-long cylinder. Place in the freezer. *(The chile butter can be prepared up to 2 months in advance and stored in the freezer.)*

3. In a medium saucepan, combine the bell peppers, corn, sage, 1½ cups of water and ½ teaspoon of the salt. Bring to a boil, reduce the heat to moderately low and simmer, uncovered, until the vegetables are tender, about 10 minutes. Drain and toss the vegetables with the remaining 2 tablespoons butter.

4. In a large skillet, heat the reserved ¼ cup oil over moderate heat. In two batches, add the chicken breasts and sauté, turning, until golden brown, about 7 minutes on each side. Season with the remaining 1 teaspoon salt.

5. To serve, mound the vegetables in the center of 8 warmed dinner plates. Place a chicken breast on top of each. Cut the frozen chile butter into ½-inch rounds and set one on top of each piece of chicken. Garnish the plates with sprigs of coriander.

—*Taxi, San Francisco*

SAUTEED CHICKEN BREASTS WITH APPLES AND CALVADOS CREAM

Sautéed fresh spinach with a pinch of nutmeg and buttered wild rice or boiled potatoes would be a fine accompaniment to this rich dish.

❦ The richness of this elegant dish would be showcased by an equally rich, full-bodied Chardonnay, such as William Hill Silver Label, or a grand white Burgundy, such as Domaine Leflaive Chevalier-Montrachet.

8 Servings

¼ pound sliced bacon, cut into small dice
8 skinless, boneless chicken breast halves
  (about 5 ounces each)
Salt and freshly ground black pepper
2 tablespoons unsalted butter
7 medium Granny Smith apples, peeled and
  cut into eighths
2 tablespoons dark brown sugar
½ cup Calvados or other apple brandy
1½ cups crème fraîche
½ teaspoon caraway seeds
Pinch of cayenne pepper

1. Preheat the oven to 250°. In a large nonreactive skillet, cook the bacon over moderate heat until crisp, 8 to 10 minutes. Using a slotted spoon, transfer the bacon to paper towels to drain. Set aside.

2. Pour off all but 1 tablespoon of the bacon fat from the skillet. Lightly sprinkle the chicken breasts with salt and pepper. Set the skillet over high heat and sauté the chicken in batches, turning once, until browned, about 2 minutes per side. Transfer the cooked chicken to a baking dish in a single layer and cover with foil. Place in the low oven for 15 minutes to finish cooking.

3. Meanwhile, in the same skillet, melt the butter over moderately high heat. Add the apples, cover and cook, stirring frequently, until tender, about 5 minutes.

4. Uncover and add the brown sugar and ¼

131

cup of the Calvados. Increase the heat to high and cook, tossing gently, until the apples begin to brown, about 2 minutes longer.

5. Add the crème fraîche, caraway seeds, cayenne and the remaining ¼ cup Calvados to the apples. Stir in any accumulated juices from the chicken and bring to a boil. Cook until the sauce is thick enough to coat the back of a spoon, about 4 minutes. Season with salt and pepper to taste.

6. To serve, place the chicken on a warmed platter or plates, arrange the apples alongside and pour the cream sauce over all. Garnish with the reserved bacon.

———————

—Bob Chambers

CHICKEN SAUTE WITH RASPBERRIES AND GARLIC

Garlic with raspberries may seem an unlikely pairing, but braised until mellow, and laced together in a delicate sweet-sour sauce tinged with raspberry vinegar, they combine in a spectacular manner.

❦ California Rosé of Cabernet Sauvignon

2 Servings

16 medium garlic cloves, peeled

1 tablespoon sugar

¼ cup plus 1 teaspoon Raspberry Vinegar (recipe follows)

2 boneless chicken breast halves, with the skin on (about 6 ounces each)

2 tablespoons plus 1 teaspoon cold unsalted butter

1 teaspoon vegetable oil

¼ teaspoon salt

¼ teaspoon freshly ground pepper

¼ cup fresh raspberries

1. In a small nonreactive saucepan, combine the garlic cloves, sugar, 1 teaspoon of the vinegar and ½ cup of water. Bring to a boil over high heat. Reduce the heat to low and simmer, uncovered, until the sugar dissolves, about 3 minutes. Increase the heat to moderate, cover and cook until the garlic is tender enough to pierce with a fork, about 10 minutes.

2. Uncover the saucepan, increase the heat to high and cook until the liquid is reduced to a thick syrup and the garlic is caramelized, about 10 minutes.

3. Add the remaining ¼ cup vinegar and cook for 30 seconds to dissolve any sugar clinging to the pan. Set the sauce aside.

4. Cut each chicken breast half crosswise into 5 slices; leave the skin on. Pat dry.

5. In a large nonreactive skillet, melt 1 teaspoon of the butter in the oil over high heat until sizzling. Add the chicken pieces, skin-side down. Reduce the heat to moderate and sauté until the skin is well browned, about 3 minutes. Turn and cook until browned on the second side, about 3 minutes. Remove to a plate and cover loosely to keep warm. Pour off any fat in the pan.

6. Add the reserved sauce with garlic cloves to the skillet. Bring to a boil over high heat, scraping up any browned bits from the bottom of the pan. Continue to boil for 1 to 2 minutes, until the sauce is thick and syrupy. Remove from the heat. Season with the salt and pepper. Whisk in the remaining 2 tablespoons cold butter, 1 tablespoon at a time.

7. Return the chicken with any accumulated juices to the skillet. Toss gently to coat with the sauce. Add the raspberries and toss gently again. Serve hot.

———————

—F&W

Chicken Teriyaki (p. 89).

Chicken, Sausage and Grits Hash with Wild Mushrooms (p. 199).

Warm Chicken Salad with Oranges and Spicy Ginger Dressing (p. 236).

RASPBERRY VINEGAR
Makes About 1 Cup

1 cup white wine vinegar
1 cup fresh raspberries

1. Place the raspberries in a 3-cup glass container and pour the vinegar over them. Cover the container and let it sit undisturbed at room temperature for 5 days, until the color and flavor have been extracted from the berries.

2. Strain the vinegar through a fine sieve; discard the raspberries. Pour the vinegar into a glass bottle, cover tightly and store in a cool, dry place.

———

—*F&W*

BREAST OF CHICKEN PECAN
At the restaurant, this is served with an apricot-mustard sauce and roasted rosemary potatoes.
♥ Cabernet Sauvignon such as Jordan
2 Servings

½ cup all-purpose flour
½ teaspoon salt
¼ teaspoon freshly ground pepper
1 egg white, beaten until frothy
3 tablespoons grainy mustard, such as
 Pommery
½ cup finely ground pecans
½ cup fresh bread crumbs
2 large skinless, boneless chicken breast halves
 (6 ounces each)
2 tablespoons unsalted butter
¼ cup heavy cream

1. In a shallow bowl, combine the flour, salt and pepper. In a second shallow bowl, blend the egg white with 2 tablespoons of the mustard. In a third shallow bowl, combine the pecans and bread crumbs.

2. One at a time, dredge each chicken breast in the flour and shake off the excess. Next, dip in the egg white mixture to coat. Finally, dip into the pecan-bread crumb mixture, pressing so the coating adheres to both sides. Set aside on a rack. *(The recipe can be prepared to this point up to 2 hours ahead. Place the chicken, on the rack and uncovered, in the refrigerator.)*

3. In a medium skillet, melt the butter over moderately high heat. When the foam subsides, add the chicken breasts. Cook on one side until crisp and brown, about 3 minutes. Then turn, reduce the heat to moderately low and cook until the chicken has just lost its pinkness inside, about 5 minutes.

4. Meanwhile, in a small saucepan, warm the cream over moderate heat. Add the remaining 1 tablespoon mustard and a pinch of pepper; cook until warmed through, 3 to 5 minutes.

5. To serve, slice the breasts on the diagonal and fan out decoratively on 2 warmed serving plates. Pass the sauce on the side.

———

—*The Lion's Rock, New York City*

CURRIED CAIN CHICKEN
♥ The soft spicy character of Cain Cellars Merlot or Cain Five goes well with this.
6 Servings

4 tablespoons unsalted butter
1 small onion, coarsely chopped
2 large celery ribs, coarsely chopped
1 medium carrot, chopped
1 small green bell pepper, chopped
2 medium garlic cloves, minced
2 tablespoons all-purpose flour
2 tablespoons curry powder
1 medium tart green apple, such as Granny
 Smith, cored and chopped
2 medium plum tomatoes, chopped
1 large bay leaf
4 cups Chicken Stock (p. 10) or 1 can (13¾
 ounces) broth diluted with 2¼ cups water
2 tablespoons fresh lemon juice

½ teaspoon Worcestershire sauce
3 dashes of hot pepper sauce
6 boneless chicken breast halves, with the skin
  on (about 2¼ pounds total)

1. In a large saucepan, melt 3 tablespoons of the butter over moderate heat. Add the onion, celery, carrot and green pepper. Cook, stirring occasionally, until the vegetables start to turn brown, about 5 minutes.

2. Reduce the heat to low. Stir in the garlic, flour and curry powder and cook until the flavors are blended, about 2 minutes. Add the apple, tomatoes, bay leaf and chicken stock. Bring to a simmer over moderately low heat and cook until the vegetables fall apart when pressed with a spoon, about 45 minutes.

3. Strain the sauce through a sieve into a medium saucepan, pressing through as much vegetable pulp as possible. Stir in the lemon juice, Worcestershire sauce and hot pepper sauce. Cover to keep warm. *(The recipe can be made to this point up to 1 day ahead. Pour into a nonreactive bowl, cover and refrigerate.)*

4. In a large heavy skillet, melt the remaining 1 tablespoon butter over moderately high heat. When the butter begins to foam, add the chicken breasts, skin-side down, and cook until the skin is browned and crisp, about 10 minutes.

5. Turn the breasts and cook until browned on the bottom and firm to the touch, about 10 minutes longer. Reheat the sauce if necessary. Transfer the chicken to warm dinner plates and ladle some of the curry sauce over each portion. Serve hot.

—Joyce Cain, Cain Cellars, St. Helena, California

SAUTEED GEWURZTRAMINER CHICKEN WITH CABBAGE AND LEEKS

The chicken thighs for this dish are marinated for 24 hours, so plan accordingly.

❦ This dish requires a fragrant Alsace Gewürztraminer with good acidity to cut through the richness of bacon and sautéed cabbage. Look for less ripe vintages, such as Zind-Humbrecht or Willm. Do not use the sweeter versions labeled either Vendange Tardive or Sélection de Grains Nobles.

4 Servings

8 chicken thighs, boned, with the skin on
¾ teaspoon salt
¾ teaspoon freshly ground pepper
2 cups plus 4 teaspoons young Alsace
  Gewürztraminer
7 slices of smoked bacon
2 garlic cloves, minced
2 medium leeks (white part only), cut into
  thin julienne strips
3 pounds savoy, nappa or Chinese cabbage (1
  large head), shredded
¼ teaspoon freshly grated nutmeg
1 cup all-purpose flour, for dredging
7 tablespoons unsalted butter
1 cup Chicken Stock (p. 10) or canned broth
1 tablespoon chopped parsley

1. Season the chicken thighs with ½ teaspoon of the salt and ¼ teaspoon of the pepper. Place in a shallow nonreactive dish just large enough to hold the thighs. Pour in enough Gewürztraminer to cover, approximately 2 cups. Cover with plastic wrap and refrigerate for 24 hours.

2. Remove the chicken from the marinade, reserving the liquid. Pat dry with paper towels. Cut eight 2-inch-long pieces of bacon from the bacon slices. Tuck 1 piece under the skin of each thigh. Cut the remaining bacon crosswise into ½-inch pieces. Season the thighs with ¼ teaspoon

of the pepper and the remaining ¼ teaspoon salt.

3. In a large heavy skillet, preferably cast iron, cook the bacon pieces over moderate heat until crisp, 5 to 7 minutes. Remove the bacon with a slotted spoon and drain on paper towels. Pour off all but 1 tablespoon of the fat and return the skillet to the heat.

4. Add the garlic and leeks to the skillet and cook over moderately low heat until softened but not browned, about 5 minutes.

5. Increase the heat to high and add the cabbage and nutmeg. Cook, tossing well, until wilted, about 3 minutes. (Add ¼ cup of water to the skillet if it seems dry.)

6. Stir in the remaining 4 teaspoons wine and ¼ teaspoon pepper; remove from the heat. Transfer the cabbage to a bowl. Add the reserved bacon and toss well. Cover and keep warm.

7. Wipe out the skillet with a paper towel. Place the flour in a shallow dish. Dredge the chicken thighs in the flour, shaking off the excess. Add 3 tablespoons of the butter to the skillet and melt over moderately high heat until foaming. Add the chicken, skin-side down. Cook over high heat until browned, about 5 minutes. Turn and brown the other side, 3 to 4 minutes longer. Remove and drain on paper towels. Cover the chicken with foil to keep warm while preparing the sauce.

8. In a small nonreactive skillet, boil the stock over high heat until reduced by half, about 3 minutes. Add ½ cup of the reserved Gewürztraminer marinade and bring just to a boil. Remove from the heat. Whisk in the remaining 4 tablespoons butter, 1 tablespoon at a time, moving the pan on and off the heat until the butter is absorbed by the sauce.

9. To serve, divide the cabbage among 4 dinner plates. Nestle 2 chicken thighs on top of each mound of cabbage. Pour the sauce over the chicken and cabbage and sprinkle the parsley on top.

—David Rosengarten

CHICKEN, SAUSAGE, SWEET PEPPERS AND OLIVES

The chicken must marinate for at least 6 hours before cooking, so plan accordingly.

6 Servings

*4 skinless, boneless chicken breast halves
  (1¼ pounds total), cut lengthwise into
  ½-inch strips*
1 cup milk
*¼ cup hot pepper sauce, preferably Louisiana
  hot sauce*
1¼ pounds bulk pork sausage
2 large garlic cloves, halved and crushed
1 cup dry red wine
*1 can (28 ounces) Italian peeled tomatoes,
  drained and coarsely chopped*
½ cup beef stock or canned broth
2 tablespoons olive oil
*4 medium yellow bell peppers, cut into
  ½-inch dice*
24 oil-cured black olives, halved

1. In a medium bowl, combine the chicken, milk and hot sauce. Cover and refrigerate for 6 hours or overnight.

2. Form the sausage meat into 18 patties. In a large nonreactive skillet, fry the patties over high heat, turning once, until very brown, 2 to 3 minutes on each side. Drain on paper towels.

3. Pour out the fat. Return the sausage patties to the pan. Add the garlic and wine. Cover and simmer over moderate heat, turning the patties once, until the liquid is reduced to ¼ cup, about 12 minutes.

4. Add the tomatoes and stock and simmer, uncovered, for 5 minutes.

5. Meanwhile, in a large heavy skillet, heat 1 tablespoon of the olive oil over high heat. Add the yellow peppers and toss to coat well. Sauté, stirring occasionally, until lightly browned and crisp-tender, about 5 minutes. Add the peppers to the sausage patties. Cover and set aside.

6. Drain the chicken and pat dry with paper towels. Discard the marinade. In the large skillet used to fry the peppers, heat the remaining 1 tablespoon olive oil. Add the chicken and cook over high heat, turning constantly, until just white throughout, 3 to 5 minutes. Using a slotted spoon, add the chicken to the sausage patties and peppers. Add the olives and stir to combine.

—*Lee Bailey*

BREAST OF CHICKEN WITH LEEKS, COMTE CHEESE AND PINK PEPPERCORNS

This dish is a beautifully orchestrated and unexpected blending of flavors and textures. If you can't find Comté cheese, substitute a Swiss Gruyère.

❦ Italian white, such as Antinori Galestro

4 Servings

7 tablespoons unsalted butter
4 medium leeks (white and tender green), cut
  crosswise into ½-inch slices
¾ cup crème fraîche
¾ teaspoon salt
Freshly ground black pepper
4 skinless, boneless chicken breast halves
  (about 5 ounces each)
¼ cup Cognac
1 cup Chicken Stock (p. 10) or canned broth
1 tablespoon chopped fresh tarragon or 1
  teaspoon dried
2 tablespoons pink peppercorns
½ cup grated Comté cheese
1 tablespoon minced chives, for garnish

1. In a large skillet or sauté pan with a lid, melt 3 tablespoons of the butter over moderate heat. Add the leeks, cover the pan and reduce the heat to moderately low. Cook, stirring occasionally, until the leeks are tender, about 15 minutes.

2. Stir in 3 tablespoons of the crème fraîche, ¼ teaspoon of the salt and a pinch of black pepper. Set aside and keep warm.

3. Remove the fillet from each chicken breast half. Cut each breast diagonally into strips approximately the same size as the fillets. Season the chicken with the remaining ½ teaspoon salt and ¼ teaspoon of black pepper.

4. In a large skillet, melt 3 tablespoons of the butter over moderate heat. Working in two batches, add the chicken and cook over moderate heat, turning occasionally, until the pieces are browned but still springy to the touch, about 3 minutes. Remove from the pan and drain on paper towels. Cover loosely with foil and return to a low oven to keep warm.

5. Pour off the fat from the pan and return it to moderate heat. Add the Cognac and bring to a boil, scraping up any browned bits from the bottom of the pan. Pour in the stock and the remaining crème fraîche. Increase the heat to high and boil until the mixture is slightly thickened, about 4 minutes.

6. Stir in the tarragon, pink peppercorns and ¼ cup of the cheese. Cook, stirring, until the cheese is melted. Off the heat, stir in the remaining 1 tablespoon butter. Taste the sauce and adjust seasonings if necessary.

7. To serve, make a bed of leeks on each of four dinner plates. Arrange one-fourth of the chicken on top of each. Pour the sauce over each and garnish each plate with some of the remaining cheese and the chives.

—*Chef Hubert, Le Bistro d'Hubert, Paris*

POULET AU POIVRE

♟ Zinfandel, such as Sebastiani Proprietor's Reserve

2 Servings

2 tablespoons golden raisins
2 tablespoons Cognac or other brandy
One 3½-pound chicken, quartered
1 tablespoon coarsely cracked peppercorns
½ teaspoon salt
2 tablespoons unsalted butter
1 tablespoon vegetable oil
¼ cup Brown Chicken Stock (p. 11) or canned broth

1. Place the raisins in a small bowl. Cover with boiling water and let soak until softened, about 5 minutes. Drain, then toss with the brandy and macerate until ready to use.

2. Pat the chicken dry. Sprinkle on both sides with the pepper and salt, pressing the peppercorns so that they will adhere to the chicken.

3. In a large skillet, melt 1 tablespoon of the butter in the oil over moderately high heat. When sizzling, add the chicken, skin-side down. Fry until well browned, turning once, about 8 minutes per side.

4. Cover and cook until the breasts are tender, 8 to 10 minutes. Remove the breasts to a warm plate and cover loosely with foil to keep warm. Cook the legs 5 minutes longer; add to the breasts.

5. Pour off any fat in the skillet. Add the raisins and brandy. Carefully ignite with a match. Shake the pan until the flames subside. Add the stock and bring to a boil, scraping up any browned bits from the bottom of the pan. Cook until reduced by one-third, about 2 minutes.

6. Remove from the heat and swirl in the remaining 1 tablespoon butter. Season to taste, adding more salt if necessary. Pour the sauce over the chicken.

—Jean-Pierre Goyenvalle, Le Lion d'Or, Washington, D.C.

SAUTEED POUSSINS WITH CARROTS AND DILL

Either brown or wild rice or a simple pilaf would be a nice complement to this dish.

6 Servings

3 poussins (about 1 pound each)
1 teaspoon salt
1 teaspoon freshly ground pepper
¼ cup olive oil
1 medium onion, chopped
1 pound carrots, halved lengthwise and sliced ¼ inch thick
2 celery ribs, sliced ¼ inch thick on the diagonal
1 cup Chicken Stock (p. 10) or canned low-sodium broth
½ cup dry white wine
½ cup chopped fresh dill

1. Using kitchen shears, cut along both sides of the poussins' backbones and remove. Quarter the birds and pat dry. Sprinkle both sides with the salt and pepper.

2. In a very large, high-sided nonreactive skillet, heat 2 tablespoons of the olive oil over high heat until it begins to smoke. Add the leg quarters, skin-side up, and sauté until browned, about 3 minutes. Turn the pieces and sauté for 3 minutes longer. Transfer to a large plate and cover loosely with foil to keep warm. Repeat with the breast quarters.

3. Pour the fat from the skillet; wipe out the pan if there's any dark sediment on the bottom. Add the remaining 2 tablespoons olive oil and heat over high heat until just beginning to smoke. Add the onion and sauté for 1 minute. Add the carrots and celery and sauté until beginning to brown, about 5 minutes.

4. Deglaze the pan with the chicken stock and wine, scraping up any browned bits from the bottom. Bring to a boil and stir in the dill. Place the leg quarters on top of the vegetables and ar-

SAUTES

range the breast quarters over the legs. Reduce the heat to moderate, cover and simmer until the meat is cooked through, about 20 minutes. Transfer the poussins to a warmed serving platter and spoon the vegetables alongside.

—*Bob Chambers*

SAUTEED JAMBONNEAUX WITH MUSHROOM AND WILD RICE STUFFING

For step-by-step photographs that show how to make *jambonneaux*, see page 18.

🍷 California White Zinfandel, such as Sutter Home

8 Servings

8 large chicken legs with thighs attached, at least 10 ounces each
½ cup wild rice, well washed
¼ pound sliced bacon
2 tablespoons unsalted butter
1 medium shallot, minced
1 cup finely chopped mushrooms (about 6 ounces)
1 tablespoon finely chopped parsley
½ teaspoon salt
¼ teaspoon freshly ground pepper
2 tablespoons vegetable oil

1. Using a boning knife, cut through the meat down the inside of each thigh to expose the bone. Starting at the top and scraping against the bone, gently work the thigh meat down to expose the leg joint. Carefully cut the tendons at the joint, taking care not to pierce the skin. Continue to scrape the meat off the leg bone, turning it inside out as you go. As you reach the lower part of the drumstick where the meat is thin, use your fingers to pull the meat downward around the bone. Cut through the skin and remove the bones, reserving them for stock. Remove the white tendons by pulling them out with small pliers or your fingers while scraping against the tendon with a knife.

2. Place the wild rice in a medium saucepan and add 1½ cups of cold water. Bring to a boil over moderately high heat; reduce the heat to low and simmer, uncovered, stirring frequently, until tender, about 30 minutes. Drain the rice and set aside in a medium bowl.

3. In a large heavy skillet, sauté the bacon over moderate heat until crisp, about 5 minutes. Drain the bacon on paper towels. Drizzle 2 tablespoons of the fat in the skillet over the wild rice; reserve the remainder.

4. In a large skillet, melt the butter over moderate heat. When the foam subsides, add the shallot and mushrooms and sauté until the mushrooms release their juice and it evaporates, about 5 minutes.

5. Add the mushroom mixture to the rice. Crumble in the bacon and add the parsley and ¼ teaspoon of the salt and ⅛ teaspoon of the pepper. Mix lightly to blend. Let the stuffing cool to room temperature.

6. Season each leg with the remaining ¼ teaspoon salt and ⅛ teaspoon pepper and turn the meat skin-side out. Spoon 2 rounded tablespoons of the stuffing into the cavity of each leg. Fold down the top flap of the thigh, wrapping the meat around the stuffing so that each leg resembles a small ham, and tuck the thigh flap into the skin of the leg. With a trussing needle and butcher's twine, sew the skin together to seal.

7. Place the skillet with the remaining bacon fat over moderately high heat and add the vegetable oil. Add the *jambonneaux* and sauté, turning frequently, until golden and lightly crisped, about 20 minutes. Drain on paper towels. Remove the strings before serving.

—*John Robert Massie*

Fries
and
Stir-Fries

CHICKEN KIEV

When properly made, chicken Kiev is one of the greatest of culinary achievements. The coating should be crisp, the meat inside moist, and the hot parsley butter should gush out when the chicken is cut.

4 Servings

1 stick (4 ounces) unsalted butter, softened to
   room temperature
2 tablespoons minced parsley
2 teaspoons minced scallions
¼ teaspoon tarragon
¼ teaspoon cayenne
½ teaspoon salt
2 teaspoons fresh lemon juice
4 skinless, boneless chicken breast halves
   (about 5 ounces each)
¼ cup all-purpose flour
2 eggs, lightly beaten
½ cup dry bread crumbs
Vegetable oil, for deep-frying

1. In a small bowl, blend together the butter, parsley, scallions, tarragon, cayenne, salt and lemon juice until smooth. On a sheet of waxed paper, shape the parsley butter into a rectangle 2 by 3 inches and place in the freezer while you prepare the chicken.

2. Trim away and discard any fat, tendons and gristle from the breasts. Working with one breast half at a time, lay it flat between two sheets of waxed paper. Pound or roll the chicken until it is slightly thicker than ⅛ inch, taking care not to tear the flesh. Repeat with the remaining pieces.

3. Remove the butter from the freezer and cut it crosswise into four ½-by-3-inch pieces. Place each one lengthwise on a flattened chicken breast. Fold the short ends of the chicken over the butter and then fold over the long ends to form a roll.

4. Gently roll one stuffed chicken breast in the flour, then in the eggs and finally in the bread crumbs. Set it aside on a plate, seam-side down.

Repeat with the remaining chicken rolls and then refrigerate them for 1 hour.

5. In a deep-fryer with a deep-frying basket inserted, heat about 3 inches of vegetable oil to 375°. Using a slotted spoon, lower two of the chicken rolls into the basket in the oil. Fry for exactly 5 minutes, remove with the basket and drain. Repeat with the remaining two rolls. Serve immediately.

———

—F&W

CHICKEN IN WHOLE-WHEAT LEMON BATTER

4 Servings

1¼ cups all-purpose flour
½ cup cornstarch
½ cup whole-wheat flour
2 teaspoons salt
1¼ cups ice water
¼ cup fresh lemon juice
Vegetable oil, for deep-frying
¼ teaspoon freshly ground pepper
One 3½-pound chicken, cut into serving pieces

1. Combine ½ cup of the flour, the cornstarch, whole-wheat flour and 1 teaspoon of the salt in a large mixing bowl; blend with a slotted spoon. Combine the water and lemon juice and pour the mixture over the flour all at once. Quickly beat the mixture with a wire whisk to form a smooth batter.

2. Tightly cover the bowl with plastic wrap and refrigerate for at least 1 hour. Whisk the batter just before using.

3. In a deep-fryer with a deep-frying basket inserted, heat about 3 inches of oil to 375°.

4. Combine the remaining ¾ cup flour and 1 teaspoon salt with the pepper. Working with half the chicken parts, dip the chicken first into the seasoned flour and then into the batter.

5. Using tongs, carefully lower each piece of chicken into the basket in the oil. Fry for 10 to 12 minutes, or until crisp and golden. Raise the basket and remove the chicken pieces with tongs; drain. Repeat with the remaining chicken. Serve hot.

———

—F&W

SMOKED CHICKEN CROQUETTES

Plain cooked chicken can easily be used in place of the smoked chicken here. If you make this with regular chicken, use the same quantities as listed below, but substitute ¼ cup of diced smoked ham for ¼ cup of the diced chicken. The croquette mixture should be chilled for at least 3 hours, so plan accordingly.

🍷 Pinot Noir Blanc, such as Sebastiani

6 to 8 Servings

CROQUETTE MIXTURE:

1 cup milk
1 medium onion, quartered
1 bay leaf
6 black peppercorns
2 tablespoons unsalted butter
2 tablespoons all-purpose flour
2 egg yolks
½ teaspoon salt
⅛ teaspoon freshly ground white pepper
Pinch of freshly grated nutmeg
1 cup minced smoked chicken plus 1 cup diced
* (¼-inch) smoked chicken*
2 tablespoons chopped parsley

COATING MIXTURE:

1 cup all-purpose flour
2 eggs, beaten
2 cups fresh bread crumbs (made from 5 or 6
* slices of firm-textured white bread, crusts*
* removed)*
1½ to 2 quarts peanut oil, for deep-frying

1. Prepare the croquette mixture: Place the milk, onion, bay leaf and peppercorns in a medium saucepan. Bring to a boil over moderately high heat. Immediately reduce the heat to low and simmer for 10 minutes.

2. Meanwhile, in another medium saucepan, melt the butter over moderate heat. Add the flour and cook, stirring, for 2 minutes without browning to make a roux. Remove from the heat.

3. Whisking constantly, strain the hot milk slowly into the roux. Bring to a boil, whisking, over moderately high heat. Beat in the egg yolks, salt, white pepper and nutmeg. Reduce the heat to low and simmer for 5 minutes; the mixture will be quite thick. Pour into a bowl and let cool to room temperature.

4. Fold in the minced and diced chicken and the parsley. Cover and refrigerate until well chilled, about 3 hours or overnight.

5. Form and coat the croquettes: Place the flour in a shallow dish, the eggs in a second dish and the bread crumbs in a third shallow dish. To make each croquette, scoop out 2 tablespoons of the chicken mixture and shape into a cylinder, about 2½ inches long, by rolling it between your palms. Roll the cylinders in the flour to coat all over; shake lightly on your fingers to remove any excess. Dip into the beaten eggs, letting the excess drip back into the dish. Roll in the bread crumbs until completely coated. Roll lightly between your palms to remove excess crumbs.

6. Fry the croquettes: Heat 2½ inches of oil in a deep-fat fryer or deep heavy saucepan to 375°. Fry the croquettes in batches without crowding for about 3 minutes, or until golden brown. Remove and drain on paper towels. Serve hot.

———

—F&W

COUNTRY FRIED CHICKEN

4 Servings

1 egg
⅓ cup milk
1 cup all-purpose flour
1 tablespoon salt
1 teaspoon freshly ground pepper
1 teaspoon paprika
One 3-pound chicken, cut into 8 pieces
1 pound lard
¼ cup rendered bacon fat

1. In a medium bowl, lightly beat the egg and milk together. Set aside.

2. In a brown paper or plastic bag, combine the flour, salt, pepper and paprika.

3. Dip each piece of chicken in the egg-milk mixture. Allow the excess to drip off, then place one piece at a time in the bag with the seasoned flour. Close the bag and shake it gently to evenly coat each piece. Remove the chicken and shake off the excess flour.

4. In a large skillet, preferably cast iron, melt the lard over moderate heat. (It should be about ½ inch deep.) Add the rendered bacon fat. Increase the heat to moderately high and bring the fat to 375°, just below the smoking point.

5. Carefully place the chicken pieces, skin-side down, in the hot fat. Cook for 15 minutes, adjusting the heat if necessary to keep the fat at about 375°. Turn each piece and cook for about 15 minutes longer, until the chicken is golden brown. Remove and drain, preferably on brown paper bags, before serving.

—*John Robert Massie*

SESAME OAT CHICKEN

Ground oats make a crunchy coating for boneless chicken breasts. They can be applied equally well to fish fillets. Sesame seeds, which provide more fiber, add a nice texture and flavor to chicken. Thyme is a delicious seasoning for poultry, but feel free to substitute any dried herb.

4 Servings

⅔ cup old-fashioned rolled oats
6 tablespoons olive, sunflower or safflower oil
1 teaspoon thyme
½ teaspoon freshly ground white pepper
1 tablespoon sesame seeds
1½ pounds skinless, boneless chicken breast
Salt (optional)
Lemon wedges, for accompaniment

1. In a food processor, process the rolled oats until finely ground.

2. In a large heavy skillet, preferably cast iron, heat about 3 tablespoons of the oil (the amount will depend on the size of the pan) over moderately high heat until hot but not smoking.

3. Meanwhile, on a plate or in a pie pan, toss together the ground oats, thyme, white pepper and sesame seeds. Dredge the chicken in the oat mixture, pressing to coat well.

4. Place half of the chicken breasts in the hot pan and fry until browned, 3 to 4 minutes per side. Drain on paper towels and blot lightly. Keep warm in a low oven. Repeat with the remaining oil and chicken. Serve with a sprinkling of salt if desired and the lemon wedges.

—*Tracey Seaman*

YAMATO'S SESAME CHICKEN

The combination of a ginger-spiked marinade and a crisp coating with the flour of sesame seeds gives this Japanese chicken dish its special character. For the full recipe, it s easier to use a deep-fryer: otherwise haul out your biggest frying pan.

6 Servings

½ cup soy sauce plus additional soy sauce for
*   serving*
2 tablespoons sugar
2 tablespoons sake or dry sherry
½ teaspoon grated fresh ginger
2 chickens (about 2½ to 3 pounds each),
*   hacked into 1½-inch pieces*
1½ cups cornstarch
6 tablespoons sesame seeds, toasted
2 cups oil
Hot mustard, for accompaniment

1. Blend the soy sauce, sugar, sake and ginger. Toss the chicken pieces in this marinade and let them sit for 30 to 40 minutes.

2. Combine the cornstarch and sesame seeds in a bowl or a large plate. Dredge the chicken pieces in the mixture. (Or use a paper bag: Put the cornstarch and sesame in the bag and toss the chicken in the bag.) Let the pieces sit for 10 minutes.

3. In a frying pan or deep-fryer, heat the oil to 360° to 370°. In batches, fry the chicken until it is golden brown, 2 to 3 minutes for boneless chicken, 5 to 8 minutes for chicken with bone. Do not overfill the pan. Drain on paper towels and keep warm in the oven until serving time.

4. Serve the chicken with little bowls of soy sauce and hot mustard for dipping.

—————

—Yamato, San Francisco

SESAME-FRIED LEMON CHICKEN

❡ Because mild and lemony flavors are predominant in this dish, a refreshing, fruity white, such as a Chenin Blanc, would be a good match. Look for a Dry Creek or Hacienda.

4 Servings

1½ cups milk
2½ tablespoons fresh lemon juice
4 large skinless, boneless chicken breast halves
*   or thighs (about 6 ounces each)*
¼ cup plus 2 tablespoons yellow cornmeal
¼ cup plus 2 tablespoons all-purpose flour
¼ cup plus 1½ teaspoons sesame seeds
2 teaspoons grated lemon zest
1 teaspoon salt
¼ teaspoon freshly ground pepper
3 tablespoons unsalted butter
3 tablespoons vegetable oil
¾ cup Chicken Stock (p. 10) or canned broth
¾ cup heavy cream
1 tablespoon chopped chives
Thin lemon slices, for garnish

1. In a shallow nonreactive dish, combine the milk and 1½ tablespoons of the lemon juice. Add the chicken and marinate, covered, in the refrigerator for about 1 hour, turning 2 or 3 times.

2. In a shallow dish, combine the cornmeal, flour, sesame seeds, lemon zest, salt and pepper. Remove the chicken from the milk but do not pat dry. Dredge the chicken in the cornmeal mixture to coat completely.

3. In a large skillet, melt the butter in the oil over moderately high heat. Add the chicken and fry, turning once, until deep golden brown on both sides, 8 to 10 minutes for breasts or 10 to 12 minutes for thighs. Drain on paper towels and transfer to a warm platter.

4. Pour off the fat from the skillet. Add the chicken stock and bring to a simmer over moderate heat, scraping up any browned bits in the pan. Add the cream, chives and the remaining

147

tablespoon lemon juice and boil until the gravy thickens slightly, 3 to 5 minutes. Season with additional salt and pepper to taste.

5. Garnish the chicken with lemon slices. Pass the gravy separately.

—*Melanie Barnard & Brooke Dojny*

FRIED CHICKEN WITH THYME-CREAM GRAVY

This thyme-flavored fried chicken is served with a thick gravy made from milk, onions and rice. It is delicious served with mashed potatoes or biscuits. Note that the chicken must sit overnight, so plan accordingly.

♟ Full-bodied California Chardonnay

4 Servings

1 bunch of thyme, large stems removed
4 whole chicken legs, divided into drumsticks
   and thighs
2¼ cups milk
2 tablespoons unsalted butter
1 medium onion, sliced
2 tablespoons rice, preferably basmati
1 tablespoon plus 1 teaspoon minced fresh
   thyme
⅓ cup all-purpose flour
1 teaspoon salt
½ teaspoon freshly ground pepper
⅔ cup corn oil
2 tablespoons heavy cream

1. Separate the bunch of thyme into sprigs and, using your fingers, rub them to release the oils. Place the chicken pieces in a medium bowl. Add 2 cups of the milk and the thyme sprigs. Cover and refrigerate overnight.

2. Let the chicken return to room temperature. Meanwhile, in a medium saucepan, melt the butter over moderate heat. Add the onion and reduce the heat to low. Cook until the onions are softened but not browned, about 10 minutes.

3. Add the rice to the onions in the saucepan. Strain the milk in which the chicken has marinated into the pan. Increase the heat to moderate and bring just to a simmer. Reduce the heat to low, cover and simmer, stirring occasionally, until the rice is soft, about 25 minutes.

4. Transfer the mixture to a blender and puree until smooth, about 20 seconds. Return the gravy to the pan and stir in 1 teaspoon of the minced thyme. Remove the gravy from the heat and set aside.

5. Preheat the oven to 400°. Pat the chicken pieces dry with paper towels. In a shallow bowl, combine the flour, ½ teaspoon of the salt, ¼ teaspoon of the pepper and the remaining 1 tablespoon minced thyme. Dredge half of the chicken pieces in the seasoned flour. In a large heavy skillet, heat the corn oil over high heat. Add the coated chicken, reduce the heat to moderate and cook, turning, until browned and crisp, about 5 minutes on each side. Transfer to a baking sheet and repeat with the remaining chicken.

6. Bake the chicken in the preheated oven until white throughout but still moist and juicy, 12 to 15 minutes. Set aside, loosely covered with foil to keep warm.

7. Add the remaining ¼ cup milk and the cream to the gravy. Season with the remaining ½ teaspoon salt and ¼ teaspoon pepper. Reheat over low heat and pour over the chicken.

—*Marcia Kiesel*

PEANUT-FRIED DRUMSTICKS WITH CURRIED CUCUMBERS

Double dipping these drumsticks ensures an even coating, and chopped peanuts give them a special crunch. They're started in a skillet and finished in the oven to avoid deep-frying.

8 Servings

1⅓ cups all-purpose flour
3 tablespoons plus 1½ teaspoons curry powder
4½ teaspoons dried dillweed
2½ teaspoons freshly ground black pepper
2 teaspoons salt
16 chicken drumsticks, skinned and patted dry
1 jar (8 ounces) unsalted dry-roasted peanuts
1½ teaspoons crushed hot red pepper
2 eggs
2 tablespoons milk
1 cup olive oil
2 European cucumbers
2 medium shallots, minced
1 teaspoon dill seeds

1. Preheat the oven to 400°. In a medium bowl, combine the flour with 3 tablespoons of the curry powder, 4 teaspoons of the dillweed, 2 teaspoons of the black pepper and 1½ teaspoons of the salt. Dredge the drumsticks in the flour mixture to coat thoroughly. Shake off the excess flour and set the chicken aside on a rack. Reserve the flour mixture.

2. In a food processor, combine the peanuts, hot pepper and 2 tablespoons of the reserved flour mixture. Pulse until the nuts are finely chopped, then transfer the mixture to a shallow bowl.

3. In another shallow bowl, beat the eggs with the milk. Dredge the drumsticks in the flour mixture once more, then dip them in the egg mixture and then into the ground peanuts, turning to coat completely.

4. Set aside 1½ tablespoons of the olive oil. In a large, high-sided skillet, heat half of the remaining oil over moderately high heat until it just begins to smoke. Add half of the drumsticks and fry, turning, until evenly browned, 10 to 12 minutes. Be careful not to break the delicate crust as you turn the legs. Transfer the chicken to a clean rack set over a baking sheet. Repeat with the remaining oil and drumsticks.

5. Bake the chicken on the rack in the middle of the oven for 35 to 40 minutes, until tender when pierced with a fork.

6. Meanwhile, cut the cucumbers lengthwise into eighths, then slice them crosswise at 1½-inch intervals.

7. In a large skillet, heat the reserved 1½ tablespoons olive oil over moderate heat. Add the shallots and cook until translucent, 2 to 3 minutes. Add the cucumbers and sprinkle with the dill seeds and the remaining 1½ teaspoons curry powder and ½ teaspoon each dillweed, black pepper and salt. Cover and cook, stirring frequently, until the cucumbers are tender, 4 to 6 minutes. Remove from the heat.

8. To serve, reheat the cucumbers if necessary. Mound the cucumbers on a serving platter and arrange the drumsticks alongside.

———————

—*Bob Chambers*

SPICY CHICKEN WITH SPRING PEANUT SAUCE

Great for picnics. Serve this piquant chicken with fresh radishes, scallions, tomatoes and cucumbers, sprinkled lightly with black pepper and coarse salt.

🍷 English ale, such as Samuel Smith

4 Servings

½ cup finely chopped unsalted dry-roasted
  peanuts
6 slices of bacon—cooked until crisp, drained
  and finely chopped
¼ teaspoon coarse (kosher) salt
½ to 1 teaspoon crushed hot red pepper,
  to taste
2 eggs, separated
4 skinless, boneless chicken breast halves
  (about 5 ounces each), pounded ⅜ inch thick
½ cup corn oil
Spring Peanut Sauce (recipe follows)
Lemon wedges, for accompaniment

1. Combine the chopped nuts, bacon, salt and hot pepper flakes.

2. Beat the egg whites until soft peaks form; then beat in the egg yolks. Spread a thick layer of egg on one side of each chicken breast. Sprinkle about 1½ tablespoons of the nut-bacon mixture over each and press firmly so that it adheres. Refrigerate for 30 minutes.

3. Repeat to coat the second side of each chicken breast with the nut mixture. Chill for 15 minutes longer.

4. In a large skillet, heat the oil until shimmering. Add the breasts and cook over moderately high heat for about 5 minutes until the nuts are brown on the bottom. Turn carefully and brown on the second side for 5 minutes. Drain on paper towels. Serve hot or at room temperature with the Spring Peanut Sauce and lemon wedges.

—Anne Disrude

SPRING PEANUT SAUCE
Makes About 1½ Cups

3 tablespoons smooth peanut butter
1 cup chicken broth
1 tablespoon fresh lemon juice
1 teaspoon Oriental sesame oil
2 scallions, minced
1 large garlic clove, crushed through a press
¼ teaspoon coarse (kosher) salt
¼ teaspoon freshly ground black pepper
⅛ to ¼ teaspoon hot pepper sauce, to taste
½ to 1 teaspoon crushed hot red pepper,
  to taste

Put the peanut butter in a medium bowl and gradually stir in the chicken broth until smooth. Add the lemon juice, sesame oil, scallions, garlic, salt, black pepper, hot sauce and hot pepper. Cover and let stand at room temperature to let the flavors develop for at least 1 hour. *(The sauce can be made 1 day ahead. Cover and refrigerate. Let return to room temperature before serving.)*

—Anne Disrude

CRISPY CHICKEN STRIPS WITH LEMON-SOY DIPPING SAUCE

These quickly sautéed strips of chicken breast are tender and succulent. Their flavor is enhanced by a zippy lemon-soy dipping sauce.

4 Servings

1½ pounds skinless, boneless chicken breast
4 tablespoons all-purpose flour
About 4 tablespoons vegetable oil
½ teaspoon freshly ground pepper
Lemon-Soy Dipping Sauce (recipe follows)

1. Cut the chicken into 3-by-½-inch strips.

2. In a paper or plastic bag, combine the chicken with the flour, shake to coat the chicken.

3. In a large heavy skillet, heat 2 tablespoons of the oil. When the oil is hot but not smoking, add as much of the floured chicken as will fit in a single layer without crowding. Sauté over moderately high heat until crisp and golden brown on the bottom, 1 to 2 minutes. Turn and cook the remaining side until just cooked, about 15 seconds. Drain on paper towels. Fry the remaining chicken in batches, adding more oil as necessary.

4. Sprinkle the chicken with the pepper and serve with individual bowls of the Lemon-Soy Dipping Sauce.

———————

—Jim Fobel

LEMON-SOY DIPPING SAUCE
Makes About 1 Cup

½ cup soy sauce
¼ cup fresh lemon juice
1 garlic clove, minced or crushed through
* a press*
1 tablespoon sugar
1 tablespoon Oriental sesame oil
2 scallions, minced (about 3 tablespoons)

In a small bowl, combine the soy sauce, lemon juice, garlic, sugar, sesame oil and scallions. Stir until the sugar dissolves.

———————

—Jim Fobel

STIR-FRY OF CHICKEN WITH ASPARAGUS
2 Servings

½ egg white (see Note)
1½ teaspoons dry vermouth
1½ teaspoons cornstarch
½ teaspoon coarse (kosher) salt
½ pound skinless, boneless chicken breast, cut
* into 1-inch squares*
1 teaspoon vegetable oil
2 tablespoons olive oil
1 tablespoon minced parsley
1 tablespoon minced onion
2 medium garlic cloves, minced
Pinch of crushed hot red pepper
1¼ cups 2-inch pieces of thin asparagus
¼ teaspoon table salt
Pinch of sugar
1 tablespoon minced black olives
½ teaspoon grated orange zest
¼ teaspoon basil
Freshly ground black pepper, to taste

1. In a medium bowl, whisk together the egg white, vermouth, cornstarch and coarse salt. Add the chicken and toss to mix well. Cover and refrigerate for at least 1 and up to 12 hours.

2. Add the vegetable oil to a large pot of simmering water. Add the chicken and cook, stirring gently, until almost cooked through but still pink in the center, about 1 minute. Drain and rinse off any excess cornstarch under cold running water; pat dry and set aside. *(The recipe can be prepared up to 3 hours ahead to this point. Refrigerate, covered. Let the precooked chicken pieces return to room temperature before proceeding.)*

3. Warm a wok or large heavy skillet over high heat until a drop of water evaporates on contact. Pour in the olive oil in a thin stream around the edge; it will smoke immediately.

4. Add the parsley, onion, garlic and hot pepper all at once. Cook, stirring, until fragrant, about 10 seconds; do not let the garlic brown.

5. Add the asparagus to the wok. Sprinkle with the salt and sugar and toss until almost crisp-tender, 1½ to 2 minutes. (If the asparagus begins to dry out or burn, add 1 tablespoon of water.)

6. Add the precooked chicken to the wok and toss over heat until warmed through, about 30 seconds.

7. Add the olives, orange zest, basil and black pepper and toss to blend the flavors, about 20 seconds. Remove from the heat and season to taste with more salt and pepper if desired.

NOTE: To obtain half an egg white, lightly beat 1 whole egg white and then measure out 1 tablespoon.

———————

—F&W

CHICKEN STIR-FRY WITH CELERY, CARROTS AND DILL

2 Servings

½ egg white (see Note)
1½ teaspoons dry vermouth
1½ teaspoons cornstarch
½ teaspoon coarse (kosher) salt
½ pound skinless, boneless chicken breast, cut
  into 1-inch squares
1 teaspoon vegetable oil
2 tablespoons olive oil
1 tablespoon minced parsley
1 tablespoon minced onion
2 medium garlic cloves, minced
Pinch of crushed hot red pepper
1¼ cups sliced celery
¼ cup julienned carrot
¼ teaspoon table salt
Pinch of sugar
2 tablespoons minced fresh dill
Freshly ground black pepper, to taste

1. In a medium bowl, whisk together the egg white, vermouth, cornstarch and coarse salt. Add the chicken and toss to mix well. Cover and re-

frigerate for at least 1 and up to 12 hours.

2. Add the vegetable oil to a large pot of simmering water. Add the chicken and cook, stirring gently, until almost cooked through but still pink in the center, about 1 minute. Drain and rinse off any excess cornstarch under cold running water; pat dry and set aside. *(The recipe can be prepared up to 3 hours ahead to this point. Refrigerate, covered. Let the precooked chicken pieces return to room temperature before proceeding.)*

3. Warm a wok or large heavy skillet over high heat until a drop of water evaporates on contact. Pour in the olive oil in a thin stream around the edge; it will smoke immediately.

4. Add the parsley, onion, garlic and hot pepper all at once. Cook, stirring, until fragrant, about 10 seconds; do not let the garlic brown.

5. Add the celery and carrot to the wok. Sprinkle with the salt and sugar and toss until almost crisp-tender, 1½ to 2 minutes. (If the vegetables begin to dry out or burn, add 1 tablespoon of water.)

6. Add the precooked chicken to the wok and toss over heat until warmed through, about 30 seconds.

7. Add the dill and black pepper and toss to blend the flavors, about 20 seconds. Remove from the heat and season to taste with more salt and pepper if desired.

NOTE: To obtain half an egg white, lightly beat 1 whole egg white and then measure out 1 tablespoon.

———————

—Anne Disrude

*Above, Chicken, Sausage, Sweet
Peppers and Olives (p. 139). Left,
Chicken Breasts with Artichoke Hearts,
Olives and Bacon (p. 180).*

Pan-Fried Noodles with Chicken and Chinese Vegetables (p. 163).

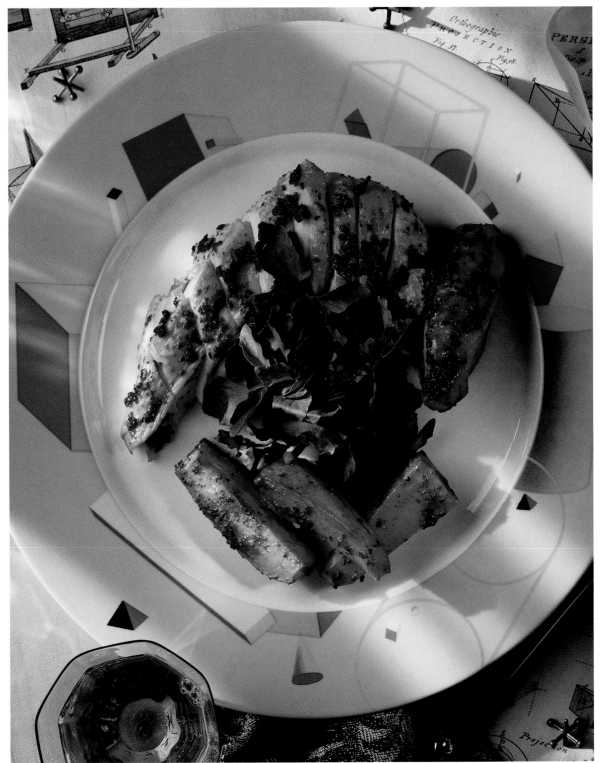

Roasted Chicken with Achiote and Garlic Sauce (p. 61).

*Above, Citrus Cornish Hens
(p. 77). Right, Spicy Stuffed Chicken
Breasts (p. 111).*

CHICKEN STIR-FRY WITH SUMMER SQUASHES

Light and summery, this colorful green and yellow dish needs only some sliced ripe red tomatoes and good bread.

♟ Chenin Blanc, such as Dry Creek

4 Servings

1¼ pounds skinless, boneless chicken breast
1 egg white
1 tablespoon dry white wine
¾ teaspoon salt
1 tablespoon cornstarch
3 tablespoons olive oil
½ medium onion, finely chopped
2 or 3 garlic cloves, finely chopped
½ pound small zucchini (about 2), cut into
  2-by-¼-inch julienne strips
½ pound small yellow summer squash (about
  2), cut into 2-by-¼-inch julienne strips
¼ teaspoon freshly ground pepper
¼ cup coarsely chopped fresh basil
Fresh spinach leaves, for garnish

1. Remove the small fillet section underneath each breast and cut it lengthwise into strips ¼ inch wide. Cut the chicken breasts crosswise on the diagonal into long strips about ¼ inch wide.

2. Combine the egg white, wine, ½ teaspoon of the salt and the cornstarch in a food processor and mix until it becomes a very smooth emulsion, about 1 minute, scraping down the sides after 30 seconds.

3. Pour the egg white mixture into a bowl, add the chicken and toss to coat. Let marinate, covered, in the refrigerator for 3 hours or overnight. *(The recipe can be prepared ahead to this point.)*

4. When ready to assemble the dish, bring a large pot of water to a boil, reduce to a simmer and add the chicken, stirring gently to separate the pieces. Simmer until the chicken is almost done but still slightly pink in the center, about

2 minutes. Do not let the water boil. Drain into a colander and rinse under cold running water to cool; drain well. Dry on paper towels.

5. In a wok or large skillet, heat the oil. Add the onion and sauté over moderate heat for 1 minute. Add the garlic and cook for 30 seconds. Add the zucchini and yellow squash and stir-fry until just warmed through, about 3 minutes. Add the chicken and stir-fry to warm through and finish cooking, about 1 minute. Add the remaining ¼ teaspoon salt, the pepper and basil and toss well; then turn out onto a spinach-lined platter. Serve warm or at room temperature.

———————

—Anne Disrude

SZECHUAN STIR-FRIED LEEKS AND CHICKEN

♟ California Gewürztraminer, such as Rutherford Hill

3 to 4 Servings

3 medium leeks (white and about 1 inch of
  tender green)
3 tablespoons peanut oil
4 garlic cloves, minced
1 pound skinless, boneless chicken breast, cut
  into strips
½ green or red bell pepper, cut into thin
  strips
1 cup (4 ounces) thinly sliced mushrooms
1 teaspoon minced fresh ginger
1 teaspoon crushed hot red pepper
1 tablespoon sugar
1 tablespoon rice vinegar
2 tablespoons Oriental sesame oil
¼ cup chicken broth

1. Cut the leeks into thin slices crosswise on the diagonal. Wash thoroughly and drain well; dry on paper towels.

2. In a wok, heat the peanut oil over moderately high heat until shimmering; reduce the heat to moderate. Add the garlic and sauté for a few

seconds, until fragrant. Add the chicken and stir-fry until the chicken turns white, about 1 minute.

3. Add the leeks, bell pepper, mushrooms, ginger and hot pepper. Continue to stir-fry for 1 minute longer, until the vegetables are barely tender. Add the sugar, vinegar, sesame oil and broth; increase the heat to moderately high and continue to cook until the vegetables are just tender, about 2 minutes.

—*Geraldine Duncann*

STIR-FRY OF CHICKEN, RED PEPPERS, ARUGULA AND PROSCIUTTO

The marinating and precooking techniques used in this recipe can also be used for any poultry, fish or shellfish stir-fry.

Remember that except for the final cooking, all of the chopping, shredding, julienning and marinating can be done in advance. To make the final frying easier, have all the prepared ingredients that get added together in a single bowl. This way adding them is fast and simple.

🍷 California Sauvignon Blanc, such as Kendall-Jackson

2 Servings

½ egg white (see Note)
1½ teaspoons dry vermouth
1½ teaspoons cornstarch
½ teaspoon coarse (kosher) salt
½ pound skinless, boneless chicken breast, cut into 1-inch squares
1 teaspoon vegetable oil
2 tablespoons olive oil
1 tablespoon minced parsley
1 tablespoon minced onion
2 medium garlic cloves, minced
Pinch of crushed hot red pepper
1 large red bell pepper, cut into ¼-inch-wide strips or ¾-inch squares (about 1¼ cups)
¼ teaspoon table salt
Pinch of sugar
1 cup shredded arugula
1 tablespoon finely chopped prosciutto
¼ teaspoon oregano
Freshly ground black pepper, to taste

1. In a medium bowl, whisk together the egg white, vermouth, cornstarch and coarse salt. Add the chicken and toss to mix well. Cover and refrigerate for at least 1 and up to 12 hours.

2. Add the vegetable oil to a large pot of simmering water. Add the chicken and cook, stirring gently, until almost cooked through but still pink in the center, about 1 minute. Drain and rinse off any excess cornstarch under cold running water; pat dry and set aside. *(The recipe can be prepared up to 3 hours ahead to this point. Refrigerate, covered. Let the precooked chicken pieces return to room temperature before proceeding.)*

3. Warm a wok or large heavy skillet over high heat until a drop of water evaporates on contact. Pour in the olive oil in a thin stream around the edge; it will smoke immediately.

4. Add the parsley, onion, garlic and hot pepper all at once. Cook, stirring, until fragrant, about 10 seconds; do not let the garlic brown.

5. Add the red bell pepper to the wok. Sprinkle with the table salt and sugar and toss until almost crisp-tender, 1½ to 2 minutes. (If the bell pepper begins to dry out or burn, add 1 tablespoon of water.)

6. Add the precooked chicken to the wok and toss over heat until warmed through, about 30 seconds.

7. Add the arugula and prosciutto, oregano and black pepper and toss to blend the flavors, about 20 seconds. Remove from the heat and season to taste with more salt and pepper if desired.

NOTE: To obtain half an egg white, lightly beat 1 whole egg white and then measure out 1 tablespoon.

—*Anne Disrude*

HOT-AND-SOUR CHICKEN WITH RED AND GREEN PEPPERS

Serve this spicy chicken dish with rice.

4 Servings

3 tablespoons rice vinegar
2 tablespoons soy sauce
1 tablespoon sugar
2 teaspoons cornstarch
¾ teaspoon crushed hot red pepper
1 teaspoon Oriental sesame oil
1 pound skinless, boneless chicken breast
* halves, sliced crosswise into ¼-inch strips*
2 tablespoons peanut oil
1 tablespoon minced fresh ginger
1 large onion, sliced lengthwise into
* ¼-inch strips*
1 large red bell pepper, sliced lengthwise into
* ¼-inch strips*
1 large green bell pepper, sliced lengthwise into
* ¼-inch strips*
⅓ cup Chicken Stock (p. 10) or low-sodium
* canned broth*
½ teaspoon salt
¼ teaspoon freshly ground black pepper

1. In a medium bowl, whisk the rice vinegar, soy sauce, sugar, cornstarch and hot pepper. Whisk in the sesame oil. Add the chicken and toss to coat. Let marinate at room temperature for about 5 minutes.

2. Meanwhile, heat a large cast-iron skillet or wok over high heat. Add the peanut oil, then add the ginger and onion and stir-fry until the onion is slightly softened, about 1 minute. Add the red and green bell peppers and stir-fry until slightly softened, about 1 minute. Add the chicken and its marinade and the chicken stock and stir-fry until the chicken is just cooked through, about 3 minutes. Season with the salt and black pepper and serve hot.

—*Jim Fobel*

DILLED CHICKEN AND VEGETABLE STIR-FRY IN PITA BREAD

Makes 3 Sandwiches

3 tablespoons peanut oil
½ pound skinless, boneless chicken breast, cut
* into ½-inch dice*
½ medium onion, thinly sliced
1 celery rib, thinly sliced
1 small garlic clove, minced
8 medium mushrooms, quartered
3 tablespoons minced fresh dill
½ teaspoon fresh lemon juice
4 drops of hot pepper sauce, or to taste
½ teaspoon salt
¼ teaspoon freshly ground pepper
1 medium tomato—peeled, seeded and
* coarsely chopped*
3 pita bread rounds, warmed

1. In a medium skillet, heat 1 tablespoon of the oil until almost smoking. Add the chicken and toss over high heat to coat with oil; reduce the heat to moderate. Cook, stirring, until lightly browned, about 2 minutes. Remove the chicken to a medium bowl.

2. Add the onion to the skillet and stir-fry over moderate heat until soft, about 3 minutes. Add the celery and garlic and cook for 30 seconds longer. Add to the chicken.

3. Add the remaining 2 tablespoons oil to the skillet and heat until almost smoking. Add the mushrooms and stir-fry over moderately high heat until well browned, about 3 minutes.

4. Add the mushrooms to the vegetables and chicken and toss with 2 tablespoons of the dill, the lemon juice, hot sauce, salt and pepper.

5. In a separate bowl, toss the remaining 1 tablespoon dill with the chopped tomato and a pinch of salt.

6. To assemble, fill the pita breads with the chicken mixture, then top with the dilled tomato.

———

—F&W

VIETNAMESE CHICKEN

Serve this fragrant chicken dish with steamed long-grain rice or with a short-grained Oriental variety.

6 to 8 Servings

*3 stalks lemon grass★ or 1 teaspoon grated
　lemon zest*
*2 pounds chicken thighs, skinned and boned to
　yield 1 pound meat*
1 pound skinless, boneless chicken breast
5 garlic cloves, finely chopped
4 tablespoons fish sauce (nuoc mam)★
3½ tablespoons sugar
½ teaspoon freshly black ground pepper
1 teaspoon fresh lemon juice
1 tablespoon peanut oil
½ teaspoon crushed hot red pepper
★Available at Asian markets

1. If using dried lemon grass, soak the stalks in hot water for 2 hours.

2. Cut the chicken into 1-inch pieces. Finely chop 2 teaspoons of the bulblike portion of the lemon grass's inner stalk and combine it (or the lemon zest) with half the garlic, 3 tablespoons of the fish sauce, ½ tablespoon of sugar and the black pepper; pour over the chicken. Cover and marinate for up to 1 hour.

3. Meanwhile, combine the remaining 3 tablespoons sugar and 2 tablespoons cold water in a small saucepan and cook over moderate heat for 3 minutes, or until the mixture begins to brown. Stir constantly for 1 minute more, or until the sugar is amber and steaming. Remove from the heat immediately and stir in the lemon juice;

set aside. (If necessary, the caramel can be resoftened by carefully warming over low heat.)

4. In a wok or heavy skillet, heat the oil over high heat. Add the remaining garlic and stir for about 10 seconds. Immediately add the chicken and marinade and cook 3 to 5 minutes. Reduce the heat to moderate and add the remaining 1 tablespoon fish sauce, the hot pepper and 2 teaspoons of the caramel mixture. Continue to cook, stirring, for 5 more minutes.

———

—F&W

CHICKEN IN SWEET
WINE SAUCE

Although not typical of Chinese cuisine in general, this wine-flavored dish is common to the province of Fukien and the Hakka who live there. Its special character comes not from potable wine, but from the fermented, red-stained wine lees, which are left at the bottom of the crock when rice wine is put aside to age. The chicken should marinate for at least 8 hours, so plan accordingly.

❧ Rheinphalze Spätlese

2 Servings

¾ pound skinless, boneless chicken breast
1 large egg white (2 tablespoons)
1 teaspoon coarse (kosher) salt
*3 tablespoons plus 1 teaspoon Chinese rice
　wine or dry sherry*
1 tablespoon plus 2 teaspoons cornstarch
2 teaspoons Chinese wine paste (see Note)
*½ cup plus 1 tablespoon rich, unsalted chicken
　stock or canned low-sodium broth*
¼ teaspoon Oriental sesame oil
2 tablespoons sugar, or more to taste
*2 tablespoons plus 1 teaspoon corn or
　peanut oil*
⅓ cup thinly sliced scallion
1 tablespoon minced fresh ginger
1 tablespoon minced garlic

1. Cut the chicken into ¾-inch cubes and place in a shallow bowl. In a blender, combine the egg white, salt, 1 tablespoon of the wine and 1 tablespoon of the cornstarch; mix until smooth, about 1 minute. Scrape this marinade over the chicken and toss well until coated. Wrap tightly and refrigerate for 8 to 24 hours; the longer the chicken marinates, the plumper and more flavorful it will be.

2. In a small bowl, blend the wine paste, the remaining 2 tablespoons plus 1 teaspoon wine, ½ cup of the stock and the sesame oil, mashing the paste to dissolve it thoroughly. Add the sugar; taste and add more if required to obtain a full, sweet flavor. Set this sauce mixture aside.

3. About 10 minutes before serving, bring 1 quart of water and 1 teaspoon of the corn oil to a simmer over high heat. Reduce the heat so the water is just below the simmer. Stir the chicken briskly with your fingers to loosen the pieces, then slide them into the water. Stir gently until the chicken is mostly white but some parts are still translucent, about 15 to 20 seconds. Immediately drain into a colander.

4. Heat a wok or large skillet over high heat until hot enough to evaporate a bead of water on contact. Add the remaining 2 tablespoons corn oil; reduce the heat to moderately high. Add the scallion, ginger and garlic. Stir-fry until fully fragrant, about 10 seconds, adjusting the heat so the mixture sizzles without scorching; add more oil if necessary to prevent sticking. Add the chicken and toss to combine. Add the sauce mixture and bring to a boil, stirring for about 30 seconds.

5. Dissolve the remaining 2 teaspoons cornstarch in the remaining 1 tablespoon stock. Add to the wok and stir until the sauce turns glossy and thickens, about 10 seconds.

6. Transfer the chicken to a platter and serve with rice or a hot loaf of good French bread.

NOTE: Wine paste is vailable at Chinese markets; it must be kept refrigerated.

———————————

—*Barbara Tropp*

CHICKEN SOONG

This popular Cantonese dish is eaten much like Moo Shu Pork, using a lettuce leaf, instead of a pancake, as a wrapper for the filling.

6 Servings

½ pound skinless, boneless chicken breast,
  partially frozen
1 egg white
2 tablespoons medium-dry sherry
1½ teaspoons water chestnut powder★
  or cornstarch
½ ounce dried Chinese mushrooms★ (about 4)
2 tablespoons hoisin sauce★
1 tablespoon dark soy sauce★
¼ teaspoon freshly ground pepper
2 cups peanut oil
⅓ cup minced shallots
¼ cup diced (¼-inch) carrots
1 medium garlic clove, minced
1 teaspoon minced fresh ginger
¼ cup diced (¼-inch) red bell pepper
½ cup diced (¼-inch) water chestnuts,
  preferably fresh★
½ cup diced (¼-inch) snow peas
1 teaspoon Oriental sesame oil
¼ cup pine nuts, lightly toasted
1 head of iceberg lettuce—cored and cut in
  half, with individual leaves loosened
★Available at Asian markets

1. Cut the chicken into small dice.

2. In a medium bowl, combine the chicken with the egg white, ½ tablespoon of the sherry and the water chestnut powder. Stir to coat. Cover and refrigerate for at least 1 hour, or up to 12 hours.

3. Rinse the mushrooms under cold running water. Put them in a bowl and cover them with 2 cups of cold water. Soak until soft, about 1 hour. Squeeze the excess moisture out of the mushrooms. Remove the stems and discard. Cut the mushroom caps into ¼-inch dice.

4. In a small bowl, combine the remaining 1½ tablespoons sherry, the hoisin sauce, soy sauce and pepper. Blend well.

5. Place a wok over high heat for about 1½ minutes. Pour in the oil and heat to 325°. Stir the marinated chicken and carefully add it to the hot oil. Cook, stirring constantly, until the chicken turns opaque, about 1 minute. Turn off the heat. Pour the chicken and the oil into a colander set over a large bowl. Shake to drain off as much oil as possible. Reserve 1 tablespoon of the oil. If desired, the remaining oil can be strained and reserved for other frying.

6. Put the wok over moderate heat and add the 1 tablespoon reserved oil along with the shallots, carrots and mushrooms. Stir-fry for 1 minute. Add the garlic and ginger and stir-fry for 1 minute longer.

7. Increase the heat to high and add the bell pepper, water chestnuts and snow peas. Stir-fry for 1 minute and then remove the vegetables from the wok.

8. Return the wok to high heat. Stir the seasoning sauce and add it to the wok. Cook, stirring, for 30 seconds.

9. Return the cooked chicken to the wok. Stir-fry for about 30 seconds. Add the cooked vegetable mixture to the wok and stir-fry for 30 seconds longer, until all the ingredients are heated through.

10. Turn off the heat and add the sesame oil. Stir to blend. Transfer the mixture to a heated platter. Sprinkle the pine nuts on top. Serve hot, with the leaves of lettuce.

—*Karen Lee & Alaxandra Branyon*

STIR-FRIED CHICKEN AND MELON

This recipe contains both honeydew and cantaloupe, which the Chinese call by the same name, *mut gua,* literally "honey melon." The melons should be ripe and sweet but very firm.

❦ Light, fruity white, such as Chateau Ste. Michelle Chenin Blanc

6 Servings

2 teaspoons oyster sauce
1½ teaspoons dry white wine
1 teaspoon light soy sauce
1 teaspoon Oriental sesame oil
¾ teaspoon grated fresh ginger
2 teaspoons cornstarch
¾ teaspoon sugar
¾ teaspoon salt
Pinch of freshly ground white pepper
½ pound skinless, boneless chicken breast, cut across the grain on the diagonal into 2-inch slices ¼ inch thick
3 tablespoons peanut oil
½ cup snow peas, cut crosswise on the diagonal into 3 pieces each
4 scallions (white part only), cut into ½-inch pieces
½ honeydew melon, cut into 1-inch-square pieces ¼ inch thick (about 1¼ cups)
½ cantaloupe, cut into 1-inch-square pieces ¼ inch thick (about 1¼ cups)
1 tablespoon minced garlic

1. In a medium bowl, combine the oyster sauce, wine, soy sauce, sesame oil, ginger, cornstarch, sugar, ½ teaspoon of the salt and the white pepper. Add the chicken, stir well and let marinate at room temperature for 1 hour.

2. Place a wok over high heat for about 45 seconds. Add 1 tablespoon of the peanut oil. Swirl it around with a metal spatula to coat the sides of the wok. Add the remaining ¼ teaspoon salt and heat until a wisp of white smoke appears. Add the snow peas and scallions. Cook, stirring constantly, until the snow peas turn bright green, about 1 minute. Add the honeydew and cantaloupe and stir-fry just until hot, about 1 minute. Remove from the wok and set aside.

3. Carefully rinse the wok and spatula with very hot water. Wipe dry. Reheat the wok over high heat. Add the remaining 2 tablespoons peanut oil, swirl again with the spatula to coat the wok and heat until a wisp of white smoke appears. Add the garlic and stir-fry until light brown, about 30 seconds. Add the chicken, spreading it out in a thin layer. Cook without stirring for 1 minute. Turn the chicken over, stir and cook until white, 30 to 60 seconds. Add the reserved melons and vegetables. Stir-fry until well mixed and hot, 30 to 60 seconds. Serve at once.

———————————

—*Eileen Yin-Fei Lo*

PAN-FRIED NOODLES WITH CHICKEN AND CHINESE VEGETABLES

This traditional preparation from Shanghai is often referred to as double-fried noodles, because the noodles are fried on both sides.

❦ To balance the soy-flavored sauce and refresh the palate, choose a California Riesling, such as Jekel, or a German white, such as Sichel Novum.

6 Servings

½ pound fine fresh Chinese egg noodles★ or
  fresh or dried capellini
6 ounces skinless, boneless chicken breast, cut
  into thin strips
2 teaspoons Oriental sesame oil
1¾ teaspoons sugar
1½ teaspoons distilled white vinegar
1½ teaspoons dry white wine

¾ teaspoon cornstarch
¼ teaspoon freshly ground white pepper
½ teaspoon light soy sauce
½ teaspoon salt
2 teaspoons dark soy sauce★
⅔ cup Chicken Stock (p. 10) or canned broth
6 to 7 tablespoons peanut oil
1 teaspoon grated fresh ginger
1 garlic clove, minced
½ cup snow peas (about 2 ounces), cut
  crosswise on the diagonal into thin strips
3 water chestnuts, preferably fresh,★ cut into
  thin strips
¼ cup bamboo shoots, cut into thin strips
2 scallions, cut into ½-inch lengths (white part
  quartered lengthwise)
★Available at Asian markets

1. In a large pot of boiling water, cook the noodles until tender but firm, about 15 seconds for fresh or about 2 minutes for dried. Run cold water into the pot and drain the noodles. Return to the pot, add cold water and drain again, turning and separating the noodles occasionally until they are quite dry, about 30 minutes. Dry completely on a kitchen towel.

2. In a medium bowl, combine the chicken with 1 teaspoon of the sesame oil, ¾ teaspoon of the sugar, ½ teaspoon of the vinegar, 1 teaspoon of the white wine, ¼ teaspoon of the cornstarch, ⅛ teaspoon of the white pepper, the light soy sauce and the salt. Let marinate for 30 minutes.

3. In a small bowl, combine the remaining 1 teaspoon each of sesame oil, sugar and vinegar, ½ teaspoon wine, ½ teaspoon cornstarch and ⅛ teaspoon white pepper with the dark soy sauce and chicken stock. Set this sauce aside.

4. Pour ¼ cup of the peanut oil into a 9- or 10-inch cast-iron frying pan and set over high heat. When a wisp of white smoke appears, arrange the noodles in the pan in an even layer that covers the entire bottom. Cook, rotating the pan on the burner, until the bottom is evenly browned and crisp, about 4 minutes.

5. Slide the noodle cake onto a dish. Place another dish on top of it and invert so that the cooked side is up. Slide the cake back into the pan and cook, adding another 1 tablespoon oil, if necessary, to prevent sticking, until the second side is browned, about 2 minutes. Turn out the noodle cake onto a large plate or platter and cover loosely with foil to keep warm.

6. Heat a wok over high heat for 30 seconds. Add 2 tablespoons of the peanut oil and swirl with a spatula to coat the pan. Add the ginger and garlic. Cook, stirring, until the garlic begins to brown, about 45 seconds. Add the chicken with its marinade and spread in a thin layer. Cook for 2 minutes, turn over and mix well.

7. Add the snow peas, water chestnuts, bamboo shoots and scallions. Cook, stirring occasionally, until the vegetables soften slightly, about 3 minutes. Make a well in the center and stir in the sauce. Cook until the sauce thickens, about 1 minute. Spoon the chicken, vegetables and sauce on top of the browned noodle cake. Serve by cutting the cake into wedges.

———————————

—*Eileen Yin-Fei Lo*

Braises,
Poaches
and
Steams

BRAISED CAPON WITH TRUFFLES

🍷 Margaux, such as Giscours, or full-bodied California Chardonnay, such as Matanzas Creek

8 Servings

2½ sticks (10 ounces) unsalted butter, softened
4 medium onions, finely diced
4 medium carrots, finely diced
4 large celery ribs, finely diced
2 large leeks (white and tender green),
  finely diced
¼ pound Black Forest ham, finely diced
  (about 1 cup)
1 teaspoon salt
½ teaspoon freshly ground pepper
⅛ teaspoon freshly grated nutmeg
One 7- to 8-pound capon—neck, gizzard and
  large pieces of fat reserved
½ lemon
2 medium black truffles, preferably fresh,
  thinly sliced
2½ cups Rich Chicken Stock (p. 11)
7 ounces truffle essence★
2 tablespoons all-purpose flour
★Available at specialty food shops

1. In a large oval flameproof casserole, melt 6 tablespoons of the butter over moderate heat. Add the onions, carrots, celery, leeks and ham. Cook until the vegetables are softened but not browned, about 15 minutes. Add ½ teaspoon of the salt, ¼ teaspoon of the pepper and the nutmeg.

2. In a small saucepan, melt 1 stick of the butter. Remove the butter from the heat and let cool to lukewarm.

3. Meanwhile, rub the capon all over with the cut lemon. With your fingers, carefully loosen the skin from the breast, thighs and legs without tearing it. Stuff 4 tablespoons of the softened butter under the skin and massage it into the bird. Sprinkle the inside and outside of the bird with the remaining ½ teaspoon salt and ¼ teaspoon pepper.

4. Reserve 6 slices of truffle for decoration. Slip the remainder under the skin of the bird, working them carefully onto the legs, thighs and breast. Truss the bird and place it on top of the vegetables in the casserole. Tuck a sheet of cheesecloth over and around the bird. Pour the lukewarm butter over the top of the bird, completely moistening the cheesecloth. *(The recipe can be prepared ahead to this point. Cover and refrigerate overnight. Let return to room temperature before proceeding.)*

5. Preheat the oven to 325°. Lay a piece of parchment paper or buttered brown paper over the bird and cover with a tight-fitting lid. Cook in the middle of the oven, basting thoroughly with the pan juices every 30 minutes, for about 1½ hours, or until an instant-reading thermometer measures 150° when inserted in the thigh of the bird.

6. Meanwhile, put the capon neck, gizzard and pieces of fat in a medium saucepan. Add the stock and simmer slowly for 1 hour. Do not let boil, or the sauce will become greasy.

7. Transfer the capon to a heatproof platter. Cover loosely with aluminum foil and let rest in a warm oven while you finish the sauce.

8. Strain the stock into the vegetables and butter in the casserole. Add the truffle essence and simmer over low heat for 20 minutes. (Do not let boil.) Strain, reserving the vegetables. Skim off the fat from the surface (see Note). Return the vegetables to the broth.

9. Knead the remaining 2 tablespoons butter with the flour to make a beurre manié. Bring the broth and vegetables to a simmer over moderate heat. Gradually whisk in the beurre manié. Bring to a boil and cook, stirring, until thickened, 1 to 2 minutes. Season the sauce with salt and pepper to taste. Set aside over low heat.

10. Remove the trussings from the bird. Add any juices that have accumulated on the platter to the sauce. Decoratively arrange the reserved truffle slices on top of the breast. Serve the capon with the sauce on the side.

NOTE: This flavorful fat can be saved for cooking potatoes or other poultry.

—*Anne Disrude*

BRAISED CHICKEN WITH LEEKS

This represents a very simple type of braise, made with cut-up poultry. The chicken marries well with the leeks and Madeira. The sauce can be served as is, or it may be enriched as described below.

3 to 4 Servings

½ cup all-purpose flour
2 teaspoons coarse (kosher) salt
Freshly ground black pepper
One 3½- to 4-pound chicken, quartered
About 3 tablespoons unsalted butter
1 tablespoon vegetable oil
6 to 8 leeks, depending on size, or 10 to 12
  large scallions
1 garlic clove, minced (optional)
Pinch of thyme
Salt and freshly ground white pepper
8 to 12 baby carrots or 1 cup carrot pieces
  (2-inch)
⅔ cup Madeira wine
¾ to 1 cup Rich Chicken Stock (p. 11),
  as needed
¼ cup crème fraîche or heavy cream (optional)
A few drops of lemon juice
1 tablespoon minced parsley, for garnish

1. On a plate, combine the flour, coarse salt and black pepper and dredge the chicken lightly in the seasoned flour, shaking off the excess.

2. In a large flameproof casserole, heat 1 tablespoon of the butter in the oil. Add the chicken pieces and sauté over moderately high heat until lightly golden on all sides. Set aside the pieces as they brown. Set the casserole aside.

3. Cut the leeks (or scallions) into 1-inch lengths.

4. Preheat the oven to 375°. If the butter in the casserole has become too dark after browning the chicken, rinse out the pan, wipe it and add 2 tablespoons of additional butter. Toss the leeks or scallions in the butter over fairly low heat until well coated, then add the garlic, thyme and a sprinkling of salt and white pepper. Stew over low heat for about 4 minutes, until the leeks begin to wilt. Add the carrots, raise the heat and toss the vegetables for another 2 minutes.

5. Add the Madeira to the pan over the heat and scrape up any browned bits on the bottom.

6. Arrange the chicken in the casserole with the vegetables, burying the leg-thigh portions at the bottom. Place the breast pieces on top and carefully spoon a layer of vegetables over them. Add chicken stock to half the depth of the chicken pieces. Cover the casserole with foil or parchment, then with the lid. Bring the liquid to a boil on top of the stove, then bake 25 to 45 minutes, or until the thigh portions are tender when poked with a sharp knife. Remove the casserole from the oven.

7. Arrange the chicken pieces on a heated platter. Lift the vegetables from the liquid with a slotted spoon and arrange them around the chicken. Keep warm. Place the casserole over fairly high heat on top of the stove and degrease the juices thoroughly as the mixture bubbles. *(The recipe can be prepared ahead to this point; in fact, degreasing the juices will be simpler, since the fat will lift off easily after chilling. Refrigerate the chicken and vegetables separately from the sauce.)*

8. Allow the sauce to boil down until slightly thickened. The sauce may be served as is, or you may enrich it by adding the optional crème fraîche and reducing the mixture further. Taste the sauce and correct the seasoning, adding, if needed, salt, pepper and/or a few drops of lemon juice and

Madeira. Pour the sauce over the chicken and vegetables. Garnish with a sprinkling of chopped parsley and serve hot.

—*F&W*

CHICKEN IN BEER WITH LEEKS

🍷 California Chardonnay, such as Beringer Private Reserve

4 Servings

One 4-pound broiler-fryer chicken
1½ tablespoons unsalted butter
3 medium shallots, chopped
1 bottle (12 ounces) dark beer
¼ teaspoon thyme
1 bay leaf, preferably imported
1 teaspoon salt
½ teaspoon freshly ground pepper
4 large leeks (white part only), cut into
 1-inch slices
¼ cup Chicken Stock (p. 10) or canned broth
1 cup crème fraîche or heavy cream
1 tablespoon chopped chives

1. Remove the chicken giblets and chop them coarsely. Quarter the chicken.

2. In a large skillet, melt the butter over moderately high heat. Add the giblets and chopped shallots and sauté, stirring, for 3 minutes.

3. Add the chicken and sauté, turning, until browned on both sides, about 10 minutes. Add the beer, thyme, bay leaf, ½ teaspoon of the salt and ¼ teaspoon of the pepper. Cover and cook over low heat until no longer pink but still juicy, about 12 minutes for the breast and wings, 20 minutes for the legs and thighs. Remove from the heat and return all the chicken to the pan; set aside.

4. Meanwhile, in a large saucepan of boiling salted water, cook the leeks until tender, about 12 minutes. Drain well.

5. In a medium saucepan, combine the leeks, stock, ½ cup of the crème fraîche, and the re-maining ½ teaspoon salt and ¼ teaspoon pepper. Bring to a boil over moderately high heat. Boil for 4 minutes. Reduce the heat to low and keep warm.

6. Remove the skin from the pieces of chicken. Return the chicken to the skillet. Add the remaining ½ cup crème fraîche and cook over high heat for 5 minutes, until the chicken is hot and the sauce is slightly thickened. Remove and discard the bay leaf.

7. To serve, arrange the chicken on a warm platter. Add the leeks with their sauce to the platter. Spoon the sauce from the skillet over the chicken and sprinkle with the chives.

—*Dominique Nahmias, l'Olympe, Paris*

COQ AU RIESLING

🍷 California Johannisberg Riesling, such as Jekel

6 to 8 Servings

½ pound lean slab bacon, thickly sliced and
 cut crosswise into ¼-inch-thick
 matchsticks (lardons)
1 stick (4 ounces) unsalted butter, softened
2 chickens (2½ to 3 pounds each), quartered
1 medium onion, coarsely chopped
1 large garlic clove, coarsely chopped
1 medium carrot, coarsely chopped
3 cups dry Riesling wine
1 cup Chicken Stock (p. 10) or canned broth
2 pounds mushrooms, quartered
¼ cup Cognac or other brandy
½ teaspoon fresh lemon juice
Salt and freshly ground pepper
2 tablespoons all-purpose flour
1 tablespoon minced parsley, for garnish

1. In a large flameproof casserole, cook the bacon over moderate heat, stirring occasionally, until golden, about 3 minutes. Drain on paper towels and set aside. Pour off the fat from the pan, reserving 2 tablespoons.

2. Heat 4 tablespoons of the butter and 1 tablespoon of the reserved bacon fat in the same casserole. Working in 2 batches, sauté the chicken over moderately high heat, turning once, until golden on both sides, about 10 minutes per batch. As it cooks, transfer the chicken to a platter.

3. Add the onion, garlic and carrot to the casserole and sauté over moderate heat until the carrot is soft, 10 to 15 minutes.

4. Preheat the oven to 200°. Add the wine and stock to the sautéed vegetables and bring to a boil, scraping up any browned bits from the bottom of the pan. Reduce the heat to moderately low, return the chicken to the casserole, cover and simmer for about 15 minutes, until the breast meat is just cooked through. Remove the breasts to a heatproof platter and keep warm in the oven. Continue cooking the dark meat for 10 minutes longer, or until the juices run clear. Add to the platter in the oven. Cover the casserole and continue to simmer the sauce for 5 minutes.

5. Meanwhile, in a large skillet, melt 2 tablespoons of the butter in the remaining 1 tablespoon bacon fat over moderately high heat. Add the mushrooms and sauté until they are soft and have absorbed all of the liquid in the skillet, about 5 minutes.

6. Pour in the Cognac and ignite with a match, shaking the skillet until the flames subside. Season with the lemon juice and salt and pepper to taste. Spoon the mushrooms around the chicken. Pour the juices on top.

7. In a small bowl, mash the remaining 2 tablespoons butter into the flour until smooth to form a beurre manié. Gradually stir the beurre manié into the simmering sauce ½ teaspoon at a time until the sauce thickens slightly. Simmer for 3 minutes longer.

8. To serve, sprinkle the bacon over the chicken. Pour the sauce on top and garnish with the minced parsley.

———————

—Anne Disrude

CHICKEN WITH
HUNGARIAN PAPRIKA
SAUCE
The smooth-textured sauce for this chicken dish is thickened entirely with a puree of vegetables cooked in stock and flavored with sharp Hungarian paprika. Be sure to use the imported spice for this dish if you want authentic flavor.

4 Servings

One 3½-pound chicken, cut into 8
  serving pieces—neck, back, gizzard and
  heart reserved
Salt and freshly ground pepper
About 6 tablespoons unsalted butter
2 tablespoons oil
2 medium onions, coarsely chopped
2 garlic cloves, chopped
1 carrot, coarsely chopped
1 rib celery, coarsely chopped
½ medium or 1 very small green bell
  pepper, diced
¾ pound mushrooms—½ cup coarsely
  chopped, the remainder sliced
¼ cup medium or hot Hungarian paprika
2 tomatoes—peeled, seeded and coarsely
  chopped
About 3 cups Chicken Stock (p. 10) or
  canned broth
1 teaspoon coarse (kosher) salt
1 cup sour cream
2 teaspoons minced parsley

1. Sprinkle the chicken pieces lightly with salt and pepper.

2. In a large skillet, heat 2 tablespoons of the butter in the oil and sauté the chicken pieces over high heat until well browned on all sides.

(Do not omit the neck, back and giblets—these add flavor and can be removed later; treat yourself to the tender gizzard.) Remove to a plate and cover loosely to keep warm.

3. In the skillet, heat the pan drippings until very hot but not smoking. Add the onions, garlic, carrot, celery, green pepper and chopped mushrooms and sauté, stirring, for about 3 minutes, just until the vegetables lose their rawness. If necessary, add another tablespoon of butter.

4. Add the paprika to the sautéed vegetables and stir to coat them well. Cook for about 3 minutes more over fairly high heat to release and mingle the flavors. Add the tomatoes and cook over high heat, stirring, until most of the moisture has evaporated.

5. In a large saucepan, bring the stock to a simmer. Add the vegetables and the salt and bring the mixture to a boil.

6. Add the chicken pieces, placing the giblets on the bottom, then the legs and thighs, and putting the breasts on top so they do not overcook. Lower the heat to a simmer, cover the saucepan and cook about 20 minutes, or until the chicken is cooked through and the carrots are very tender.

7. Meanwhile, in a medium skillet, heat the remaining 3 tablespoons butter until hot but not smoking. Add the sliced mushrooms and sauté until softened and lightly browned.

8. Remove the chicken to a plate and cover loosely to keep warm. Skim off excess fat from the top of the sauce. Strain the sauce over a fine strainer into a saucepan and remove any last drops of fat from the strained liquid; reserve the solids.

9. In a blender or food processor, puree the solids until they are completely smooth. (You may wish to add a bit of the sauce to facilitate this.) Strain the puree through the fine strainer back into the sauce, rubbing with the back of a wooden spoon to force the puree through.

10. Beat in ½ cup of the sour cream until the sauce is smooth. Adjust the seasoning with salt and pepper to taste. Reheat the sauce before using, but do not allow it to boil or the sour cream will curdle. If the sauce seems too thick, thin it with additional chicken stock, adding more salt and pepper if necessary.

11. Place the heated chicken pieces on a warmed platter or serving plates. Top with the sautéed mushrooms, then coat lightly with the sauce. Top each portion with a dollop of the remaining ½ cup sour cream and the parsley.

———

—F&W

MEDITERRANEAN CHICKEN WITH LEMONS AND OLIVES
4 Servings

2 cups boiling water
1 pound Greek or Italian green olives
1 lemon, thinly sliced
½ cup all-purpose flour
2 teaspoons salt
1 teaspoon freshly ground pepper
One 3½-pound chicken, cut into 10
  serving pieces
3 tablespoons olive oil
2 medium onions, finely chopped
  (about 1½ cups)
2 garlic cloves, chopped
1 tablespoon coriander seed, crushed
½ cup chopped parsley
¼ teaspoon ground saffron
1½ cups Chicken Stock (p. 10) or canned
  broth
2 tablespoons fresh lemon juice

1. In a medium bowl, pour 1½ cups of boiling water over the olives and let them steep for 20 minutes. Drain, cover and set aside.

2. Place the lemon slices in a small bowl, sprinkle them with ½ teaspoon of the salt, pour ½ cup boiling water over them and let them steep for 2 to 3 minutes. Drain, cover and set aside.

3. In a paper bag, combine the flour with ½ teaspoon of the salt and ½ teaspoon of the pepper. Shake the chicken pieces in the bag of flour until lightly coated.

4. In a large nonreactive skillet, warm the oil for a minute or two over moderate heat. Add the chicken, a few pieces at a time, and brown lightly on both sides. Remove the chicken pieces with a slotted spoon and set aside.

5. Add the onions, garlic, coriander, parsley, saffron and the remaining 1 teaspoon salt and ½ teaspoon pepper. Sauté over low heat for 4 to 5 minutes. Return the chicken to the skillet, add the chicken stock and bring it to a boil over moderately high heat. Lower the heat, cover and simmer the chicken until the juices run clear when a thigh is pierced with a fork, 15 to 20 minutes.

6. Remove the skillet from the heat and stir in the reserved sliced lemon and olives. Blend in the lemon juice. Transfer to a serving dish and serve hot.

———

—F&W

BRESSE CHICKEN IN CREAM A LA GRANDMERE BLANC

🍷 Riesling from Alsace, such as Trimbach

4 Servings

One 3½-pound chicken
4 tablespoons clarified butter
Salt and freshly ground pepper
3 tablespoons all-purpose flour
About 4 cups Chicken Stock (p. 10) or
*   canned broth*
1 medium onion stuck with 1 clove
1 medium garlic clove
1 sprig of fresh thyme or ½ teaspoon dried
1 bay leaf

4 cups heavy cream, reduced by half (see Note)
3 egg yolks
½ teaspoon fresh lemon juice

1. Cut the chicken into 8 pieces as follows: Cut off the legs and separate the drumsticks from the thighs. Using a very sharp boning knife, lift the complete breasts off the carcass. Cut each breast in half crosswise. You now have 8 pieces that you will serve, all the rest of the chicken is to provide flavor for the sauce. Cut off the wings and divide them into their sections. Chop the carcass into fairly large but manageable pieces and set aside.

2. In a large skillet, heat 2 tablespoons of the butter. Add the 8 chicken serving pieces. Salt and pepper them and sauté over high heat, turning, until golden in color, about 5 minutes. Remove with a slotted spoon and set aside.

3. Add the remaining 2 tablespoons butter to the skillet and warm over moderately high heat. Add the reserved chicken wings and bones and cook, tossing, for about 2 minutes, to coat on all sides with butter. Sprinkle the pieces evenly with the flour. Continue to cook, tossing, until the flour is well browned, about 2 minutes longer.

4. Pour in enough stock (about 3½ cups) to cover the wings and bones. Increase the heat to high and cook, stirring constantly, until the stock boils and thickens slightly, about 6 minutes. Reduce the heat to a gentle simmer, move the wings and bones to the sides of the skillet and place the browned serving pieces in the center of the pan. Make sure the pieces are covered by the stock, add more if necessary.

5. Tuck the onion, garlic, thyme and bay leaf around the serving pieces and simmer gently, uncovered, until the serving pieces are perfectly cooked: the breast meat about 6 minutes, the thighs and legs about 15 minutes. If the stock reduces too quickly, or if any of the pieces are not covered, add more stock to cover. As each piece is done, remove to a warm platter and keep warm.

6. When all the serving pieces are cooked, strain the cooking liquid through a fine sieve into a bowl. Spoon off any excess grease and place 1½ cups of the liquid in a medium saucepan (reserve the remainder for another use).

7. Warm the 1½ cups cooking liquid over low heat just to a simmer. In a medium bowl, whisk the reduced cream with the egg yolks until blended. Remove the pan from the heat and beat the cream and egg yolk mixture into the warmed liquid. Stirring constantly, warm the sauce over low heat until it thickens enough to lightly coat the back of a spoon; do not allow it to boil. If the sauce becomes too thick, add more stock, 1 tablespoon at a time. Taste and adjust the seasonings, then add the lemon juice.

8. Return the serving pieces to the sauce just to heat through. Divide the chicken among 4 plates and coat lightly with some of the sauce. Pass the remaining sauce separately.

NOTE: Simmer the cream until reduced by half, about 1 hour.

—*Georges Blanc, La Mère Blanc, Vonnas, France*

BRAISED CHICKEN WITH CIDER-CREAM GRAVY

The apple cider you use for this recipe should be hard (alcoholic), not sweet. Try to find a good imported French cider (many liquor stores now carry it) because it will have just the proper crispness and intense apple flavor.

❦ California Chardonnay, such as Beringer Private Reserve

6 Servings

3 tablespoons unsalted butter
2 chickens (about 2½ pounds each), cut into 8
  serving pieces each
5 large shallots, minced (about ½ cup)
1 pound small mushrooms
½ cup Calvados

½ cup hard apple cider, preferably French
1 cup heavy cream
½ teaspoon salt
⅛ teaspoon freshly ground pepper
3 tablespoons minced parsley

1. In a large nonreactive skillet, melt 2 tablespoons of the butter over moderately high heat. When the butter is sizzling, add half the chicken pieces (don't crowd) and sauté until browned, about 5 minutes per side. Remove to a platter and brown the second half.

2. In the same skillet, melt the remaining 1 tablespoon butter. Add the shallots and mushrooms and cook, stirring, until lightly browned, 2 to 3 minutes. Reduce the heat to low. Cover the skillet and cook until the shallots are soft, about 10 minutes.

3. Return the chicken to the skillet and spoon the mushroom mixture on top. Pour the Calvados over the chicken, warm gently over low heat and ignite with a match. When the flames subside, pour in the cider, cover the skillet and simmer over very low heat for 15 minutes. Remove the chicken breasts and mushrooms to an ovenproof platter, cover loosely and keep warm in a 250° oven. Continue cooking the dark meat for 10 minutes longer, then add to the platter in the oven.

4. Boil the liquid in the skillet until it is reduced to a thin glaze, 12 to 15 minutes. Pour in the cream and continue to boil, uncovered, until the sauce is the consistency of moderately thin gravy, 4 to 5 minutes. Add the salt and pepper and half of the parsley.

5. To serve, spoon the sauce evenly over the chicken and mushrooms, then sprinkle with the remaining parsley.

—*Jean Anderson*

Chicken Salad with Shrimp and Fennel (p. 233).

Chicken Tacos (p. 253).

CHICKEN WITH APPLE AND CALVADOS SAUCE

♟ California Chardonnay, such as Franciscan Napa

4 Servings

2 tablespoons clarified butter
2 tablespoons peanut oil
One 3-pound chicken, cut into 8 serving pieces
1 teaspoon salt
½ teaspoon freshly ground white pepper
½ cup Calvados
¼ cup cider vinegar
1 bay leaf
1 pound tart red apples, preferably Winesap or Cortland, cored and cut into eighths
1 cup Chicken Stock (p. 10) or canned broth
¼ cup heavy cream
2 tablespoons cold unsalted butter

1. Preheat the oven to 350°. In a large nonreactive skillet, heat the clarified butter and oil until shimmering. Add the chicken in batches and sauté without crowding, turning, over moderately high heat until well browned, 6 to 8 minutes. Remove to a plate and season with ½ teaspoon of the salt and ⅛ teaspoon of the white pepper.

2. Pour off the fat from the skillet. Add ¼ cup of the Calvados and the vinegar and bring to a boil, scraping up any browned bits from the bottom of the pan. Add the bay leaf and remove from the heat.

3. Place the apples in a medium, nonreactive casserole. Arrange the chicken on top. Pour the Calvados-vinegar mixture over the chicken and bake uncovered for 30 to 35 minutes, until the juices run clear when the thigh of the chicken is pierced.

4. Remove the chicken pieces and cover loosely with foil to keep warm. Discard the bay leaf. Pass the apples and the cooking juices through a food mill or puree in a food processor or blender. Pass through a fine sieve.

5. Pour the sauce into a nonreactive saucepan; add the stock and cream. Bring to a boil over moderately high heat and cook until the sauce is slightly thickened and darker in color, about 5 minutes. Add the remaining ¼ cup Calvados and remove from the heat. Stir in the cold butter. Season with the remaining salt and white pepper. Spoon about ¼ cup of the sauce onto each serving plate and arrange the chicken on top.

———————————

—*John Robert Massie*

CHICKEN IN CHAMPAGNE SAUCE

4 Servings

3½- to 4-pound broiler-fryer chicken, cut into 8 serving pieces
½ teaspoon salt
½ teaspoon freshly ground pepper
10 tablespoons unsalted butter
2 tablespoons olive oil
3 large shallots, minced (about ⅓ cup)
1¼ cups brut Champagne
1 cup Chicken Stock (p. 10) or canned broth
1 cup crème fraîche
½ pound mushrooms, quartered and sautéed (optional)

1. Preheat the oven to 375°. Season the chicken all over with the salt and pepper.

2. In a large ovenproof skillet, melt 4 tablespoons of the butter in the oil over moderate heat. When the foam begins to subside, add the chicken and sauté, turning once, until golden, about 5 minutes per side. Remove the chicken and set aside.

3. Add the shallots to the skillet, reduce the heat to moderately low and sauté, shaking the pan frequently, until just softened, about 1 minute. Return the chicken to the pan and stir to coat with the shallot butter. Pour the chicken, shallots and butter into a colander; let drain for 2 to 3 minutes to remove excess fat and return to the skillet.

4. Add the Champagne and bring to a boil over moderate heat. Cook for 2 minutes; turn the chicken and partially cover the skillet. Boil until the Champagne is reduced by half, about 5 minutes.

5. Add the stock, bring to a boil and cover tightly. Transfer the skillet to the oven and bake until the chicken is tender and its juices run clear when pierced with a fork, about 10 minutes.

6. Remove the chicken to a platter and cover loosely with foil to keep warm. Add the crème fraîche to the skillet and boil over moderate heat until the sauce is thick enough to coat a spoon lightly, 15 to 20 minutes.

7. Reduce the heat to low. Gradually whisk in the remaining 6 tablespoons butter, 1 or 2 table-spoons at a time, until the sauce is smooth and thickened. (Squeeze the butter into the sauce through your fingers so that it softens slightly and breaks into small bits. Then a simple stir or shake of the pan will form a smooth emulsion.) Season with salt and pepper to taste. Add the mush-rooms, if you are using them, and the chicken. Serve hot.

—*Gérard Boyer, Les Crayères, Reims, France*

BREAST OF CHICKEN CHARENTE

Napa Valley Chardonnay

4 Servings

¼ cup all-purpose flour
1 tablespoon tarragon
1½ teaspoons salt
½ teaspoon freshly ground pepper
4 skinless, boneless chicken breast halves
* (about 5 ounces each)*
4 tablespoons unsalted butter
1 tablespoon corn oil
½ cup brandy
1 cup Chicken Stock (p. 10) or canned broth
3 tablespoons Dijon-style mustard
2 tablespoons fresh lemon juice
¼ cup capers, drained

1. On a sheet of waxed paper, combine the flour, tarragon, salt and pepper. Lightly dredge the chicken in the mixture, shaking off the excess.

2. In a large skillet, heat the butter and oil over moderate heat. When the foam begins to subside, add the chicken and sauté for 3 minutes on each side, or until lightly browned.

3. In a small saucepan, warm the brandy over moderate heat. Remove the skillet from the heat, pour the brandy over the chicken and return the skillet to the heat. If the brandy does not ignite from the heat source, light with a match. Shake the pan constantly until the flames subside. Add the chicken stock, mustard and lemon juice. Bring to a boil, cover, reduce the heat to low and sim-mer for 7 to 10 minutes, turning once, until the breasts are just cooked through.

4. Arrange the chicken breasts on a warm plat-ter. Boil the sauce over high heat for about 1 minute, until reduced to a coating consistency slightly thicker than heavy cream. Season with salt and pepper to taste. Pour the sauce over the chicken and sprinkle on the capers.

—*W. Peter Prestcott*

CHICKEN SAUCE PIQUANT

If you like your chicken with a very flavorful sauce, this is for you. Since the recipe creates a generous amount of sauce, it can be stretched to accommodate any last-minute guests. All you have to do is throw in a few more pieces of chicken.

🍷 Spicy California Zinfandel, such as Chateau Montelena

6 to 8 Servings

⅓ *cup safflower or corn oil*
4 large chicken breast halves
12 chicken thighs
2 medium onions, coarsely chopped
4 celery ribs, coarsely chopped
1 large green bell pepper, coarsely chopped
⅓ *cup all-purpose flour*
1 can (28 ounces) crushed Italian peeled tomatoes
¼ *cup tomato paste*
2 large imported bay leaves
2 large garlic cloves, minced
1 tablespoon fresh lemon juice
1 teaspoon hot pepper sauce
1 teaspoon salt
½ *teaspoon freshly ground black pepper*
4 cups Chicken Stock (p. 10) or canned broth
2 tablespoons chopped scallion greens
2 tablespoons minced parsley
12 pimiento-stuffed olives, sliced

1. In a large flameproof casserole, heat the oil over moderately high heat. Add the chicken pieces in batches and sauté, turning, until browned, 4 to 5 minutes on each side. With a slotted spoon, transfer the chicken to a plate.

2. Add the onions, celery and green pepper to the casserole and cook over moderate heat, stirring, until softened but not browned, 5 to 10 minutes. With a slotted spoon, transfer the vegetables to another plate.

3. Whisk the flour into the remaining oil in the casserole and cook over moderate heat, stirring and scraping up the browned bits from the bottom of the pan, until the roux turns a rich brown, about 10 minutes.

4. Stir in the tomatoes with their juice, ½ cup of water, the tomato paste, bay leaves, garlic, lemon juice, hot sauce, salt, pepper and stock. Bring to a boil. Add the chicken and reserved sautéed vegetables to the casserole and simmer, uncovered, stirring and skimming the top occasionally, until the chicken is tender and the sauce thickened, about 1 hour. *(The recipe can be prepared to this point up to 1 day ahead. Let cool, then cover and refrigerate.)*

5. A few minutes before serving, stir in the scallions, parsley and olives.

———

—*Lee Bailey*

INDONESIAN CHICKEN IN A SPECIAL SAUCE

This is one of Indonesia's finest chicken preparations. The key is the balanced combination of spices and seasonings that are simmered in coconut milk until reduced to a thick paste.

12 Servings

2 whole chickens (3 pounds each)
12 macadamia nuts
8 shallots, sliced
3 garlic cloves, sliced
1-inch piece of fresh ginger, peeled and sliced
2 teaspoons salt
¼ *teaspoon turmeric*
1 tablespoon brown sugar
1 to 2 teaspoons crushed hot red pepper, to taste

3 cups Coconut Milk (p. 56), or 1½ cups
  canned unsweetened coconut milk★ mixed
  with 1½ cups water
1 tablespoon corn oil
3 slices of laos root (galingale)★
2 slices of lemon
★Available at Asian markets

1. Cut the backbone off both chickens. Cut each bird into 10 serving pieces: separate the drumsticks and thighs and the wings; cut each breast crosswise into 2 pieces. Pull off all the skin you can and trim off any excess fat.

2. Preheat the broiler. Broil the chicken pieces about 4 inches from the heat, turning once, for 3 minutes on each side to sear the outside. Set aside.

3. In a food processor, grind the macadamia nuts to a smooth paste. Add the shallots, garlic, ginger, salt, turmeric, brown sugar, hot pepper and ½ cup of the coconut milk. Puree the spice paste until smooth.

4. In a large flameproof casserole, heat the oil. Add the coconut spice paste and stir-fry over moderate heat until the liquid evaporates, about 2 minutes. Add the remaining 2½ cups coconut milk, the laos root and the lemon. Boil until reduced by one-third, about 5 minutes.

5. Add the chicken, reduce the heat to moderately low and simmer, uncovered, until the chicken is tender, about 30 minutes. Boil until the liquid in the pan is reduced to a thick sauce, about 10 minutes. *(The recipe can be prepared up to 2 days ahead and refrigerated. Reheat before serving.)* Serve warm.

———————————

—Copeland Marks

CHICKEN BREASTS WITH ARTICHOKE HEARTS, OLIVES AND BACON

Frozen artichoke hearts retain their flavor, texture and color when thawed and cooked. This mélange of artichokes, olives and chicken is easily assembled and surprisingly elegant. Serve an unexpected grain, such as steamed couscous or bulgur, as an accompaniment.

❦ Since artichokes can make wine taste sweeter, serve a simple, clean-flavored white, such as Domaines Ott Bandol Blanc, Parducci French Colombard or Mirafiore Soave.

  6 Servings

6 tablespoons unsalted butter
1 tablespoon olive oil
1½ cups coarsely chopped onions
2 packages frozen artichoke hearts, thawed and
  halved lengthwise
¾ cup dry white wine
¾ teaspoon salt
½ teaspoon freshly ground pepper
¼ pound sliced bacon, finely diced
6 skinless, boneless chicken breast halves
6 Calamata olives, pitted and thinly sliced
1 tablespoon fresh lemon juice
1 teaspoon grated lemon zest
½ cup minced parsley

1. In a large nonreactive skillet, melt 2 tablespoons of the butter in the oil. Add the onions, cover and cook over moderately low heat until softened, about 10 minutes.

2. Add the artichoke hearts, wine, ½ teaspoon of the salt and the pepper to the skillet. Cover and cook, stirring occasionally, until the artichoke hearts are tender, about 10 minutes.

3. Meanwhile, in another large nonreactive skillet, fry the bacon over moderate heat until browned and crisp, about 5 minutes. Transfer to paper towels to drain. Set aside.

4. Increase the heat under the bacon fat to moderately high. Add the chicken breasts to the skillet and sauté, turning once, until golden brown, 2 to 3 minutes per side. Pour off the bacon fat, but do not wash the skillet.

5. Place the chicken breasts on top of the artichoke hearts. Cover and cook over moderate heat until the chicken is just cooked through, 7 to 9 minutes. Transfer the chicken breasts to a warmed platter and sprinkle with the remaining ¼ teaspoon salt. Cover with foil to keep warm.

6. Drain as much liquid as possible from the artichoke hearts into the skillet the chicken was sautéed in. Bring to a boil and cook over high heat until thick and syrupy, about 3 minutes. Remove from the heat. Cut the remaining 4 tablespoons butter into pieces and gradually whisk them into the reduced liquid. Spoon the sauce over the chicken.

7. Add the olives to the artichoke hearts and cook over moderate heat until warmed through, about 1 minute. Add the lemon juice, lemon zest and parsley and toss well. Spoon the artichoke hearts around the chicken and sprinkle with the reserved bacon.

—*W. Peter Prestcott*

PIMIENTO CHICKEN WITH MUSHROOMS

❦ Fruity red, such as Castello d'Albola Chianti Classico

6 to 8 Servings

6 tablespoons all-purpose flour
¼ teaspoon salt
¼ teaspoon freshly ground pepper
6 large skinless, boneless chicken breast halves
3 tablespoons safflower oil
2 tablespoons unsalted butter
1 large onion, coarsely chopped
2 medium shallots, minced
12 ounces mushrooms, sliced
⅓ cup dry white wine
2 cups Chicken Stock (p. 10) or canned low-sodium broth
½ cup low-fat sour cream
2 jars (4 ounces each) pimientos, drained and diced
2 tablespoons minced parsley

1. In a small bowl, place 2 tablespoons of the flour. In a medium bowl, combine the remaining ¼ cup flour with the salt and pepper. Add the chicken pieces to the seasoned flour and toss to coat, shaking off any excess.

2. In a large heavy flameproof casserole, heat 2 tablespoons of the oil over moderately high heat. Add half of the chicken and cook until well browned and partially cooked, about 3 minutes per side. Transfer the chicken to a bowl or platter and repeat with the remaining 1 tablespoon oil and the chicken pieces.

3. Reduce the heat to moderate and melt the butter in the casserole. Add the onion and cook, stirring to scrape up any browned bits from the bottom of the pan, until the onion is softened and slightly browned, about 5 minutes.

4. Add the shallots and let cook for 1 minute. Add the mushrooms and cook, stirring, until the juices have evaporated, 6 to 8 minutes.

5. Increase the heat to moderately high and add the white wine. Cook until the liquid has reduced by half. Sprinkle in the reserved 2 tablespoons of flour and stir to incorporate; the mushroom mixture will become thick and pasty. Gradually add the chicken stock, stirring. Bring to a simmer and let bubble, until thickened slightly, about 2 minutes. (*The recipe can be made to this point up to 1 day ahead. Wrap and refrigerate the partially cooked chicken breasts with their juices, cover the casserole and refrigerate. To reheat, place the pot over moderate heat, stirring occasionally, until warm.*)

6. Stir in the sour cream and adjust with additional salt and pepper to taste. Stir in the pimientos and parsley. Add the chicken to the sauce and let cook, stirring occasionally, until the chicken is cooked through, 3 to 5 minutes.

—*Lee Bailey*

STUFFED CHICKEN LEGS WITH CURRY SAUCE

For step-by-step photographs that show how to bone a chicken leg, see page 18.

6 Servings

STUFFED CHICKEN LEGS:

6 whole chicken legs (drumsticks with thighs)
½ cup plus 1 tablespoon grated fresh coconut
6 tablespoons mango chutney
6 tablespoons coarsely chopped, dry-roasted salted peanuts
6 tablespoons raisins
¼ cup clarified butter

CURRY SAUCE:

1 garlic clove, bruised
⅓ cup finely chopped green bell pepper
¼ teaspoon crushed hot red pepper
½ teaspoon cumin
½ teaspoon cardamom
½ teaspoon mace
½ teaspoon cinnamon
¾ teaspoon ground ginger
1½ teaspoons turmeric
1½ teaspoons ground fenugreek
1 tablespoon poppy seeds, lightly crushed
1½ cups Chicken Stock (p. 10) or canned broth
½ cup plain yogurt, at room temperature

1. Bone the chicken legs: Using a boning knife and starting at the top of a thigh, free the meat from the bone, keeping the meat in one piece and turning the leg as you scrape. When you reach the joint between the thigh and drumstick, you may have to make a small cut or two through the flesh toward the bones in order to continue scraping down the drumstick. When all the flesh has been scraped off the bones, free it completely by pulling it over the ankle joint with your hands. The leg meat will now be inside out. Cut away any tendons and cartilage and then turn the meat right-side out. Bone all the legs in this way and set them aside.

2. Stuff the chicken legs: In a small bowl, combine the coconut, chutney, peanuts and raisins. Using about ¼ cup of the mixture for each leg, stuff them, dividing the filling evenly between the leg and thigh areas. Close the openings with toothpicks and set aside.

3. In a large skillet, heat the clarified butter over moderate heat. Add the stuffed chicken legs and lightly brown them on each side for about 2 minutes. Reserving the fat in the pan, remove the chicken and set it aside.

4. Prepare the curry sauce: Add the garlic clove and green pepper to the skillet and cook for about 1 minute over moderate heat. Add the spices and poppy seeds and cook another minute; remove and discard the garlic.

5. Return the chicken to the pan, add the chicken stock, bring it to a boil, reduce the heat slightly and simmer, covered, for 20 to 25 minutes, or until tender, turning once. Transfer the chicken to a serving platter and keep warm. Turn the heat to high and cook the sauce 3 to 4 minutes, or until reduced to 1⅓ cups.

6. Place the yogurt in a small bowl and very slowly stir into it about ¼ cup of the sauce. Stir this mixture back into the sauce in the pan. Pour the sauce over the chicken and serve. *(The recipe can be made completely ahead. Cover and refrigerate. Rewarm by simmering over low heat, covered, for about 10 minutes, or until heated through.)*

—*F&W*

CHICKEN THIGHS WITH TARRAGON WINE VINEGAR

This recipe is a variation of a French classic. With its tangy sauce, the best accompaniment is buttered noodles with lots of black pepper.

☙ The tart notes contributed by the vinegar and tomatoes suggest a medium-bodied, unfussy red, such as Rioja. A Bodegas Muga or a Marqués de Cáceres would be a fine choice.

4 Servings

2 tablespoons all-purpose flour
1 teaspoon salt
½ teaspoon freshly ground pepper
½ teaspoon celery seeds
8 chicken thighs
2 tablespoons olive oil
1 head of garlic, cloves peeled
1 cup tarragon wine vinegar
1 can (14 ounces) crushed Italian peeled
  tomatoes
1 can (10½ ounces) low-sodium chicken broth
1 tablespoon tomato paste
1½ teaspoons tarragon
¼ cup chopped parsley

1. In a shallow bowl, combine the flour, salt, pepper and celery seeds. Dredge the thighs in the flour mixture.

2. In a large nonreactive flameproof casserole, heat the oil over moderately high heat. Add the chicken, skin-side up, and cook, turning once, until well browned all over, 8 to 10 minutes.

3. Reduce the heat to low. Add the garlic, cover and cook until tender, turning the chicken once, about 15 minutes.

4. Tip the pan and drain off all the fat. Add the tarragon vinegar and bring to a boil over high heat; boil until the vinegar reduces by half, 5 to 7 minutes. Add the tomatoes, chicken broth, tomato paste and tarragon to the casserole and return to a boil. Reduce the heat to moderate and simmer the chicken, turning once, until tender, about 15 minutes.

5. Transfer the chicken to a warmed platter and cover with foil to keep warm. Pass the sauce through a food mill or sieve. Alternatively, transfer the sauce to a food processor or blender and puree until smooth. *(The recipe can be prepared to this point up to 2 days ahead. Cover and refrigerate. Reheat before serving.)* Stir the parsley into the sauce and pour it over the chicken. Serve hot.

—*Bob Chambers*

THAI CHICKEN AND FRESH BASIL

This version of a popular Thai dish takes up an entire plate. It is served on a bed of shredded cabbage with bowls of rice.

4 Servings

2 tablespoons peanut oil
8 to 10 small fresh red or green chile peppers,
  seeded and minced
2 tablespoons dried chopped lemon grass,★ tied
  in a cheesecloth bag, or 2 teaspoons grated
  lemon zest
½ cup Coconut Milk (p. 56) or canned
  unsweetened coconut milk★
2 pounds skinless, boneless chicken breast, cut
  crosswise into ½-inch strips
3 tablespoons fish sauce (nuoc mam)★
2 tablespoons minced fresh basil or 1½
  tablespoons minced cilantro (fresh coriander)
2 cups finely shredded cabbage
★Available at Southeast Asian and many
  Chinese markets

1. In a large skillet, warm the oil over moderate heat until shimmering. Add the chile peppers and sauté, stirring, for 3 minutes.

2. Add the lemon grass and coconut milk, increase the heat to high and boil until the sauce is slightly thickened, about 2 minutes.

3. Reduce the heat to moderate. Add the chicken and cook, stirring occasionally, until opaque throughout, about 5 minutes. Stir in the fish sauce and basil. Discard the lemon grass.

4. To serve, make a bed of cabbage on a large platter. Pour the chicken and sauce on top.

———

—Keo Sananikone, Keo's Thai Cuisine, Honolulu, Hawaii

ROSE BLANQUETTE OF CORNISH HEN

♟ Bordeaux, such as Château d'Angludet

6 to 8 Servings

1 onion, peeled and stuck with 2 cloves
1 carrot, quartered
1 celery rib, halved
Bouquet garni: 6 parsley stems, 2 large bay
  leaves, 1 teaspoon peppercorns and 1
  tablespoon thyme tied in cheesecloth
6 cups Chicken Stock (p. 10) or canned broth
1 stick (4 ounces) plus 3 tablespoons
  unsalted butter
¼ cup olive oil, preferably extra-virgin
6 Cornish game hens, quartered
1½ pounds small mushrooms, stemmed
1½ pounds small white boiling onions
1 tablespoon sugar
¼ cup all-purpose flour
¼ cup tomato paste
1 cup minced dry, unmarinated sun-dried
  tomatoes
4 egg yolks
1 cup crème fraîche
3 tablespoons minced parsley, for garnish

1. In a medium stockpot, combine the onion, carrot, celery, bouquet garni and chicken stock. Bring to a boil over high heat. Reduce the heat to a simmer.

2. In a large skillet, melt 4 tablespoons of the butter in 2 tablespoons of the oil over high heat. Sauté the hen pieces in batches, turning until golden brown, about 3 minutes per side.

3. When the hen pieces are browned, add them to the stock. Simmer until tender, about 20 minutes. With a slotted spoon, transfer the hens to an ovenproof platter. Cover loosely with foil.

4. Strain the stock through a fine-mesh sieve set over a medium saucepan. Press on the vegetables to extract as much liquid as possible. Bring the stock to a boil over high heat. Add the mushroom caps and cook for 5 minutes. With a slotted spoon, transfer the caps to a small bowl. Continue boiling the stock until reduced to 4 cups, about 15 minutes.

5. Meanwhile, in a large ovenproof skillet, melt 2 tablespoons of the butter in the remaining 2 tablespoons oil over moderate heat. Add the onions and sugar. Sauté, shaking the pan from time to time, until the onions are golden and tender, about 15 minutes.

6. Preheat the oven to 300°. In a medium saucepan, melt the remaining 5 tablespoons butter over moderately high heat. Add the flour and cook, whisking, for about 2 minutes without coloring. Gradually whisk in the stock and bring to a boil. Stir in the tomato paste, sun-dried tomatoes and mushroom caps. Reduce the heat to low and simmer for 10 minutes. *(The recipe can be prepared ahead to this point. Reheat the sauce before proceeding.)*

7. Place the hens and onions in the oven to reheat.

8. In a medium bowl, whisk together the egg yolks and crème fraîche. Slowly stir in ½ cup of the hot sauce. Gradually whisk this mixture back into the sauce. Remove from the heat.

9. To serve, ladle the sauce over the hens. Arrange the onions around the platter and sprinkle with the parsley.

———

—W. Peter Prestcott

POULE AU POT

The best-beloved French king, Henry IV, was born in 1553 in the southwestern region of France then called Navarre. The legend is that when he was only an hour old, his lips were rubbed with garlic and he was given a tablespoonful of Jurançon wine to make him strong. The procedure seems to have worked well. When he became king, he said that his aim was to improve the condition of *all* French people, so that they could have *poule au pot* every Sunday. Such a dish—a stuffed, poached chicken—was a great luxury at that time.

6 Servings

2½ quarts Chicken Stock (p. 10) or
  canned broth
2 bay leaves
½ teaspoon rosemary
½ teaspoon thyme
3 large onions
4 cloves
1 cup dry white wine, such as Mâcon Blanc
One 5-pound roasting chicken, liver reserved
6 tablespoons unsalted butter
3 shallots, chopped
3 links of Italian sweet sausage, casings
  removed
2 slices rye bread, crusts removed, processed to
  coarse crumbs
3 whole eggs plus 3 egg yolks
3 tablespoons milk
2 tablespoons Cognac or other brandy
8 medium carrots, cut into 1-inch pieces
2 ribs celery, with leaves, cut into 1-inch pieces
2 cups rice
1 cup coarsely chopped mushrooms
2 tablespoons all-purpose flour
1 teaspoon fresh lemon juice
Pinch of freshly ground pepper
Salt

1. In a large saucepan or stockpot, combine the chicken stock, bay leaves, rosemary and thyme.

Stud one of the onions with the cloves and add it to the pot. Bring the stock to a boil, then add the wine. Let the stock simmer while you prepare the remaining ingredients.

2. Coarsely chop the remaining 2 onions and set aside. Dice the chicken liver and set aside. Trim as much fat as possible from the chicken; set the chicken aside.

3. In a large skillet, warm 2 tablespoons of the butter over moderately high heat until hot but not smoking. Add the shallots and cook, stirring, until softened, about 1 minute. Crumble in the sausage meat. Add the chicken liver. Cook over moderate heat, stirring frequently, until the sausage is golden, about 1 minute. Scrape the meat mixture into a bowl.

4. Remove about one-third of the meat mixture to a food processor or blender and puree to a paste. Return the paste to the bowl and thoroughly combine with the rest of the meat mixture.

5. Stir in the rye bread crumbs. Add the 3 whole eggs, milk and Cognac and mix the stuffing thoroughly.

6. Take two pieces of double-thickness cheesecloth, 12 to 15 inches long, and overlap at right angles to form a cross. Gather the 4 ends of the cross together to form a pouch. Line the chicken cavity with the pouch, making sure it remains intact inside the bird. There should be some excess cheesecloth extending from the cavity and hanging over the sides of the opening.

7. Gently fill the cavity with the stuffing. Roll the excess cheesecloth into the cavity, sealing off the stuffing.

8. Return the broth to a boil. Place the chicken in the broth. Add the chopped onions, carrots and celery. Simmer the chicken, covered, until the chicken is cooked through, 45 to 55 minutes. Meanwhile, preheat the oven to "warm," or its lowest setting.

9. Remove the chicken to an ovenproof serving dish, cover loosely with foil and place in the oven to keep warm. Keep the remaining broth at a simmer.

10. Measure out 5 cups of the chicken broth into a saucepan and bring to a boil. Add the rice, reduce the heat to a simmer and cook until the rice is tender and all of the liquid has been absorbed, about 20 minutes.

11. Meanwhile, in a medium skillet, warm 2 tablespoons of the butter until hot. Add the mushrooms and sauté until softened. Set aside.

12. In a small saucepan, melt the remaining 2 tablespoons butter. Sprinkle in the flour and stir over medium heat until the flour is no longer visible, about 1 minute. Measure out 2 cups of the simmering broth and stir it gradually into the butter and flour mixture in the saucepan. Cook, stirring, until the sauce comes to a boil, about 2 minutes.

13. Stir in the sautéed mushrooms and remove the sauce from the heat. Season the sauce with the lemon juice, pepper and salt to taste.

14. Place the egg yolks in a heatproof bowl. Whisk the sauce in gradually.

15. To serve, remove the cheesecloth bag of stuffing from the chicken. Spoon the rice, some of the vegetables from the broth and the stuffing around the chicken on the serving platter. Serve the sauce on the side.

—*Monique Guillaume*

POACHED CHICKEN AND WINTER VEGETABLES
4 to 6 Servings

One 3½-pound chicken
3 quarts Chicken Stock (p. 10) or
 canned broth
1 pound white turnips, cut into 1-inch cubes
3 carrots, cut into 1-inch pieces
4 small onions, halved
1 pound green cabbage, cut into wedges

1. Truss the chicken and place it in a large stockpot, breast-side down. Add the stock, partially cover the pot and bring the stock to a boil over moderate heat. Reduce the heat and simmer the chicken for 20 to 30 minutes, or until the juices run clear when the thigh is pierced with a fork or a meat thermometer inserted into the thickest part of a thigh registers 165°.

2. Remove the chicken from the stock and set aside. Add the turnips, carrots and onions. Cook over moderate heat, uncovered, for 10 minutes.

3. Add the cabbage wedges, cover the pot and cook for an additional 5 minutes, or until the vegetables are tender.

4. To serve, carve the chicken and place the pieces in shallow soup bowls; ladle some of the broth and vegetables over it. Serve the remaining broth and vegetables as a soup course.

—*F&W*

CHICKEN AND DUMPLINGS
♟ California Zinfandel, such as Ridge
4 Servings

One 3-pound chicken, cut into 8 serving
 pieces, giblets reserved
1 teaspoon salt
½ teaspoon freshly ground pepper
2 medium carrots, thinly sliced
2 medium onions, thinly sliced
2 celery ribs, thinly sliced
3 garlic cloves, crushed through a press
2 cups sifted all-purpose flour
1 tablespoon baking powder
1 teaspoon salt
2 eggs, lightly beaten
⅔ cup milk
½ cup chopped parsley

1. Place the chicken pieces and giblets in a large flameproof casserole. Season with the salt and pepper. Add the carrots, onions, celery, 2 of the garlic cloves and water to cover. Bring to a

boil over high heat. Reduce the heat to moderately low and simmer for about 1 hour, or until the chicken is very tender. With a slotted spoon, remove the chicken pieces and giblets to a deep platter and cover with foil to keep warm.

2. In a medium bowl, combine the flour, baking powder and salt. Add the eggs, milk, parsley and the remaining clove of garlic and stir to blend well.

3. Over moderately high heat, return the chicken stock to a boil. Drop the batter by rounded teaspoons into the broth. Cover the casserole and cook for 15 minutes.

4. To serve, place the dumplings on the platter around the chicken and pour on the cooking liquid and vegetables.

—John Robert Massie

POACHED CAPON WITH SPRING HERB SAUCE

With so few ingredients, make sure they are of the best quality. Canned chicken broth will not be satisfactory for this recipe.

♟ White Zinfandel or Rosé of Cabernet

8 to 10 Servings

One 8- to 10-pound capon
4 quarts Chicken Stock (p. 10)
Bouquet garni: 10 parsley stems, 1 bay leaf,
  10 peppercorns and ½ teaspoon thyme
  tied in cheesecloth
Spring Herb Sauce (recipe follows)

1. Put the capon, breast-side up, in a large stockpot. Pour the chicken stock over the bird. Add the bouquet garni. Cover and bring to a boil over moderately high heat. Reduce the heat and simmer for 2 hours (see Note).

2. Carefully remove the bird from the stock, draining the liquid from its cavity. Cover loosely with foil and set aside to cool to room temperature. Discard the bouquet garni. Reserve the stock for the Spring Herb Sauce.

3. Serve the capon at room temperature with a sauceboat of warm or hot Spring Herb Sauce on the side.

NOTE: If the stock does not cover the bird completely, turn the bird after 1 hour to ensure even cooking.

—John Robert Massie

SPRING HERB SAUCE

If you can't find all of the fresh herbs, rather than substitute dried herbs, increase the quantity of the fresh herbs you *do* have.

Makes About 2½ Cups

2 quarts chicken stock (see Note)
3 tablespoons minced shallots
2 tablespoons minced fresh chives
2 tablespoons minced fresh tarragon
2 tablespoons minced fresh parsley
2 tablespoons minced fresh thyme
½ teaspoon minced fresh marjoram
½ teaspoon salt
¼ teaspoon freshly ground pepper
1 stick (4 ounces) unsalted butter, at room
  temperature
2 tablespoons all-purpose flour

1. In a large saucepan, combine the stock with 2 tablespoons of the shallots, 1 tablespoon of the chives, 1 tablespoon of the tarragon, 1 tablespoon of the parsley and 1 tablespoon of the thyme. Bring to a boil over high heat and cook until reduced to about 2 cups, 15 to 20 minutes. Strain through a fine-mesh sieve into another, smaller saucepan.

2. Meanwhile, in a food processor, combine the remaining 1 tablespoon each of shallots, chives, tarragon, parsley and thyme, the marjoram, salt and pepper with 6 tablespoons of the butter. Process to a smooth paste. Set the herb butter aside.

3. Blend the remaining 2 tablespoons butter with the flour until smooth to form a beurre manié. Bring the reduced stock to a boil over

moderately high heat. Whisk in the beurre manié, 1 tablespoon at a time, and boil until the sauce thickens, 1 to 2 minutes. Remove from the heat and whisk in the herb butter, 1 tablespoon at a time.

NOTE: If you're making this sauce to go with Poached Capon with Spring Herb Sauce (at left), use the poaching liquid instead of chicken stock.

—John Robert Massie

BREAST OF CHICKEN WITH JULIENNE OF VEGETABLES IN CREAM SAUCE

Fresh herbs impart a marvelously delicate flavor to the sauce. By all means, if you have them, use about a teaspoon of minced fresh herbs instead of the pinch of dried.

🍷 California Sauvignon Blanc, such as Dry Creek
  4 Servings

  8 small skinless, boneless chicken breast halves
    (about 4 ounces each)
  ⅔ cup dry white wine
  ⅔ cup dry sherry
  1 bay leaf
  2 medium carrots, cut into julienne strips
  1 medium leek (white part only), cut into
    julienne strips
  2 medium celery ribs, cut into julienne
    strips
  Pinch of crushed fennel seeds
  Pinch of basil
  Pinch of mint
  Pinch of thyme
  1 teaspoon minced fresh chives
  1¼ cups heavy cream
  ¾ teaspoon salt
  ⅛ teaspoon freshly ground pepper
  Sprigs of parsley, for garnish

1. Place the chicken breasts in a large nonreactive skillet. Pour in the wine and sherry; add the bay leaf. Arrange the julienned carrots, leek and celery over the chicken.

2. Cover the skillet and simmer over moderate heat for about 15 minutes, or until the chicken is tender and the juices run clear when pierced with a knife.

3. With a slotted spoon, transfer the chicken to a platter. Scatter the vegetables over the chicken. Cover with foil to keep warm.

4. Add the fennel seeds, basil, mint, thyme and chives to the skillet and boil the mixture over high heat until reduced by half, about 6 minutes.

5. Add the cream and boil again until the sauce thickly coats the back of a spoon, about 6 minutes longer. Season with the salt and pepper. Pour the hot sauce around the chicken breasts. Garnish with sprigs of parsley.

—Ston Easton Park, Bath, England

CHICKEN BREASTS WITH ORANGE SAUCE AND TOASTED ALMONDS

🍷 California Chardonnay, such as Sebastiani
  4 to 6 Servings

  6 skinless, boneless chicken breast halves, at
    room temperature
  2 large oranges
  1 egg yolk
  1 tablespoon plus 1 teaspoon white
    wine vinegar
  ½ teaspoon Dijon-style mustard
  ½ teaspoon salt
  Pinch of sugar
  Pinch of freshly ground white pepper
  1¼ cups safflower oil
  2 or 3 small zucchini, sliced into ¼-inch
    rounds and blanched for 30 seconds
  2 or 3 small yellow squash, sliced into ¼-inch
    rounds and blanched for 30 seconds

⅓ cup toasted slivered almonds,
    coarsely chopped
2 tablespoons finely chopped parsley

1. Lightly pound the thicker end of the chicken breasts for more even cooking.

2. In a pan that will hold the breasts comfortably in a single layer, bring enough water to cover them by about ½ inch to 140°.

3. Add the chicken breasts. Poach for 20 to 25 minutes, until the flesh is springy to the touch and the internal temperature is 140°. Remove the breasts to a platter, cover loosely and let cool to room temperature. *(The recipe can be prepared to this point up to 1 day ahead. Wrap well and refrigerate.)*

4. Grate the zest from the oranges; there will be about 1½ tablespoons. Squeeze ¼ cup juice. In a medium bowl, whisk together 1 tablespoon of the zest, the egg yolk, orange juice, vinegar, mustard, salt, sugar and pepper.

5. Gradually whisk in the oil, beginning with a few drops at a time; when the sauce thickens and becomes emulsified, whisk in the remaining oil in a thin stream. Cover and refrigerate the sauce overnight or until ready to use.

6. To serve, cut each chicken breast crosswise on the diagonal into 5 or 6 slices. Fan them out on the platter and sprinkle lightly with salt.

7. In separate small bowls, toss the zucchini and squash slices in 1 to 2 tablespoons each of the sauce to coat. Taste and add salt and pepper if needed. Arrange alternating green and yellow slices in rows around the chicken.

8. Spoon some sauce down the length of each chicken breast. Toss together the almonds, parsley and remaining orange zest and sprinkle over the sauce. Serve the remaining sauce on the side.

—————

—F&W

CHICKEN BREAST WITH ANCHOVY-CELERY SAUCE
6 Servings

6 skinless, boneless chicken breast halves, at
    room temperature
5 anchovy fillets, rinsed and finely chopped
    (1½ tablespoons)
½ cup minced celery
½ cup minced green bell pepper
1 tablespoon minced fresh hot green chile
1 small garlic clove, minced
¼ cup plus 1 tablespoon olive oil
2 tablespoons white wine vinegar
¼ teaspoon freshly ground black pepper
2 tablespoons finely chopped parsley
Salt
4 or 5 plum tomatoes, thinly sliced

1. Lightly pound the thicker end of the chicken breasts for more even cooking.

2. In a pan that will hold the breasts comfortably in a single layer, bring enough water to cover them by about ½ inch to 140°.

3. Add the chicken and poach for 20 to 25 minutes, until the flesh is springy to the touch and the internal temperature is 140°. Remove the breasts to a platter, cover loosely and let cool to room temperature. *(The recipe can be prepared to this point up to 1 day ahead. Wrap the chicken well and refrigerate.)*

4. In a medium bowl, combine the anchovies, celery, bell and chile peppers, garlic, oil, vinegar and black pepper. Let stand for 1 hour or overnight to allow the flavors to blend. Just before serving, stir in the parsley and salt to taste.

5. To serve, cut each chicken breast crosswise on the diagonal into 5 or 6 slices. Fan them out on the platter and sprinkle lightly with salt. Then spoon the sauce in a band over the top. Garnish with the tomato slices.

—————

—F&W

SAKE-STEAMED CHICKEN WITH SESAME SAUCE

You can also serve this sake-steamed chicken without the sesame sauce, hot or cold, for a simple low-calorie dish. For a quick low-fat sauce to go with it, reserve about ½ cup of the broth from the steamer and stir in 1 tablespoon of dark soy sauce and 2 tablespoons of lemon juice. Spoon this light sauce over the chicken before serving.

4 Servings

1 pound chicken thighs
Salt
6 tablespoons sake
2 tablespoons Oriental sesame paste★ or
  peanut butter
¼ cup chicken broth
1 tablespoon dark shoyu (Japanese soy sauce)★
½ tablespoon fresh lemon juice
¼ teaspoon sugar
★Available at Asian markets

1. Score the skin side of the thighs fairly deeply, with cuts placed about ½ inch apart to allow the sake to penetrate as the meat steams. Lay skin-side up in a baking pan, salt lightly and splash on the sake.

2. Fill a steamer, large pot or wok fitted with a rack with water to a level 1 inch below the rack, cover and bring to a boil. Place the baking pan on the rack and cover immediately. Steam 15 to 20 minutes over high heat Remove the chicken to a plate and cover loosely to keep warm. *(The recipe can be prepared well ahead to this point. If serving the chicken cold, cover and refrigerate; remove from the refrigerator shortly before serving.)*

3. In a small bowl, blend the sesame paste and chicken broth (you can use some of the broth from steaming the chicken if it is flavorful enough). Add the soy sauce, lemon juice and sugar and blend well. Add more chicken broth if you would prefer a thinner sauce.

4. Cut the chicken off the bone and cut the meat into bite-size pieces. Spoon the sauce over the chicken and serve.

———

—F&W

STEAMED CHICKEN WITH ORIENTAL VINAIGRETTE

4 Servings

One 3½-pound chicken
5 tablespoons red wine vinegar
3 tablespoons soy sauce
1 tablespoon cider vinegar
1½ tablespoons Oriental sesame oil
·1 teaspoon peanut oil
1 teaspoons finely chopped garlic
1 thinly sliced scallion

1. Truss the chicken. Add water to a steamer to 1 inch below the rack and bring to a full, rolling boil. Place the chicken on the rack, cover and, over moderate heat, steam for 25 to 30 minutes, adding more boiling water if necessary. The chicken is done when the juice runs clear when the thigh is pierced with a fork or a meat thermometer inserted into the thickest part of a thigh registers 165°.

2. In a small bowl, whisk together the red wine vinegar, soy sauce, cider vinegar, sesame oil, peanut oil and garlic. Stir in the scallion.

3. Serve the steamed chicken with the sauce on the side.

———

—F&W

Casseroles and One-Dish

BAKED ACORN SQUASH STUFFED WITH CURRIED CHICKEN

This recipe calls for no curry powder, but for plenty of its component spices. Also, both butternut and acorn squash are used. There's a good reason for this: The butternut squash meat adds color to the curry, and the acorn squash, when halved, makes a perfect receptacle for baking the curry. If you prefer to make this recipe in stages, the chicken curry can be prepared and the squash baked ahead.

6 Servings

4 tablespoons clarified butter
1½ pounds skinless, boneless chicken breast,
    cut into 1½-by-¼-inch strips
1 large Spanish onion, coarsely chopped
1 small red bell pepper, cut into ¼-inch-wide
    strips
1 large garlic clove, crushed through a press
½ teaspoon turmeric
¼ teaspoon cinnamon
¼ teaspoon ground cardamom
¼ teaspoon cumin
¼ teaspoon ground coriander
¼ teaspoon crushed hot red pepper
Pinch of ground cloves
½ cup Chicken Stock (p. 10) or canned broth
½ cup apple juice or cider
1 tablespoon tomato paste
3 small acorn squash (about ¾ pound each)
1 small butternut squash (about 1 pound)
½ cup heavy cream
½ teaspoon salt
Freshly ground black pepper

1. Preheat the oven to 350°. In a large heavy skillet, heat 2 tablespoons of the clarified butter. Add the chicken and stir-fry over high heat until golden brown, 3 to 5 minutes. Remove to a bowl with a slotted spoon and reserve.

2. Add another tablespoon clarified butter to the skillet and reduce the heat to moderate. Add the onion, red bell pepper and garlic and stir-fry until the onion is softened and translucent, about 5 minutes.

3. Blend in the turmeric, cinnamon, cardamom, cumin, coriander, hot pepper and cloves and cook, stirring, over moderate heat until fragrant, about 2 minutes. Stir in the stock, apple juice and tomato paste. Return the chicken to the skillet and adjust the heat so that the liquid just barely bubbles. Cover and cook for 45 minutes.

4. Meanwhile, place the acorn and butternut squashes in a baking dish and bake for 20 minutes. Turn and cook for 20 to 25 minutes longer, or until they feel fairly soft to the touch. Remove from the oven and let stand until cool enough to handle. Leave the oven on.

5. Halve the butternut squash and scoop out the seeds and strings; peel and cut the flesh into ¾-inch cubes. Add the butternut squash and cream to the curried chicken. Season with the salt and black pepper to taste.

6. Halve each acorn squash and scoop out all the seeds and stringy portions; brush the cut surfaces with the remaining 1 tablespoon butter. Place the acorn squash, cut-sides up, in a large shallow baking pan. Mound the hollows with the curried chicken. Cover loosely with foil and bake for 30 minutes, or until the acorn squash is tender.

———————————

—*Jean Anderson*

*Above, Chicken and Canadian Bacon
Salad with Toasted Pecans (p. 225).
Left, Chicken and Pasta Salad with
Roasted Peppers (p. 247).*

Cassoulet Rapide (p. 203).

Above, Herbed Cornish Game Hens (p. 78). Right, Fricassee of Cornish Hens with Cherry Tomatoes and Glazed Shallots (p. 264).

CHICKEN WITH ARTICHOKES

8 Servings

3½ tablespoons unsalted butter
5½ teaspoons peanut oil
¼ cup minced shallots or ½ cup minced onions
Salt
2 packages frozen artichoke hearts, thawed and patted dry
¾ pound mushrooms, sliced
¾ teaspoon freshly ground white pepper
3 pounds skinless, boneless chicken breast, cut into bite-size pieces
½ cup dry white wine
½ teaspoon tarragon
¾ cup Bel Paese cheese, in ¼-inch cubes
1½ teaspoons chopped parsley

1. In a large skillet, heat 1½ teaspoons of butter and 1½ teaspoons of oil over high heat. Add the shallots and a pinch of salt and sauté only until translucent. Scrape the shallots into a baking dish and set aside.

2. Add 1 tablespoon of butter to the skillet. Add half the artichokes and ¼ teaspoon of salt and cook over very high heat, until light golden, but not cooked through, about 3 minutes. Add to the shallots in the baking dish. Repeat with another 1 tablespoon butter, ¼ teaspoon salt and the second package of artichokes.

3. Add 1 teaspoon of the butter and 2 teaspoons of the oil to the skillet. Add the mushrooms and ¼ teaspoon of the pepper and stir-fry until lightly colored, but before the mushrooms give off any liquid. Add the mushrooms to the baking dish.

4. Melt 1 teaspoon of butter in 2 teaspoons of oil. Add half the chicken and ½ teaspoon of salt and cook only until lightly colored. Add the chicken to the baking dish. Pour the cooking juices out of the skillet into a small bowl and reserve. Repeat with the remaining chicken, another 1 teaspoon butter and ½ teaspoon salt.

5. Return the reserved cooking juices to the skillet and bring to a boil. Cook until only fat and browned bits remain. Pour off the excess fat, add the wine and bring to a boil, scraping up the browned bits. Pour the juices over the chicken and vegetables in the baking dish. Sprinkle with the tarragon. *(The recipe can be prepared ahead up to this point.)*

6. Preheat the oven to 350°. Cover the baking dish and bake, stirring the contents occasionally, until thoroughly hot and chicken is done, 30 to 45 minutes.

7. Five minutes before the dish is ready, add the Bel Paese and toss. Re-cover the dish and bake for 5 minutes, or until the cheese is just soft but not melted. Sprinkle with the chopped parsley and serve at once.

————

—F&W

BAKED EGGS AND CHICKEN HASH

The chicken for the hash is poached and the resulting stock is used to make the gravy. The stock will be easier to degrease if refrigerated overnight. The potatoes can be cooked ahead as well.

8 Servings

3 large baking potatoes (about 1½ pounds), scrubbed
One 3½-pound chicken, gizzard and neck reserved
2 onions—1 medium, cut into 1-inch chunks, and 1 large, chopped
2 large celery ribs with leaves, cut into 1-inch chunks
2 medium carrots, cut into 1-inch chunks
1 large garlic clove, lightly crushed
1 large bay leaf
½ teaspoon thyme

3 sprigs of parsley plus 2 tablespoons minced
1 teaspoon whole peppercorns
2 teaspoons salt
7 tablespoons unsalted butter
2 tablespoons vegetable oil
1 teaspoon freshly ground pepper
8 eggs
2 tablespoons all-purpose flour
¼ cup heavy cream

1. Preheat the oven to 400°. Pierce the potatoes in several places with a fork and bake for 1 hour. Set aside to cool. Then peel the potatoes, wrap them in foil and refrigerate .

2. Place the chicken in a small flameproof casserole. Add the gizzard and neck. Add the medium onion, celery, carrots, garlic, bay leaf, thyme, parsley sprigs, peppercorns and 1 teaspoon of the salt. Pour in 6 cups of water and bring to a boil over high heat. Reduce the heat to moderately low, cover and simmer for 1 hour. Transfer the chicken to a platter and set aside to cool to room temperature.

3. Increase the heat to moderately high and boil the stock for 35 minutes. Strain the stock into a large measuring cup, pressing on the solids with a spoon to extract any liquid. If you have more than 1¾ cups, boil again to reduce; if you have less, add enough water to compensate. Let the stock cool to room temperature, then cover and refrigerate.

4. Remove the skin from the cooled chicken and discard. Pull the meat from the bones, tearing it into bite-size pieces, and place in a medium bowl. Cover and refrigerate. *(The recipe can be prepared to this point up to 1 day ahead.)*

5. In a 10-inch ovenproof skillet, preferably cast iron, melt 2 tablespoons of the butter over moderate heat. Add the chopped onion and cook until softened, about 5 minutes. Using a slotted spoon, transfer the onion to a medium bowl and set aside.

6. Increase the heat to moderately high and add 1 tablespoon of the butter. When the butter begins to foam, add the chicken. Cook, turning once, until the meat is browned and crisp in spots, about 10 minutes. Add the chicken to the onions in the bowl and mix.

7. Preheat the oven to 350°. Cut the potatoes into ½-inch dice. Add 1 tablespoon of the oil and 1 tablespoon of the butter to the skillet and increase the heat to high. When the butter has melted, add half of the potatoes. Cook, stirring only occasionally, until golden and crisp, about 10 minutes. Season with ½ teaspoon each of the salt and pepper and add to the chicken and onion in the bowl. Repeat with 1 more tablespoon of the butter and the remaining 1 tablespoon oil, potatoes, ½ teaspoon salt and ½ teaspoon pepper. Return all the chicken and potato mixture to the skillet and smooth the surface with the back of a spoon.

8. Using a spoon, make 8 indentations about 2½ inches wide and ½ inch deep in the hash. One at a time, crack the eggs into the indentations. Cover loosely with foil and bake for about 25 minutes, until the eggs are cooked through.

9. Meanwhile, skim the congealed fat from the surface of the stock. In a medium skillet, melt the remaining 2 tablespoons butter over moderately high heat. Whisk in the flour and cook, whisking constantly until thick and pasty, 2 to 3 minutes. Gradually whisk in the stock and cook, whisking frequently, for 5 minutes. Add the cream and bring to a boil. Reduce the heat to very low, stir in the minced parsley and keep the sauce warm until the eggs are cooked. (If the sauce gets too thick, stir in water by the tablespoon.) Serve the hash hot from the oven and pass the gravy on the side.

———————

—Tracey Seaman

CHICKEN, SAUSAGE AND GRITS HASH WITH WILD MUSHROOMS

If you're making the hash with leftovers, you will need three cups of cooked chicken meat. But there is also a method for starting from scratch. Do not use quick-cooking grits here, for the results will be less than satisfactory.

❣ For an exciting contrast to this new-style hash, try a big, oaky California Chardonnay, such as Cuvaison.

6 Servings

6 medium chicken thighs (about 2½
  pounds total)
Salt and freshly ground pepper
3¼ cups canned chicken broth
¾ cup enriched white hominy grits
½ pound sage-seasoned breakfast sausage,
  casings removed if in links
2 tablespoons unsalted butter
1 large onion, chopped
½ teaspoon thyme
½ pound white mushrooms, thinly sliced
½ pound assorted wild mushrooms, such as
  chanterelles, morels, cèpes (porcini) or
  shiitakes, thinly sliced
2 tablespoons vegetable oil

1. Preheat the oven to 375°. Place the chicken thighs in a roasting pan. Season with salt and pepper and bake for about 40 minutes, until the juices run clear when a thigh is pierced with a knife. Set aside to cool.

2. Meanwhile, lightly grease a small baking sheet with oil or vegetable cooking spray and set aside. In a medium saucepan, bring the chicken broth to a boil over high heat. Gradually pour in the grits in a steady stream, stirring constantly. Reduce the heat to low and simmer, stirring occasionally, for 15 minutes. Let cool slightly, then scrape the grits onto the prepared baking sheet and, using a rubber spatula, spread evenly to a ½-inch thickness. Set aside to cool completely, about 30 minutes. *(The recipe can be prepared to this point up to 1 day ahead; cover and refrigerate the chicken and grits separately.)*

3. While the grits cool, cook the sausage meat in a large skillet over moderately high heat, stirring occasionally with a wooden spoon or spatula to break up the clumps, until well browned and crusty in spots, about 10 minutes. Using a slotted spoon, transfer the meat to a large bowl.

4. Reduce the heat to moderate and melt 1 tablespoon of the butter in the skillet. Add the onion and cook, stirring often, until softened and browned, about 8 minutes. Stir in the thyme, white mushrooms and wild mushrooms. Increase the heat to moderately high and cook, stirring occasionally, until the mushrooms are soft, browned and dry, 10 to 12 minutes. Transfer to the bowl with the sausage.

5. Cut the cooled grits into ¾-inch cubes. Using a spatula, transfer the grits to the bowl with the sausage and mushrooms.

6. Remove and discard the skin from the cooled chicken. Pull the meat from the bones and shred into ¾- to 1-inch pieces. Add the chicken to the bowl of mushrooms and grits and season with ½ teaspoon pepper and ¼ teaspoon salt. Toss gently.

7. Heat a large heavy skillet over moderately high heat until hot but not smoking. Add the oil and the remaining 1 tablespoon butter. When the butter is melted, spoon in the hash, distributing it evenly in the pan and pressing down lightly with the back of a spoon or spatula to pack it in. Cook the hash, without disturbing it, for 10 minutes. Remove the skillet from the heat and let rest for 3 minutes.

8. Preheat the broiler. Place the skillet under the broiler or as close to the heat as possible for about 3 minutes, rotating the pan as necessary, until the top of the hash is browned. Serve at once directly from the skillet.

———

—*Lee Bailey*

CHICKEN POT PIES

A good addition to a cook's chicken repertoire is this version of an American classic. In most pot pie recipes, the chicken is cooked twice: It is usually boiled before making the pie filling and then baked within the pie. We have found this double-cooking unnecessary; when uncooked chicken is added to the filling, the result is meat that is tender as well as tasty. To make the recipe, you will need eight 5-inch pie pans.

8 Servings

PASTRY:

4 cups all-purpose flour

1 teaspoon salt

6 tablespoons lard, chilled

*1 stick (4 ounces) unsalted butter, chilled and
 cut into pieces*

8 tablespoons vegetable shortening

10 to 12 tablespoons ice water

CHICKEN FILLING:

1 pound skinless, boneless chicken breast

3 cups Chicken Stock (p. 10) or canned broth

*2 medium carrots, cut into ⅛-inch slices
 (about 1 cup)*

*1 medium boiling potato, cut into ⅜-inch dice
 (about 1 cup)*

1 cup peas

*1 small to medium white turnip, peeled and
 cut into ⅜-inch dice (about 1 cup)*

7 tablespoons unsalted butter

1 medium onion, finely diced (about ¾ cup)

7 tablespoons all-purpose flour

½ cup dry sherry

GLAZE:

1 egg

1. Prepare the pastry: In a large mixing bowl, combine the flour and salt. Using a pastry blender or two knives, cut in the lard, butter and vegetable shortening until the mixture resembles coarse meal.

2. Sprinkle 10 tablespoons of the ice water over the mixture and stir rapidly with a fork to blend. If the pastry will not gather into a ball, stir in up to 2 additional tablespoons of water. Do not overmix or the pastry will be tough. Divide the dough into two portions, flatten them and wrap separately in waxed paper. Chill for 30 minutes.

3. Meanwhile, prepare the chicken filling: Cut the breast halves lengthwise into thirds. Cut the strips across the grain into ½-inch pieces. Cover and refrigerate.

4. In a 3-quart saucepan, bring the chicken stock to a boil over high heat. Add the carrots and potato. When the boiling resumes, cook for 3 minutes. With a slotted spoon, transfer the vegetables to a large bowl; set aside.

5. Return the broth to a boil, add the peas and turnip and cook for 3 minutes. Transfer the vegetables to the bowl with the carrots and potato. Measure the chicken stock; you should have 2 cups. If you have less, add broth or water; reserve.

6. In a medium skillet, melt the butter over moderate heat. Add the onion and sauté until translucent, about 5 minutes. Stir in the flour and cook, stirring for 2 minutes.

7. Combine the sherry with the reserved stock and add it all at once to the skillet. Stirring constantly with a wire whisk or a fork, cook the sauce over moderate heat until it thickens, 3 to 4 minutes. Remove the skillet from the heat, cover the sauce with a round of waxed paper and cool it to room temperature (this can be done in the refrigerator if desired).

8. Prepare the pie pans: Have ready eight 5-inch pie pans. On a lightly floured surface and using a lightly floured rolling pin, roll out half the pastry to a ⅛-inch thickness. For each pie, you will need one 7-inch round to line the pan and one 6-inch round for the top crust. Cut out as many 7-inch rounds as possible and carefully fit them into the pie pans without stretching the dough. Stack the prepared pie pans, wrap them in

foil and chill until needed. Gather the scraps and refrigerate them. Roll out the remaining half of the dough in the same manner and cut as many 6-inch rounds as possible. Stack these between sheets of waxed paper and refrigerate. Gather the scraps and combine them with the chilled scraps. Roll out the dough and cut as many 6- and 7-inch rounds as needed to complete the pies. Again gather the scraps, roll them ⅛ inch thick, place between sheets of waxed paper and chill.

9. Preheat the oven to 400°. Combine the chicken with the reserved vegetables, add the sauce and gently toss the mixture to blend the ingredients evenly. Remove the pastry-lined pie pans, the 6-inch pastry rounds and the rolled scraps from the refrigerator. Using the small end of a funnel or a ¼-inch cutter, cut a steam hole in the center of each 6-inch round. As optional garnish, use the reserved rolled-out scraps of pastry and a small petal-shaped cutter or a paring knife to cut out 72 petal shapes.

10. Glaze the pies: In a small bowl, beat the egg with 1 tablespoon cold water. Using a small pastry brush, paint a ½-inch circle of the egg wash around each steam hole; attach nine petals around each hole to form a flower.

11. Place about ¾ cup of the chicken filling in each prepared pie pan. Working with one pie at a time, moisten the top surface of the pastry in the pans all around. Then center a 6-inch round of pastry over the top and press the seam together to seal in the filling. Tuck the excess pastry under all around and crimp to make a fluted edge.

12. Brush the top of each pie with some of the remaining egg glaze and place on a heavy cookie sheet. Bake for about 40 minutes, or until the crust is crisp and golden brown. Serve hot accompanied with a tossed green salad if desired.

———

—F&W

GAME BIRD POT PIE

My father always made this recipe with wild birds, but for convenience, I usually use poussins (baby chickens) or Cornish game hens. If you decide to make this with wild game birds, substitute a dry red wine for the white wine called for below.

4 Servings

2 poussins (baby chickens) or Cornish game
  hens (1 to 1¼ pounds each)
⅓ cup all-purpose flour
½ teaspoon salt
¼ teaspoon freshly ground pepper
2 tablespoons unsalted butter
2 tablespoons olive oil
½ pound carrots (3 or 4 medium), diced
3 medium leeks (white and tender green),
  chopped
½ cup dry white wine
2½ cups Chicken Stock (p. 10) or
  canned broth
¾ pound small red potatoes, unpeeled and cut
  into 1-inch cubes
1 cup peas
1 garlic clove, minced
1 tablespoon minced fresh thyme or
  1 teaspoon dried
Baking Powder Biscuits (recipe follows)
Chopped fresh thyme or parsley, for garnish

1. Preheat the oven to 375°. Cut the birds lengthwise in half. In a shallow dish, combine the flour, salt and pepper. Dust the birds with the seasoned flour, reserving the excess.

2. In a large skillet, melt the butter in the oil over moderately high heat. Add the chickens, skin-side down, in batches if necessary, and sauté, turning, until nicely browned, 3 to 5 minutes. Remove and set aside.

3. Add the carrots and leeks; cook for 2 minutes. Sprinkle the reserved seasoned flour over the vegetables and toss to coat. Cook, stirring, for 1 to 2 minutes without browning. Add the

wine and stock and bring to a boil, scraping up any browned bits from the bottom of the pan. Add the potatoes, peas, garlic and thyme. Increase the heat to high and bring to a boil. Cook, stirring frequently, until the mixture is nicely thickened, 3 to 5 minutes.

4. Pour the vegetables and sauce into a large casserole. Arrange the chickens in a single layer on top of the sauce. Cover the casserole and bake for 20 minutes. *(The recipe can be prepared to this point up to 1 day ahead. Let cool, then cover and refrigerate. Reheat to lukewarm before proceeding.)*

5. Meanwhile, prepare the Baking Powder Biscuits through Step 4.

6. After the casserole has baked for 20 minutes, increase the oven temperature to 425°. Arrange the biscuits over the birds. Return the casserole to the oven and bake, uncovered, until the biscuits are fluffy and golden brown, 12 to 15 minutes.

7. To serve, remove the biscuits; split if desired and divide among 4 warmed serving plates. Place a half chicken on each plate and cover generously with sauce and vegetables. Garnish with chopped thyme or parsley.

—*Gayle Henderson Wilson*

BAKING POWDER BISCUITS

Serve these biscuits on their own, or use them to top Game Bird Pot Pie (above).

Makes 8 to 10

4 tablespoons unsalted butter
2 cups all-purpose flour
1 tablespoon baking powder
1 teaspoon salt
¾ cup milk

1. Preheat the oven to 450°. In a food processor, thoroughly blend the butter, flour, baking powder and salt until the mixture resembles coarse meal.

2. Add the milk and mix until the dough begins to mass together; do not overblend.

3. Turn the dough out onto a lightly floured surface and knead briefly, dusting lightly with additional flour if it sticks, until a soft, smooth dough forms, about 10 seconds.

4. Roll out the dough ½ inch thick on a clean lightly floured surface. Cut into 2-inch rounds.

5. Arrange the biscuits on a greased baking sheet and bake for 12 minutes, or until golden brown.

—*Gayle Henderson Wilson*

MEXICAN CASSOULET

A great party casserole, this dish needs nothing but a green salad to make a substantial meal. For added spice, you could serve an icy-cold fresh tomato salsa on the side.

8 to 10 Servings

1½ cups dried small red beans
1½ cups dried pea beans (or other small white bean)
8 large dried ancho chiles★
1 pound chorizo (Mexican fresh sausage)★ or hot Italian sausage
One 3½-pound chicken, cut into 8 serving pieces, or 3 pounds chicken parts
1 teaspoon salt
2 teaspoons freshly ground pepper
1 tablespoon chili powder
1 tablespoon cumin
3 cups Chicken Stock (p. 10) or canned broth
2 medium onions, cut into wedges
2 small fresh serrano chiles★ or jalapeños, minced, or 2 teaspoons minced pickled jalapeños
4 garlic cloves, crushed through a press
2 tablespoons chopped fresh oregano or 2 teaspoons dried
¼ teaspoon hot pepper sauce
2 medium chayote★ (about 1 pound), or 3 medium zucchini

1 can (28 ounces) Italian peeled tomatoes, cut
  in half and drained, liquid reserved
1½ cups fresh bread crumbs
3 tablespoons melted unsalted butter
*Available at Latin American markets

1. In a large flameproof casserole, combine the beans with 8 cups of lightly salted water. Bring to a boil over moderately high heat and continue to boil for 40 minutes; remove from the heat. The beans will still be crunchy.

2. Meanwhile, rinse, stem and seed the ancho chiles. Soak in 2 cups of boiling water for 20 minutes. Puree the chiles and their soaking liquid in a blender or food processor. Set the chile puree aside.

3. Prick the sausages all over. In a large skillet, sauté the sausages over moderate heat, turning, until browned, 8 to 10 minutes. Transfer the sausages to a plate to cool slightly; reserve 2 tablespoons of fat in the skillet. Halve the sausages lengthwise, then slice crosswise ½ inch thick.

4. Preheat the oven to 350°. Rub the chicken pieces with the salt and pepper. Combine the chili powder and cumin. Sprinkle some over each piece of chicken. Reserve any that is not used.

5. Heat the 2 tablespoons reserved fat in the skillet. Add the chicken, skin-side down, in batches if necessary. Sauté over moderately high heat, turning once, until golden brown, 3 to 5 minutes on each side. Remove the browned chicken to a plate and pour off the fat in the skillet.

6. Mix 2 cups of the stock with the chile puree and add to the skillet. Bring to a boil over high heat, scraping up any browned bits from the bottom of the pan. Remove from the heat and set aside.

7. Cover the beans in the casserole with the onions, serrano chiles, garlic, oregano and hot sauce. Add the sausage and lay the chicken on top, wedging the pieces snugly together. Reserve 1 cup of the chile puree and pour the remainder into the casserole. Sprinkle any remaining chili powder and cumin over the top.

8. Cover the casserole and bake in the oven until the beans are just tender, about 2 hours; check the cassoulet after 1 hour and add the reserved 1 cup stock and chile puree if the beans look dry. (The recipe can be prepared ahead to this point. Let cool, then cover and refrigerate for up to 2 days, or freeze for up to 1 month. Thaw the cassoulet, if frozen, and reheat before proceeding.)

9. Meanwhile, peel and cut the chayote into 1-inch slices or slice the zucchini. Quarter each piece into pie-shaped wedges.

10. Remove the cassoulet from the oven and gently transfer the chicken to a plate. Add the chayote and tomatoes and enough of the reserved tomato juices to moisten the beans. Toss gently to mix. Return the chicken to the top of the casserole and bake for 20 to 30 minutes, until the chayote is tender and the beans are soft but not mushy.

11. Preheat the broiler. Mix the bread crumbs with the melted butter. Scatter the crumbs over the top of the cassoulet. Place the casserole under the broiler until the crumbs are browned, about 2 minutes, watching carefully.

—Gayle Henderson Wilson

CASSOULET RAPIDE

There are as many versions of cassoulet as there are cooks who prepare it. This one takes all the shortcuts except the one on taste.

♟ Hearty red, such as C.U.N.E. Rioja Clarete or California Zinfandel, such as Kendall-Jackson

   6 to 8 Serving

2 cups dried navy beans
1 pound chicken gizzards
2 medium onions, coarsely chopped
Bouquet garni: 8 sprigs of parsley, 3 garlic
  cloves, 2 tablespoons thyme, 4 whole cloves
  and 2 bay leaves tied in cheesecloth

*1 pound very lean bacon, cut into
   julienne strips*

*1 pound boneless smoked chicken or duck, cut
   into 2-inch chunks*

*1 pound smoked Polish sausage, sliced
   ¼ inch thick*

1 tart apple, peeled and cut into ½-inch dice

½ cup dry red wine

½ cup Armagnac or other brandy

3 tablespoons tomato paste

½ teaspoon freshly ground pepper

2 cups fresh bread crumbs

½ cup finely chopped parsley

4 tablespoons unsalted butter, melted

1. In a large heavy saucepan or flameproof casserole, bring 8 cups of water to a boil. Add the beans and cook for 1 minute. Remove from the heat and let stand, covered, for 1 hour.

2. Meanwhile, in a medium saucepan, cover the gizzards with 4 cups of water and bring to a simmer. Reduce the heat to low and cook for 1 hour. Strain the stock; discard the gizzards. Boil the stock over high heat until it is reduced to 1 cup. Set the reduced stock aside.

3. Add the onions and bouquet garni to the beans and bring to a boil over high heat. Reduce the heat to moderate and simmer for 1 hour. Drain the beans and discard the bouquet garni.

4. In a small saucepan, cover the bacon with cold water and bring to a boil. Cook for 3 minutes, then drain the bacon.

5. Preheat the oven to 400 . In a large bowl, combine the beans, reserved stock, smoked chicken, sausage, bacon, apple, wine, Armagnac, tomato paste and pepper. Toss to mix well. Turn into a large casserole.

6. In a medium bowl, toss the bread crumbs with the parsley and melted butter. Sprinkle evenly over the top of the casserole and bake, uncovered, for 20 minutes.

7. Reduce the oven temperature to 350° and bake for 1 hour longer.

———————————

—W. Peter Prestcott

PESTO CHICKEN CASSOULET

This hearty one-dish meal needs nothing more in the way of accompaniment than a loaf of bread or lightly buttered noodles.

❡ Full-bodied white, such as Clos du Bois Chardonnay, or fruity red, such as Louis M. Martini Pinot Noir

8 Servings

⅔ cup all-purpose flour

2 teaspoons salt

2½ teaspoons freshly ground black pepper

8 chicken thighs

8 chicken drumsticks

3 tablespoons olive oil

2 pounds small zucchini

6 shallots, thinly sliced

3 garlic cloves, crushed

4 red bell peppers, cut into ¼-inch strips

4 yellow bell peppers, cut into ¼-inch strips

1 jar (7 ounces) pesto (¾ cup)

1½ cups crème fraîche

*1 cup freshly grated Parmesan cheese (about
   4 ounces)*

1½ cups fresh bread crumbs

1½ teaspoons thyme

¼ teaspoon cayenne pepper

1. In a shallow bowl, combine the flour, salt and 2 teaspoons of the black pepper. Dredge the chicken parts in the flour mixture. Shake off any excess.

2. In a large flameproof casserole, heat 2 tablespoons of the olive oil over moderately high heat. Add the chicken in batches and cook, turning often, until evenly browned, about 15 minutes. Transfer the chicken to paper towels to drain. Wipe out the casserole.

3. Meanwhile, quarter the zucchini lengthwise, then slice crosswise into ½-inch pieces.

4. In a large skillet, heat the remaining 1 tablespoon olive oil over moderately high heat. Add the shallots and cook until translucent, 2 to 3 minutes. Add the garlic and cook for 1 minute longer, then add the red and yellow bell peppers and the zucchini and cook until softened, 5 to 7 minutes. Remove from the heat.

5. In a small bowl, combine the pesto with the crème fraîche and whisk until blended. In another bowl, toss the Parmesan cheese with the bread crumbs, thyme, cayenne and the remaining ½ teaspoon black pepper.

6. Preheat the oven to 375°. Return the chicken to the casserole and spread the vegetable mixture evenly on top. Spread the pesto cream over the vegetables. *(The recipe can be prepared to this point up to 2 days ahead and refrigerated. Let return to room temperature before proceeding.)*

7. Sprinkle the Parmesan crumbs evenly over the casserole and bake in the middle of the oven for 45 minutes. Heat the broiler. Broil the cassoulet for 2 to 3 minutes to brown the topping. Serve hot, directly from the casserole.

—Bob Chambers

BAKED SAFFRON CREPES WITH CHICKEN FILLING

These crêpes are especially attractive, tinted a delicate yellow by the saffron, which appears as threads of crimson.

4 Servings

CREPES:

3 tablespoons unsalted butter
¾ teaspoon saffron threads
1½ tablespoons dry vermouth
3 eggs
1⅓ cups milk
½ teaspoon salt
2 cups all-purpose flour

CHICKEN FILLING:

½ cup all-purpose flour
½ teaspoon coarse (kosher) salt
¼ teaspoon freshly ground black pepper
1½ pounds skinless, boneless chicken breast,
  cut into ¾-inch dice
1 stick (4 ounces) unsalted butter
1½ teaspoons minced garlic
⅔ cup thinly sliced scallions
¼ pound mushrooms, halved and thickly sliced
1 teaspoon thyme or basil
About 3 tablespoons Pernod
1½ teaspoons thick tomato paste
¼ to ½ cup sour cream
Pinch of cayenne pepper
½ cup sliced almonds, toasted

1. Make the crêpes: In a small saucepan, melt the butter over low heat.

2. In a small bowl, moisten the saffron in the vermouth. Let steep for about 10 minutes.

3. Meanwhile, in a food processor, lightly beat the eggs. Add the milk, 1 cup of water, the saffron, vermouth and salt and blend. Gradually add the flour, blending thoroughly. Blend in the melted butter. Cover and set aside in the refrigerator to rest for an hour or two.

4. Stir the batter and add enough water (about ½ cup) to thin the batter to the consistency of heavy cream.

5. Preheat a crêpe pan. When it is hot enough for a drop of water to sizzle, grease it with a light film of oil. Ladle about 3 tablespoons of batter into the pan and quickly swirl the pan to coat the surface lightly (pour any excess batter back into the bowl). Cook the crêpe until lightly browned on one side. Use your fingers to flip the crêpe over and cook on the second side for about 30 seconds, or until scattered with brown spots. Remove the crêpe to a plate. Repeat with the remaining batter, stacking the crêpes on top of one another (cover loosely with foil to keep warm); regrease the pan if necessary.

6. Make the chicken filling: In a bowl, combine the flour, salt and black pepper. Toss the chicken pieces in the mixture to coat them very lightly and evenly. Put the floured chicken into a sieve.

7. In a large skillet, heat 4 tablespoons of the butter until it stops foaming. Shake all excess flour from the chicken in the sieve then add to the skillet and stir-fry for about 2 minutes. Add the garlic, scallions, mushrooms and thyme and toss and cook 1 to 2 minutes longer, or until the mushrooms just lose their raw look.

8. Add the Pernod, heat it for a moment, then light it with a match, standing well back. Shake the pan until the flames die out. Add the tomato paste and toss to combine. Remove from the heat.

9. Add just enough sour cream to the chicken to bind the mixture lightly. Taste and carefully adjust seasonings, adding the cayenne and enough additional salt, black pepper, thyme and/or drops of Pernod to flavor the mixture assertively. Cool the mixture slightly.

10. Preheat the oven to 375°. Lightly butter a shallow baking dish large enough to hold the crêpes after they are rolled. In a small saucepan, melt the remaining 4 tablespoons butter.

11. Assemble the crêpes: Spoon a generous amount of the filling onto the spotty underside of each crêpe, arranging it in a long row, off-center. Fold the closer edge of the crêpe over the filling and carefully roll it up, evening the shape as you go. Place seam-side down in the baking dish. Repeat until all crêpes have been filled. Drizzle a small amount of the melted butter over the crêpes, sprinkle the almonds on top and drizzle the remaining butter over the almonds. Bake 10 to 12 minutes, or until the crêpes are heated through and sizzling. Serve at once.

———

—F&W

CHICKEN ENCHILADA CASSEROLE WITH SALSA VERDE

You can make this up to three months ahead and freeze it, or up to three days ahead and refrigerate it.

6 Servings

One 3½- to 4½-pound roasting chicken
1 medium carrot, coarsely chopped
2 thick slices of Spanish onion
2 garlic cloves, coarsely chopped
1 teaspoon salt
4 cups corn oil
12 corn tortillas (6 inches in diameter)
1 cup heavy cream
½ cup sour cream
Salsa Verde (recipe follows)
1 cup chopped scallions (white and tender green)
1½ cups coarsely grated Monterey Jack cheese (about 6 ounces)
1½ cups coarsely grated sharp Cheddar cheese (about 6 ounces)
6 lettuce leaves and 6 radish roses, for garnish

1. Put the chicken in a large heavy stockpot or flameproof casserole. Add the carrot, onion, garlic, salt and enough water to cover and bring to a boil. Reduce the heat to a simmer, cover and cook until the chicken is very tender, about 1½ hours.

2. Remove the pot from the heat, uncover and let the chicken cool in the poaching liquid for 1 hour.

3. Pull the chicken off the bones; discard the bones and skin. Tear the meat into ½-by-2-inch strips. Reserve the broth for another use.

4. In a skillet, heat the oil to 375°. Quickly fry the tortillas in the hot oil, 2 or 3 at a time, until crisp. Drain well on paper towels.

5. Preheat the oven to 375°. Lightly oil the bottom of a large shallow baking dish. In a small bowl, combine the heavy cream and sour cream and blend well.

6. Spread ½ cup of the Salsa Verde over the bottom of the baking dish and cover with 6 of the tortillas. Drizzle the tortillas with ½ cup of the salsa and arrange the chicken on top. Spread half the sour cream mixture over the chicken and sprinkle with half the scallions and 1 cup of each cheese. Arrange the remaining 6 tortillas on top and cover with the remaining salsa and cheese. Pour the remaining sour cream mixture on top and sprinkle with the remaining scallions. *(The dish can be prepared ahead to this point. Cover well with plastic wrap and refrigerate for up to 3 days or freeze for up to 3 months. Return to room temperature before baking.)*

7. Bake, uncovered, for 30 to 35 minutes, until the casserole is heated through and the cheese is melted. Garnish each dish with a lettuce leaf and radish rose.

—*Jane Butel*

SALSA VERDE

This tart, piquant sauce is good on anything, but is often served with chicken and sour cream.

Makes About 2½ Cups

1 can (13 ounces) tomatillos, drained
1 cup chopped scallions (white and
　tender green)
½ cup chopped hot green New Mexico chiles
　(roasted and peeled, fresh or frozen) or 1 can
　(4 ounces) chopped hot green chiles, drained
1 large garlic clove, minced
½ teaspoon salt

Combine all the ingredients in a blender or food processor and puree.

—*Jane Butel*

GREEN CHILE CHICKEN

Fresh green chiles add a lively flavor to this dish, and the dried green chile provides a deep, smoky flavor. Look for corn tortillas labeled "for soft tacos"—they're relatively thick and have an earthy, true corn taste.

6 Servings

One 3-pound chicken, quartered
2 tablespoons olive oil or vegetable oil
1 large onion, chopped
½ pound poblano★ or other fresh mild green
　chiles, chopped
8 garlic cloves, minced
1 Idaho potato (about ½ pound), peeled and
　cut into ½-inch dice
½ ounce dried green chile★ (optional)
4 fresh tomatillos,★ chopped
⅓ cup chopped cilantro (fresh coriander)
2 teaspoons salt
Freshly ground black pepper
2 tablespoons unsalted butter
9 corn tortillas (6 inches in diameter)
6 ounces Monterey Jack cheese, grated (about
　1½ cups)

*6 ounces sharp Cheddar cheese, grated (about
  1½ cups)*
⅛ teaspoon chili powder or paprika
*Available at Latin American markets

1. In a large saucepan, pour 4 cups of water over the chicken and bring to a boil over high heat. Reduce the heat to low and simmer for 15 minutes. Turn the chicken pieces over and simmer for 15 minutes longer. Remove the breast pieces and cook the legs for another 10 minutes. Remove the legs.

2. Strain the broth into a bowl and skim off any fat that rises to the surface. Pour the broth into a medium saucepan and boil over high heat until it reduces to 2 cups, about 20 minutes. Pour the reduced broth into a bowl and set aside.

3. Meanwhile, return the large saucepan to high heat and add the oil. When it's hot, add the onion, poblanos and garlic and reduce the heat to low. Cover and cook, stirring occasionally, until the vegetables are softened, about 15 minutes.

4. In a small saucepan, cover the diced potato with water and boil over high heat until tender, about 5 minutes. Drain well.

5. Put the dried green chile, if using, in a small bowl and cover with 1 cup boiling water. Let soak until softened, about 10 minutes. Drain and chop.

6. When the vegetables in the saucepan are soft, add the diced potato, reconstituted dried chile and the reserved chicken broth and simmer over low heat, mashing some of the potatoes, until the mixture thickens slightly and the flavors blend, about 10 minutes. Remove from the heat and stir in the tomatillos, cilantro, salt and black pepper to taste.

7. Meanwhile, remove all the meat from the chicken, discarding the skin and bones. Cut the meat into 2-inch pieces. Stir the chicken into the sauce.

8. In a small skillet, heat 1 tablespoon of the butter over moderately high heat. Add 1 corn tortilla and fry until lightly browned, about 1 minute per side. Drain on paper towels. Add the remaining 1 tablespoon butter to the skillet and fry 2 more tortillas, one at a time. Drain well. Cut the fried tortillas in half and set aside.

9. Preheat the oven to 425°. In a bowl, combine the Monterey Jack and Cheddar cheeses. Set aside 1 tablespoon. Spoon one-third of the chicken mixture into a deep 3-quart casserole. Halve the remaining 6 unfried tortillas and arrange 4 halves over the chicken layer. Sprinkle one-third of the mixed cheeses on top. Continue layering in this order until the chicken, unfried tortilla halves and cheese are used up. Decoratively arrange the 6 fried tortilla halves on top and sprinkle with the reserved 1 tablespoon cheese and the chili powder.

10. Bake in the upper third of the oven until bubbly and crisp on top, about 25 minutes. Remove the casserole from the oven and let rest for 15 minutes before serving. Spoon hefty helpings onto 6 warmed plates, making sure to include a crisp tortilla half for each serving.

———

—Marcia Kiesel

ORANGE AND CORIANDER CHICKEN WITH RICE

This flavorsome combination makes a great dish for last-minute entertaining. I've substituted left-over roast pork for the chicken with great results.

🍷 California Chardonnay, such as Rodney Strong "Chalk Hill" or Viansa

6 Servings

⅓ cup fresh lemon juice
3 tablespoons tamari or soy sauce
2 teaspoons grated fresh ginger
2 dashes of hot pepper sauce
*2 broiled chickens, cut into 6 serving
  pieces each*
3 tablespoons olive oil
1 medium onion, thinly sliced

1 garlic clove, minced
¾ pound mushrooms, thinly sliced
½ teaspoon ground ginger
½ teaspoon salt
⅛ teaspoon freshly ground pepper
2 cups rice
2 cups Chicken Stock (p. 10) or canned broth
1 cup dry white wine
½ cup minced cilantro (fresh coriander)
1 tablespoon grated orange zest

1. In a large bowl, combine the lemon juice, tamari, grated ginger and hot pepper sauce. Add the chicken pieces and toss well to coat.

2. Preheat the oven to 375°. In a large flame-proof casserole, heat the oil. Add the onion and garlic and cook over moderate heat until softened, about 5 minutes.

3. Add the mushrooms and cook, stirring, until softened, about 5 minutes. Stir in the ground ginger, salt and pepper.

4. Add the rice to the casserole and increase the heat to moderately high. Cook, stirring constantly, until the rice is translucent, about 3 minutes. Stir in the chicken stock, wine and ½ cup of water. Bring to a boil and stir well. Cover tightly and bake for 10 minutes.

5. Uncover and arrange the chicken pieces on top of the rice. Pour on any marinade and sprinkle with the cilantro and orange zest. Cover and bake until the chicken is heated through and the rice is tender, about 10 minutes.

—*W. Peter Prestcott*

MOROCCAN PASTA
4 Servings

2 pounds fresh spinach, stemmed
¼ cup olive oil
¼ cup pine nuts
½ cup raisins
1 teaspoon sugar
¼ teaspoon ground cardamom
Zest of 1 lemon, cut into thin julienne strips
1 teaspoon fresh lemon juice
¾ teaspoon salt
½ teaspoon freshly ground pepper
3 tablespoons unsalted butter
10 ounces skinless, boneless chicken breast, cut crosswise into ½-inch pieces
¼ cup dry white wine
½ pound spaghetti or linguine

1. Rinse the spinach well but do not drain. In a large nonreactive saucepan over high heat, steam the spinach in the water clinging to its leaves until just wilted, about 2 minutes. Drain, rinse under cold running water, then squeeze in a clean linen towel or between several layers of paper towels to remove as much water as possible. Finely chop and set aside.

2. In a medium skillet, warm the oil over moderate heat. Add the pine nuts, raisins, sugar and cardamom. Cook, tossing, until the nuts are golden, about 2 minutes. Add the lemon zest and continue to sauté until the pieces of zest begin to brown around the edges, about 1 minute.

3. Add the spinach and cook, mixing with a fork to evenly distribute the ingredients, for 2 minutes. Season with the lemon juice, ½ teaspoon of the salt and the pepper and set aside.

4. In a medium skillet, melt 1 tablespoon of the butter over moderately high heat. Add the chicken and sauté, tossing, until lightly browned all over, 3 to 4 minutes. Season with the remaining ¼ teaspoon salt and add to the spinach mixture.

5. Pour the wine into the skillet and bring to a boil over high heat, scraping up any browned

bits from the bottom to deglaze the pan. Boil until the liquid is reduced to 2 tablespoons, about 2 minutes. Add to the spinach and chicken.

6. Cook the pasta in a large pot of boiling salted water until al dente, 10 to 12 minutes; drain. In a large bowl, toss the hot pasta with the remaining 2 tablespoons butter. Add the spinach and chicken and toss until mixed. Serve warm or at room temperature.

———

—*F&W*

CHICKEN LASAGNA

♒ Light Italian white, such as Galestro, or Italian red, such as Dolcetto or Bardolino

12 Servings

10 tablespoons unsalted butter

4 tablespoons olive oil

3 medium onions, minced

2 small garlic cloves, finely chopped

½ cup plus 2 tablespoons all-purpose flour

2½ cups hot milk

2½ cups hot Chicken Stock (p. 10) or canned broth

1 tablespoon tarragon

1½ teaspoons salt

½ teaspoon freshly ground white pepper

½ teaspoon freshly grated nutmeg

4 eggs

2½ to 3 pounds tomatoes—peeled, seeded and chopped

2 tablespoons tomato paste

½ cup dry red wine

1 tablespoon basil

½ teaspoon sugar

½ teaspoon red wine vinegar

2 pounds skinless, boneless chicken breast

1½ pounds chicken livers, trimmed

1 tablespoon oregano

1 package (16 ounces) lasagna noodles

2 cups freshly grated Parmesan cheese (about 8 ounces)

1. In a large saucepan, melt 5 tablespoons of the butter in 1 tablespoon of the oil over moderate heat. Add the onions and garlic and sauté until softened and translucent, about 5 minutes.

2. Stir in the flour. Reduce the heat to low and cook, stirring, for 3 minutes without coloring to make a roux. Off the heat, gradually whisk in the hot milk and hot chicken stock. Return to moderate heat, bring to a boil and cook, stirring, for 5 minutes.

3. Add the tarragon, 1 teaspoon of the salt, the pepper and the nutmeg. Remove from the heat and, one at a time, briskly whisk in the eggs. Cover partially and set the béchamel sauce aside.

4. In a large nonreactive skillet, combine the tomatoes with the tomato paste, red wine, basil, sugar, vinegar and the remaining ½ teaspoon salt. Cook, stirring frequently, over moderate heat until thick, about 15 minutes. Remove from the heat and set aside.

5. In a large skillet, melt the remaining 5 tablespoons butter in 1 tablespoon of the oil over moderate heat. Add the chicken, cover and cook, turning once, for 5 minutes on each side. Remove with tongs, leaving any fat in the pan. Let the chicken cool, then cut crosswise into ½-inch slices.

6. Add the chicken livers to the same skillet and sauté over moderately high heat, tossing, until nicely browned on the outside, 3 to 4 minutes. Add the oregano and let cool slightly. Mince the livers fine.

7. Bring a large pot of water to a boil and add the remaining 2 tablespoons oil. Cook the lasagna noodles until al dente, about 12 minutes. Drain and return the pasta to the pot; add warm water to cover (it will keep the noodles soft to facilitate handling).

8. Preheat the oven to 375°. Picking the noodles out of the water, arrange one layer in a well-buttered large, shallow baking dish. Cover the pasta with about 1¼ cups of the béchamel sauce. Top with half of the sliced chicken and then with ⅓ cup of the Parmesan cheese. Add another layer of pasta, all of the tomato sauce and ⅓ cup of the cheese. Add another layer of pasta, spread all of the chicken livers over the pasta and cover with 1¼ cups of the béchamel and then ⅓ cup of the cheese. Form another layer of pasta, then 1¼ cups béchamel, the remaining chicken and ⅓ cup cheese. Top with a final layer of pasta, the remaining béchamel and the remaining cheese. *(The lasagna can assembled to this point ahead of time. Cover well and refrigerate. Let return to room temperature before proceeding.)*

9. Bake for 45 minutes to 1 hour, until the top is golden brown and somewhat crusty. Let stand for 15 minutes before serving. *(If preparing the lasagna ahead of time, bake and set aside to cool completely. Cover with plastic and refrigerate overnight. Next day, let return to room temperature and reheat at 300° for 30 minutes. Let stand for 15 minutes before serving.)*

————————

—*W. Peter Prestcott*

CORIANDER CHICKEN WITH TUBETTI

The chicken and pasta cook together in one pot. This dish is best served with simply prepared vegetables such as steamed broccoli or cauliflower or broiled tomatoes.

8 Servings

8 chicken drumsticks
8 chicken thighs
¼ cup olive oil
1 tablespoon Chinese chili sauce
2 teaspoons cumin seeds
1 teaspoon (loosely packed) saffron threads
1 teaspoon salt

Juice of 1 lemon
½ cup coarsely chopped cilantro (fresh coriander)
4 cups Chicken Stock (p. 10) or canned broth
2 cups tubetti or other small dried pasta

1. Place the chicken drumsticks and thighs in a glass baking dish. In a bowl, combine the oil, chili sauce, cumin seeds, saffron, salt, lemon juice and ¼ cup of the cilantro. Pour this mixture over the chicken and turn to coat. Cover and marinate at room temperature for 1 hour or for up to 4 hours in the refrigerator.

2. Heat two deep heavy skillets over moderate heat. Add half of the chicken pieces to each pan and cook, turning frequently, until evenly browned, about 15 minutes. Remove the chicken and set aside.

3. Pour off all the fat from the pans. Add 2 cups of the stock to each pan and bring to a boil over high heat, scraping to dislodge any browned bits from the bottoms. Pour all the stock into one pan, add the pasta and cook for 2 minutes, stirring frequently.

4. Return the chicken to the pan. Reduce the heat to moderately low, cover tightly and simmer until the pasta and chicken are cooked through, about 20 minutes.

5. Transfer the chicken to a warmed platter or plates and sprinkle the remaining ¼ cup chopped cilantro on top. Serve the pasta alongside.

————————

—*Bob Chambers*

GLAZED CHICKEN DOMBURI

In Japanese *domburi* means "big bowl," which refers to both a deep ceramic dish and to the heaping portion of rice topped with sauced meat, fish and vegetables that is served in it. As the history of domburi goes back several hundred years, it might be considered Japan's first contribution to the fast food scene. In this example, a richly sauced and glazed chicken sauté is served with crisp snow peas over rice and sprinkled with toasted sesame seeds.

4 Servings

2 cups short-grain rice (such as Blue Rose or
  California Rose)
¾ pound skinless, boneless chicken breast
2 tablespoons sake
½ teaspoon salt
1 tablespoon sesame seeds
½ pound fresh snow peas
1 tablespoon cornstarch
2 tablespoons vegetable oil
¼ cup canned chicken broth or water
2 tablespoons soy sauce
2 tablespoons mirin (sweet rice wine)★
1 teaspoon sugar
8 sweet pickled scallions (rakkyo)★ or pickled
  pearl onions
★Available at Asian markets

1. Rinse the rice in a colander under cold running water until the water runs clear. Drain the rice well, then place it in a deep 3-quart saucepan with straight sides and a tight-fitting lid. Add 2⅓ cups of cold water, cover and let the rice soak for 10 minutes before cooking.

2. Be sure to keep the saucepan tightly covered throughout the cooking and steaming process. If you must check, do so quickly to lose as little moisture and steam pressure as possible. Bring the rice and water to a boil over high heat (about 6 minutes). Reduce the heat to low and simmer until all the water has been absorbed, about 6

minutes. Return to high heat, still covered, for 20 seconds. Remove the pan from the heat and let the rice steam undisturbed for 15 minutes.

3. Slice the chicken crosswise on the diagonal into ½-inch slices and then into bite-size pieces, about 1 inch square. Place the chicken in a small bowl and add the sake and salt. Marinate for 5 to 10 minutes, while you finish the preparations.

4. Place the sesame seeds in a heavy skillet or saucepan over moderately high heat. Dry roast, shaking the pan once or twice, until the seeds turn pale beige, about 20 seconds. Empty the toasted seeds onto a cutting board and mince them with a large, sharp knife.

5. Blanch the snow peas in rapidly boiling salted water for 10 seconds and drain immediately; refresh in cold water and pat dry.

6. Remove the chicken from the marinade and pat dry with paper towels. Place in another small bowl, sprinkle with the cornstarch and toss lightly to coat evenly.

7. In a medium skillet, heat the oil and add the chicken. Sauté over moderately high heat, stirring, until all the pieces are white. Add the broth and stir with a wooden spoon to scrape up any browned bits sticking to the bottom of the skillet. Reduce the heat to low, add the soy sauce, mirin and sugar and simmer until the sauce is reduced by two-thirds, about 5 minutes. Increase the heat to high and cook, stirring, for about 10 seconds to glaze the chicken with the sauce. Sprinkle half of the sesame seeds over the chicken and stir to mix them in.

8. To serve, divide the rice among 4 deep bowls or soup plates. Cover three-fourths of the rice in each bowl with chicken, dividing evenly. Cover the remaining rice with snow peas, standing them up on an angle to look like leaves. On the side of the bowl, arrange a couple of pickled scallions. Sprinkle with the remaining sesame seeds.

—Elizabeth Andoh

Lemon Chicken with Capers and Pine Nuts (p. 129).

Thai Chicken Salad (p. 243).

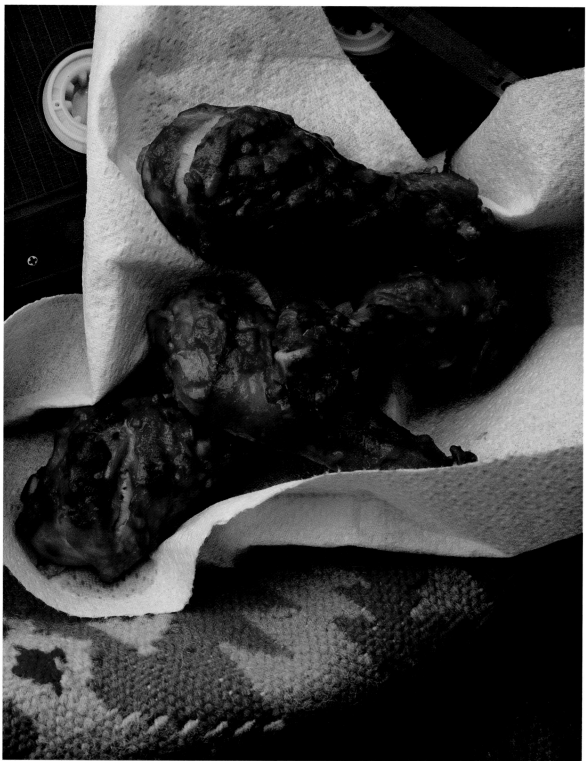

Drumsticks Along the Mohawk (p. 103).

CHICKEN OMELET DOMBURI

In Japanese this rice dish is called *oyako domburi*. *Oyako* means "mother and child" and is a Japanese culinary joke celebrating that famous question, "Which came first, the chicken or the egg?" Here, the chicken comes first, along with bamboo shoots—all simmered in a smoky amber broth. Then comes the egg, poached in the broth with green beans. Everything is served over steaming rice.

4 Servings

2 cups short-grain rice (such as Blue Rose or
   California Rose)
1 large can (15 ounces) bamboo shoots
1½ cups Chicken Stock (p. 10) or
   canned broth
3 tablespoons soy sauce
2 tablespoons sugar
1 tablespoon sake
¾ pound skinless, boneless chicken breast
4 eggs, beaten with a pinch of salt
8 to 10 (about 2 ounces) fresh green beans,
   trimmed and cut on the diagonal into
   1-inch pieces
5-inch square of nori (dried seaweed), cut with
   scissors into thin strips (1 by ⅛ inch)
   (optional)

1. Rinse the rice in a colander under cold running water until the water runs clear. Drain the rice well, then place it in a deep 3-quart saucepan with straight sides and a tight-fitting lid. Add 2⅓ cups of cold water, cover and let the rice soak for 10 minutes before cooking.

2. Be sure to keep the saucepan tightly covered throughout the cooking and steaming process. If you must check, do so quickly to lose as little moisture and steam pressure as possible. Bring the rice and water to a boil over high heat (about 6 minutes). Reduce the heat to low and simmer until all the water has been absorbed, about 6 minutes. Return to high heat, still covered, for 20 seconds. Remove the pan from the heat and let the rice steam undisturbed for 15 minutes.

3. Slice the bamboo shoots into thin wedges ⅛ inch thick. Rinse them well and remove any white deposits that may be caught between the "teeth" of the rippled bamboo edges. (These deposits are harmless but unpleasantly gritty.) Drain the wedges and pat them dry.

4. In a 10- to 12-inch skillet, heat the stock, soy sauce, sugar and sake over low heat, stirring to dissolve the sugar. Add the bamboo shoot wedges and simmer uncovered for 5 minutes.

5. Meanwhile, slice the chicken crosswise on a slight diagonal into ½-inch slices; cut the slices into bite-size pieces, about 1 inch square. Add the chicken to the skillet, cover and increase the heat to moderate. Cook until the chicken is just opaque throughout, about 4 minutes.

6. Pour the eggs into the skillet and reduce the heat to moderately low. Scatter the green beans on top, cover the skillet and poach the omelet for 2 minutes. Remove the skillet from the heat and let the omelet steam, tightly covered, for 1 to 3 minutes, depending on how firm you like your eggs.

7. To serve, divide the rice among 4 deep bowls or soup plates. Top each portion of rice with one-fourth of the omelet cut into a large wedge. Garnish each serving with a small mound of the seaweed strips.

———————————

—*Elizabeth Andoh*

ARROZ CON POLLO WITH SHRIMP AND ARTICHOKES

All this hearty dish needs beforehand is a small selection of nibbles—some olives and toasted almonds, perhaps. Sliced hard sausage or prosciutto would not be amiss, and you might enjoy trying some of the Spanish cheeses now available in this country, such as the rich blue-veined Cabrales, which often comes wrapped in grape leaves. For a simple but striking cool dessert, try a scoop of good-quality mango sherbet doused with Grande Passion, a light passion fruit liqueur.

🍷 Spanish white, such as Marqués de Cáceres

10 to 12 Servings

3 large artichokes (see Note)
2 tablespoons fresh lemon juice
12 chicken thighs (about 3½ pounds)
2¾ teaspoons salt
¾ teaspoon freshly ground black pepper
4 tablespoons olive oil
3 medium onions, chopped
1½ pounds chorizo or hot Italian sausage, cut into 1-inch lengths
3 garlic cloves, finely chopped
1 can (35 ounces) Italian peeled tomatoes, with their juice
1½ bottles (12 ounces each) lager beer
1 can (13¾ ounces) chicken broth
2 imported bay leaves
1½ teaspoons oregano
½ teaspoon crushed hot red pepper
½ teaspoon (loosely packed) saffron threads (.2 grams)
3 cups converted rice
1½ pounds medium shrimp, shelled and deveined
1 package (10 ounces) frozen peas, thawed
Strips of roasted red pepper, preferably homemade, for garnish

1. Trim the stems off the artichokes. Cut off two-thirds of the top to leave about 1½ inches of artichoke. Bend back and pull off all the tough outer dark green leaves. As each artichoke is trimmed, drop into a bowl of cold water with 1 tablespoon of the lemon juice to prevent discoloration.

2. In a large saucepan of boiling salted water, cook the artichokes with the remaining 1 tablespoon lemon juice until tender, 15 to 20 minutes. Drain and rinse under cold running water. *(The artichokes can be cooked 1 day ahead.)* Remove the chokes and cut each artichoke into 8 to 12 wedges.

3. Preheat the oven to 350°. Season the chicken with ¾ teaspoon of the salt and ¼ teaspoon of the pepper. In a very large (8-quart) flameproof casserole, heat 3 tablespoons of the oil. Add as many thighs as will fit in a single layer and fry over moderately high heat, turning once, until lightly browned, 3 to 5 minutes on each side. Transfer to a plate and repeat with the remaining thighs. Set the chicken aside. (If you do not have a big enough casserole, all the ingredients can be sautéed in a large skillet and transferred to a large covered turkey roaster for baking.)

4. Remove all but 3 to 4 tablespoons of fat from the casserole. Add the onions and sauté over moderate heat until softened and beginning to brown, about 10 minutes.

5. Meanwhile, in a large skillet, heat the remaining 1 tablespoon oil. Add the chorizo and cook over moderate heat, turning occasionally, until lightly browned, 5 to 10 minutes.

6. Add the garlic to the onions and sauté until fragrant, about 2 minutes. Add the tomatoes and their juice, the beer, chicken broth, bay leaves, oregano, hot pepper, saffron and the remaining 2 teaspoons salt and ½ teaspoon pepper. Bring to a boil over high heat. Stir in the rice. With a slotted spoon, transfer the chorizo to the casserole. Add the chicken and any juices that have collected on the plate.

7. Cover the casserole tightly and bake for 25 minutes, or until the rice has absorbed most of the liquid.

8. Add the shrimp and stir to bury in the rice. Bake for 5 minutes. Add the peas and artichokes and bake for 5 to 10 minutes longer, until the shrimp are pink and loosely curled. Serve on a large deep platter, garnished with strips of roasted pepper.

NOTE: To save time, you can substitute 1 package frozen artichoke hearts, thawed. Skip Steps 1 and 2 and add the artichokes with the shrimp at the beginning of Step 8.

—*Susan Wyler*

CHICKEN WITH RICE AND OLIVES

4 Servings

3 tablespoons olive oil
3 garlic cloves, lightly crushed
One 3- to 3½-pound chicken, cut into 8
  serving pieces
½ pound smoked ham, cut into ¼-inch dice
2 medium onions, chopped
½ green bell pepper, chopped
1½ cups converted rice
1 can (14 ounces) Italian peeled tomatoes,
  drained and coarsely chopped
1½ cups Chicken Stock (p. 10) or unsalted
  canned broth
1½ cups lager beer
½ cup pitted green olives, chopped
¼ cup chopped pimientos
1 teaspoon salt
½ teaspoon freshly ground black pepper

1. Preheat the oven to 375°. In a large skillet, heat the oil with the garlic cloves. Add the chicken pieces and cook over moderate heat until browned, about 10 minutes. Transfer the chicken and garlic to a flameproof casserole.

2. Add the ham, onions and bell pepper to the skillet. Cook over moderate heat until softened, 5 to 7 minutes. Add to the casserole.

3. Add the rice to the skillet and cook, stir-ring constantly, until translucent, 2 to 3 minutes. Add the rice, tomatoes, chicken stock, beer, olives, pimientos, salt and black pepper to the casserole, stirring to combine. Bring to a boil over moderate heat. Stir once, cover the casserole and bake until the rice and chicken are tender, about 25 minutes.

—*Mary Lynn Mondich*

CHICKEN BIRYANI

This Indo-Persian dish is perhaps one of the world's most elegant rice dishes. Partially cooked rice and spicy chunks of chicken are layered, and saffron-infused milk is poured over the top. The pot is then sealed and the dish bakes slowly in the oven. If you want the biryani to remain tri-colored—white, saffron and brown—do not mix the rice until ready to serve. In a warm place, a covered pot of biryani will keep its heat for a good hour.

6 Servings

2 teaspoons lightly packed saffron
  threads
3 tablespoons hot milk
3 cups basmati rice
2½ tablespoons salt
2-inch piece of fresh ginger, peeled and
  coarsely chopped
5 garlic cloves
2 cups plain yogurt, preferably
  whole-milk
½ cup coarsely chopped fresh mint
½ cup coarsely chopped cilantro (fresh
  coriander)
1 to 2 fresh green chiles, thinly sliced
½ cup vegetable oil
3 medium onions—2 halved lengthwise and
  thinly sliced, 1 finely chopped
¼ cup slivered almonds
¼ cup golden raisins
4 cinnamon sticks
12 cardamom pods

10 whole cloves

2 bay leaves

1 teaspoon black cumin seeds or ½ teaspoon
regular cumin seeds

6 chicken drumsticks, skinned

6 chicken thighs, skinned

2 tablespoons fresh lemon juice

1 teaspoon ground cumin

½ teaspoon cayenne pepper

½ teaspoon freshly ground black pepper

3 hard-cooked eggs, quartered

1. Set a small cast-iron skillet over moderate heat. When hot, add the saffron and stir until the threads turn a few shades darker, about 1 minute. Pour the hot milk into a small cup and crumble in the saffron threads. Set aside for 3 hours.

2. Meanwhile, place the rice in a large bowl and wash in several changes of cold water. Add enough water to the bowl to cover the rice by 2 inches. Add 1 teaspoon of the salt, mix and set aside to soak for at least 3 hours.

3. In a blender, combine the ginger, garlic and 1 tablespoon water. Blend on low speed, scraping down the sides a few times, until a fine paste forms.

4. In a bowl, beat the yogurt lightly until smooth. Stir in the mint, cilantro and chiles.

5. In a large, straight-sided skillet, heat the oil over moderately high heat. Add the sliced onions and fry, stirring once or twice, until well browned and crisp, about 5 minutes. With a slotted spoon, transfer the onions to paper towels to drain.

6. Add the almonds to the skillet and fry, stirring, until golden, about 30 seconds. Transfer to paper towels to drain. Add the raisins to the skillet; they will plump up immediately. Quickly transfer them to paper towels to drain.

7. Add 2 cinnamon sticks, 6 cardamom pods, 5 cloves and 1 bay leaf to the skillet. Stir once and add the cumin seeds. Stir once and add the chopped onion. Increase the heat to moderately high and fry until the onion is browned at the edges, about 1 minute. Add the ginger-garlic paste and stir-fry for 1 minute. Add the chicken pieces and fry for 1 minute. Add half of the yogurt mixture, half of the fried almonds and raisins, 1¼ teaspoons of the salt and the lemon juice, ground cumin and cayenne.

8. Stir ¼ cup water into the skillet and bring to a simmer. Reduce the heat to low. Cover and simmer gently for 10 minutes, then uncover and add half of the fried onions. Increase the heat to moderate and cook, stirring frequently, until the sauce is dark and thickened and the chicken is just tender, about 5 minutes.

9. Add the black pepper and season the sauce with salt to taste. Transfer the chicken and sauce to a large ovenproof casserole. *(The recipe can be prepared to this point up to 6 hours ahead.)*

10. Preheat the oven to 375°. Stir ¼ teaspoon of the salt and 2 teaspoons of the reserved saffron milk into the remaining yogurt. Spread this mixture over the chicken.

11. In a large pot, bring 10 cups of water to a rolling boil. Add the remaining 5 teaspoons salt, 2 cinnamon sticks, 6 cardamom pods, 5 cloves and 1 bay leaf. Drain the rice and slowly pour it into the pot. When the water returns to a rapid boil, cook the rice until just barely tender, 7 to 8 minutes; drain quickly, leaving in the spices.

12. Pour the rice over the chicken in a heap, making a small mound. Working quickly, use a chopstick or a long spoon to make a well in the center of the rice all the way down to the bottom of the pot. Drizzle the remaining saffron milk on the sides of the mound. Lay a clean, dampened dish cloth over the rice and cover the casserole tightly, first with a piece of foil and then with a lid. Bake for 35 minutes.

13. To serve, have a large, warmed platter ready. Stir the rice gently with a slotted spoon to mix and spoon the biryani onto the platter. Garnish with the remaining fried onions, almonds, raisins and the hard-cooked eggs.

———————————

—Madhur Jaffrey

Salads

MINTED CHICKEN SALAD WITH TROPICAL FRUITS

This is a delicate salad that is cooled by the mint and fresh fruits. It is a pleasant and refreshing lunch or supper dish when served in crisp lettuce cups with a marinated green bean and shallot salad, and a chilled Gewürztraminer alongside.

6 Servings

3½ tablespoons vegetable oil
2 teaspoons minced fresh ginger
1 teaspoon minced garlic
¼ teaspoon crushed hot red pepper
1 pound skinless, boneless chicken breast, cut
   into 1-inch pieces
½ teaspoon salt
Freshly ground black pepper
⅓ cup Chicken Stock (p. 10), canned
   broth or water
¼ cup chopped fresh mint
¼ cup mayonnaise
¼ cup plain yogurt
1 tablespoon fresh lemon juice
1¼ teaspoons grated lemon zest
½ mango, peeled and diced
½ papaya, peeled and diced
1 medium banana, sliced
⅓ cup diagonally sliced scallions
Fresh mint sprigs, for garnish

1. In a large skillet or wok, heat the oil. Add 1 teaspoon of the ginger, ½ teaspoon of the garlic and the hot pepper and cook over moderately high heat for 10 seconds. Add the chicken and stir-fry until just cooked through, about 2 minutes; transfer to a sieve placed over a bowl to catch any juices. Season the chicken with the salt and black pepper to taste.

2. Add the chicken stock, 1 tablespoon of the chopped mint and any juices from the chicken to the skillet. Boil over high heat until reduced to about 1 tablespoon, scraping the bottom of the pan to loosen any browned bits.

3. Strain the reduced liquid into a medium bowl and let cool slightly. Stir in the mayonnaise, yogurt, lemon juice, lemon zest, the remaining 1 teaspoon ginger, ½ teaspoon garlic and chopped mint. Season with additional salt and pepper to taste.

4. Toss the cooled chicken with the dressing. Add the mango, papaya, banana and scallions and toss gently. Place in a serving dish, cover and refrigerate for at least 2 hours to chill and to allow the flavors to meld. Serve at room temperature, garnished with fresh mint sprigs.

———————————————

—Jane Helsel Joseph

POTATO AND CHICKEN SALAD WITH SHREDDED ZUCCHINI

This is a great dish to make with leftovers. You could boil a chicken for chicken stock and use the meat in this salad or use leftover meat from fried or roasted chicken (remove the skin first). Likewise, bake some extra potatoes to have on hand.

10 to 12 Servings

6 cups diced (½-inch) baked red potatoes
   (about 2 pounds) or 2 pounds uncooked red
   potatoes, cut into ½-inch dice
3 cups shredded cooked chicken (from 1 small
   frying chicken)
4 small zucchini, shredded (about 4 cups)
6 hard-cooked eggs, coarsely chopped
¼ cup minced fresh tarragon or parsley
¾ teaspoon salt
¼ teaspoon freshly ground pepper
¾ cup mayonnaise
¼ cup Chicken Stock (p. 10) or canned broth
1 tablespoon white wine vinegar

1. If not using leftover baked potatoes, cook the diced raw potatoes in a large pot of boiling salted water until tender when pierced with a fork, about 15 minutes. Drain and let cool to room temperature.

2. In a large bowl, toss together the potatoes, chicken, zucchini, eggs, tarragon, salt and pepper.

3. In a small bowl, whisk together the mayonnaise, chicken stock and vinegar until blended. Pour over the salad. Toss well and serve the salad at room temperature.

—*Anne Disrude*

MEDITERRANEAN CHICKEN SALAD WITH BROCCOLI

♟ California Chenin Blanc

6 Servings

4 tablespoons unsalted butter
8 skinless, boneless chicken breast halves (about 5 ounces each)
½ cup dry white wine
2 garlic cloves, minced
1 bunch of broccoli
1 cup mayonnaise
1 tablespoon fresh lemon juice
½ teaspoon thyme
¼ teaspoon basil
¼ teaspoon oregano
½ teaspoon salt
½ teaspoon freshly ground pepper
1 medium red onion, quartered and thinly sliced
Sliced tomatoes, toasted slivered almonds and slivered oil-cured black olives, for accompaniment

1. In a large skillet, melt the butter over moderately low heat. Add the chicken breasts in a single layer, and pour in the wine. Lay a round of waxed paper over the chicken and cover the skillet with a tight-fitting lid. Cook for 8 to 10 min-

utes, until the chicken breasts are springy to the touch. Remove the chicken, cover loosely and set aside to cool.

2. Add the garlic to the skillet and cook over moderately low heat until fragrant, about 1 minute. Strain, reserving both the garlic and ⅓ cup of the cooking liquid. Set aside to cool.

3. Peel and trim the broccoli stems and cut into ½-inch dice; separate the tops into 1-inch florets. In a medium saucepan of boiling salted water, blanch the broccoli just until bright green, about 30 seconds. Drain and rinse under cold running water until cool; drain well.

4. In a small bowl, combine the mayonnaise, lemon juice, thyme, basil and oregano; blend well. Whisk in the reserved garlic and cooking liquid. Season with the salt and pepper.

5. Cut the chicken breasts into ¾-inch cubes. In a large bowl, combine the chicken, broccoli and onion. Add the dressing and toss well. Cover and refrigerate for at least 2 hours, or overnight.

6. To serve, arrange the tomato slices decoratively around the salad on a serving dish or individual plates. Sprinkle with the slivered almonds and olives.

—*Rick Ellis*

MINTED CHICKEN AND RAW ARTICHOKE SALAD IN PITAS

The unusual addition of raw artichoke gives this salad a special flavor and texture. If you like, warm the pita in a low oven before stuffing.

4 Servings

¼ cup fresh lemon juice
⅓ cup minced fresh mint
½ teaspoon salt
½ teaspoon freshly ground pepper
¼ cup extra-virgin olive oil
1 large artichoke

¾ pound cooked chicken, cut into 1-inch pieces
   (about 3 cups)
⅓ cup finely chopped or coarsely grated
   Parmesan cheese (about 1½ ounces)
½ cup mayonnaise
4 pita breads (6 inches in diameter)

1. In a large bowl, combine the lemon juice, mint, salt and pepper. Gradually whisk in the oil.

2. Using a sharp knife, remove the tough outer leaves from the artichoke. Peel the stem. Cut the artichoke into quarters and, using a teaspoon, remove the hairy choke and the purple inner leaves. Using a very sharp stainless steel knife, thinly slice the artichoke quarters crosswise. Alternatively, slice the artichoke quarters, stem-end down, in a food processor fitted with a slicing disk. (You should have about 1½ cups.)

3. Immediately toss the artichoke with the lemon mixture. Add the chicken and Parmesan and mix well. Stir in the mayonnaise and blend the ingredients thoroughly.

4. Cut a 1-inch slice from the top of each pita and stuff the pockets with the salad.

—Molly O'Neill

CHICKEN SALAD WITH NEW POTATOES AND DILL

I like to cook the chicken the day before I prepare the salad so that I can skim all the fat from the broth.

8 Servings

One 3- to 3½-pound chicken
2 medium carrots, chopped
2 celery ribs, chopped
2 large onions, chopped
1 imported bay leaf
10 whole black peppercorns
3 whole cloves
3 cans (10½ ounces each) low-sodium
   chicken broth

2 pounds small new potatoes
2 tablespoons grainy mustard
1 tablespoon Dijon-style mustard
3 tablespoons fresh lemon juice
2 tablespoons red wine vinegar
¼ cup heavy cream
½ cup extra-virgin olive oil
¾ teaspoon salt
½ teaspoon freshly ground pepper
2 tablespoons chopped fresh dill

1. Place the chicken in a large saucepan, breast-side up. Add the carrots, celery, onions, bay leaf, peppercorns, cloves and chicken broth. Add enough water to cover the chicken and bring to a boil. Reduce the heat to moderately low and simmer for 40 minutes. Turn the chicken over and simmer for 20 minutes longer.

2. Remove from the heat and let the chicken cool to room temperature in the liquid. Refrigerate for about 5 hours or overnight, until the fat solidifies on the surface of the broth.

3. Skim the fat from the broth. Remove the chicken and set aside. Bring the broth to a boil. Strain through a fine sieve.

4. Return the broth to the pan. Add the potatoes and bring to a boil. Reduce the heat to moderate and simmer until a knife inserted in the largest potato is easily removed, 15 to 20 minutes. Drain the potatoes, reserving the broth for another use. Let cool for 10 minutes, then cut into 1-inch chunks.

5. Meanwhile, in a small bowl, whisk together the grainy mustard, Dijon-style mustard, lemon juice, vinegar, cream, oil, salt, pepper and dill.

6. Remove the skin from the chicken and discard. Remove the meat from the bones and cut it into 1-inch chunks. In a large bowl, toss the chicken with the warm potatoes and the dressing. Cover and refrigerate. Serve the salad at room temperature.

—Bob Chambers

CHICKEN SALAD WITH CRÈME FRAÎCHE

In this variation on the classic chicken salad, the crème fraîche binds the ingredients and marries their flavors. A confetti of red and green bell peppers and a bed of radicchio leaves provide the crunch.

🍷 Alsace Riesling, such as Trimbach

4 Servings

One 3-pound chicken
Salt and freshly ground black pepper
3 tablespoons vegetable oil
⅔ cup crème fraîche
⅓ cup diced (½-inch) red bell pepper
1 cup diced (½-inch) green bell pepper
2 tablespoons minced cilantro (fresh coriander)
1 head of Bibb lettuce
2 heads of radicchio (about ½ pound) or an equal quantity of tender red cabbage leaves

1. Preheat the oven to 375°. Season the chicken inside and out with salt and pepper.

2. In a roasting pan just large enough to hold the chicken, warm the oil over moderate heat. Place the chicken on its side in the pan and roast for 20 minutes. Turn onto the other side and roast for 20 minutes. Turn onto its back and roast, basting often with the pan juices, for 20 to 25 minutes longer, until the juices run clear when the thigh is pierced with a fork. Remove the chicken from the pan, let cool to room temperature and refrigerate, covered, until chilled.

3. Remove the meat from the carcass, discarding the skin and bones. Cut the meat into ½-inch chunks.

4. In a medium bowl, combine the chicken, crème fraîche, red and green peppers, cilantro, ½ teaspoon salt and ¼ teaspoon pepper. Toss well to coat. Refrigerate, covered, until ready to serve.

5. Arrange the lettuce leaves on each of four plates. Arrange the radicchio leaves in a circle within the lettuce. Mound the chilled chicken mixture in the center of the lettuces and serve.

—Windows on the World, New York City

CHICKEN AND CANADIAN BACON SALAD WITH TOASTED PECANS

This chicken salad is perfect for the buffet table, but you can easily halve the ingredients for a smaller number of servings.

🍷 Chianti Classico

12 to 16 Servings

6 whole boneless chicken breasts, with the skin on (about 12 ounces each)
3 tablespoons peanut oil
½ pound pecan halves (2⅓ cups)
2 teaspoons cumin
2 packages (10 ounces each) frozen baby peas
2 pounds Canadian bacon or lean ham, cut into ½-inch dice
2 pounds mushrooms, cut into ½ dice
⅓ cup fresh lemon juice
2 cups thinly sliced scallions (about 2 bunches)
1½ cups plain yogurt
1½ cups sour cream
¼ cup Dijon-style mustard
2 tablespoons salt
2 teaspoons freshly ground pepper

1. Place the chicken breasts in a large wide saucepan or heatproof casserole with water to cover. Bring to a simmer over moderate heat. Reduce the heat to very low and poach the chicken at a bare simmer until firm to the touch, about 45 minutes. Remove from the heat and let cool in the poaching liquid. Drain the chicken, remove the skin and cut the meat into ½-inch cubes.

2. Meanwhile, in a large skillet, heat the oil. Add the pecans, sprinkle with the cumin and sauté over moderately high heat, tossing constantly, until aromatic and lightly toasted, about 4 minutes. Transfer the pecans to paper towels to drain.

3. Blanch the peas in boiling salted water for 30 seconds; drain and let cool.

4. In a large bowl, combine the chicken, pecans, Canadian bacon and mushrooms. Add the lemon juice and toss until coated. Add the scallions and all but ⅓ cup of the peas.

5. In a medium bowl, combine the yogurt, sour cream, mustard, salt and pepper and mix well. Pour the dressing over the salad and toss to coat.

6. Transfer the salad to a large decorative serving bowl or platter and garnish with the remaining peas. Serve at room temperature.

———————————

—*W. Peter Prestcott*

CURRIED CHICKEN SALAD WITH YOGURT DRESSING

This light salad gets its heat from the curry, its cool from the yogurt and crunch from the carrots, apples and zucchini.

6 to 8 Servings

1 cup plain yogurt
3 tablespoons sour cream
2 teaspoons curry powder
1 teaspoon thyme
½ teaspoon ground coriander
1 teaspoon cumin
½ teaspoon celery seeds
1 teaspoon salt
2 tablespoons fresh lemon juice
3 cups cooked chicken (½-inch pieces)
½ cup dried currants
2 medium carrots, grated
2 small zucchini, cut lengthwise into eighths,
   then sliced 1 inch thick

2 Granny Smith apples, cut into ½-inch cubes
Crisp greens, for garnish
½ cup roasted cashews (about 2½ ounces)

1. In a large bowl, combine the yogurt, sour cream, curry powder, thyme, coriander, cumin, celery seeds, salt and lemon juice. Add the chicken and toss well. Cover and set aside at room temperature for 15 minutes.

2. Meanwhile, in a small bowl, cover the currants with hot water and set aside to plump for 10 minutes. Drain well.

3. Add the carrots, zucchini, apples and plumped currants to the chicken and toss well to combine. Mound the salad on a platter or plates lined with crisp greens and sprinkle the cashews on top. Serve immediately.

———————————

—*Bob Chambers*

CHICKEN-POTATO SALAD WITH OLIVES AND WALNUTS

8 to 10 Servings

2 large red bell peppers
1 celery rib with leaves, coarsely chopped
1 carrot, coarsely chopped
½ onion, sliced
4 to 6 parsley sprigs
1 bay leaf
2½ pounds skinless, boneless chicken breast
½ cup olive oil
3 tablespoons red wine vinegar
1¼ cups (4 ounces) coarsely chopped walnuts
1 bunch scallions, thinly sliced (use part
   of green)
1 tablespoon tarragon
½ pound medium-small mushrooms, quartered
2 pounds (about 8) medium new potatoes
½ cup dry white wine
4 anchovy fillets, rinsed and finely chopped
½ cup Calamata olives, slivered, or ¼ cup
   pitted, slivered oil-cured black olives

1 teaspoon salt

¼ teaspoon freshly ground black pepper

2 tablespoons fresh lemon juice, or more
   to taste

Leaf lettuce

1. Place the peppers directly on a gas burner or under the broiler. Turn them until the skin is blackened all over. Place them in a plastic bag, close it and let them stand for 5 or 10 minutes. Halve the peppers lengthwise and seed and derib them. Scrape off all the blackened skin with a knife. Cut the roasted peppers into lengthwise strips. Halve the strips crosswise.

2. In a large saucepan, combine the celery, carrot, onion, parsley, bay leaf and 5 cups of water. Bring to a boil, cover and simmer for 10 minutes. Add the chicken breasts and poach them for 10 minutes, or until barely cooked. Remove the chicken to a cutting board. Reserve the poaching liquid.

3. Cut the chicken into 3-inch strips ¼ to ½ inch thick. Toss with the peppers, oil, vinegar, walnuts, scallions and tarragon.

4. Strain the poaching liquid into a saucepan and heat to simmering. Add the mushrooms and simmer 2 minutes. Drain the mushrooms and add them to chicken. (Save the broth for another use.)

5. Cook the potatoes in rapidly boiling water until just tender, 15 to 20 minutes. Peel, cut into ½-inch cubes and combine with the wine while warm. Let stand until the wine is absorbed, tossing twice.

6. Add the potatoes to the chicken. Add the anchovies, olives, salt, black pepper and 2 tablespoons lemon juice (or more, to taste). Toss gently. Let stand at least 30 minutes, then serve in a shallow bowl lined with the lettuce.

—*W. Peter Prestcott*

ARTICHOKE SALAD WITH CHICKEN AND DRIED MONTEREY JACK

4 Servings

2 tablespoons fresh lemon juice

4 large uncooked artichoke bottoms, with 20
   leaves reserved

2 cups Chicken Stock (p. 10) or canned broth

2 skinless, boneless chicken breast halves

3 tablespoons olive oil, preferably Californian

¼ teaspoon salt

¼ teaspoon freshly ground pepper

¼ cup coarsely grated dried Monterey Jack
   cheese or mild Parmesan

2 tablespoons finely chopped parsley

1. Place 1 tablespoon of the lemon juice in a small bowl. One at a time, cut each artichoke bottom into ⅛-inch julienne strips and add to the bowl, tossing until coated with the lemon juice to prevent discoloration.

2. In a medium, nonreactive saucepan, bring 1 quart of water to a boil. Add the julienned artichokes (with lemon juice) and the 20 reserved leaves. Blanch until barely tender, about 1 minute. Drain and rinse under cold running water; drain well. Transfer to a medium bowl.

3. In a medium saucepan, bring the stock and 2 cups of water to a boil over moderately high heat; reduce to a simmer. Add the chicken and poach 10 minutes, or until firm to the touch. Let cool, then cut into ¼-inch julienne strips. Add to the artichokes.

4. In a small bowl, whisk together the olive oil, remaining 1 tablespoon lemon juice, the salt and pepper. Pour over the artichokes and chicken and toss to coat. Arrange 5 artichoke leaves around the edge of each of 4 plates. Pile one-fourth of the artichoke-chicken mixture on each plate. Sprinkle each serving with 1 tablespoon Monterey Jack, a grind of pepper and ½ tablespoon parsley.

—*John Robert Massie*

TUSCAN CHICKEN AND BEAN SALAD

Beans are cooked here without presoaking. It takes a little longer on the stove but less time overall.

4 to 6 Servings

2 cups dried white beans, such as
  Great Northern
1 bay leaf
1 medium onion, chopped
1 whole chicken breast, bone in, preferably
  free-range
3 garlic cloves, unpeeled
1 red bell pepper
1½ teaspoons salt
2 tablespoons red wine vinegar
½ cup extra-virgin olive oil
2 tablespoons minced fresh thyme or 1
  teaspoon dried
3 tablespoons minced flat-leaf parsley
½ teaspoon freshly ground black pepper
3 scallions, minced

1. Place the beans, bay leaf and onion in a large heavy pot with 8 cups of cold water. Bring to a simmer over moderate heat and cook until tender, about 1½ hours. Drain the beans and let cool.

2. Preheat the oven to 350°. Place the chicken, garlic cloves and red pepper in a lightly oiled, medium baking pan. Bake for about 35 minutes, turning the garlic and pepper after 15 minutes, until the skin on the chicken is golden brown and the meat is white throughout. Remove from the oven and let stand for about 10 minutes until cool enough to handle.

3. Using a sharp knife, peel the pepper and discard the skin and seeds. Cut the pepper into ½-inch dice.

4. Squeeze the roasted garlic from its skin and place in a large bowl. Using a fork, mash the roasted garlic with 1 teaspoon of the salt. Whisk in the vinegar and then the olive oil. Add the thyme, parsley and black pepper.

5. Skin and shred the roasted chicken, add to the vinaigrette and toss well to coat. Add the beans, minced scallions, diced roasted pepper, the remaining ½ teaspoon salt and additional black pepper to taste. Serve warm or chilled.

—*Molly O'Neill*

GOAT CHEESE-STUFFED GRILLED CHICKEN WITH TOMATO VINAIGRETTE

This salad can be served just out of the oven, warm or at room temperature.

♟ California Fumé Blanc, such as Chateau St. Jean

4 Servings

2 whole chicken breasts, with wings attached
4 ounces mild goat cheese, at room temperature
1½ tablespoons unsalted butter, at room
  temperature
¼ teaspoon thyme
Salt and freshly ground pepper
10 large basil leaves, finely chopped
10 sprigs of cilantro (fresh coriander), finely
  chopped, plus the leaves from 2 sprigs
2 tablespoons finely chopped chives
8 tablespoons olive oil, preferably extra-virgin
1 small shallot, minced
1 small garlic clove, minced
1 jalapeño—roasted, seeded and minced
2 tablespoons champagne vinegar or white
  wine vinegar
2 large tomatoes—peeled, seeded and
  coarsely chopped
About 4 cups mixed salad greens (see Note),
  torn into pieces
1 red bell pepper, cut into julienne strips
1 yellow bell pepper, cut into julienne strips

1. Preheat the oven to 350°. Carefully bone the chicken breasts, leaving the wing bone and skin attached.

2. In a small bowl, blend the goat cheese, 1 tablespoon of the butter, the thyme, a pinch of salt and pepper and all but a pinch of the basil, chopped cilantro and chives. Reserve the pinches of chopped herbs for the vinaigrette.

3. Using your finger, carefully make a pocket between the skin and the meat of each chicken breast with as small an opening to the outside as possible. Stuff the herbed cheese mixture in a thin layer under the skin.

4. In a large skillet, warm 2 tablespoons of the oil and the remaining ½ tablespoon butter over moderately high heat. When the foam subsides, add the chicken breasts, skin-side down, and sauté, turning once, until well browned, 6 to 8 minutes.

5. Transfer the chicken to a baking pan and roast in the oven for about 5 minutes. Remove from the oven and let rest for about 10 minutes.

6. Meanwhile, make the tomato vinaigrette. In a bowl, whisk the remaining 6 tablespoons olive oil, the shallot, garlic, jalapeño, vinegar, ¼ teaspoon salt and ¼ teaspoon pepper. Stir in the tomatoes. Just before serving, add the reserved herbs and the whole cilantro leaves.

7. Arrange the greens on 4 large plates. Slice the chicken breasts on the diagonal, leaving the wing on, and fan out the slices in the middle of the plate. Arrange the bell peppers around the edge of the greens. Dot the plate with the vinaigrette, spooning some around the chicken for color contrast.

NOTE: Use a combination of sweet and bitter salad greens, such as Boston, Bibb or limestone lettuce with arugula, chicory or radicchio.

—*Michael's, Santa Monica, California*

GRILLED CHICKEN BALSAMICO
6 Servings

1½ pounds boneless chicken breasts or thighs
⅓ cup fresh lemon juice
½ cup plus 3 tablespoons olive oil, preferably extra-virgin
2 teaspoons coarsely cracked black pepper
¾ teaspoon salt
¼ teaspoon hot pepper sauce
3 tablespoons balsamic or red wine vinegar
1 tablespoon Dijon-style mustard
1½ teaspoons minced fresh thyme or ½ teaspoon dried
2 tablespoons minced flat-leaf parsley
¾ pound green beans, cut into 2-inch pieces
2 Belgian endives, trimmed and separated into leaves
1 head of romaine lettuce
2 large red bell peppers, cut into 2-by-¼-inch strips
3 firm-ripe tomatoes, cut into wedges
3 scallions, thinly sliced

1. Place the chicken in a shallow bowl. Combine the lemon juice, 3 tablespoons of the olive oil, the black pepper, ½ teaspoon of the salt and the hot sauce. Pour over the chicken and marinate at room temperature, turning occasionally, for 1 hour.

2. Light the charcoal or preheat the broiler. Grill or broil the chicken 3 to 4 inches from the heat, turning once, until the skin is crisp and the meat is no longer pink, about 12 minutes for the breasts and 5 minutes longer for the thighs. *(The recipe can be prepared ahead to this point. Let the chicken cool to room temperature, wrap and refrigerate. Let return to room temperature before continuing.)*

3. In a large bowl, combine the vinegar, mustard, thyme, parsley and the remaining ¼ teaspoon salt. Gradually whisk in the remaining ½ cup olive oil.

4. Cut the chicken into bite-size pieces (keep

the skin on for its flavor unless you are watching your calorie intake) and toss to coat well with half of the dressing.

5. Bring a large saucepan of salted water to a boil. Add the green beans and cook until crisp-tender, about 3 minutes. Drain and rinse under cold water; drain well.

6. On a large serving platter, arrange some of the endive and romaine leaves; tear the rest into bite-size pieces. Just before serving, combine the torn lettuce with the green beans, peppers, tomatoes, scallions and chicken. Add the remaining dressing and toss until coated. Serve on the bed of endive and romaine leaves.

—*Beverly Cox*

CHICKEN BREASTS WITH MUSTARD AND SESAME SAUCE

In this chicken salad, the pungency of ginger and scallions infuses the chicken as it poaches. Mustard dressing is mellowed with sherry and sesame oil and the earthy taste of cilantro. The flavor, at once French and Chinese, is so intense that it belies the ease with which the dish is made.

🍷 White Châteauneuf-du-Pape, such as Château de Beaucastel

4 Servings

2 whole chicken breasts (about 3 pounds)
4 scallions, cut into 4-inch lengths
5 slices (quarter-size) peeled fresh ginger
½ cup Dijon-style mustard
½ cup vegetable oil
1 tablespoon Oriental sesame oil
1½ teaspoons dry sherry
4 leaves of crisp lettuce, such as romaine or iceberg, cut into julienne strips
Cilantro leaves (fresh coriander), for garnish

1. Place the chicken breasts, skin-side down, in a pot just large enough to hold them in a single layer.

2. In a blender or food processor, puree the scallions and ginger with 1 cup of water and add to the pot. Add cold water to cover the chicken by 1 inch. Bring to a boil over high heat. Reduce the heat to low and simmer until just cooked through, about 20 minutes. Plunge the chicken into a large bowl of ice water to cool it quickly to room temperature. Remove the breast meat in 4 intact halves, discarding the skin and bones. Cut each breast crosswise on the diagonal into ½-inch slices. Arrange one breast on each of four plates.

3. In a medium bowl, whisk together the mustard, vegetable oil, sesame oil and sherry. Spoon about 3 tablespoons of the dressing over each serving of chicken and serve the remainder in a sauceboat.

4. Garnish each plate with one-fourth of the lettuce and cilantro leaves.

—*The Ginger Man, New York City*

HOT CHICKEN SALAD WITH WALNUT OIL DRESSING

This hot chicken salad is an exuberant expression of summer. Lettuces are shredded and mounded high, with a fan of sautéed chicken flowing down from the top. A dressing of nuts and herbs is spiked with the sharpness of good wine vinegar. This recipe takes only minutes to prepare.

🍷 Italian white, such as Gavi

4 Servings

2 pounds skinless, boneless chicken breast
8 cups shredded mixed greens, such as Bibb, romaine, red leaf lettuce and watercress
2 tomatoes, cut into julienne strips
Salt and freshly ground pepper
3 tablespoons vegetable oil
2 teaspoons coarsely chopped fresh tarragon or dill
2 teaspoons coarsely chopped parsley

2 teaspoons coarsely chopped chives
¼ cup thinly sliced scallion greens
1 tablespoon plus 1 teaspoon red wine vinegar
2 tablespoons pine nuts
Walnut Oil Dressing (recipe follows)

1. Cut each chicken breast lengthwise into ½-inch slices, keeping the shape of the breast. Place each breast between two layers of waxed paper and pound until ½ to ¾ inch thick.

2. Arrange the greens and tomatoes in a mound in the center of each of four plates.

3. Season the chicken lightly with salt and pepper. In a large nonreactive skillet, heat the oil over moderately high heat. Add the chicken and sauté, turning once, until lightly browned outside and opaque throughout, about 1½ minutes on each side. Fan out each breast half on top of the greens on each plate.

4. Add the tarragon, parsley, chives, scallions, vinegar and pine nuts to the skillet and reduce the heat. Cook, stirring, for 1 minute. Drizzle over the chicken. Serve with Walnut Oil Dressing on the side.

—F&W

WALNUT OIL DRESSING
Makes About ½ Cup

1 teaspoon minced garlic
2 tablespoons Dijon-style mustard
2 tablespoons plus 2 teaspoons red
  wine vinegar
½ teaspoon salt
¼ teaspoon freshly ground white pepper
¼ cup walnut oil

In a medium bowl, mix the garlic, mustard, vinegar, salt and white pepper. Gradually whisk in the oil until well blended.

—F&W

CHICKEN SALAD WITH CHILI DRESSING

In this salad, chilled chicken is mixed with shredded lettuce and cabbage and tossed with a thick dressing tinged with chili sauce and pungent with chopped watercress.

🍷 Spanish Rioja, such as Domecq Privilegio

4 Servings

2 whole chicken breasts (about 3 pounds)
½ egg yolk
Pinch of dry mustard
2 tablespoons cider vinegar
½ teaspoon Worcestershire sauce
½ teaspoon salt
⅛ teaspoon freshly ground pepper
⅓ cup olive oil
½ cup chili sauce
½ cup coarsely chopped watercress
1 small head of crisp lettuce, such as romaine
  or iceberg, finely shredded (about 4 cups)
1 small head (1 pound) of green cabbage,
  finely shredded (about 4 cups)
Capers, for accompaniment

1. Place the chicken breasts skin-side down in a pot just large enough to hold them with cold water to cover by 1 inch. Bring to a boil over high heat. Reduce the heat to low and simmer until just cooked through and no longer pink in the center, about 20 minutes. Remove from the pot and set the chicken aside to cool to room temperature; cover and refrigerate until chilled. Discard the skin and bones and cut the meat into julienne strips.

2. Meanwhile, in a medium bowl, beat the egg yolk and mustard with 1½ tablespoons of the vinegar, the Worcestershire sauce, salt and pepper.

3. Slowly beat in the oil drop by drop until the mixture begins to thicken. Continue to beat in the oil in a thin stream. Add the remaining ½ tablespoon vinegar and blend well.

4. Stir in the chili sauce and the watercress.

5. In a large salad bowl, combine the chicken with the lettuce and cabbage. Add the dressing and toss well. Serve chilled, with capers passed separately.

—*F&W*

AVOCADO STUFFED WITH CHICKEN AND ARTICHOKE HEARTS

Served on a bed of lettuce, this makes a fine summer supper.

🍷 Alsace Gewürztraminer, such as Trimbach or Hugel

2 Servings

1 teaspoon salt
1 tablespoon fresh lemon juice
½ teaspoon freshly ground pepper
3 tablespoons olive oil, preferably extra-virgin
1 tablespoon capers
4 artichoke hearts (canned in brine), quartered
2 cooked whole chicken breasts—skinned, boned and cut into bite-size pieces
2 medium avocados, preferably Hass
Lettuce leaves and lemon wedges, for serving

1. In a medium bowl, dissolve the salt in the lemon juice. Add the pepper and whisk in the olive oil to make a vinaigrette. Add the capers, artichoke hearts and chicken.

2. Cut each avocado in half lengthwise and remove the pit. Keeping the skin intact, gently run a paring knife between the skin and the fruit to loosen. Without piercing the shell, cut the fruit lengthwise at ½-inch intervals and then horizontally to form bite-size pieces. Using a teaspoon, lift the pieces of avocado from the shell and add to the chicken mixture. Toss gently to mix. Season with additional salt and pepper to taste.

3. Spoon the mixture back into the avocado shells, heaping generously. Serve on a bed of lettuce and garnish with lemon wedges.

—*Molly O'Neill*

CHICKEN AND POTATO SALAD WITH PESTO AND RED PEPPER

6 Servings

2½ pounds skinless, boneless chicken breast
1 pound small red potatoes
1 red bell pepper, cut into thin strips
½ cup fresh basil leaves
2 garlic cloves
½ cup olive oil, preferably extra-virgin
¼ cup white wine vinegar
3 tablespoons freshly grated Parmesan cheese
½ teaspoon oregano
Salt and freshly ground black pepper

1. In a large saucepan of simmering salted water, poach the chicken breasts until white throughout but still juicy, about 15 minutes. Remove the chicken and let cool. *(The chicken can be prepared 1 day ahead. Wrap tightly and refrigerate.)*

2. Put the potatoes in a large saucepan of cold salted water. Bring to a boil and cook until tender, 10 to 15 minutes. Drain and rinse under cold running water. Remove the skins.

3. Cut the chicken and potatoes into 1-inch cubes. In a large bowl, combine the chicken, potatoes and red pepper.

4. In a blender or food processor, combine the basil, garlic, oil, vinegar, cheese and oregano. Puree until smooth. Season with salt and black pepper to taste.

5. Pour the basil dressing over the salad and toss to coat. Serve slightly chilled or at room temperature.

—*Jeanette Ferrary & Louise Fiszer*

CHICKEN SALAD WITH SHRIMP AND FENNEL

Fresh fennel and endive and a light lemony dressing make this a refreshing salad for a hot summer day.

6 to 8 Servings

1½ pounds large shrimp, shelled and
   deveined, shells reserved
2 pounds skinless, boneless chicken breast
2 large fennel bulbs with tops
⅓ cup fresh lemon juice
½ cup olive oil
1 teaspoon salt
½ teaspoon freshly ground pepper
1½ pounds Belgian endives (4 to 6)

1. In a medium saucepan, cover the shrimp shells with 3 cups of water and bring to a boil over high heat. Reduce the heat to low and simmer for 5 minutes. Strain the broth and return it to the saucepan; discard the shrimp shells.

2. Add the shrimp to the broth and cook over high heat just until opaque throughout, about 3½ minutes. Drain the shrimp, reserving the broth. Transfer the shrimp to a plate to cool, then refrigerate, covered, until chilled.

3. Pour the broth into a large, straight-sided skillet. Add the chicken and bring to a simmer over moderate heat. Cook until firm and white throughout, about 10 minutes. Transfer the chicken to a plate to cool, then refrigerate, covered, until chilled. *(The recipe can be prepared to this point up to 1 day ahead.)*

4. Trim the fennel, reserving the feathery tops. Halve the bulbs lengthwise and cut out the cores. Thinly slice the fennel crosswise. Mince most of the feathery tops, reserving a few for garnish.

5. In a large bowl, whisk the lemon juice with the oil, salt and pepper. Add the shrimp, fennel and minced fennel tops; toss well.

6. Slice the chicken breasts crosswise ¼ inch thick. Add the chicken to the shrimp and toss well.

7. Separate the endive spears and arrange them around a platter or individual serving plates, yellow tips pointing out. Mound the salad on top, garnish with the reserved fennel tops and serve chilled.

———

—*Bob Chambers*

CHICKEN, MUSHROOM AND NAPPA CABBAGE SALAD WITH FRESH CORIANDER

The mushrooms are marinated first to absorb the flavor of the tangy dressing, but the cabbage is tossed in at the very last moment to keep it crisp.

8 to 10 Servings

4 scallions, thinly sliced
Juice of 1 lemon
⅓ cup plus 2 tablespoons olive oil
2 tablespoons coarsely chopped cilantro (fresh
   coriander), plus additional sprigs for garnish
1 teaspoon salt
½ teaspoon freshly ground pepper
½ pound firm white mushrooms, stems
   removed, caps sliced ⅛ inch thick
6 cups cubed (½-inch) cooked chicken
1 small nappa cabbage (about 1½ pounds),
   quartered lengthwise and sliced crosswise ⅛
   inch thick

1. In a large bowl, combine the scallions, lemon juice, olive oil, chopped cilantro, salt and pepper. Add the mushrooms and toss well. Cover and set aside for 1 hour, stirring occasionally.

2. Add the chicken to the mushrooms and toss well. *(The recipe can be prepared to this point up to 4 hours ahead and refrigerated, covered.)* Just before serving, add the cabbage and toss again. Mound the chicken salad on a platter and garnish with the cilantro sprigs.

—*Bob Chambers*

TARRAGON CHICKEN SALAD WITH MELON AND CUCUMBER

Crisp cucumbers and juicy melon make this a cooling summer salad that's best served as soon as it's made.

8 to 10 Servings

> 2 tablespoons tarragon wine vinegar
> 2 tablespoons minced fresh tarragon
> ¾ teaspoon salt
> ½ teaspoon freshly ground pepper
> ¼ cup plus 2 tablespoons light olive oil
> ¼ cup minced red onion
> 6 cups cooked chicken breast, cut into slices
> 1 cantaloupe (about 2½ pounds)
> 2 cucumbers—peeled, seeded and sliced
>   crosswise ¼ inch thick
> Radicchio leaves, for garnish

1. In a large bowl, combine the vinegar, tarragon, salt, pepper and oil. Add the onion and chicken, toss gently and set aside while you prepare the melon.

2. Halve the cantaloupe and scoop out the seeds. Using a sharp knife, cut each half into 4 wedges. Slice the melon off the peel and cut into ½-inch dice.

3. Add the melon and cucumbers to the bowl and toss well to coat. Serve the salad on a platter or plates on a bed of radicchio leaves.

—*Bob Chambers*

CHICKEN SALAD WITH BITTER GREENS, PANCETTA AND CHICKEN LIVER CONFIT

In this hearty salad, the richness of the liver confit is balanced by the bitter greens and sweet-tart balsamic dressing.

❦ The rich confit of chicken livers with the flavorful balsamic dressing would be best matched by a fruity, lively red. A Rhône, such as a Paul Jaboulet Aîné St-Joseph Le Grand Pompée, or a Kendall-Jackson Zinfandel from California would be a good match.

6 to 8 Servings

> ½ pound pancetta, sliced ⅛ inch thick, cut
>   into 1-inch pieces
> 1 tablespoon vegetable oil
> Chicken Liver Confit (recipe follows)
> 4 scallions, thinly sliced
> ⅓ cup balsamic vinegar
> 1 teaspoon salt
> ½ teaspoon freshly ground pepper
> 3 cups cooked chicken (1-inch pieces)
> ¼ cup pine nuts (about 1¼ ounces)
> 8 cups mixed bitter greens (about 1 pound),
>   such as curly endive, radicchio and
>   dandelion, torn into pieces

1. In a medium skillet, cover the pancetta with water and bring to a boil over high heat. Drain well and wipe the skillet dry. Add the oil to the skillet and fry the pancetta over high heat, stirring occasionally, until crisp, about 7 minutes. Drain the pancetta on paper towels. Set aside.

2. Remove the chicken livers from their oil, reserving the oil. Cut the livers into ½-inch cubes.

3. In a large bowl, combine the scallions, balsamic vinegar, salt and pepper. Add the chicken, the cubed chicken livers and their oil and toss well. Set aside for 15 minutes to 1 hour to blend the flavors.

4. Meanwhile, in a small dry skillet, toast the pine nuts over moderate heat, shaking the pan frequently, until lightly browned, about 5 minutes. Set aside.

5. Just before serving, add the greens to the chicken and toss well. Mound the salad on plates or a platter and garnish with the reserved pancetta and the toasted pine nuts. Serve immediately.

——————

—*Bob Chambers*

CHICKEN LIVER CONFIT

This is a great method for putting up delicate chicken livers. They're seasoned first, then cooked slowly in olive oil.

Makes 1 Pound

1 pound chicken livers, lobes separated and
  trimmed of fat and membrane
1 tablespoon fresh thyme or 1½ teaspoons
  dried
1 teaspoon coarse (kosher) salt
½ teaspoon coarsely ground pepper
⅔ cup olive oil

1. In a small bowl, toss the livers with the thyme, salt and pepper. Cover and refrigerate for 1 hour.

2. In a medium skillet, spread the livers out in a single layer and pour the olive oil on top. Cook over very low heat, turning once, until the livers feel firm to the touch, about 14 minutes. Transfer the livers to a glass jar and pour the oil on top. Let cool completely, then cover tightly and refrigerate for up to 1 week.

——————

—*Bob Chambers*

LEMON-CHICKEN SALAD WITH WILD RICE AND GRAPES

Sweet-tart, juicy grapes are the perfect counterpoint to the tender chicken and chewy, nutty rice.

6 to 8 Servings

1 cup wild rice (about 6½ ounces)
4 cups Chicken Stock (p. 10) or canned low-
  sodium broth
1 teaspoon herbes de Provence
1 teaspoon salt
¾ teaspoon freshly ground pepper
⅓ cup fresh lemon juice
1 teaspoon Dijon-style mustard
2 tablespoons olive oil
3 cups cooked chicken (½-inch pieces)
1 celery rib, minced
½ pound seedless red grapes, halved lengthwise
½ pound seedless green grapes, halved
  lengthwise
Red leaf lettuce, for garnish

1. In a medium bowl, soak the rice in 3 cups of warm water for 1 hour. Drain the rice, rinse well and transfer it to a heavy medium saucepan. Add the chicken stock and bring to a boil over high heat, skimming the surface as necessary.

2. Add the herbes de Provence, ½ teaspoon of the salt and ¼ teaspoon of the pepper. Reduce the heat to low and simmer, covered, for 25 minutes. Uncover and continue to cook until the rice is tender and the liquid has been absorbed, about 30 minutes longer. Transfer the rice to a bowl to cool slightly.

3. In another bowl, whisk together the lemon juice, mustard, olive oil and the remaining ½ teaspoon each of salt and pepper. Add this dressing to the rice along with the chicken, celery and red and green grapes. Toss well to combine. Line

a platter or plates with the red leaf lettuce and mound the salad on top. Serve warm or at room temperature.

———

—*Bob Chambers*

CHICKEN SALAD WITH ONIONS AND POTATO CRISPS

Here chicken teams up with crisp potatoes, caramelized onions and garlic. Peppery watercress offsets the sweetness of the onions, and a pungent mustard dressing brings all of the elements together.

8 Servings

2 pounds small red potatoes, unpeeled

¾ cup plus 2 tablespoons olive oil

2 teaspoons salt

1 teaspoon freshly ground pepper

2 pounds Spanish onions, halved lengthwise and sliced ¼ inch thick

2 garlic cloves, crushed through a press

1 tablespoon grainy mustard

2 tablespoons Dijon-style mustard

⅓ cup fresh lemon juice

⅓ cup chopped flat-leaf parsley

2 teaspoons minced fresh rosemary

6 cups cooked chicken (½-inch pieces)

2 bunches of watercress, large stems removed

2 tomatoes, quartered, for garnish

1. Preheat the oven to 450°. Using a mandoline or a food processor, slice the potatoes ⅛ inch thick. Place in a bowl, add 3 tablespoons of the olive oil and toss until coated. Season with ½ teaspoon each of the salt and pepper.

2. Spray 4 baking sheets with vegetable spray. Arrange the potato slices in a single layer on the baking sheets and roast in the oven, 2 sheets at a time, for 10 minutes. Then switch the sheets and bake for 5 to 7 minutes longer, until the potatoes are nicely browned and crisp. Loosen the potatoes from the sheets as soon as they are done

and transfer to paper towels to cool. Repeat with the remaining potatoes.

3. Meanwhile, in a large casserole, heat 3 tablespoons of the olive oil over moderate heat. Add the onions and ½ teaspoon of the salt. Cover tightly and cook, stirring occasionally, until translucent, about 10 minutes. Uncover, increase the heat to moderately high and cook, stirring frequently, until the onions are well browned, about 10 minutes. Add the garlic and cook for 2 minutes longer.

4. In a bowl, combine the grainy and Dijon mustards with the lemon juice, parsley, rosemary and the remaining 1 teaspoon salt and ½ teaspoon pepper. Whisk in the remaining ½ cup olive oil; set aside ¼ cup of this dressing. Add the remainder to the onions and stir well to blend, scraping up any browned bits adhering to the bottom of the casserole. Scrape the onions into a bowl. Add the chicken and potato crisps and toss well.

5. In a bowl, toss the watercress with the reserved ¼ cup dressing. Arrange the watercress on a platter or plates and mound the salad on top. Garnish with the tomato wedges and serve immediately.

———

—*Bob Chambers*

WARM CHICKEN SALAD WITH ORANGES AND SPICY GINGER DRESSING

Serve this sweet, pungent, gingery salad while the chicken is still slightly warm. For a colorful touch, garnish the dish with edible flowers such as nasturtiums.

❦ Citrus and ginger tend to clash with subtle wines; choose a more straightforward white, such as Trefethen Eschol White.

6 Servings

4 small skinless, boneless chicken breast halves (about 4 ounces each)

2 tablespoons fresh lime juice

1 teaspoon crushed hot red pepper

2 medium navel oranges

4 ounces fettuccine, dry or fresh

Spicy Ginger Dressing (recipe follows)

1 tablespoon peanut oil

2 tablespoons chopped cilantro (fresh coriander)

½ medium red bell pepper, cut into thin
  julienne strips

1 head of romaine lettuce, leaves separated

1 bunch of radishes, sliced, for garnish

1. In a small nonreactive dish, combine the chicken breasts with the lime juice and hot red pepper; turn to coat. Cover and marinate in the refrigerator for at least 4 hours or overnight.

2. With a small sharp knife, peel the oranges, cutting off all the bitter white pith. Working over a bowl, cut in between the membranes to release the sections. Set aside.

3. In a large saucepan, bring 2 quarts of salted water to a boil over high heat. Add the fettuccine and cook until al dente, 10 to 12 minutes for dry and about 3 minutes for fresh. Drain and rinse under cool water for several seconds to remove starch and cool slightly. Transfer the pasta to a medium bowl and toss with ½ cup of the Spicy Ginger Dressing. Set aside.

4. In a large heavy skillet, heat the peanut oil over moderately high heat. Add the chicken breasts and cook, turning once, until golden brown and just cooked through, 3 to 4 minutes per side. Transfer the chicken to a cutting board and slice the meat across the grain ½ inch thick. Toss the chicken with the remaining ½ cup dressing and the cilantro, red pepper and oranges.

5. Arrange the lettuce leaves on a platter. Mound the fettuccine on the lettuce and top with the warm chicken salad. Garnish the platter with the radish slices and serve at once.

—Michel Stroot

SPICY GINGER DRESSING
Makes About 1 Cup

¼ cup coarsely chopped fresh ginger

2 tablespoons red wine vinegar

1 tablespoon rice vinegar

1 tablespoon mirin (sweet rice wine)★

1 tablespoon honey

1 tablespoon reduced-sodium soy sauce

1 tablespoon minced fresh basil

½ teaspoon crushed hot red pepper

½ cup peanut oil

★Available at Asian markets

In a blender, combine the ginger, red wine vinegar, rice vinegar, mirin, honey, soy sauce, basil, hot red pepper and 1 tablespoon of water. With the machine on, gradually pour in the peanut oil in a thin stream and continue to blend until smooth. (The dressing can be made up to 1 week ahead and refrigerated in a jar. Remove from the refrigerator at least 20 minutes before using.)

—Michel Stroot

SHREDDED CHICKEN SALAD WITH GINGER AND SESAME
🍷 A hearty California red, such as Petite Sirah
4 to 6 Servings

2 slices (quarter-size), plus 1 tablespoon finely
  shredded fresh ginger

3 tablespoons sherry wine vinegar

Green tops from 1 bunch of scallions

3 peppercorns

1 teaspoon salt

1 pound skinless, boneless chicken breasts

¾ pound carrots, cut into 2-by-¼-inch sticks

½ pound green beans, cut into 2-inch lengths

1 tablespoon Dijon-style mustard

2 tablespoons soy sauce

½ teaspoon freshly ground pepper

237

2 tablespoons Oriental sesame oil
2 tablespoons vegetable oil

1. In a large nonreactive skillet or flameproof casserole, put the ginger slices, 1 tablespoon of the vinegar, the scallion tops, peppercorns, salt and 6 cups of water. Bring to a boil, reduce the heat and simmer for 15 minutes.

2. Add the chicken, reduce the heat to low and simmer until the chicken is almost cooked through but still slightly pink in the center (it will finish cooking as it cools), about 10 minutes. Remove the chicken to a rack and let cool.

3. Meanwhile, in a medium saucepan of boiling salted water, cook the carrots until crisp-tender, about 2 minutes. Drain and rinse under cold running water; drain well.

4. In another medium saucepan of boiling salted water, cook the green beans until crisp-tender, about 2 minutes. Drain and rinse under cold running water; drain well.

5. In a small bowl, whisk the mustard, soy sauce, pepper and remaining 2 tablespoons vinegar until blended. Slowly whisk in the sesame and vegetable oils in a thin stream to make a dressing.

6. With your fingers, tear the chicken into shreds about the same size as the carrots. In a large bowl, combine the chicken with the carrots, green beans and shredded ginger. Pour on the dressing, toss well to coat and serve at room temperature.

—*Mitchell Cobey Cuisine, Chicago, Illinois*

MA LA CHICKEN

A Chinese version of chicken salad includes shredded chicken and strips of scallion green atop a bed of slivered aromatic vegetables. A dressing of soy, sesame oil and hot oil comes next, and the ground red Szechuan peppercorns that blanket the top are just hot enough to make your tongue tingle.

4 Servings

One 3-pound chicken
1 large cucumber
¼ cup Szechuan peppercorns★
½ carrot, cut into 3-by-⅛-inch julienne strips
3 celery ribs, cut into 3-by-⅛-inch julienne strips
¼ teaspoon salt
2½ tablespoons soy sauce, preferably dark★
1 tablespoon Oriental sesame oil
1½ teaspoons Chinese chile oil★
½ teaspoon vinegar
½ teaspoon sugar
⅛ teaspoon freshly ground white pepper
4 scallions (green part only), cut into 3-by-⅛-inch julienne strips
1 tablespoon minced garlic
★Available at Asian markets

1. Place the whole chicken in a pot just large enough to hold it with water to cover by 1 inch. Bring to a boil over high heat. Reduce the heat to low and simmer until cooked through and no longer pink near the bone, 30 to 35 minutes. Remove the chicken from the pot and let stand until cool enough to handle. Remove the meat from the carcass, discarding the skin and bones. Tear the meat into ¼- to ½-inch-thick shreds. Cover and keep warm.

2. Meanwhile, peel the cucumber and halve it lengthwise. Remove the seeds with a spoon. Cut into 3-by-⅛-inch julienne strips; drain on paper towels.

3. In a small dry skillet, toast the peppercorns over high heat until they begin to smoke.

Remove from the heat and grind to a powder in a coffee mill blender or food processor.

4. In a bowl, combine the carrot, celery and cucumber. Toss with the salt and mound in the center of a serving dish. Arrange the shredded chicken over the vegetables.

5. In a small bowl, whisk together the soy sauce, sesame oil, chile oil, vinegar, sugar and white pepper. Pour over the chicken.

6. Garnish the chicken with the scallion greens. Pass the ground Szechuan pepper and minced garlic separately.

———

—*F&W*

CHINESE CHICKEN WITH CARROTS AND STAR ANISE

Use only the sweetest carrots for this light, room-temperature salad.

2 Servings

3 tablespoons light (thin) soy sauce
2 teaspoons sugar
⅜ teaspoon Oriental sesame oil
2 star anise pods, crumbled
1½-inch piece of fresh ginger, peeled and
*   thinly sliced lengthwise*
½ pound skinless boneless chicken breast
2 small carrots, thinly sliced on the diagonal
1 tablespoon rice vinegar
1½ tablespoons peanut oil
1 scallion, green part only, thinly sliced

1. In a bowl, combine the soy sauce, sugar and ⅛ teaspoon of the sesame oil. Stir in the star anise and the ginger. Add the chicken breasts, turning to coat with the marinade. Cover and refrigerate for at least 2 hours or overnight.

2. Transfer the chicken and marinade into a medium saucepan. Add 1 cup of water and bring to a boil over high heat. Reduce the heat to low, turn the chicken over and simmer for 3 minutes. Remove from the heat and set aside to cool.

3. Transfer the chicken to a work surface and thinly slice crosswise; set aside. Return the poaching liquid to a boil over high heat and cook until reduced to ¼ cup, about 3 minutes. Strain the liquid into a small bowl and let cool to room temperature.

4. Meanwhile, in a small saucepan of boiling salted water, cook the carrots until barely tender, about 2 minutes. Drain and set aside to cool.

5. Whisk the rice vinegar into the reduced poaching liquid, then gradually whisk in the remaining ¼ teaspoon sesame oil and the peanut oil.

6. To serve, decoratively arrange the chicken and carrots on 2 small plates. Spoon the dressing over the salads and let stand for about 5 minutes to let it soak in. Sprinkle the scallion on top.

———

—*David Rosengarten*

WATERCRESS SALAD WITH SMOKED CHICKEN AND WALNUT CROUTONS

In the South, wild watercress ("creasy greens") gives this salad an arresting flavor and texture. Elsewhere, the peppery cultivated green still contrasts nicely with the sweet-tangy mustard. The walnut oil and croutons add richness.

❦ The bite of the greens and smoky flavor of the meat dictate a spicy white wine, such as an Alsace Gewürztraminer from Willm or Trimbach, to stand up to the flavors.

6 Servings

5 tablespoons walnut oil
1 tablespoon unsalted butter
3 large garlic cloves, slivered
3 slices of stale, firm-textured white bread, cut
*   into ½-inch cubes (about 1 cup)*
½ teaspoon salt
2 teaspoons Honeycup or other sweet-spicy
*   mustard*
2 teaspoons fresh lemon juice

2 teaspoons red wine vinegar

2 tablespoons olive oil

1 tablespoon vegetable oil

¼ teaspoon freshly ground pepper

2 large bunches of watercress, wild if available,
tough stems removed (about 6 cups)

1 small head of radicchio, torn into
bite-site pieces

6 ounces smoked chicken, shredded into bite-
size pieces

1. In a large skillet, heat 2 tablespoons of the walnut oil with the butter over moderately low heat. Add the garlic and cook until fragrant, about 1 minute.

2. Add the bread cubes to the skillet and cook, tossing often, until crisp and golden brown, 5 to 8 minutes. Season with ¼ teaspoon of the salt and set aside.

3. In a small bowl, blend the mustard, lemon juice, vinegar and remaining ¼ teaspoon salt. Whisk in the olive oil, vegetable oil, remaining 3 tablespoons walnut oil and the pepper.

4. In a large bowl, toss the watercress, radicchio and smoked chicken with the dressing. Top with the croutons.

—Sarah Belk

SMOKED CHICKEN
WITH APPLES
AND ARUGULA

Fragrant wood smoke, the tart snap of a crisp apple and the play of walnuts and walnut oil against the pungent flavor of arugula produce a richly flavorful combination in this chicken salad.

❦ Gewürztraminer, such as DeLoach

4 Servings

⅓ cup coarsely chopped walnuts

Juice of 1 lemon

2 Red Delicious or other crisp apples

4 skinless, boneless smoked chicken breast
halves (about 1 pound)

6 cups arugula, stems removed

Walnut Vinaigrette (recipe follows)

1. Preheat the oven to 300°. In a shallow pan, bake the walnuts in the oven, shaking the pan occasionally, until toasted, 25 to 30 minutes. Set aside to cool. Reserve 1 tablespoon of the nuts for the Walnut Vinaigrette.

2. In a small bowl, combine the lemon juice with 1 cup of cold water. Core, peel and thinly slice the apples and dip the slices into the mixture to prevent discoloration; drain.

3. Cut the chicken crosswise on the diagonal into thin slices. Arrange the chicken and apple slices on one side of each of four plates, alternating and overlapping the slices. Arrange the arugula on the other half of the plates. Spoon 1½ tablespoons of Walnut Vinaigrette over each serving of arugula, and drizzle 1 tablespoon of the vinaigrette over the chicken. Garnish each serving with about 1 tablespoon of the toasted walnuts. Pass the remaining vinaigrette in a sauceboat.

—One Fifth, New York City

WALNUT VINAIGRETTE

Makes About 1½ Cups

1 hard-cooked egg yolk

2 tablespoons Dijon-style mustard

¼ cup white wine vinegar

1 teaspoon salt

¼ teaspoon freshly ground pepper

1 cup walnut oil

1 tablespoon chopped toasted walnuts
(see Note)

In a medium bowl, whisk together the egg yolk and mustard. Mix in the vinegar, salt and pepper. Gradually whisk in the oil. Add the walnuts and serve at room temperature.

NOTE: Use the walnuts reserved from Step 1 of Smoked Chicken with Apples and Arugula (above).

———————

—*One Fifth, New York City*

SMOKED CHICKEN AND APPLE SALAD

This salad is a colorful, crunchy combination of chicken, red peppers, tart green apples and toasted pecans all tossed with a mustard vinaigrette.

3 to 4 Servings

1 small garlic clove, minced
1 tablespoon Dijon-style mustard
1 tablespoon white wine vinegar or rice vinegar
2 tablespoons minced winter savory
¼ teaspoon salt
¼ teaspoon freshly ground black pepper
¼ cup plus 2 tablespoons olive oil
1 small red onion, thinly sliced
1 cup pecans
2 large tart green apples, such as Granny Smith—peeled, quartered and cut into ½-inch chunks
1 medium red bell pepper, cut into thin julienne strips
¾ pound smoked chicken, turkey or pheasant, cut into 1-inch pieces

1. Preheat the oven to 400°. In a small bowl, combine the garlic, mustard, vinegar, savory, salt and black pepper. With a fork, whisk in the oil. Set aside.

2. Put the onion slices in a small bowl. Cover with cold water and soak for 5 to 10 minutes; then drain well.

3. Spread the pecans on a baking sheet and cook in the oven until fragrant and toasted, about 4 minutes. Let cool and crumble into smaller pieces.

4. In a large bowl, combine the onion, apples, red pepper and chicken. Pour the vinaigrette over the salad and toss well. Spoon the salad onto a serving platter, or divide among 6 plates. Sprinkle with the toasted pecans and serve.

———————

—*Marcia Kiesel*

WARM SMOKED CHICKEN SALAD

For this meaty, delicious salad, strips of smoked chicken and sliced scallions are sautéed and then mounded on a bed of lettuce; a fresh tomato vinaigrette is spooned over, and the salad is sprinkled with parsley and toasted sesame seeds.

4 Servings

½ head of Boston lettuce
½ head of red leaf lettuce
1 bunch of scallions, sliced diagonally into 1-inch lengths
6 tablespoons olive oil
¾ pound thinly sliced smoked chicken, cut into 3-by-1-inch strips
¾ pound plum tomatoes, seeded and minced
3 tablespoons red wine vinegar
Salt and freshly ground pepper
Chopped parsley and toasted sesame seeds, for garnish

1. Arrange the lettuces on a platter. Set aside about 10 pieces of scallion for garnishing.

2. In a large skillet, heat 4 tablespoons of the oil until shimmering. Add the chicken and scallions and cook over moderately high heat, stirring, until warmed through, about 3 minutes. Remove from the heat and mound in the center of the platter.

3. Warm the remaining 2 tablespoons oil in the skillet over high heat. Add the tomatoes and

vinegar. Cook until the liquid is evaporated, about 2 minutes. Season with salt and pepper to taste. Spoon the sauce over the chicken and sprinkle with the reserved scallions, the parsley and toasted sesame seeds. Serve warm or at room temperature.

—F&W

MEDITERRANEAN CHICKEN-RATATOUILLE SALAD

The base of this recipe is a light ratatouille made with roasted eggplant.

8 to 10 Servings

2 eggplants (1 to 1¼ pounds each)
2 teaspoons salt
½ cup plus 2 tablespoons olive oil
2 medium onions, chopped
2 red bell peppers, cut into 1-by-½-inch strips
2 yellow bell peppers, cut into 1-by-½-inch strips
3 small zucchini, quartered lengthwise and sliced 1 inch thick
3 small yellow summer squash, quartered lengthwise and sliced 1 inch thick
2 garlic cloves, crushed through a press
1 teaspoon fresh thyme or ½ teaspoon dried
½ pound plum tomatoes, halved lengthwise and sliced ½ inch thick
1 teaspoon freshly ground black pepper
6 cups cubed (¾-inch) cooked chicken
1 cup shredded fresh basil, plus whole leaves for garnish
⅓ cup fresh lemon juice

1. Halve the eggplants lengthwise. Set them on a work surface, cut-sides down, and slice lengthwise into eighths. Cut the eggplant slices into 1-inch pieces and place in a colander. Sprinkle 1 teaspoon of the salt on top, toss and set them over a bowl to drain for at least 1 hour at room temperature or overnight, covered.

2. Preheat the oven to 450°. Pat the eggplant dry between paper towels. Transfer the eggplant to a jelly-roll pan and toss with ¼ cup of the olive oil. Spread the eggplant out in a single layer and bake for 40 to 45 minutes, until well browned. Let cool slightly in the pan.

3. Meanwhile, in a large flameproof casserole, heat 2 tablespoons of the olive oil over moderately high heat. Add the onions and cook, stirring frequently, until beginning to brown, about 5 minutes.

4. Add the bell peppers, zucchini and summer squash and cook, stirring frequently, until slightly tender but still crisp, 12 to 15 minutes.

5. Stir in the garlic and cook for 1 minute longer. Stir in the thyme, tomatoes and ½ teaspoon of the black pepper and remove from the heat.

6. Transfer the cooked vegetables to a large bowl and let cool slightly. Fold in the eggplant, chicken, shredded basil, lemon juice and the remaining ¼ cup olive oil, 1 teaspoon salt and ½ teaspoon pepper. Mound the salad on a platter or plates and serve warm or at room temperature, garnished with the basil leaves.

—Bob Chambers

CASHEW CHICKEN SALAD

The chicken breasts can be sautéed whole, instead of in strips, and then sliced shortly before serving.

❡ To harmonize with the somewhat sweet flavors of the chicken and the nuts, try a light white wine with fruity flavors, such as California Dry Chenin Blanc from Hacienda or Dry Creek.

6 Servings

2½ pounds skinless, boneless chicken breast, sliced crosswise ¼ inch thick
½ teaspoon salt
½ teaspoon freshly ground black pepper
2 tablespoons olive oil
1 cup dry white wine

½ pound sliced smoked bacon

1 cup salted whole cashews plus 2 tablespoons chopped cashews

3 garlic cloves, minced

3 tablespoons cider vinegar

1½ teaspoons Dijon-style mustard

1½ teaspoons anchovy paste

⅛ teaspoon cayenne pepper

½ head of red cabbage, thinly sliced

3 carrots, cut into 2-by-¼-inch sticks

1 large cucumber—peeled, halved, seeded and sliced crosswise ¼ inch thick

2 hard-cooked eggs, quartered

1. Season the chicken strips with ¼ teaspoon of the salt and ¼ teaspoon of the black pepper. In a large nonreactive skillet, heat 1 tablespoon of the olive oil over high heat. When the oil starts to smoke, add half of the chicken pieces in a single layer and fry until browned, about 2 minutes. With a metal spatula, turn the pieces and brown well on the other side, about 2 minutes longer. Transfer the chicken to a large plate and repeat with the remaining oil and chicken strips.

2. Return the skillet to high heat and add the wine. Scrape up any browned bits from the bottom of the pan and boil until the liquid is reduced to ½ cup, about 2 minutes. Stir in any accumulated juices from the chicken.

3. In a large skillet, fry the bacon over moderate heat until crisp, about 7 minutes. Drain on paper towels. Break into small pieces and set aside.

4. In a food processor, combine the whole cashews, garlic, vinegar, mustard, anchovy paste and cayenne. Puree until smooth. Scrape down the sides of the bowl and add the reduced wine and the remaining ¼ teaspoon each of salt and black pepper; process until blended.

5. On a large platter, arrange the sliced red cabbage in an even layer. In a large bowl, combine the chicken, carrots, cucumber and dressing; toss well. Spoon the chicken over the cabbage and sprinkle with the reserved bacon bits and the chopped cashews. Arrange the egg quarters around the edge of the salad.

———————————

—Marcia Kiesel

THAI CHICKEN SALAD

On our first night in Bangkok several years ago, we had dinner at a small, out-of-the-way restaurant. One of the dishes we ate that evening was a delicious chicken salad. Here is my version, reassembled from notes I scribbled on a napkin.

6 Servings

3 cups vegetable oil, for frying

20 wonton skins,★ cut into ¼-inch strips

8 cups shredded mixed salad greens

4 cups of bite-size pieces of barbecued or roast chicken (from a 3-pound bird)

1 cup bean sprouts

1 large yellow bell pepper, cut into thin julienne strips

½ European seedless cucumber (about 8 ounces), cut into thin julienne strips

6 tablespoons fresh lime juice

¼ cup fish sauce (nuoc mam)★

¼ cup (packed) light brown sugar

4 serrano chiles,★ seeded and minced

½ teaspoon freshly grated nutmeg

1 tablespoon finely minced fresh lemon grass★ (optional)

1 tablespoon finely minced fresh ginger

¼ cup minced fresh mint

3 tablespoons minced fresh basil

¼ cup dry-roasted unsalted peanuts, coarsely chopped

★Available at Asian markets

1. In a large skillet, heat the oil over moderately high heat until a strip of wonton bounces across

243

the surface. Add the wonton strips in batches and fry, turning, until crisp and golden, about 1 minute. Transfer to paper towels; drain well.

2. In a large bowl, combine the mixed salad greens, chicken, bean sprouts, yellow pepper and cucumber.

3. In a medium bowl, whisk together the lime juice, fish sauce, brown sugar, chiles, nutmeg, lemon grass, ginger, mint and basil. Add the dressing to the salad and toss well. Gently fold in the crisp wonton strips. Turn out onto a serving platter and sprinkle with the peanuts.

—*Hugh Carpenter*

BROILED THAI CHICKEN SALAD

The special taste of *yom gai* is in the marinade. Try this same marinade with thin slices of pork for an unusual and delicious barbecue.

♥ Although cold beer is an obvious choice for this salad, a fruity, off-dry white, such as Folie à Deux Dry Chenin Blanc or Hogue Cellars Chenin Blanc, would also work nicely.

6 Servings

3½ ounces cellophane noodles (wun sen)★
4 large garlic cloves, chopped
2 teaspoons peppercorns
¼ cup chopped cilantro (fresh coriander)
¼ cup plus 1 tablespoon soy sauce
2 tablespoons plus 1 teaspoon fish sauce (nam pla)★
1¼ pounds skinless, boneless chicken breast, cut into 1-inch cubes
4 cups Chicken Stock (p. 10) or canned broth
1½ teaspoons sugar
3 tablespoons fresh lime juice
1 head of leaf lettuce, leaves separated
4 medium tomatoes, cut into wedges
3 scallions, chopped
1 European seedless cucumber, cut into 1-inch dice
1 tablespoon chopped roasted peanuts

1 lime, thinly sliced
★Available at Asian markets

1. Place the cellophane noodles in a bowl with hot water to cover. Let soak for 30 minutes to soften.

2. In a blender or food processor, combine the garlic, peppercorns and 2 tablespoons of the cilantro. Blend or process to a paste. Scrape down the sides of the bowl and add ¼ cup of the soy sauce and 2 tablespoons of the *nam pla*. Pour the marinade into a shallow pan and add the chicken cubes. Toss well and let marinate for 30 minutes.

3. Preheat the broiler. In a medium saucepan, bring the chicken stock to a boil. Drain the cellophane noodles. Add the noodles to the pan and boil until softened, about 5 minutes. Drain well. Cut the noodles into 4 pieces. Reserve the stock for another use.

4. Remove the chicken from the marinade and place on a baking sheet in a single layer. Broil for 4 to 7 minutes, stirring the pieces from time to time, until browned and cooked through.

5. In a small bowl, stir together the sugar, lime juice and the remaining 1 tablespoon soy sauce and 1 teaspoon *nam pla*.

6. To assemble the salad, line a large platter with the lettuce leaves. Spread the noodles over the lettuce and top with the tomato wedges, chopped scallions and diced cucumber. Arrange the broiled chicken on the salad and pour on the dressing. Sprinkle the remaining 2 tablespoons cilantro and the peanuts on top. Garnish with the lime slices.

—*Jeffrey Alford*

Low-Calorie Dishes

CRISPY BALSAMIC CHICKEN WINGS

The rich, sweet balsamic vinegar marinade caramelizes to form a crisp glaze on these wings as they cook. They can be baked or grilled if you prefer.

4 First-Course Servings
254 Calories per Serving

2 pounds chicken wings
⅔ cup balsamic vinegar
3 large scallions, thinly sliced

1. In a large bowl, combine the chicken wings, vinegar and scallions. Toss well to evenly coat the wings. Cover and let marinate at room temperature for 6 hours, stirring occasionally, or refrigerate overnight.

2. Preheat the oven to 450°. Let the chicken wings return to room temperature if refrigerated. Lift them out of the marinade and place on a baking sheet in a single layer. Bake the wings until crisp and deep brown, about 25 minutes. Alternatively, grill the chicken wings over a medium-hot fire, about 5 inches from the heat, for about 8 to 10 minutes per side. Serve hot or at room temperature.

—*Marcia Kiesel*

CORN CREPES STUFFED WITH CHICKEN AND POBLANOS

6 Servings
350 Calories per Serving

2 chicken breast halves (about 8 ounces each),
  bone in
2 large garlic cloves—1 halved, 1 minced
1 bay leaf
1 pound fresh poblano peppers
  (about 5 medium)
1 cup milk
⅓ cup all-purpose flour

1 teaspoon crumbled oregano
1 teaspoon cumin
1 teaspoon salt
⅛ teaspoon freshly ground black pepper
1 cup corn kernels, fresh or thawed frozen
Corn Crêpes (recipe follows)
1 cup grated Monterey Jack cheese
  (about 4 ounces)
¼ cup sour cream
1 large tomato, finely diced

1. In a heavy medium saucepan, combine the chicken with 1½ cups water, the halved garlic clove and the bay leaf. Cover and bring to a boil over moderate heat. Reduce the heat to low and simmer until the chicken is just cooked through, about 15 minutes. Transfer the chicken to a plate and let sit until cool. Discard the bay leaf and strain the broth through a sieve. Reserve 1½ cups of the broth (save the rest for another use) and let it cool.

2. Meanwhile, roast the poblanos directly over a gas flame or under a broiler as close to the heat as possible, turning with tongs until charred all over. Enclose the peppers in a plastic bag and chill until cool enough to handle, 5 to 10 minutes. Working under running water, carefully rub the skins off. Halve the poblanos and remove the stems, seeds and ribs; coarsely chop the poblanos.

3. Preheat the broiler. Lightly coat 6 individual gratin dishes with vegetable cooking spray.

4. In a heavy medium saucepan, combine the reserved chicken broth and the milk. Sift the flour into the saucepan, whisking constantly until all the flour has been added and the mixture is smooth. Add the minced garlic, oregano, cumin, salt and black pepper and bring to a boil over moderately high heat, whisking constantly. Reduce the heat to moderate and simmer, stirring, for 3 minutes.

5. Spoon ⅓ cup of the sauce into a bowl. Add the corn and half of the chopped poblanos to the remaining sauce in the pan and simmer for 2 minutes. Pull the meat from the chicken breast,

discarding the skin and bones. Tear the meat into fine shreds and stir it into the sauce in the bowl.

6. To assemble, place one Corn Crêpe on a work surface with the speckled side down. Spoon about 2 tablespoons of the chicken mixture and 1 tablespoon of the chopped poblanos on the crêpe and loosely roll up. Place in the dish seam-side down. Repeat with the remaining Corn Crêpes, chicken and chopped poblanos, arranging 2 in each dish.

7. Spoon a scant ½ cup of the poblano-corn sauce over the crêpes in each dish and top with the cheese and sour cream. *(The recipe can be prepared to this point up to 1 hour ahead and kept, covered, at room temperature.)* Place 3 of the dishes under the broiler for 3 to 5 minutes to melt and lightly brown the cheese and heat the crêpes through. Repeat with the remaining 3 dishes. Garnish with the diced tomato and serve one gratin dish per person.

—*Jim Fobel*

CORN CREPES

Makes 12 Crêpes
54 Calories per Crêpe

2 large eggs
1 cup skim milk
½ cup masa harina★
¼ cup all-purpose flour
1 tablespoon unsalted butter, melted
¼ teaspoon salt
★*Available at Latine American markets and specialty food stores*

1. In a large bowl, lightly beat the eggs. Gradually whisk in the milk and masa harina. Whisk in the flour, melted butter and salt. Let stand at room temperature for 30 minutes.

2. Spray a heavy 7-inch crêpe pan (or 8-inch nonstick skillet with a 6½-inch bottom) with vegetable cooking spray and place over moderate heat. When the pan is hot, ladle in 2 tablespoons of the batter, quickly swirling to coat. Cook the crêpe until it's speckled brown on the bottom, 30 seconds to 1 minute. Flip and cook for 15 to 20 seconds longer. Transfer the crêpe to a sheet of waxed paper. Repeat with the remaining batter, spraying the pan between crêpes. Stack the crêpes between sheets of waxed paper and cover to keep warm. *(The crêpes can be frozen. Thaw at room temperature before using.)*

—*Jim Fobel*

CHICKEN AND PASTA SALAD WITH ROASTED PEPPERS

This is a recipe for bell pepper aficionados—the peppers not only garnish the salad, but form the base for the dressing as well.

2 Servings
349 Calories per Serving

1 medium red bell pepper
1 large green bell pepper
1 large yellow bell pepper
2 cups Chicken Stock (p. 10) or canned broth
½ cup (about 2 ounces) dry tripolini pasta or very small shells
1 teaspoon extra-virgin olive oil
1 tablespoon chopped chives
1 tablespoon chopped parsley
1 garlic clove
¼ teaspoon thyme
½ teaspoon freshly ground black pepper
2 skinless, boneless chicken breast halves (about 4½ ounces each)
10 small romaine lettuce leaves

1. Roast the red, green and yellow bell peppers over a gas flame or under the broiler, turning, until charred all over. Place the peppers in a bag and let steam for 10 minutes. Peel the peppers over a bowl. Remove the cores, seeds and ribs; strain and reserve any pepper juices. Slice the entire red pepper and one-third of the green and

yellow peppers into fine julienne strips. Coarsely chop the remaining green and yellow peppers.

2. In a medium saucepan, bring the stock to a boil over high heat. Add the tripolini and cook until al dente, 6 to 8 minutes. Drain the pasta in a colander set over a medium saucepan to reserve the stock. In a small bowl, toss the pasta with the olive oil.

3. Return the chicken stock to a boil over high heat. Add the chives, 1½ teaspoons of the parsley, the garlic, thyme and black pepper. Add the chicken breasts and reduce the heat to moderate. Simmer, turning frequently, until the chicken is just white throughout but still moist, 7 to 10 minutes. Remove from the heat and let cool in the stock.

4. In a blender or food processor, puree the chopped green and yellow peppers with 2 tablespoons of the stock and any pepper juices. Cut the chicken into ½-inch cubes and place in a medium bowl. Add the pepper puree and toss. Add the pasta and toss to coat well.

5. Line 2 plates with the lettuce leaves. Mound the chicken and pasta salad in the center and garnish each serving with the reserved pepper strips and the remaining parsley.

—Bob Chambers

MARINATED SZECHUAN CHICKEN SALAD

This chicken salad is highly spiced with hot pepper, Szechuan peppercorns and garlic and tastes just like Chinese sesame chicken. Serve this delicious dish for lunch or as a light supper.

6 Servings
265 Calories per Serving

5 large basil leaves or ½ teaspoon dried
⅛ teaspoon crushed hot red pepper
⅛ teaspoon Szechuan peppercorns★
¼ cup grated fresh ginger
1 teaspoon minced garlic
2 tablespoons honey

¼ cup soy sauce
¼ cup red wine vinegar
¼ cup Oriental sesame oil
6 small skinless, boneless chicken breast halves (about 4 ounces each)
1 large head of romaine lettuce, leaves separated
1½ cups finely shredded cabbage
1½ cups grated carrot
6 scallions, finely chopped
★Available at Asian markets

1. In a blender, combine the basil, hot pepper, Szechuan peppercorns, ginger, garlic, honey, soy sauce, wine vinegar, sesame oil and ½ cup of water. Blend until smooth, about 1 minute. Reserve ¾ cup of this marinade.

2. In a glass dish, combine the remaining marinade and the chicken breasts. Let stand at room temperature, turning once or twice, for 1 to 2 hours.

3. Preheat the oven to 350°. Remove the chicken breasts from the marinade and pat dry with paper towels. In a large nonstick skillet over high heat, brown the chicken breasts until golden in color, about 15 seconds on each side. Place the chicken on a baking sheet and bake until white throughout but still juicy, 15 to 20 minutes.

4. Divide the romaine among 6 plates. Arrange ¼ cup each of the cabbage and carrots on top of the lettuce on each plate. Slice the chicken lengthwise into thin strips and divide it and the scallions evenly among the plates. Spoon 2 tablespoons of the reserved marinade over each salad.

—Golden Door Spa, Escondido, California

Watercress Salad with Smoked Chicken and Walnut Croutons (p. 239).

Grilled Marinated Chicken Breasts (p. 86).

Above, Orange and Coriander Chicken with Rice (p. 208). Right, Grandpa's Hearty Chicken Soup (p. 42).

CANTONESE CHICKEN SALAD

Salads featuring meats and poultry are popular in Hong Kong's "New Cantonese Cooking." Though chicken is used here, duck is often the preferred ingredient in Hong Kong, perhaps with melon or pistachio nuts. These salads are served at room temperature, a departure from Cantonese tradition in which dishes come to the table hot.

6 Servings
219 Calories per Serving

*1½ cups shredded Cantonese Roast Chicken
  (p. 65)*
1 tablespoon distilled white vinegar
1 tablespoon Oriental sesame oil
1 teaspoon Shao-Hsing wine★ or dry sherry
1½ teaspoons sugar
¾ teaspoon salt
Pinch of freshly ground white pepper
*3 fresh water chestnuts★ or 4 sliced canned
  water chestnuts*
1 tablespoon sesame seeds
5 cups peanut oil
1 ounce rice noodles★ or capellini
*½ small, ripe honeydew melon, cut into ½-
  inch pieces*
1 celery rib, cut into thin julienne strips
1 carrot, cut into thin julienne strips
*1 small red bell pepper, cut into thin julienne
  strips*
★Available at Asian markets

1. After roasting the Cantonese Roast Chicken, let it cool to room temperature. (*It can be roasted up to 1 day ahead.*) To shred the chicken: Pull the meat off the bone; with a rolling pin, pound the meat and roll over it to break the fibers. Then shred it with your fingers, setting aside 1½ cups. (Reserve the remainder of the chicken for another use.)

2. In a small bowl, combine the vinegar, sesame oil, wine, sugar, salt and white pepper. Whisk together until well blended and set aside.

3. With a small sharp knife, peel the rough brown outer skin from the water chestnuts. Rinse under cool water. Pat dry with paper towels. Cut into matchstick-size pieces and set aside.

4. Heat a wok over high heat for 30 seconds. Add the sesame seeds, reduce the heat to very low and toast, stirring constantly, until the seeds are brown and fragrant, about 1 minute. Transfer to a plate and set aside.

5. Return the wok to high heat. After 20 seconds, add the peanut oil and heat until it is rippling and reaches about 350° on a deep-fat thermometer, about 12 minutes. Add the rice noodles and cook, turning once, until crisp and golden brown, 5 or 6 seconds. With a wire or perforated strainer, remove the noodles and drain well in the strainer over a large bowl. Spread the drained noodles on a serving platter.

6. In a large bowl, combine the chicken, melon, celery, carrot, red pepper, and the reserved water chestnuts and toasted sesame seeds. Pour in the reserved dressing and toss thoroughly to mix. Spoon the salad over the bed of rice noodles and serve at once.

———————————

—Eileen Yin-Fei Lo

CHICKEN TACOS

So simple and fresh-tasting, these low-cal soft tacos can be thrown together in practically no time at all. And if you prefer, turkey can be used in place of the chicken.

12 Servings
102 Calories per Serving

1 teaspoon vegetable oil
2 large garlic cloves, minced
*½ pound skinless, boneless chicken breast, cut
  into 2-by-¼-inch strips*
½ teaspoon cumin
½ teaspoon crumbled oregano
Pinch of salt
¼ teaspoon freshly ground pepper
1 medium onion, finely chopped

⅓ cup chopped cilantro (fresh coriander)
12 corn tortillas
2 medium tomatoes, finely diced
1 cup shredded romaine lettuce

1. In a large, nonstick skillet, heat the oil over moderate heat. Add the garlic and cook for 30 seconds. Add the chicken, cumin, oregano, salt and pepper. Increase the heat to high and sauté until the chicken is almost cooked through, 2 to 3 minutes. Add the onion and cook to warm through, about 1 minute. Remove from the heat; stir in the cilantro.

2. Place another medium skillet over moderate heat. Moisten each corn tortilla with drops of water on each side. Add the tortillas to the skillet, one at a time, and flip several times until hot, softened and the water has been absorbed.

3. Spoon 2 tablespoons of the chicken filling across the center of each hot tortilla. Top with the tomatoes and lettuce and fold in half. Serve 1 taco per person.

—Jim Fobel

CURRIED CHICKEN WITH FRAGRANT BASMATI RICE TIMBALES

Deep spicy flavors in a rich and plentiful sauce are complemented with timbales of nutty basmati rice. Instead of chutney, serve cubes of fresh mango on the plate, next to the timbale.

4 Servings
328 Calories per Serving

½ cup basmati rice
12 cardamom pods
12 whole cloves
1 cinnamon stick
1 teaspoon grated fresh ginger plus 1 tablespoon minced fresh ginger
½ teaspoon salt
1 tablespoon vegetable oil
1 cup finely chopped onion
1 garlic clove, minced
2 teaspoons garam masala,★ or substitute 1 teaspoon curry powder mixed with ½ teaspoon each ground coriander and cumin and a dash of cayenne pepper
1 teaspoon curry powder
2 tablespoons all-purpose flour
2 cups Chicken Stock (p. 10) or canned broth
¾ pound skinless, boneless chicken breasts, cut crosswise on the diagonal into ⅛- to ¼-inch-thick slices
½ cup plain low-fat yogurt
2 tablespoons chopped cilantro (fresh coriander)
Pinch of cayenne pepper
1 large mango or small papaya (½ pound), cut into ½-inch dice, for accompaniment
★Available at Indian markets and specialty food shops

1. Place the rice in a medium bowl and fill with cold water; pour off the water. Repeat 3 or 4 times, until the water runs clear. Drain the rice in a sieve. Place in a small heavy saucepan and add 1 cup of cold water. Add 4 of the cardamom pods, 4 of the cloves, the cinnamon stick, grated ginger and ¼ teaspoon of the salt. Let the rice soak for 30 minutes.

2. Place the saucepan of rice over high heat and bring to a boil. Reduce the heat to low, cover and simmer until the water is absorbed, about 12 minutes. Remove from the heat, and let stand, tightly covered, for at least 15 minutes. *(The rice will hold for at least 30 minutes.)*

3. Meanwhile, in a heavy medium saucepan, heat the oil over moderate heat. Add the onion, minced ginger and garlic. Cook until the onion is soft and lightly colored, about 5 minutes. Add the garam masala, curry powder and remaining 8 cardamom pods and 8 cloves. Cook, stirring, for 1 minute. Add the flour and stir to moisten with the oil; the mixture will be dry. Cook, stirring, for 1 minute.

4. Gradually whisk in the chicken stock and bring to a boil, stirring constantly. Simmer uncovered for 15 minutes. Use a skimmer to remove the cardamom pods and cloves. Add the chicken slices and the yogurt and cook until the chicken is just cooked through, 3 to 5 minutes. Remove from the heat and stir in the cilantro, cayenne and remaining ¼ teaspoon salt.

5. For each serving, pack a scant ½ cup of the rice into a ½-cup measure and invert onto a dinner plate. Spoon one-fourth of the chicken and sauce onto each plate. Garnish with the mango.

———————

—*Jim Fobel*

SOUTHWESTERN-STYLE CHICKEN WITH YELLOW RICE

Bright red-orange annatto seeds add a wonderful color and flavor to the rice.

2 Servings

338 Calories per Serving

¼ cup seeded and chopped dried ancho or
* mulato chiles★*
½ teaspoon ground cumin
½ teaspoon oregano
½ teaspoon salt
2 skinless, boneless chicken breast halves
* (about 4½ ounces each)*
2 teaspoons achiote seeds (annatto seeds)★
¼ cup rice
2½ tablespoons chopped cilantro
* (fresh coriander)*
¼ teaspoon cumin seeds
¼ teaspoon freshly ground black pepper
½ cup Chicken Stock (p. 10) or canned broth
½ teaspoon minced garlic
⅔ cup coarsely chopped scallions
½ head of iceberg lettuce, finely shredded
2 tablespoons grated Monterey Jack or
* Cheddar cheese*
1 medium plum tomato, seeded and chopped
★Available at Spanish and Latin American
* markets and in spice shops*

1. In a small saucepan, combine the dried chiles with 1 cup of water. Bring to a boil over high heat. Remove from the heat, cover and let stand for 1 hour.

2. Meanwhile, in a small bowl, combine the ground cumin with the oregano and ¼ teaspoon of the salt. Rub over the chicken breasts and set aside.

3. In a small saucepan, combine the achiote seeds with ¾ cup of water. Bring to a boil. Remove from the heat, cover and let stand for 20 minutes.

4. Place the rice in a medium saucepan. Strain the achiote seed water over the rice (discard the seeds). Add 1 tablespoon of the cilantro, the cumin seeds, black pepper and remaining ¼ teaspoon salt. Bring to a boil over high heat. Reduce the heat to moderate, cover and cook until the water is absorbed and the rice is fluffy, 18 to 20 minutes.

5. Meanwhile, transfer the chiles and their soaking liquid to a blender and puree until smooth. Strain the puree into a medium skillet. Add the chicken stock, garlic, 1 tablespoon of the cilantro, and ⅓ cup of the scallions. Bring to a boil over high heat. Reduce the heat to moderate. Add the chicken breasts and cook, turning frequently, until just white throughout but still moist, 7 to 10 minutes.

6. Divide the lettuce between 2 serving plates. Using a slotted spoon, place the chicken breasts on the lettuce. Sprinkle 1 tablespoon grated cheese over each.

7. Blend the tomato with the remaining ½ tablespoon cilantro. Spoon the rice onto the plates and top with the chopped tomato. Drizzle any remaining chile sauce over the chicken and sprinkle each serving with the remaining ⅓ cup scallions.

—*Bob Chambers*

CHICKEN BREAST STUFFED WITH GOAT CHEESE AND SUN-DRIED TOMATOES

Make sure to cut a deep enough pocket in the chicken breasts to prevent the cheese from seeping out.

🍷 Sauvignon Blanc, such as Sam J. Sebastiani

2 Servings
323 Calories per Serving

- *2 tablespoons mild, creamy goat cheese, such as Montrachet*
- *2 teaspoons chopped dry, unmarinated sun-dried tomatoes (well drained and pressed between paper towels if oil-packed)*
- *2 teaspoons chopped parsley*
- *¼ teaspoon minced garlic*
- *¾ teaspoon freshly ground pepper*
- *2 skinless, boneless chicken breast halves (about 4½ ounces each)*
- *¼ cup dry bread crumbs*
- *½ teaspoon salt*
- *1 egg white, beaten*
- *1 pound fresh spinach, stemmed*
- *¼ teaspoon freshly grated nutmeg*
- *2 teaspoons unsalted butter*

1. In a small bowl, mash the goat cheese with the sun-dried tomatoes, parsley, garlic and ¼ teaspoon of the pepper.

2. Cut a 2-inch-long pocket in the side of each chicken breast. Fill the pockets with the goat cheese stuffing.

3. On a sheet of waxed paper, toss the bread crumbs with ¼ teaspoon of the salt and ¼ teaspoon of the pepper. Brush the stuffed breasts with the egg white and dredge in the seasoned crumbs. Set the breasts on a plate and refrigerate for 15 minutes.

4. In a heavy, medium, nonreactive saucepan, sprinkle the spinach with the nutmeg and the remaining ¼ teaspoon each of salt and pepper. Cover tightly and cook over moderately low heat until the spinach is wilted and has given off its liquid, 3 to 5 minutes. Drain the spinach. Return to the pan, cover and keep warm.

5. In a medium skillet, melt the butter over moderately high heat. Add the chicken breasts and turn until evenly coated with the butter. Reduce the heat to low, cover and cook for 3 minutes. Turn the breasts over, cover and cook until the chicken is just white throughout but still moist, about 4 minutes longer. Transfer the chicken to warmed plates and serve the spinach alongside.

—*Bob Chambers*

GREEK-STYLE CHICKEN WITH DILLED CUCUMBERS, GOAT CHEESE AND PHYLLO CRESCENTS

The Anise-Phyllo Crescents are an indulgent accompaniment to this fresh-tasting chicken dish. Without them, this dish will only cost you 244 calories a serving.

2 Servings
346 Calories per Serving

- *1 large cucumber*
- *2 cups Chicken Stock (p. 10) or unsalted canned broth*
- *2 tablespoons chopped fresh dill*

¼ teaspoon freshly ground pepper

½ teaspoon minced garlic

2 skinless, boneless chicken breast halves
  (about 4½ ounces each), pounded ½ inch
  thick and cut crosswise into ½-inch strips

1 ounce Montrachet or other mild goat cheese,
  crumbled

Anise-Phyllo Crescents (recipe follows)

Sprigs of dill, for garnish

1. Peel the cucumber, leaving some lengthwise strips of skin attached for decoration (if the skin is heavily waxed, peel completely). Halve lengthwise and scoop out the seeds. Cut the cucumber crosswise into ¼-inch-thick slices.

2. In a medium saucepan, cover the cucumber slices with the chicken stock. Add 1 tablespoon of the chopped dill and the pepper. Bring to a boil over high heat. Immediately remove the cucumbers with a slotted spoon and set aside to cool.

3. Add the remaining 1 tablespoon dill and the garlic to the saucepan and return the stock to a boil. Add the chicken strips and simmer over moderate heat until just white throughout but still moist, about 1 minute after the stock returns to a boil. With a slotted spoon, remove the chicken and set aside. Boil the stock until reduced to ¼ cup, about 10 minutes. Strain the stock.

4. To serve, divide the cucumbers between 2 plates and mound the chicken strips on top. Sprinkle with the goat cheese and pour 2 tablespoons of the reduced stock over each serving. Garnish each plate with Anise-Phyllo Crescents and a sprig of fresh dill.

—Bob Chambers

ANISE-PHYLLO CRESCENTS

  2 Servings
  102 Calories per Serving

2 sheets of phyllo dough

1½ teaspoons olive oil

½ teaspoon anise seeds

Preheat the oven to 425°. Spread 1 sheet of the phyllo dough out on a work surface and brush lightly with oil. Sprinkle with ¼ teaspoon of the anise seeds. Cover with the second sheet of phyllo. Lightly brush one half of the sheet with oil and sprinkle with the remaining ¼ teaspoon anise seeds. Fold the stacked sheets in half and brush the top lightly with any remaining oil. Cut the layered phyllo into crescent shapes. Place on a nonstick baking sheet and bake for 3 to 5 minutes, or until golden brown.

—Bob Chambers

CHICKEN WITH VERMOUTH

This low-calorie, low-sodium (155 mg per serving) chicken dish is from the Ambassador Grill in Manhattan.

  4 Servings
  247 Calories per Serving

Vegetable cooking spray, such as Pam

4 large skinless, boneless chicken breast halves
  (about 7 ounces each)

¾ teaspoon freshly ground white pepper

1 medium carrot, cut into 2-inch
  julienne strips

1 celery rib, cut into 2-inch julienne strips

1 medium leek (white and tender green), cut
  into 2-inch julienne strips

½ cup unsalted chicken stock or low-sodium
  canned broth

3 tablespoons dry vermouth

1. Put a large skillet over moderately high heat. Coat lightly with the cooking spray. Season the chicken breasts with ½ teaspoon of the white pepper. Add to the skillet and sauté, turning once, until browned on the outside and opaque throughout, about 10 minutes. Remove and set aside.

2. Add the carrot, celery and leek to the skillet. Season with the remaining ¼ teaspoon pepper and cook for 1 minute. Pour in the stock and vermouth, partly cover and simmer until the vegetables are tender and the liquid thickens to the consistency of light syrup, about 10 minutes.

3. Return the chicken to the skillet and cook until heated through, 3 to 5 minutes.

—*Ambassador Grill, New York City*

GRAPEFRUIT CHICKEN WITH LEEKS AND FENNEL SEED

Grapefruit and grapefruit juice provide a sweet-tart counterpoint to the caramelized leeks and the sautéed chicken.

❦ Crisp white, such as Dry Creek Fumé Blanc

2 Servings

343 Calories per Serving

2 tablespoons plus 1 teaspoon dry vermouth

1 teaspoon oregano

¼ teaspoon salt

¼ teaspoon freshly ground pepper

2 skinless, boneless chicken breast halves (about 4½ ounces each), pounded ¼ inch thick

1 tablespoon unsalted butter

1 teaspoon fennel seeds

3 small leeks (white and tender green), cut into thin julienne strips (about 6 ounces)

2 teaspoons sugar

⅔ cup fresh grapefruit juice

1 pink grapefruit

1. In a small bowl, combine 1 tablespoon of the vermouth with the oregano, salt and pepper. Rub the chicken with this mixture. Cover with plastic wrap and refrigerate for at least 2 hours.

2. In a heavy medium saucepan, melt 2 teaspoons of the butter over high heat. Add the fennel seeds and sauté until the butter browns, about 1 minute. Immediately add the leeks and stir to coat with the butter. Reduce the heat to moderate and cover tightly. Cook, stirring occasionally, until the leeks are nicely browned, 8 to 10 minutes.

3. In a small nonreactive saucepan, combine the sugar, remaining 1 tablespoon plus 1 teaspoon dry vermouth and the grapefruit juice. Bring to a boil over moderately high heat and cook until reduced to ¼ cup, about 7 minutes.

4. Meanwhile, using a sharp knife, peel the grapefruit, cutting off all of the bitter white pith. Slice in between the membranes to release the sections; set aside in a bowl.

5. In a large nonstick skillet, melt the remaining 1 teaspoon butter over moderately high heat. Add the chicken and sauté, turning once, until lightly browned outside and white but still moist inside, about 1½ minutes on each side.

6. Reheat the leeks briefly if necessary. Make a bed of the leeks on each plate and place a chicken breast on top. Garnish each serving with grapefruit sections and spoon the sauce over all.

—*Bob Chambers*

ORANGE-GINGER CHICKEN WITH OVEN-BAKED SCALLIONS

The pungent flavors of ginger, garlic, chile and orange zest do a superb job of making you forget that this dish has so few calories.

2 Servings
231 Calories per Serving

½ cup fresh orange juice
1 tablespoon finely chopped fresh ginger
1 teaspoon sugar
¼ teaspoon Chinese chili paste with garlic★
2 skinless, boneless chicken breast halves
 (about 4½ ounces each), pounded
 ¼ inch thick
2 tablespoons dry sherry
1 tablespoon soy sauce
1 tablespoon grated orange zest
12 scallions—white and tender green left
 whole, dark green tops chopped
¼ teaspoon freshly ground pepper
★Available at Asian markets

1. In a small saucepan, bring the orange juice, ginger and sugar to a boil over high heat. Reduce the heat and boil until reduced to ¼ cup, 5 to 7 minutes. Remove from the heat and stir in the chili paste; let cool.

2. Place the chicken in a baking dish and pour on the orange-ginger mixture; turn to coat. Cover with plastic wrap and refrigerate for at least 2 hours.

3. Meanwhile, in a medium baking dish, combine the sherry, soy sauce and orange zest. Add the whole scallions and toss to coat well. Sprinkle with the pepper. Cover with aluminum foil and set aside at room temperature for 2 hours.

4. Preheat the oven to 450°. Bake the scallions, covered, for 12 to 15 minutes, until tender. About 5 minutes before the scallions are done, place the chicken in the oven and bake uncovered for 5 minutes, until just white but still moist. Divide the scallions between 2 warmed plates. Arrange the chicken on top and sprinkle with the chopped scallion greens.

—Bob Chambers

BROILED MARINATED CHICKEN WITH VEGETABLES

The wonderful, slightly charred flavor of grilled vegetables is achieved in the broiler with little fuss or mess. The flavors improve if the vegetables are cooked several hours ahead, leaving just the marinated chicken to be broiled at dinnertime. The chicken should marinate for at least 12 hours.
❣ A mild-flavored fruity wine, such as J. Pedroncelli or Grand Cru Chenin Blanc, would set off the tart yet mild flavors of the chicken.

4 Servings
289 Calories per Serving

5 large garlic cloves, unpeeled
½ teaspoon salt
1 teaspoon freshly ground black pepper
½ teaspoon oregano
½ teaspoon cumin
⅛ teaspoon ground cloves
2 tablespoons fresh lime juice
4 small skinless, boneless chicken breast halves
 (about 4 ounces each)
2 medium green bell peppers
4 medium zucchini (6 ounces each),
 halved lengthwise
4 small eggplants (4 ounces each),
 halved lengthwise
4 small onions, halved crosswise, plus ½ cup
 finely chopped onion
4 small plum tomatoes, halved lengthwise
1 tablespoon vegetable oil

2 teaspoons all-purpose flour
1 cup Chicken Stock (p. 10) or canned broth
¼ cup dry white wine
¼ cup chopped parsley

1. Place the garlic cloves on a heavy griddle or in a cast-iron skillet over moderate heat and toast, turning frequently, until spotted dark brown on the outside and soft inside, 15 to 20 minutes. Let cool slightly. Peel and chop on a cutting board. Add the salt and work into a paste.

2. Scrape the garlic paste into a small bowl and stir in the black pepper, oregano, cumin and cloves. Gradually stir in the lime juice. Spread this seasoned paste all over the chicken breast halves, wrap tightly and refrigerate for 12 to 24 hours.

3. Roast the green peppers directly over a gas flame or under the broiler as close to the heat as possible, turning, until charred all over. Place in a bag and let steam for 5 minutes. Peel the peppers under gently running warm water. Remove the cores and seeds; cut the peppers into ½-inch strips.

4. Preheat the broiler. Deeply score the cut sides of the zucchini and the eggplants in diagonal lines about ½ inch apart. Working in 2 batches, if necessary, arrange the zucchini, eggplants, halved onions and tomatoes in a single layer on a foil-lined broiler pan. Brush the zucchini, eggplants, onions and tomatoes with 2 teaspoons of the oil. Broil about 4 inches from the heat until the vegetables are slightly blackened on top and soft and tender inside, 5 to 7 minutes. Remove, cover with foil and set aside.

5. Let the chicken return to room temperature before broiling. Remove the chicken from the marinade; reserve the marinade for the sauce. Broil the chicken on a foil-lined broiler pan until speckled dark brown, about 3 minutes on top. Turn and broil until just cooked through, 1 to 2 minutes longer. Wrap in foil to keep warm and pour any drippings into the marinade.

6. Put the remaining 1 teaspoon vegetable oil in a small heavy skillet, preferably nonstick. Add the chopped onion and sauté over moderate heat until lightly colored, about 3 minutes. Add the flour and cook, stirring, for 1 minute. Whisk in the reserved marinade, the chicken stock and the wine. Bring to a boil, whisking, until thickened slightly. Simmer, stirring frequently, until reduced to 1 cup, about 5 minutes. Remove from the heat and stir in the parsley. Season with salt to taste.

7. To serve, thinly slice the chicken breasts across the grain and fan in the center of each dinner plate; divide the vegetables among the plates and drizzle the sauce over the chicken and vegetables. Serve warm or at room temperature.

———————

—*Jim Fobel*

MIDDLE EASTERN CHICKEN WITH EGGPLANT AND TOMATOES

In this recipe, the spiced yogurt marinade tenderizes the chicken and helps it brown in a mere ¼ teaspoon of oil.

2 Servings
271 Calories per Serving

2 tablespoons plain yogurt
½ teaspoon ground cumin
½ teaspoon cumin seeds
½ teaspoon cinnamon
½ teaspoon salt
2 skinless, boneless chicken breast halves
   (about 4½ ounces each), pounded
   ¼ inch thick
Freshly ground pepper
1 teaspoon olive oil
1 large eggplant (about 1⅓ pounds)
3 large shallots, finely chopped
1 teaspoon minced garlic

12 cherry tomatoes

1½ teaspoons chopped fresh oregano, or ⅜
   teaspoon dried

1. In a small bowl, blend the yogurt with the ground cumin, cumin seeds, cinnamon and salt; set aside half the yogurt mixture. Rub the chicken breasts with the remaining mixture and season lightly with pepper. Set the chicken on a plate, cover with plastic wrap and refrigerate for at least 2 hours.

2. Meanwhile, preheat the oven to 450°. Brush ¼ teaspoon of the oil on a nonstick baking sheet. Prick the eggplant with a fork, center on the sheet and bake in the middle of the oven for 45 minutes to 1 hour, until the eggplant is very soft to the touch. Let cool for 15 minutes. Cut the eggplant open and scoop the pulp from the skin; chop well.

3. In a medium nonstick skillet, heat ¼ teaspoon of the oil. Add the shallots and garlic and cook over moderate heat, stirring constantly, until very fragrant but not brown, about 1 minute. Add the chopped eggplant and cook for 1 minute. Remove from the heat and stir in the remaining seasoned yogurt. Keep warm.

4. In another medium nonstick skillet, heat ¼ teaspoon of the oil over moderately high heat. Add the chicken breasts and sauté, turning once, until browned outside and white but still moist inside, 1½ minutes per side. Spoon the eggplant puree onto 2 plates and set the chicken on top.

5. Add the remaining ¼ teaspoon olive oil to the skillet. Add the cherry tomatoes and sauté over moderately high heat, tossing frequently, until they are heated through but still hold their shape, about 2 minutes. Season with pepper to taste and the oregano. Spoon the tomatoes onto the plates and serve hot.

———————

—Bob Chambers

CHICKEN BREASTS WITH ARTICHOKES AND PORCINI MUSHROOMS

🍷 California Sauvignon Blanc, such as Beringer

2 Servings

295 Calories per Serving

½ ounce dried porcini mushrooms

2 large artichokes

½ lemon

½ teaspoon olive oil

2 skinless, boneless chicken breast halves
   (about 4½ ounces each)

1 garlic clove, minced

⅓ cup canned crushed Italian peeled tomatoes

¼ teaspoon crushed rosemary

¼ teaspoon salt

¼ teaspoon freshly ground pepper

1½ teaspoons unsalted butter

Chopped parsley, for garnish

1. In a small bowl, soak the porcini in 1 cup of hot water until softened, about 30 minutes. Drain the mushrooms and strain the soaking liquid through a fine sieve. Coarsely chop the mushrooms.

2. Meanwhile, trim the artichokes by first snapping off the outer leaves. Using a stainless steel knife, cut off the stems. Cut the crowns to about 1½ inches of the base. Rub all over with the lemon. Cook the artichokes in a large saucepan of boiling water over moderately high heat until the bottom is tender when pierced with a fork, about 12 minutes. Remove from the water and let stand until cool enough to handle. Scoop out and discard the hairy chokes and trim off any tough outer skin. Return the artichokes to their cooking liquid and set aside.

3. In a large skillet, heat the olive oil over moderately high heat. Add the chicken breasts and sauté, turning once, until browned on both sides, about 1½ minutes per side. Reduce the heat to moderate and cook until the chicken is just white throughout but still moist, about 5 min-

utes; transfer to serving plates and cover with foil to keep warm.

4. Add the garlic to the skillet and cook until fragrant, about 30 seconds. Add the tomatoes, rosemary, chopped porcini mushrooms and their liquid. Increase the heat to moderately high and cook, stirring, until the liquid is reduced to 2 tablespoons, about 5 minutes. Season with the salt and pepper and remove from the heat. Swirl in the butter.

5. Remove the artichokes from the hot water and drain well; slice ¼ inch thick. Fan out an artichoke bottom on each plate next to the chicken. Spoon the sauce over the chicken and sprinkle with the chopped parsley.

—*Marcia Kiesel*

GRATINEED CHICKEN BREAST WITH ROASTED GARLIC AND POTATO PUREE

Roasting unpeeled garlic slowly in the oven turns the pungent cloves mild and creamy.

♀ Fruity red, such as Beaujolais Villages

2 Servings
270 Calories per Serving

12 large garlic cloves, unpeeled
½ cup diced peeled potato
½ cup milk
¼ teaspoon salt
¼ teaspoon freshly ground pepper
1 tablespoon freshly grated Parmesan cheese
1 tablespoon dry bread crumbs
2 skinless, boneless chicken breast halves
  (about 4½ ounces each), pounded
  ½ inch thick
2 tablespoons watercress leaves, for garnish

1. Preheat the oven to 300°. Place the garlic cloves in a baking dish and roast in the oven until very soft, about 45 minutes. Let cool slightly, then squeeze the pulp into a small bowl. With a

fork, mash the garlic pulp to a smooth puree.

2. Meanwhile, in a small saucepan, cover the potato with 1 cup of water and cook over moderately high heat until tender, about 20 minutes. Remove from the heat and mash the potato and any remaining liquid until smooth. Stir in the milk, salt, pepper and the garlic puree.

3. Preheat the broiler. In a small bowl, combine the Parmesan cheese and the bread crumbs.

4. Place the chicken breasts on a baking sheet and broil about 4 inches from the heat, without turning, for 2½ to 3 minutes, or until just white throughout but still moist. Sprinkle the bread crumbs and cheese evenly over the chicken and broil for about 30 seconds, until the topping is crusty and browned.

5. Reheat the potato puree. If it is too thick, thin out with a little water. Spoon the puree onto 2 dinner plates, place the chicken breasts on top and garnish with the watercress.

—*Marcia Kiesel*

HONEY-MUSTARD CHICKEN WITH BUTTERNUT SQUASH

The honey-mustard mixture becomes a tangy glaze on both the chicken and the squash.

♀ California rosé of Cabernet Sauvignon, such as Simi

2 Servings
337 Calories per Serving

1½ tablespoons Dijon-style mustard
1 tablespoon honey
1½ teaspoons chopped fresh thyme or ½
  teaspoon dried
¼ teaspoon freshly ground pepper
½ teaspoon salt

2 skinless, boneless chicken breast halves
  (about 4½ ounces each)
1¼-pound butternut squash, peeled
1 teaspoon corn or safflower oil
2 teaspoons minced chives, for garnish

1. Preheat the oven to 425°. In a small bowl, combine the mustard and honey. Stir in the thyme, pepper and ¼ teaspoon of the salt. Rub each chicken breast with 1½ teaspoons of the honey mustard. Cover with plastic wrap and set aside.

2. Cut the squash crosswise into ¾-inch-thick slices. Scoop out any seeds and discard. Cut the squash into triangles and arrange on a heavy non-stick baking sheet. Brush with ½ teaspoon of the oil and sprinkle with the remaining ¼ teaspoon salt. Bake in the middle of the oven for 20 minutes, or until nicely browned.

3. Reduce the heat to 375°. Remove the baking sheet from the oven and turn the squash triangles over. Brush with the remaining honey mustard. Return to the oven and bake until browned and very tender, 15 to 20 minutes longer.

4. Meanwhile, about 10 minutes before the squash is done, heat the remaining ½ teaspoon oil in a nonstick skillet. Add the chicken breasts and cook over moderate heat, turning once, until browned outside and white but still moist inside, 3 to 4 minutes per side.

5. Arrange the squash triangles on 2 warm plates. Slice the chicken crosswise on the diagonal and fan out beside the squash. Sprinkle with the chives.

———————

—Bob Chambers

CHICKEN BREASTS WITH MUSHROOMS, SCALLIONS AND TOASTED ALMONDS

🍷 California Chardonnay, such as Wente

2 Servings
210 Calories per Serving

½ teaspoon olive oil
2 skinless, boneless chicken breast halves
  (about 4½ ounces each)
¼ teaspoon freshly ground pepper
2 cups sliced mushrooms (about 4 ounces)
2 tablespoons sour cream
¼ teaspoon salt
¼ cup thinly sliced scallion greens
2 teaspoons toasted sliced almonds

1. In a large nonstick skillet, heat the olive oil over high heat. Season the chicken breasts on both sides with a pinch of the pepper and add to the skillet. Sauté, turning once, until browned, about 1 minute per side.

2. Add ½ cup water to the skillet and reduce the heat to low. Cover and cook until the chicken is just white throughout but still moist, about 5 minutes. Transfer the chicken to warmed dinner plates. Pour the cooking liquid into a cup and reserve.

3. Add the mushrooms to the skillet and cook over high heat, without stirring, until browned on the bottom, about 1½ minutes. Add the reserved cooking liquid and boil until reduced to 1 tablespoon, about 2 minutes.

4. Add any juices that have drained from the chicken. Remove from the heat and stir in the sour cream. Season with the salt and the remaining pepper and stir in the scallion greens. Pour the mushrooms and their liquid over the chicken breasts and garnish with the toasted almonds.

———————

—Marcia Kiesel

FRICASSEE OF CORNISH HENS WITH CHERRY TOMATOES AND GLAZED SHALLOTS

If you can, have the butcher quarter the birds for you.

❢ This subtle, satisfying fricassee points toward light, flavorful reds, such as a Sinskey or Sterling Pinot Noir.

8 Servings
397 Calories per Serving

4 Cornish game hens (about 1 pound each)
1 teaspoon salt
Freshly ground pepper
1½ tablespoons olive oil
1½ pounds shallots, peeled
2 medium onions, finely chopped
4 garlic cloves, crushed
6 cups Chicken Stock (p. 10) or canned low-
   sodium broth
1½ pounds carrots, sliced diagonally
   ¼ inch thick
4 celery ribs, sliced diagonally
   ½ inch thick
1 teaspoon thyme
½ teaspoon mustard seeds
1 pint cherry tomatoes
½ cup chopped flat-leaf parsley

1. Cut the wing tips off the birds. Using kitchen shears, cut along both sides of the backbones and remove them. With a large sharp knife, quarter the hens so that you have 2 leg-thigh pieces and 2 breast-wing pieces per bird. Sprinkle the pieces with the salt and pepper to taste.

2. Place 4 of the leg-thigh pieces in a large nonstick skillet, skin-side up. Set the cold pan over low heat and gradually increase the heat to moderately high over a period of 3 minutes. This will melt some of the fat from the hens. Cook, turning occasionally, until all the pieces are nicely browned, about 6 minutes total. Remove from the pan and set aside. Repeat with the remaining hen pieces.

3. Meanwhile, heat ½ tablespoon of the olive oil in a large nonstick skillet. Add the shallots and toss to coat with the oil. Cook over moderately low heat, tossing frequently, until the shallots are browned and glazed, about 25 minutes. Set aside.

4. In a large heavy casserole, heat the remaining 1 tablespoon oil over moderately low heat. Stir in the onions. Cover and cook, stirring occasionally, until translucent, about 5 minutes. Add the garlic and cook for 1 minute longer. Then add 3 cups of the chicken stock.

5. Toss the carrots and celery and add half to the casserole in an even layer. Add the reserved game hen pieces and cover with the remaining carrots and celery. Sprinkle with the thyme and the mustard seeds. Pour in the remaining 3 cups chicken stock. *(The recipe can be prepared to this point up to 1 day ahead. Cover and refrigerate the casserole and the glazed shallots separately.)*

6. Place the covered casserole in the oven. Set the oven at 350° and bake for 1¼ hours (or 1½ hours if the casserole was cold). The hens will be very tender but not overcooked.

7. Strain all the cooking liquid into a medium saucepan and bring to a boil over moderately high heat. Boil, skimming frequently, until the liquid reduces to 2 cups, 20 to 25 minutes.

8. Reheat the shallots over moderate heat. When warmed through, add the cherry tomatoes and parsley and toss well. Gently stir the shallots and tomatoes into the casserole and pour in the reduced stock. Reheat the fricassee over moderately high heat until hot, 5 to 7 minutes. Transfer to a large serving dish or arrange on individual plates and serve hot.

—*Bob Chambers*

Index

Contributors

Jeffrey Alford is the author of *Tastes of Travel* (Dharma Press) and the forthcoming *The Flatbread Book* (Morrow).

Jean Anderson is a food/travel writer and the author of numerous cookbooks, including *The Food of Portugal* (Morrow) and *The Doubleday Cookbook* (with Elaine Hanna). She is currently working on a book tentatively titled *German Cooking Today*.

Elizabeth Andoh is the author of *An Ocean of Flavor: The Japanese Way with Fish and Seafood* (Morrow), *An American Taste of Japan* (Morrow) and *At Home with Japanese Cooking* (Knopf).

Lee Bailey is a designer and cookbook author currently working on several books: *Cooking for Friends, Lee Bailey's Tomatoes, Lee Bailey's New Orleans* and *Lee Bailey's Corn*.

Melanie Barnard is a food writer and co-author, with Brooke Dojny, of *Let's Eat In, Sunday Suppers* (both from Prentice Hall Press) and the forthcoming *Parties!* (HarperCollins).

Sarah Belk is a senior editor of *Bon Appétit* magazine, a culinary historian specializing in the American southeast and the author of *Around the Southern Table* (Simon and Schuster).

Gérard Boyer is chef/owner of Les Crayères in Reims, France.

Alexandra Branyon *See Karen Lee*

Jennifer Brennan is the author of numerous cookbooks, including most recently *Curries and Bugles* and an upcoming book tentatively titled *Tradewinds and Coconuts* (both HarperCollins).

Jane Butel is a cooking teacher and the author of numerous cookbooks, including *Chili Madness* and *Hot & Spicy Barbecue* (both Workman). She is currently working on a book titled *Jane Butel Cooks the Traditions of the Southwest*.

Hugh Carpenter is a cooking teacher and the author of *Pacific Flavors* and *Chopstix* (both Stewart, Tabori & Chang) and an upcoming book tentatively titled *Cooking Without Boundaries*.

Penelope Casas is a cooking teacher and the author of *The Foods and Wines of Spain, Tapas: The Little Dishes of Spain* and *Discovering Spain: An Uncommon Guide* (all from Knopf).

Patrick Clark is executive chef of Bice restaurants in Los Angeles and San Diego. He is currently working on a cookbook tentatively titled *Patrick Clark: East Coast/West Coast*.

Mitchell Cobey is chef/owner of Mitchell Cobey Cuisine in Chicago.

Bruce Cost is a food writer, Asian food scholar, restaurateur and the author of *Bruce Costs's Asian Ingredients* (Morrow) and *Ginger East to West* (Aris).

Beverly Cox is a food stylist, recipe developer and the author of *Spirit of the Harvest: North American Indian Cooking* (Stewart, Tabori & Chang).

Robert Del Grande is chef/owner of Cafe Annie in Houston.

Brooke Dojny *See Melanie Barnard*

Jeanette Ferrary is a food/travel writer and co-author, with cooking teacher Louise Fiszer, of *Season to Taste, California-American Cookbook* and the upcoming *Sweet Onions and Sour Cherries: A Cookbook for Market Day* (all Simon and Schuster).

Barbara Figueroa is executive chef at the Sorrento Hotel in Seattle.

Louise Fiszer *See Jeanette Ferrary.*

Jim Fobel is a food writer and the author of numerous books, including *The Whole Chicken Cookbook* (Ballantine) and *Diet Feasts* (Doubleday).

Joyce Goldstein is chef/owner of Square One in San Francisco, a food writer and the author of *The Mediterranean Kitchen* and *Back to Square One* (both Morrow).

Jean-Pierre Goyenvalle is chef/owner of Le Lion d'Or in Washington, D.C.

Dorie Greenspan is a food writer and the author of *Sweet Times: Simple Desserts for Every Occasion* (Morrow) and an upcoming book tentatively titled *Chocolate Through and Through*.

Paul Grimes is senior cooking instructor at Peter Kump's New York Cooking School.

Madhur Jaffrey is an actress, cooking teacher and the author of numerous cookbooks, including *Far Eastern Cookery* (Harper-Collins) and *An Invitation to Indian Cooking* (Knopf). She is currently working on an 8-part PBS series called "Madhur Jaffrey's Far Eastern Cooking."

Susan Shapiro Jaslove is a food writer and recipe developer.

Peter Kump is owner of Peter Kump's New York Cooking School and the author of *Quiche and Pâté* (Irena Chalmers) and the forthcoming *The Techniques of Home Cooking*.

Karen Lee is a caterer, cooking teacher and the co-author, with playwright and food writer Alaxandra Branyon, of *Nouvelle Chinese Cooking* (Macmillan) and *Soup, Salad and Pasta Innovations* and *Chinese Cooking Secrets* (both Doubleday).

Susan Herrmann Loomis is a food writer and the author of *Farmhouse Cooking* and *The Great American Seafood Cookbook* (both Workman).

Copeland Marks is a food historian and the author of numerous cookbooks, including *The Burmese Kitchen* and *The Exotic Kitchens of Indonesia* (both M. Evans). He is currently working on a book tentatively titled *The Exotic Kitchens of Korea.*

Lydie Marshall is a cooking teacher (A La Bonne Cocotte, New York City) and the author of *Cooking with Lydie Marshall* (Knopf) and *A Passion for Potatoes* (HarperCollins).

Michael McLaughlin is the author of *Back of the Box Gourmet* and the upcoming *Fifty-Two Meat Loaves* (both Simon and Schuster). He is also the co-author of *The Silver Palate Cookbook* (Workman) and *The El Paso Chile Company's Texas Border Kitchen Cookbook* (Morrow).

Perla Meyers is the author of numerous cookbooks, including most recently *The Art of Seasonal Cooking* (Simon and Schuster). She is currently working on two books: *The Spanish Way with Beans* (Morrow) and *Cooking from the Garden* (Potter).

Molly O'Neill is the food columnist for *The New York Times Magazine* and the author of *New York Kitchen, A Community Cookbook* (Workman).

Janice Okun is food editor and restaurant reviewer for the *Buffalo News* in Buffalo, New York.

Judith Olney is a food writer, cooking teacher, restaurant critic for *Washington Times* and the author of *Comforting Food* (Atheneum), *The Joy of Chocolate* (Barrons) and *The Farm Market Cookbook* (Doubleday).

Jacques Pépin is a cooking teacher, newspaper columnist and the author of ten cookbooks, the most recent of which are *The Short-Cut Cook* (Morrow) and *Today's Gourmet* (KQED, Inc.), the companion book to his current PBS series of the same name.

David Rosengarten is a cooking teacher, food writer, wine columnist, the author of *Food & Wine*'s "Wine & Food" column and of *Red Wine with Fish* (Simon and Schuster) and the forthcoming *Crashing the Borders* (Crown/Harmony).

Phillip Stephen Schulz is a food writer and the author of *As American as Apple Pie* (Simon and Schuster), *Cooking with Fire and Smoke* (Fireside) and *America the Beautiful Cookbook* (Collins).

Michel Stroot, the former executive chef of Cal-a-Vie Health Resort in Vista, California, is currently a private chef in Europe.

Elizabeth Terry is chef/owner of Elizabeth on 37th in Savannah, Georgia.

Barbara Tropp is chef/owner of China Moon Cafe in San Francisco and the author of *The Modern Art of Chinese Cooking* (Morrow), *The China Moon Cookbook* (Workman) and a book tentatively titled *The China Diet* to be published in 1993.

Roger Vergé is chef/owner of Amandier de Mougins and Le Moulin de Mougins, both in Mougins, France.

Anne Willan is the founder and president of La Varenne cooking school and the author of numerous cookbooks, including the upcoming *Great Cooks and Their Recipes* (Little Brown) and *Château Cuisine* (Macmillan).

Eileen Yin-Fei Lo is a cooking teacher, food writer and the author of *Eileen Yin-Fei Lo's New Cantonese Cooking* (Viking), *The Dim Sum Book* (Crown) and *The Chinese Banquet Cookbook (Crown).*

We would also like to thank the following restaurants and individuals for their contributions to this cookbook: **Ambassador Grill**, New York City; **Georges Blanc**, La Mère Blanc, Vonnas, France; **Joyce Cain**, Cain Cellars, St. Helena, California; **Cal-a-Vie Health Resort**, Vista, California; **Nora Carey; Michèle Chassagne; Citadel Grill**, Cairo, Egypt; **Ana Cotaescu; Geraldine Duncann; Golden Door Spa**, Escondido, California; **Monique Guillaume; Chef Hubert; Mary Marshall Hynson; Jane Helsel Joseph; Jean-Jacques Jouteux; Alan Lieb; Michael McCarty; Dominique Nahmias; Ridgewell's**, Bethesda, Maryland; **Alex Patout; Danforth Rogers**, The Lion's Rock, New York City; **Alain Sailhac; Keo Sananikone; Ston Easton Park**, Bath, England; **Taste**, San Francisco; **The Ginger Man**, New York City; **Gayle Henderson Wilson; Windows on the World**, New York City; **Yamato**, San Francisco.

And members of the *Food & Wine* staff, past and present: **Jim Brown, Anne Disrude, Bob Chambers, Marcia Kiesel, John Robert Massie, Mary Lynn Mondich, W. Peter Prestcott, Tracey Seaman, Elizabeth Woodson, Susan Wyler**

PHOTO CREDITS

Cover: Dennis Galante. **Pages 17-18:** Thom de Santo. **Page 19:** Frank Moscati. **Page 20:** Thom de Santo. **Pages 37-39:** Lisa Charles Watson. **Page 40:** Mark Thomas. **Pages 73-76:** Thom de Santo. **Pages 93-95:** Thom de Santo. **Pages 96, 113-116:** Maria Robledo. **Pages 133-136:** David Bishop. **Pages 153-156:** Mark Thomas. **Pages 173-175:** Rita Maas. **Page 176:** Elizabeth Watt. **Page 193:** Jerry Simpson. **Pages 194-195:** Steven Mark Needham. **Pages 196, 213-216:** Jerry Simpson. **Pages 249-252:** Dennis Galante.